Violence and Trauma in the Lives of Children

Violence and Trauma in the Lives of Children

Volume 1: Overview of Exposure

Joy D. Osofsky and
Betsy McAlister Groves,
Editors

PRAEGER™

An Imprint of ABC-CLIO, LLC
Santa Barbara, California • Denver, Colorado

Library of Congress Cataloging-in-Publication Data

Names: Osofsky, Joy D., editor. | Groves, Betsy McAlister, editor.
Title: Violence and trauma in the lives of children / Joy D. Osofsky and Betsy McAlister Groves, editors.
Description: Santa Barbara, California : Praeger, an Imprint of ABC-CLIO, LLC, [2018] | Includes bibliographical references and index.
Identifiers: LCCN 2017061841 (print) | LCCN 2018004154 (ebook) | ISBN 9781440852596 (ebook) | ISBN 9781440852589 (set : alk. paper) | ISBN 9781440852602 (vol. 1) | ISBN 9781440852619 (vol. 2)
Subjects: LCSH: Psychic trauma in children. | Psychic trauma in adolescence. | Psychic trauma in children—Treatment. | Psychic trauma in adolescence—Treatment. | Child psychotherapy.
Classification: LCC RJ506.P66 (ebook) | LCC RJ506.P66 V54 2018 (print) | DDC 616.85/2100835—dc23
LC record available at https://lccn.loc.gov/2017061841

ISBN: 978-1-4408-5258-9 (set)
978-1-4408-5260-2 (vol. 1)
978-1-4408-5261-9 (vol. 2)
978-1-4408-5259-6 (ebook)

22 21 20 19 18 1 2 3 4 5

This book is also available as an eBook.

Praeger
An Imprint of ABC-CLIO, LLC

ABC-CLIO, LLC
130 Cremona Drive, P.O. Box 1911
Santa Barbara, California 93116–1911
www.abc-clio.com

This book is printed on acid-free paper ∞

Manufactured in the United States of America

Contents

Acknowledgments

Violence and trauma take an often-unrecognized toll on children of all ages. Exposure to trauma occurs so often that many people have come to expect to hear about violence in their everyday lives. A problem that comes up frequently is how to find the appropriate language to talk to children about the violent events that have occurred in their families, communities, and their world. These volumes are designed to expand knowledge not only about the types of traumas that occur at the individual, family, community, and national levels but also to educate the reader about ways to build resilience in children. In addition, policy issues related to violence prevention are crucial in making a difference for children.

The editors of these volumes have come to the trauma field through somewhat different paths. Joy D. Osofsky, throughout her career, has had a strong commitment to prevention and intervention. With that passion came the recognition that more innovative and concentrated interventions were needed to help children exposed to violence and trauma. Through her early efforts to partner with police in the community and during summer programs for youth, the Violence Intervention Program in New Orleans represented a positive way to reach out to attempt to reduce and prevent youth violence. During her work with police and schools, nine-year-old James Darby wrote a letter to President Clinton asking him to stop the violence because he was afraid that he would be killed. Unfortunately, his fears turned out to be well grounded as he was killed shortly after he wrote the letter. Throughout the years, she has worked in establishing prevention programs and helping those impacted by violence and trauma.

For Betsy McAlister Groves, her early work with children in childcare settings in the child protection system taught powerful and sobering lessons about the impact of trauma in early childhood. These experiences led to the founding of the Child Witness to Violence Project, providing clinical intervention and advocacy for children under age eight and their families. This program was one of the first in the country to specifically focus on young children and exposure to violence. Funded since 2001 by the National Child Traumatic Network as one of four sites in the Early Trauma Treatment Network, the Child Witness to Violence Project has provided training and consultation nationally and internationally on early childhood trauma and intervention.

The editors want to express appreciation to the many individuals who supported us through the process of developing and editing *Violence and Trauma in the Lives of Children*. We give special thanks to Lucy S. King, a gifted young woman who is a graduate student in psychology at Stanford University, for her enormous help and editing skill working with us to bring the volumes to completion. We want to express much appreciation to Debbie Carvalko, senior acquisitions editor at ABC-CLIO/Praeger Publishers, who provided continual availability and assistance every step along the way toward publication. We also want to extend heartfelt thanks to the authors, all leaders in the field, who despite their many commitments for time and expertise contributed significantly to these volumes.

Both of the editors wish to acknowledge the professional and personal relationships that have been fostered over the past 18 years by the National Child Traumatic Stress Network (NCTSN), funded by the Substance Abuse Mental Health Services Administration. Over half of the authors who wrote chapters for these volumes have been funded through the NCTSN, a network that by encouraging collaborations and connections has contributed substantially to our knowledge about the effects of violence and trauma on the lives of children shared in these volumes.

Joy D. Osofsky expresses special appreciation to my colleagues in the Department of Psychiatry at Louisiana State University Health Sciences Center for their collaborative efforts to help children exposed to trauma and violence and helping me learn from their experiences. Finally, I could not do this work with trauma so effectively without the continual encouragement and support from my husband, Howard, who is not only always available to think things through with me but also endlessly patient with my long work hours. He is both a loving partner and a consistent believer in my work and contributions. I also want to add special thanks to my grown wonderful children, Hari, Justin, and Michael, who taught me so much not only about being a parent but also about the importance of love and nurturing in families.

Betsy McAlister Groves thanks her students at Harvard's Graduate School of Education who have challenged her to think more broadly about the cultural dimensions of research and intervention in this field. Appreciation also goes to my colleagues in the Department of Pediatrics at Boston Medical Center and at the Child Witness to Violence Project, who continue to inspire me. Finally, and most important, I thank my family—my husband Tim, an educator with extensive child-focused experience, and my daughters, Jeanie and Rebecca, who, along with Tim, have patiently accompanied me in the two-year evolution of this book project.

Hopefully, this book will contribute to making a difference in the lives of children, adolescents, and families now and in the future.

CHAPTER 1

Introduction

Joy D. Osofsky and Betsy McAlister Groves

When we started working on the impact of violence and trauma on children more than 25 years ago, relatively little attention was paid to the traumatic effects on children and adolescents, parents, and others who cared for them. For many, violence and trauma were accepted as "what happens." Most people knew that children were exposed to violence and trauma but assumed the children would adjust to difficult situations, be it the untimely death of a parent, being exposed to partner violence in their homes, or witnessing the community violence taking place in their neighborhoods. Further, many believed that children, especially young children, would not be impacted as they were too young to understand what was happening. However, we have learned much in recent years about the effects of violence and trauma on children of all ages. Through the Adverse Childhood Experiences Study (ACES) (Anda et al., 2006; Felitti et al., 1998), we now know not only that violence and trauma impact negatively children of all ages but also that exposure to violence and trauma during the early years can contribute to intergenerational transmission of negative behaviors and emotions.

It is also important to recognize that prevention and intervention must start early. Joy Osofsky's close colleague and friend, Bill Harris, who is dedicated to supporting sound public policies for children, emphasizes that prevention and early intervention to support healthy development in newborns and their mothers should begin during the prenatal period (personal communication, October 31, 2017). While pregnancy may bring pleasure to many, for others it can be a time of increased stress and even trauma depending on the circumstances of their lives. Heightened stress during pregnancy may lead to depression and other serious mental health problems that are sometimes dealt with through substance use. An important contributor to risk for trauma exposure is poverty, which also leads to significant disparities in care. In 2015 in the United States, 4.25 million babies were born, of whom 21 percent were born into poverty (National Center for Children in Poverty, 2017). The research tells us that 49 percent of children living in poverty have been exposed to trauma, are highly likely to have multiple ACES even at birth, and are two to five times more likely to be exposed to violence. These babies are at high risk for long-term adverse developmental outcomes, indicating the need for increased prevention and early intervention strategies.

While the focus of these two volumes is to provide caregivers, health professionals, child-serving agencies caring for and providing services for children, and the public with additional knowledge concerning the initial and long-term effects of violence and trauma on children, the two volumes differ in approach. Volume 1 provides important perspectives about the effects of different types of violence and trauma exposure on children and adolescents within the context of their caregiving and community environments. Volume 2 takes a systems perspective, describing the different ways that child-serving systems can become more trauma-informed by integrating perspectives related to the effects of trauma on children. We conclude Volume 2 with policy chapters including knowledge about the effects of violence and trauma on children and proposing the integration of such knowledge into policy. The chapters in Volume 2 support the idea that being trauma-informed is crucial and can help support children exposed to violence and trauma. Further, being trauma-informed means recognizing the signs and symptoms of trauma in clients, families, staff, and others involved. An individual, agency, or system responds by fully integrating knowledge about trauma into their policies, procedures, and practices and will seek to actively resist retraumatization (Substance Abuse and Mental Health Services Administration, 2014).

In Volume 1, Goldstine-Cole and McAlister Groves (Chapter 3) describe the exponential growth in the past decade in research on the effects of trauma and stress on the developing brain. In addition to describing the research, further advances have been made by translating this complex research on brain development into briefs, short videos, and other educational material for wider distribution. In particular, the Center for the Developing Child at Harvard provides web-based resources explaining the impact of stress and trauma on the architecture of the brain, which serves as the "building blocks" for development (see https://developingchild.harvard.edu/). An important distinction has been made between exposure to mild stress that can support positive growth, coping, and resilience; more severe stress that may be more difficult to deal with but can be buffered by a supportive environment; and chronic stress, or toxic stress, caused by persistent exposure to violence or trauma, which can "derail" a child's developmental trajectory and disrupt brain development. Toxic stress impacts cognitive, emotional, and social development early in life and, in the absence of intervention, influences health across the life span. In raising awareness about the effects of violence and trauma on children of all ages, the discourse has changed from asking a child who is behaving atypically "What did you do?" to "What happened to you?" (Raz & Burke Harris, 2017).

Unfortunately, children are rarely at the forefront of people's minds when violence occurs, be it on the streets of cities, in rural communities, in homes, or at times when a disaster occurs. Therefore, it is crucial to raise awareness and provide education for service providers and agencies about the impact of violence and trauma on children, including education regarding interventions and treatment strategies. Many adults, even parents and mental health professionals, are unsure about how to communicate with children when violence or trauma happens. Some think that if they do not talk about the experience in front of or with the children, the children will not be impacted. Others may say nothing, thinking that silence is the best way to deal with the problem and that it will "go away" if they don't talk about it. Still others may talk openly with other adults about the experience, ignoring that children can hear their discussions, believing that the children won't listen and, that if they hear, they won't pay attention or understand what is being said. The chapters in this volume reviewing the impact of different types of violence and trauma on children correct these misconceptions, providing an opportunity to learn more about the impact of violence on trauma on children and their development. Exposure to trauma and violence can change the life course for children, and how these experiences are dealt with by the adults in the children's lives is crucial.

Many of the chapters in Volume 1 emphasize the importance of the child–caregiver relationship. This crucial relationship changes from the earliest years of life, when children are extremely dependent on their caregivers to provide both nurturance and safety, to adolescence, when guidance is still needed but provided in a different manner. In fact, careful listening and promoting safe behaviors are very important throughout childhood and adolescence. Much research evidence is elaborated throughout the different chapters indicating that parenting and the child–caregiver relationship are crucial mechanisms to moderate stressful life experiences and that this type of support is key to building resilience. In fact, despite stressful life experiences, with the presence of an adult who is emotionally available and supportive, the evidence also shows that a child can recover.

To aid recovery, Brown and Frances present the principles of trauma-informed care and trauma-specific treatment in Chapter 4. It is important for the reader to recognize that growth in evidence-based, trauma-specific treatments has paralleled the growth of knowledge about the effects of violence and trauma on children and adolescents. These authors discuss the core principles of these evidence-based treatments.

Several authors review the effects of child maltreatment, violence, and trauma in the family (McAlister Groves, Chapter 5) and child sexual abuse (Many, Chapter 7). Unfortunately for children's healthy growth and development, it is important that the readers of these handbooks recognize that much interpersonal violence and trauma exposure occurs in family settings among those adults who are supposed to have the role of protecting the child. Research on childhood trauma exposure emphasizes that both proximity and familiarity may make the exposure more traumatic for the child, both of which are components of maltreatment and domestic violence. In Volume 2, several perspectives are presented related to ways to support and heal children who are exposed to traumatic events.

Throughout the two volumes, the authors have provided case examples that vividly depict the ways that multiple childhood adversities, including exposure to cumulative trauma, can place a child at increased risk for long-term problems. Some of the chapters describe ways children can recover from exposure to traumatic events, emphasizing different approaches to help children heal. All illustrate the important conceptualization of understanding violence exposure for children and adolescents through the lens of an interpersonal-developmental perspective, as is elaborated by King and Osofsky (Chapter 2). Exposure to violence and trauma impacts personal, family, group, and community relationships. One of the most important factors that helps children and adolescents heal from trauma is a supportive relationship, which, as is elaborated more fully in Volume 2, is also the key element to building resilience.

For more complex areas such as community and gang violence, adolescent suicide, and commercial sexual exploitation, there is also much added complexity to the child/adolescent–caregiver relationship. For example, McCauley and Berkowitz (Chapter 8) emphasize that for an adolescent in crisis, a supportive adult who will listen without passing judgment in a safe environment and provide sound and authentically hopeful treatment is essential for recovery. Abdul-Adil and Suarez (Chapter 6) discuss gang-involved youth, emphasizing the high levels of traumatic stress that contribute to their being at increased risk for violent victimization and perpetration of community violence. Due to the high levels of pressure, family dysfunction, and community violence that some adolescents face, they may join gangs both to protect themselves and to become members of a group. These authors poignantly emphasize the need for better integrated treatment programs to address the exposure of these youth to complex violence. Chapter 12 by Rothman and Bair-Merritt on commercial sexual exploitation of children indicates that difficulties in the child–caregiver relationship may contribute to sexual exploitation, which can lead to severe trauma symptoms and which, as has been documented through the ACES studies, can adversely impact mental and physical health. Further influenced by the adversities, relationship difficulties, their own mental health needs, and lack of safety and other complex issues, children who are sexually exploited may not perceive that they are being abused. These children may also lack established, nurturing families or supports that can help them leave the exploitative, but now familiar, environment. Like the other high-risk situations described previously, trauma-informed care is crucial in efforts to build a safe, trusting relationship.

The child–caregiver relationship is also crucial when children are exposed to events that are beyond the caregiver's control, such as illness or injury, war, military deployment of a family member, disasters and terrorism, and the death of a primary caregiver. Much recent research has shown that illness or injury can lead to both developmental delays and traumatic stress reactions in children as is elaborated in by Kassam-Adams (Chapter 13). As a result of the illness or injury itself, children may experience additional trauma by being separated from family members by medical order or when they must go through very difficult procedures. Depending on the situation, they may have to relate to new people in unfamiliar settings, the effects of which will vary by age and circumstances. In an effort to reduce the incidence of traumatic stress reactions, health-care professionals and other supportive services in hospitals and outpatient clinics must offer trauma-informed care. In addition, increased support for families is needed when they are dealing with medical illness or injury of their child in order to provide them with the additional resources they need to provide support for the child and family members. Again, the importance of the caregiver–child relationship is emphasized because the response and continuity of care provided influences the level of support for children.

Perhaps the most traumatic rupturing of the child–parent relationship comes with the loss of a parent through prolonged separation (e.g., military deployment) or death. Fortunately, telecommunication has been somewhat helpful in providing continuity and reassuring children and families about safety of the deployed services' men and women. Deployment plays a role in separating children from parents and increasing stress for both the deployed and the home-based parent. Studies have shown problems in parenting, increased anxiety, irritability, and depression and more inconsistency in parenting. The deployed parent while communicating with his or her family may also be preoccupied with being at war. At the same time, the deployed service member's family is often proud of the father's or mother's heroism, which can help offset some of the problems. With deployment, Gewirtz and Zhang (Chapter 9) elaborate that it is not uncommon for the home-front parent to feel overwhelmed with the responsibility as well as to worry about the deployed parent. For adolescents, other issues may arise with the potential of high-risk behaviors that need to be carefully monitored as older children may also have difficulty with deployment and return. The parent the child knew before deployment may now seem very different when he or she returns home due to his or her experiences during deployment. These points illustrate the importance of consistency and predictability in the child–caregiver relationship to foster positive development.

Parental loss is also a possibility during deployment. Reyes and Lieberman (Chapter 11) present this important topic in their chapter on the effects of death of a parent or caregiver on a child. For children, especially young children, loss of a parent is obviously very traumatic. The young child depends on this relationship for security, predictability, and safety. As a child progresses in development and can incorporate a more complex cognitive understanding of loss, he or she is able to have a better understanding of the meaning of loss. However, it can still be very difficult for the mature child. With the loss of a parent, a child may not only experience his or her own loss and grief, but it may also impact the surviving parent and the circumstances of his or her life. The loss of a parent may impact his or her sense of safety and stability. Further, both the economic and relationship consistencies may change dramatically. If the loss is also associated with violence or a traumatic event, the effect on the child can be more intense.

In the concluding chapter in Volume 1, Pressley and Spinazzola (Chapter 14) provide an additional opportunity for the reader to gain understanding of the impact of exposure to more than one traumatic event on children of all ages. Exposure to multiple and complex traumas can affect the children's developing expectations of behavior of others in their environment and their internalized view of themselves. Because of the impact on physiology, emotions, and behaviors, such exposure may also make it more difficult for the child or adolescent to resume a relatively normal developmental trajectory.

All the chapters in this volume review topics with important developmental implications for children; however, some of them currently may be underrecognized. They provide information to help the reader understand the importance of how violence and trauma can affect children and adolescents and the longer-term impact over time. There is little question that exposure to violence and trauma impacts children and adolescents' current and future relationships and their ability to trust. It not only can have an impact on early brain development and social, emotional, and cognitive development, but it also affects peer relationships and risk-taking behavior in adolescence and subsequent adult relationships, health, and mental health. Volume 2 will expand on our understanding of the effects of violence and trauma on children by reviewing the impact on different systems that children and families encounter and often must negotiate as well as the policy implications of this work. A fuller description of the goals and objectives of Volume 2 is elaborated in our introduction for that volume.

References

Anda, R. F., Felitti, V. J., Bremner, J. D., Walker, J. D., Whitfield, C. H., Perry, B. D., . . . & Giles, W. H. (2006). The enduring effects of abuse and related adverse experiences in childhood. *European Archives of Psychiatry and Clinical Neuroscience*, 256(3), 174–186.

Felitti, V. J., Anda, R. F., Nordenberg, D., Williamson, D. F., Spitz, A. M., Edwards, V., . . . & Marks, J. S. (1998). Relationship of childhood abuse and household dysfunction to many of the leading causes of death in adults: The Adverse Childhood Experiences (ACE) Study. *American Journal of Preventive Medicine*, *14*(4), 245–258.

National Center for Children in Poverty. (2017). *Basic facts about low income children*. Retrieved from http://www.nccp.org/publications/pub_1074.html

Raz, G. (Producer), & Burke Harris, N. (Presenter). (2017). How does trauma affect a child's DNA? *TED Radio Hour*. Retrieved from https://www.npr.org/2017/08/25/545092982/nadine-burke-harris-how-does-trauma-affect-a-childs-dna

Substance Abuse and Mental Health Services Administration. (2014). *SAMHSA's concept of trauma and guidance for a trauma-informed approach*. HHS Publication No. (SMA) 14–4884. Rockville, MD: Substance Abuse and Mental Health Services Administration.

CHAPTER 2

Violence in Childhood and Adolescence

An Interpersonal-Developmental Perspective

Lucy S. King and Joy D. Osofsky

Relative to other forms of trauma or adversity, exposure to violence in childhood and adolescence may have unique deleterious consequences for development and mental health, particularly if the perpetrator or the victim of the violence is known to the child. These experiences of violence are sometimes referred to as *interpersonal trauma*, which differs from accidental trauma or exposure to natural disasters in that human actors intentionally cause harm. As Finkelhor (2008) notes, "In interpersonal victimization, the elements of malevolence, betrayal, and injustice are more likely to be factors" (p. 23). From a developmental perspective, the experience of violence may have a distinct impact because it affects children's developing understanding of how others usually behave (Luke & Banerjee, 2013), their ability to regulate emotions in the face of an unpredictable and threatening environment (Maughan & Cicchetti, 2002), and the emotion learning circuitry in the brain that underlies this ability (McLaughlin, Peverill, Gold, Alves, & Sheridan, 2015). Disturbances in developing socioemotional systems caused by violence are likely to have cascading consequences for individuals' long-term capacities to trust others, feel safe in changing environments, and effectively regulate their physiology, emotions, and behavior (Masten & Cicchetti, 2010). Indeed, interpersonal trauma in childhood is associated with a broad range of mental health difficulties and symptoms that often co-occur (D'Andrea, Ford, Stolbach, Spinazzola, & van der Kolk, 2012). In this chapter, we present an interpersonal-developmental perspective on the impact of violence on children and adolescents. Specifically, we review research and theory characterizing interpersonal relationships as sources of both violence and protection across development, as well as the influence of violence on the development of these relationships.

Prevalence and Nature of Violence

Experiences of violence are prevalent in childhood and adolescence and take many forms. Children may be directly impacted by violence or may witness it through interactions with family members, peers, and community members. Data from the 2011 National Survey of Children's Exposure to Violence (Finkelhor, Turner, Shattuck, & Hamby, 2013) indicate that two in five children age 1 month to 17 years were physically assaulted in the previous year, including being assaulted by an adult or peer. Further, approximately 6 percent of children had been sexually victimized, with approximately 8 percent of girls age 14–17 years reporting an attempted or completed rape. Children were also victimized by their caregivers, such that about 4 percent were physically abused in the last year. In addition to directly experiencing violence, children witnessed family assaults (~8%), shootings (~4%), and community assaults (~17%). Unfortunately, these figures likely *under*estimate the true prevalence of violence in childhood. Although studies often rely on reports from parents to assess young children's experiences, parents may be unaware of certain events or incentivized to hide them (e.g., sexual or physical abuse). Older children can report their own experiences of violence, but they may nonetheless be hesitant to discuss them.

In addition to being prevalent and myriad, experiences of violence in childhood and adolescence may be chronic in nature. In the absence of intervention, children of maltreating caregivers are likely to be continuously exposed to violence until they are either removed from their homes by protective service agencies or they are old enough to leave. Indeed, research indicates that family adversity is fairly stable across the first fifteen years of life, such that it is uncommon to escape from an environment characterized by experiences such as family discord and abuse (Dunn et al., 2011). In fact, studies suggest that those who are victimized in childhood are more likely to be victimized later in life (e.g., Shields &

Cicchetti, 2001). Different types of early adversity are also interrelated. In an epidemiological sample of adults, Dong, Anda, and Felitti (2004) found that over 50 percent of individuals who reported childhood exposure to physical neglect also reported exposure to physical abuse. In addition to neglect, researchers have found that poverty, another form of deprivation, is associated with higher rates of exposure to household and community violence, as well as increased likelihood of harsh care and abuse (for a review, see Evans, 2004). Studies that document the interrelations between forms of adversity highlight the need to intervene early in order to prevent future exposure. Early intervention is especially critical given that researchers have consistently identified a *dose-response* effect between the number of types of trauma that children experience and the severity of their mental and physical health problems (e.g., Greeson et al., 2014). It can be difficult, however, to identify vulnerable children early in development. For example, parents and teachers may only identify affected children when they undergo challenging developmental transitions (e.g., puberty) and become more likely to engage in risk-taking behavior and meet diagnostic criteria for mental health disorders.

In understanding childhood experiences of violence, it is important to consider the reciprocal effects of children's interactions with their environment, the extent to which children are characterized by neurobiological susceptibility to their environment, and the multiple and evolving contexts in which children develop. Researchers have theorized that development is nonlinear and transactional, such that children's trajectories depend on interactions with a complex and changing environment (Bowlby, 1973). Although adults are responsible for providing safe and stable environments for children, children's prior experiences and existing patterns of functioning influence the quality of their interactions. For example, infants may develop more difficult temperaments following the experience of adversity, and these temperaments may elicit further negative behaviors from caregivers (for a review, see Kiff, Lengua, & Zalewski, 2011). According to *differential susceptibility theory* (Ellis, Boyce, Belsky, Bakermans-Kranenburg, & van Ijzendoorn, 2011), sensitivity to the environment is an adaptive evolutionary mechanism; children with a stable tendency toward heightened neurobiological reactivity to their environment will fare especially poorly in environments characterized by adversity, but especially well in highly enriched environments.

Bronfenbrenner's (1994) bioecological model of human development proposes that development occurs through increasingly complex, reciprocal interactions between an individual and his or her environment. Within this model, children may be affected by violence through their interactions with multiple nested systems. For example, children who develop in cultures that implicitly or directly condone the objectification of girls and women are more likely to experience sexual violence. Children developing in contemporary times, with greater access to the Internet and television, are exposed to cyberbullying and violence in the media in ways that previous generations were not. Therefore, although much of the research on childhood exposure to violence focuses on violence in the child's immediate family or community setting, it is important to consider broader historical and cultural factors in the etiology of violence.

Because experiences of violence are likely to co-occur with other types of adversity, it is challenging for researchers to identify the unique effects of violence and the distinct environmental causes of symptoms and behaviors. Recently, experts in childhood stress and trauma have moved beyond cumulative risk models of early adversity to advance frameworks that distinguish the unique effects of experiences of *threat* (e.g., violence) versus experiences of *deprivation* (e.g., poverty and neglect; Humphreys & Zeanah, 2015; McLaughlin & Sheridan, 2016; Sheridan & McLaughlin, 2014). Sheridan and McLaughlin (2014) posited that in situations of violence, the brain develops to deal with an unpredictable and dangerous world, resulting in alterations in the neurobiological systems that govern responses to fear. Researchers investigating the differential effects of unique types of adversity have found support for the theory that experiences of threat have unique associations with neurobiological reactivity (e.g., Busso, McLaughlin, & Sheridan, 2017). Others have identified subgroups of children exposed to violence and examined their distinct associations with mental health difficulties. For example, in a sample of young, high-risk children, Hagan, Sulik, and Lieberman (2016) identified a group of children who witnessed violence and another group who had been directly victimized. Even after controlling for the number of types of trauma that children had experienced, being directly victimized was associated with the most severe internalizing, externalizing, and post-traumatic stress symptoms.

Developmental Timing

In addition to identifying the distinct effects of different types of early adversity, there is interest in investigating how the developmental timing of adversity, or the developmental stage in which adversity occurs, influences subsequent functioning. Experiences in infancy, childhood, and adolescence may have different impacts because of the unique developmental processes occurring during these periods. In fact, there may be *sensitive periods* when certain experiences are likely to have the strongest and most lasting impact. At different life stages, different psychobiological systems are plastic and therefore open to alterations by the environment. In the first years of life, caregivers create and modify the environment for their infants, and infants depend on their caregivers to provide input across domains (e.g., visual, linguistic, somatosensory, socioemotional) to achieve developmental milestones. In contrast, as children enter adolescence, they transition toward independence from caregivers and require input from peers and the wider environment to develop adaptively (for a review, see Piekarski et al., 2016). In this context, experiences of violence perpetrated by caregivers may be especially consequential in early life, whereas peer and community violence may become more pertinent for outcomes during adolescence. Importantly, understanding the influence of the developmental timing of violence has implications for prevention and intervention. Developmentally informed interventions target different types of violence, psychobiological systems, and behaviors, depending on the child's developmental stage.

The Caregiver–Child Relationship in Early Life

According to John Bowlby's evolutionary theory of attachment, children come into the world biologically preprogrammed to form attachments with others to ensure their survival (Bowlby, 1969). Although infants are "prepared" to form these bonds, whether they are formed and how depends on the socioemotional input that their caregivers provide. Findings from orphanage studies of children who were deprived of individualized caregiving indicate that infancy is a sensitive period for forming attachments to caregivers. Specifically, children who were transferred from orphanages to high-quality foster-care homes earlier in their lives were more likely to form secure attachments with their new caregivers (Smyke, Zeanah, Fox, Nelson, & Guthrie, 2010). In the general population, most children demonstrate a secure attachment style (van Ijzendoorn & Kroonenberg, 1988), characterized by a safe and trusting relationship, which adaptively organizes stress and emotional regulation, enables exploration, and predicts more positive socioemotional functioning across childhood, adolescence, and adulthood (Braungart-Rieker et al., 2014; Dujardin, Bosmans, De Raedt, & Braet, 2015; Sroufe, 2005). The development of a secure attachment style, however, depends on the sensitivity and responsiveness of caregivers to child distress (Ainsworth, Blehar, Waters, & Wall, 1978).

Young children who experience violence are more likely to develop insecure attachments, characterized by behaviors that cling to, resist, or avoid parents who are perceived as unavailable or frightening (Ainsworth et al., 1978). Violence may affect the attachment relationship through multiple pathways. First, caregivers may be perpetrators of violence. Considerable research has demonstrated that children of maltreating caregivers are more likely to be classified as insecurely attached (e.g., Cicchetti, Rogosh, & Toth, 2006; Stronach et al., 2011). Although suboptimal, anxious-resistant and avoidant insecure attachment styles involve strategies for coping with stress. Unfortunately, children with particularly severe experiences, such as maltreatment, may fail to develop any attachment strategy. The *disorganized* attachment style, characterized by fear, disengagement, and dysregulation during stressful interactions with caregivers (Hesse & Main, 1999), is associated with psychobiological dysregulation and pronounced risk for psychopathology (MacDonald et al., 2008; van Ijzendoorn, Schuengel, & Bakermans-Kranenburg, 1999).

Violence may also affect the attachment relationship when caregivers are exposed to violence, and children are thus indirectly involved. By taxing the caregivers' stress and emotion regulation systems, experiences such as domestic violence are likely to affect caregiving behavior, which, in turn, will affect the attachment bond. Indeed, infants of trauma-exposed mothers with elevated posttraumatic stress disorder (PTSD) symptoms are at increased risk for developing an insecure attachment style (Bosquet Enlow, Egeland, Carlson, Blood, & Wright, 2014). Violence may also transmit generations. Research indicates that mothers exposed to maltreatment in childhood are more likely to maltreat their own children (Dixon, Browne, & Hamilton-Giachritsis, 1996; Pears & Capaldi, 2001) and that experiencing more stress as a parent may explain why mothers who have been maltreated show greater insensitivity (Pereira et al., 2012). Finally, caregivers can protect their children from threats through their positive behaviors. For example, infants whose mothers provided touch during a stressor showed less cortisol reactivity to the stressor and recovered from it faster (Feldman, Singer, & Zagoory, 2010). As such, parental behavior, including effective coregulation of children's stress responses, helps to determine the impact on the child of experiences of violence occurring outside of the attachment relationship (e.g., witnessing violence in the community or media). Interventions that support the caregiver, as well as the child, are therefore critical following exposure to violence (Appleyard & Osofsky, 2003).

A Case Example

To illustrate the impact of violence on the caregiver–child relationship as well as the importance of this relationship for recovery and resilience following exposure to violence, we present a case of two-year-old twin boys referred to the LSUHSC Infant Mental Health Program directed by Joy Osofsky following the violent shooting death of their mother. At the time of the referral, we had not previously experienced treatment related to extreme violence exposure with twins. The twins were born to Mr. and Mrs. D who prior to the shooting appeared outwardly to be loving, caring, and nurturing. However, as is so often the case, domestic violence is often hidden to the outside world beyond the family. According to the referral information, the birth of the twins to Mr. and Mrs. D. increased the level of stress in the family, leading to verbal conflict, which sometimes involved physical violence perpetrated by the twins' father. Before his wife became pregnant with the twins and even during the pregnancy, Mr. D worked hard and spent a great deal of time at home with his wife. However, after the twins were born, there was a mixed picture. Mr. D was at times very involved with the boys and even took them to their pediatric appointments. At other times, however, he lost his patience with both them and Mrs. D., shouted, and sometimes left the house for the night. By the time the twins were about two years old, Mr. D's behavior had become markedly more troubling. He frequently found excuses for not coming home for dinner and staying out late. When he did come home, he did not want to talk to his wife or play with the twins. Rather, Mr. D retreated to another room where he would drink by himself and watch television. While he preserved the appearance of "a good father" by joining his wife at times in public and taking the boys to pediatrics appointments, he spent very little time with either his wife or his sons. Mrs. D was therefore responsible for maintaining consistency and stability for the boys.

Mr. D. worried a lot about danger and violence in their neighborhood and kept a small gun in the night table drawer. His erratic behavior continued to increase. One evening, Mr. and Mrs. D's arguing escalated into fighting and, suddenly, Mr. D. became enraged, took out the gun, and shot and killed his wife. The twins, who were now a little over two years old, hid in a closet and reportedly did not witness the shooting death. They reportedly were very scared and ran out of the closet room screaming. A neighbor heard the gunshots, called the police, and ran over to the house. When the police came, they found the twins hunched in a corner crying with blood on their hands and bodies. The gun was near the twins, and reports indicated that their father had possibly placed the gun in one of their hands to suggest that one of the young children had pulled the trigger.

Both twins were extremely traumatized by witnessing the shooting death of their mother and the disorganization and violence of their father. When their mother's sister took them in to live with her after the incident, they cried continually, ran around constantly, and wouldn't communicate or play with anyone. The twins' maternal grandparents, who lived in another state, arrived to help support their daughter and the twins. After about four months, the family decided that it would be better for the twins to move to their grandparents' home, which was about four hours away; their aunt was overwhelmed with the twins, her own family, and the loss of her sister. Expectedly, the grandparents were also overwhelmed. They sought the LSUHSC Harris Center to receive treatment for the twins who had regressed and were very dysregulated emotionally and behaviorally. It was almost impossible to understand them when they spoke. This regression in language can often result from witnessing extreme trauma. According to the reports, the aunt stated that they were able to communicate understandably before the shooting death of their mother.

When the twins came to our program, we considered whether we should treat them separately or with their grandparents. However, the decision to work with them together and include the grandparents was made for us as the boys refused to be separated from each other, and at first, refused to be separated from their grandparents. Initially, they showed little emotion. They wandered often aimlessly around the playroom with little interest in playing or engaging with the therapist. When they did play, it was mainly repetitive banging; otherwise, they just sat in the room and stared into space. The therapist continually tried to interest them in different toys, and, over time, they started to pay attention. Over the course of the first month during which they had weekly sessions, progress was noted as they started to play with their grandparents. Again, at first, they had difficulty organizing their behavior, and the play was mainly posttraumatic behavior with little emotion and much repetition. During one session, when they heard a siren outside of the medical center office, they jumped and insisted on being picked up and held for at least 15 minutes. When they saw a toy doll that reminded them of their mother, they would first become disorganized and then "freeze" and stand totally still showing no emotions. Then, it appeared that they would gradually "unfreeze" and begin to play again. For over a year, individual support services and parental guidance were also provided to the grandparents weekly by another therapist to help them with feelings of being overwhelmed with taking care of the twins at the same time as they were mourning the loss of their daughter. Gradually, the boys' play become more organized and relaxed, and together with the therapist, they began to talk more about what happened, including some of the traumatic events they had witnessed, using drawing and books to help them tell the story. An important theme during play centered on "getting rid of the monster" so that they would be safe.

After about a year, the grandparents felt comfortable enrolling the twins in Head Start. They wanted the boys to be in different classrooms; however, the twins refused to separate. After they adjusted to leaving their grandparents each day to go to school, they did well and enjoyed playing with the other children. During this time, the therapist continued to see the twins monthly to check progress and provide support to the grandparents. Over time, in general, the elementary school years went smoothly. However, when they were about 10 years old, their grandmother became ill, and, in the playroom, we saw a return of both disorganized behaviors and some regression in language, play, and emotional control. At this time, therapy sessions resumed once a week to provide additional support to the boys. After about two months of more frequent sessions and continuing support from their grandfather, they were able to recover and get "back on track." While some regression was noticeable as their grandmother became sicker and then passed away, their gains remained in place. Their significant improvement and ability to adjust to difficult situations were clearly based on the consistency, routines, and love and nurturance from their grandparents. The twins built on both the stability in their early relationship with their mother and the support and consistency of their grandparents. Their warm, loving grandparents helped the twins develop the ability to depend on them as attachment figures despite the terrible trauma they had experienced early in their lives.

This case demonstrates the powerful effects of trauma and loss in early childhood, and the capacity of children, when they have access to reliable and nurturing caregivers to reestablish equilibrium and healthy functioning. It also provides an example of the developing child's changing relationships with caregivers.

Transitions in the Caregiver–Child Relationship

As children develop, they gain greater independence from their caregivers. Even the acquisition of basic skills, such as the ability to talk to other children and adults, entails the broadening of the interpersonal environment beyond caregivers. From an evolutionary perspective, by the time of adolescence, children have acquired the caregiving input necessary for early survival and have established the skills they need from the caregiving environment. Therefore, they begin to explore elsewhere to gain new input that is critical for long-term survival (Piekarski et al., 2016).

Normatively, relationships with parents have been established and are relatively stable by middle childhood. The transition to adolescence, however, is marked by changes in the caregiver–child relationship, which may have implications for exposure and resilience to violence. In two publications using a family-systems perspective to chart the trajectories of the parent–child relationship in siblings from middle childhood to late adolescence, Shanahan and colleagues identified changes in parental warmth (Shanahan, Mchale, Crouter, & Osgood, 2007) and parent–child conflict (Shanahan, Mchale, Osgood, & Crouter, 2007) that coincided with the transition to adolescence. Specifically, parental warmth remained stable in late childhood but decreased during the transition to adolescence. Furthermore, there were increases in parent–child conflict during the transition to adolescence. Interestingly, these relations depended on birth-order and gender of siblings.

The influence of caregivers on child functioning may also change during adolescence. Indeed, increasing child independence and changes in the nature of caregiving may signify the closing of a sensitive period for caregivers' behaviors and a shift in the plasticity of specific neural circuits. Animal and human studies have documented changes in "social buffering" during adolescence, such that the role of caregiver support in child biological regulation diminishes (for a review, see Hostinar, Sullivan, & Gunnar, 2014). For example, Hostinar, Johnson, and Gunnar (2015) found that children who experienced a stressor with their parent showed less cortisol reactivity compared to children who experienced a stressor with a stranger; for adolescents, however, the presence of their parent had no effect on cortisol reactivity. These findings point to a developmental shift in the role of the parent–child relationship in resilience to stressors. Researchers using functional magnetic resonance imaging (fMRI) have also found evidence for an adolescent shift in the influence of parents on the reactivity of the amygdala, which is a brain region involved in responses to threat. Gee et al. (2014) found that when *children* viewed pictures of their mother, as compared to when they viewed pictures of a stranger, they showed less reactivity of the amygdala and a more mature pattern of amygdala-prefrontal connectivity. The brains of adolescents, however, responded similarly to mother and stranger pictures.

Because parents may be less effective in moderating their children's biological reactivity and regulation to threat during adolescence, their children may be particularly vulnerable to stress, including violence, during this period. Indeed, it is possible that decreased parental moderation of threat contributes to increased rates of specific mental health disorders, including depression and anxiety, during adolescence (Centers for Disease Control and Prevention, 2013). Nonetheless, studies have shown that positive caregiving continues to serve as a protective resource during adolescence. Researchers studying parenting have used Baumrind's framework of *parenting style* (Baumrind, 1967, 1991), which delineates authoritative, permissive, and authoritarian parenting, to investigate the influence of caregiving during this developmental period. The authoritative style, defined by high levels of warmth and appropriate monitoring and limit-setting, has been consistently associated with better outcomes in adolescence compared to nonauthoritative styles. For example, the authoritative style is associated with reduced depressive symptomatology during adolescence, particularly among girls (Piko & Balazs, 2012).

Investigations of parenting styles suggest that suboptimal styles across childhood and adolescence (e.g., *indulgent* and *uninvolved* styles) are associated with the steepest increases in antisocial behavior from grades 1 to 12 (Luyckx et al., 2011). In contrast, positive parenting may help reduce adolescents' antisocial behaviors by moderating the association between violence exposure and delinquency. In a sample of early adolescent boys who were repeatedly exposed to racial discrimination (e.g., racial slurs, threats of violence), Simons et al. (2006) found that supportive parenting moderated the longitudinal relationship between discrimination and increases in delinquency by both decreasing the likelihood that discrimination would result in anger and hostile views of relationships and decreasing the likelihood that anger and hostile views would lead to violent behavior.

Finally, although caregivers may no longer serve as active regulators of child reactivity to threat during adolescence, patterns of reactivity still depend on early experiences with parents. For example, among parentally bereaved adolescents and young adults, higher levels of recent adversity were only associated with higher cortisol reactivity to an interpersonal conflict stressor for those who experienced lower levels of positive caregiving six years earlier (Hagan et al., 2011). Dysregulated cortisol has been frequently associated with risk for internalizing disorders, such as depression and anxiety (Adam et al., 2014; Colich, Kircanski, Foland-Ross, & Gotlib, 2015). Importantly, research also suggests that supportive parenting is as an explanatory mechanism in the development of internalizing problems during adolescence. Specifically, in a sample of 771 adolescents, family support at age 14 years was found to mediate the relation between childhood family adversity in the preschool years and depression at age 17 years (van Harmelen et al., 2016). In summary, despite important changes in the caregiver–child relationship during the transition to adolescence, adaptation in adolescence remains associated with current and past caregiver behavior. Indeed, experiences of abuse and domestic violence continue to influence risk for mental and physical health difficulties into adulthood (Felitti et al., 1998).

Peer Relationships

Children who experience violence in early life may be more likely to experience victimization in interactions with their peers. For example, among children aged 1 month to 17 years, being maltreated by a caregiver was associated with a 1.8 times higher likelihood of lifetime exposure to bullying (Finkelhor et al., 2013). Exposure to bullying, defined generally as repeated victimization in the context of an interpersonal power imbalance (for a detailed discussion of this definition, see van Noorden, Haselager, Cillessen, & Bukowski, 2014), is common. Indeed, data from the National Center for Education Statistics revealed that in 2013, approximately 22 percent of students age 12–18 reported being bullied at school during the school year, and 7 percent reported being cyberbullied anywhere during the school year (Zhang, Musu-Gillette, & Oudekerk, 2016). Other studies have identified even higher lifetime rates of this type of victimization, with about 40 percent of individuals age 14–17 years reporting lifetime exposure to assault by a peer (Finkelhor et al., 2013).

Researchers have identified emotion dysregulation in children as a potential mechanism for how exposure to violence in early life may confer risk for problematic peer relationships and, ultimately, increase risk for mental health difficulties. As noted previously, caregivers are powerful regulators of their children's emotions. Thus, children of maltreating caregivers may not develop adaptive emotion regulation strategies, which, in turn, places them at greater risk for problematic peer relationships. Specifically, Kim and Cicchetti (2009) found that experiencing multiple types of maltreatment and experiencing maltreatment earlier in life (infancy or toddlerhood) were associated with emotion dysregulation in children age 6–12 years attending a summer camp. Furthermore, children who showed greater emotion dysregulation also had higher externalizing symptoms (i.e., aggressive and delinquent behaviors), and higher externalizing symptoms predicted greater peer rejection at summer camp one year later. In another longitudinal study, researchers found that early adolescents who were exposed to greater peer victimization later experienced increases in emotion dysregulation, which predicted later increases in aggressive behavior (Herts, McLaughlin, & Hatzenbuehler, 2012).

Research indicates that children who have problems with emotion dysregulation also evidence issues in the development of empathy (Davidov & Grusec, 2006; Eisenberg et al., 1996). Empathy, including affective and cognitive dimensions, develops early. Indeed, children exhibited empathy for another in distress before the second year of life, and empathy at age 10 months prospectively predicted prosocial behavior (Roth-

Hanania, Davidov, & Zahn-Waxler, 2011). One way that early experiences of violence may disrupt the development of empathy is by impairing the development of emotion regulation, with lasting consequences for peer relationships. Although further studies are needed in this area to identify the associations between experiences such as maltreatment, emotion regulation, empathy, and peer relationships across development, research does indicate that deficits in empathy are associated with involvement in bullying, including both being a bully and being victimized (for a review, see van Noorden et al., 2014). On the other hand, given findings among adolescents that greater empathy is associated with increased likelihood of intervening to stop bullying (Bellmore, Ma, You, & Hughes, 2012), interventions aimed at increasing empathy may help to interrupt a developmental cascade of violence. Because cognitive empathy has been found to decrease during the transition from elementary school to middle school (Williford et al., 2016), such interventions may be particularly critical during periods of social transition.

Although peer relationships may be a source of vulnerability when they are characterized by violence or rejection, social support, including from peers, can serve as a source of protection. For example, across youth classified as bullies, victims, both bullies and victims, or uninvolved in bullying, those who were uninvolved reported the highest levels of peer social support (Holt & Espelage, 2007). Given the increasing importance of peer relationships during adolescence, peer social support may be particularly important for decreasing risk for mental health difficulties among adolescents who have experienced violence. Indeed, van Harmelen et al. (2016) found that the quality of friendships at age 14 mediated the association between relational bullying and depressive symptoms at age 17.

Conclusion

There are interventions for children across development that address issues of trauma or violence-exposure, in addition to supporting positive caregiver–child relationships. Caregiver-child interventions for young children (e.g., Child-Parent Psychotherapy [Lieberman, 2004] and the Attachment and Behavioral Catch-Up intervention [Dozier, Meade, & Bernard, 2014]) can increase positive parenting behaviors, decrease negative parenting behaviors, improve the attachment relationship, and ultimately increase child well-being following trauma and/or maltreatment. As detailed in the case study presented in this chapter, when intervention occurs early, is developmentally informed, and occurs in the context of the caregiver–child relationship, children can recover from even the most extreme experiences of violence. However, it is important to recognize that triggers may continue to occur, reminding the developing child of his or her earlier traumatic experiences. For older children and adolescents, there are interventions that are effective in addressing trauma, such as Trauma-Focused Cognitive Behavioral Therapy ([TF-CBT]; Cohen, Deblinger, Mannarino, & Steer, 2004; Cohen & Mannarino, 2008) and Cognitive Behavioral Intervention for Trauma in Schools ([CBITS]; Jaycox, Kataoka, Stein, Langley, & Wong, 2012). This widely used intervention focuses on group sessions with adolescents, building on the power of peer relationships, and includes parents in separate sessions.

Interpersonal relationships can serve both as sources of violence and sources of protection from violence across development. The experience of violence may compromise the quality of current and future relationships. The caregiver–child relationship is especially critical in the first months and years of life. While positive caregiver–child relationships are associated with well-being across development, early problems in the establishment of attachment bonds can have long-lasting negative consequences. The negative sequelae of the impact of violence on the caregiver–child relationship in early life, including impairments in the development of emotion regulation, may affect peer relationships, which are of increasing importance in adolescence as children transition toward greater independence from their caregivers. Of great concern is evidence for a cascading effect of violence, such that children who experience violence in childhood are more likely to be victimized later in life, have dysfunctional relationships, and develop externalizing and internalizing problems. However, positive relationships, in the form of positive parenting behaviors as well as high-quality friendships, may protect children and adolescents from the negative consequences of exposure to violence and help to halt this cascade of negative consequences.

References

Adam, E. K., Vrshek-Schallhorn, S., Kendall, A. D., Mineka, S., Zinbarg, R. E., & Craske, M. G. (2014). Prospective associations between the cortisol awakening response and first onsets of anxiety disorders over a six-year follow-up—2013 Curt Richter Award Winner. *Psychoneuroendocrinology*, *44*, 47–59. https://doi.org/10.1016/j.psyneuen.2014.02.014

Ainsworth, M. D. S., Blehar, M. C., Waters, E., & Wall, S. N. (1978). *Patterns of attachment: A psychological study of the strange situation*. Hillsdale, NJ: Erlbaum.

Appleyard, K., & Osofsky, J. D. (2003). Parenting after trauma: Supporting parents and caregivers in the treatment of children impacted by violence.

Infant Mental Health Journal, *24*(2), 111–125. https://doi.org/10.1002/imhj.10050

Baumrind, D. (1967). Child care practices anteceding three patterns of preschool behavior. *Genetic Psychology Monographs*, *75*(1), 43–88. https://doi.org/10.4135/9781473915435

Baumrind, D. (1991). *Effective parenting during the early adolescent transition*. Lawrence Erlbaum Associates, Inc. Retrieved from http://psycnet.apa.org/psycinfo/1991-97352-005

Bellmore, A., Ma, T. L., You, J. L., & Hughes, M. (2012). A two-method investigation of early adolescents' responses upon witnessing peer victimization in school. *Journal of Adolescence*, *35*(5), 1265–1276. https://doi.org/10.1016/j.adolescence.2012.04.012

Bosquet Enlow, M., Egeland, B., Carlson, E., Blood, E., & Wright, R.J. (2014). Mother-infant attachment and the intergenerational transmission of posttraumatic stress disorder. *Development and Psychopathology*, *26*(1), 41–65. https://doi.org/10.1017/S0954579413000515

Bowlby, J. (1969). *Attachment and loss: Attachment* (Vol. 1). New York: Basic Books. https://doi.org/10.1177/000306518403200125

Bowlby, J. (1973). *Attachment and loss: Separation, anxiety and anger* (Vol. 2). New York: Basic Books.

Braungart-Rieker, J. M., Zentall, S., Lickenbrock, D. M., Ekas, N. V., Oshio, T., & Planalp, E. (2014). Attachment in the making: Mother and father sensitivity and infants' responses during the Still-Face Paradigm. *Journal of Experimental Child Psychology*, *125*(1), 63–84. https://doi.org/10.1016/j.jecp.2014.02.007

Bronfenbrenner, U. (1994). Ecological models of human development. In T. Husen and N. Postlethwaite, eds. *International encyclopedia of education* (2nd ed.), 1643–1647. Oxford: Elsevier.

Busso, D. S., McLaughlin, K. A., & Sheridan, M. A. (2017). Dimensions of adversity, physiological reactivity, and externalizing psychopathology in adolescence. *Psychosomatic Medicine*, *79*(2), 162–171. https://doi.org/10.1097/PSY.0000000000000369

Centers for Disease Control and Prevention. (2013). Mental health surveillance among children—United States, 2005–2011. *MMWR*, *62*(Suppl 2). https://doi.org/su6202a1 [pii]

Cicchetti, D., Rogosh, F. A., & Toth, S. L. (2006). Fostering secure attachment in infants in maltreating families through preventive interventions. *Developmental Psychopathology*, *18*(3), 626–649.

Cohen, J. A., Deblinger, E., Mannarino, A. P., & Steer, R. A. (2004). A multisite, randomized controlled trial for children with sexual abuse-related PTSD symptoms. *Journal of the American Academy of Child and Adolescent Psychiatry*, *43*(4), 393–402. https://doi.org/10.1097/00004583-200404000-00005

Cohen, J. A., & Mannarino, A. P. (2008). Disseminating and implementing Trauma-Focused CBT in community settings. *Trauma, Violence, & Abuse*, *9*(4), 214–226. https://doi.org/10.1177/1524838008324336

Colich, N. L., Kircanski, K., Foland-Ross, L. C., & Gotlib, I. H. (2015). HPA-axis reactivity interacts with stage of pubertal development to predict the onset of depression. *Psychoneuroendocrinology, 55*, 94–101. https://doi.org/10.1016/j.psyneuen.2015.02.004

D'Andrea, W., Ford, J., Stolbach, B., Spinazzola, J., & van der Kolk, B.A. (2012). Understanding interpersonal trauma in children: why we need a developmentally appropriate trauma diagnosis. *The American Journal of Orthopsychiatry, 82*(2), 187–200. https://doi.org/10.1111/j.1939-0025.2012.01154.x

Davidov, M., & Grusec, J. E. (2006). Untangling the links of parental responsiveness to distress and warmth to child outcomes. *Child Development, 77*(1), 44–58.

Dixon, L., Browne, K., & Hamilton-Giachritsis, C. (1996). Risk factors of parents abused as children: A mediational analysis of the intergenerational continuity of child maltreatment (Part I). *Journal of Child Psycho, 46*(1), 47–57. https://doi.org/10.1111/j.1469-7610.2004.00339.x

Dong, M., Anda, R., & Felitti, V. (2004). The interrelatedness of multiple forms of childhood abuse, neglect, and household dysfunction. *Child Abuse & Neglect, 28*, 771–784. https://doi.org/10.1016/j.chiabu.2004.01.008

Dozier, M., Meade, E., & Bernard, K. (2014). Attachment and Biobehavioral Catch-Up: An intervention for parents at risk of maltreating their infants and toddlers. In S. Timmer & E. Urquiza (Eds.), *Evidence-based approaches for the treatment of maltreated children* (Vol. 3, pp. 43–59). Dordrecht, the Netherlands: Springer Science+Business Media. https://doi.org/10.1007/978-94-007-7404-9

Dujardin, A., Bosmans, G., De Raedt, R., & Braet, C. (2015). Children's attentional exploration of threatening information as related to trust in maternal support. *Developmental Psychology, 51*(10), 1341–1350. http://dx.doi.org/10.1037/a0039500

Dunn, V. J., Abbott, R. A., Croudace, T., Wilkinson, P., Jones, P. B., Herbert, J., & Goodyer, I. M. (2011). Profiles of family-focused adverse experiences through childhood and early adolescence: The ROOTS project a community investigation of adolescent mental health. *BMC Psychiatry, 11*, 109. https://doi.org/10.1186/1471-244X-11-109

Eisenberg, N., Fabes, R. A., Murphy, B., Karbon, M., Smith, M., & Maszk, P. (1996). The relations of children's dispositional empathy-related responding to their emotionality, regulation, and social functioning. *Developmental Psychology, 32*(2), 195–209. https://doi.org/10.1037/0012-1649.32.2.195

Ellis, B. J., Boyce, W. T., Belsky, J., Bakermans-Kranenburg, M. J., & van Ijzendoorn, M. H. (2011). Differential susceptibility to the environment: An evolutionary-neurodevelopmental theory. *Development and Psychopathology, 23*(1), 7–28. https://doi.org/10.1017/S0954579410000611

Evans, G. W. (2004). The environment of childhood poverty. *American Psychologist, 59*(2), 77–92. https://doi.org/10.1037/0003-066X.59.2.77

Feldman, R., Singer, M., & Zagoory, O. (2010). Touch attenuates infants' physiological reactivity to stress. *Developmental Science*, *13*(2), 271–278. https://doi.org/10.1111/j.1467-7687.2009.00890.x

Felitti, V. J., Anda, R. F., Nordenberg, D., Williamson, D. F., Spitz, A. M., Edwards, V., . . . Marks, J. S. (1998). Relationship of childhood abuse and household dysfunction to many of the leading causes of death in adults: The Adverse Childhood Experiences (ACE) Study. *American Journal of Preventive Medicine*, *14*(4), 245–258. https://doi.org/10.1016/S0749-3797(98)00017-8

Finkelhor, D. (2008). *Childhood victimization*. New York: Oxford University Press.

Finkelhor, D., Turner, H. A., Shattuck, A., & Hamby, S. L. (2013). Violence, abuse, and crime exposure in a national sample of children and youth. *JAMA Pediatrics*, *167*(7), 614–621. https://doi.org/10.1542/peds.2009-0467

Gee, D. G., Gabard-Durnam, L., Telzer, E. H., Humphreys, K. L., Goff, B., Shapiro, M., . . . Tottenham, N. (2014). Maternal buffering of human amygdala-prefrontal circuitry during childhood but not during adolescence. *Psychological Science*, *25*(11), 2067–2078. https://doi.org/10.1177/0956797614550878

Greeson, J. K. P., Briggs, E. C., Layne, C. M., Belcher, H. M. E., Ostrowski, S. A., Kim, S., . . . Fairbank, J. A. (2014). Traumatic childhood experiences in the 21st century: Broadening and building on the ACE studies with data from the National Child Traumatic Stress Network. *Journal of Interpersonal Violence*, *29*(3), 536–556. https://doi.org/10.1177/0886260513505217

Hagan, M. J., Roubinov, D. S., Gress-Smith, J., Luecken, L. J., Sandler, I. N., & Wolchik, S. (2011). Positive parenting during childhood moderates the impact of recent negative events on cortisol activity in parentally bereaved youth. *Psychopharmacology*, *214*(1): 231–238. https://doi.org/10.1007/s00213-010-1889-5

Hagan, M. J., Sulik, M. J., & Lieberman, A. F. (2016). Traumatic life events and psychopathology in a high risk, ethnically diverse sample of young children: A person-centered approach. *Journal of Abnormal Child Psychology*, *44*(5). https://doi.org/10.1007/s10802-015-0078-8

Herts, K. L., McLaughlin, K. A., & Hatzenbuehler, M. L. (2012). Emotion dysregulation as a mechanism linking stress exposure to adolescent aggressive behavior. *Journal of Abnormal Child Psychology*, *40*(7), 1111–1122. https://doi.org/10.1007/s10802-012-9629-4

Hesse, E., & Main, M. (1999). Second-generation effects of unresolved trauma in nonmaltreating parents: Dissociated, frightened, and threatening parental behavior. *Psychoanalytic Inquiry*, *19*(4), 481–540. https://doi.org/10.1080/07351699909534265

Holt, M. K., & Espelage, D. L. (2007). Perceived social support among bullies, victims, and bully-victims. *Journal of Youth and Adolescence*, *36*(8), 984–994. https://doi.org/10.1007/s10964-006-9153-3

Hostinar, C. E., Johnson, A. E., & Gunnar, M. R. (2015). Parent support is less effective in buffering cortisol stress reactivity for adolescents compared to children. *Developmental Science, 18*(2), 281–297. https://doi.org/10.1111/desc.12195

Hostinar, C. E., Sullivan, R. M., & Gunnar, M. R. (2014). Psychobiological mechanisms underlying the social buffering of the hypothalamic-pituitary-adrenocortical axis: A review of animal models and human studies across development. *Psychological Bulletin, 140*(1), 256–282. https://doi.org/10.1037/a0032671

Humphreys, K. L., & Zeanah, C. H. (2015). Deviations from the expectable environment in early childhood and emerging psychopathology. *Neuropsychopharmacology, 40*(1), 154–170. https://doi.org/10.1038/npp.2014.165

Jaycox, L. H., Kataoka, S. H., Stein, B. D., Langley, A. K., & Wong, M. (2012). Cognitive behavioral intervention for trauma in schools. *Journal of Applied School Psychology, 28*(3), 239–255. https://doi.org/10.1080/15377903.2012.695766

Kiff, C. J., Lengua, L. J., & Zalewski, M. (2011). Nature and nurturing: Parenting in the context of child temperament. *Clinical Child and Family Psychology Review, 14*(3), 251–301. https://doi.org/10.1007/s10567-011-0093-4

Kim, J., & Cicchetti, D. (2009). Longitudinal pathways linking child maltreatment, emotion regulation, peer relations, and psychopathology. *Journal of Child Psychology and Psychiatry, 51*(6), 706–716. https://doi.org/10.1111/j.1469-7610.2009.02202.x

Lieberman, A. F. (2004). Child-Parent Psychotherapy: A relationship-based approach to the treatment of mental health disorders in infancy and early childhood. In A. J. Sameroff, S. C. McDonough, & K. L. Rosenblum (Eds.), *Treating parent-infant relationship problems: Strategies for intervention* (pp. 97–122). New York: Guilford Press.

Luke, N., & Banerjee, R. (2013). Differentiated associations between childhood maltreatment experiences and social understanding: A meta-analysis and systematic review. *Developmental Review, 33*(1), 1–28. https://doi.org/10.1016/j.dr.2012.10.001

Luyckx, K., Tildesley, E. A., Soenens, B., Andrews, J. A., Hampson, S. E., Peterson, M., & Duriez, B. (2011). Parenting and trajectories of children's maladaptive behaviors: A 12-year prospective community study. *Journal of Clinical Child & Adolescent Psychology, 403*, 468–478. https://doi.org/10.1080/15374416.2011.563470

MacDonald, H. Z., Beeghly, M., Grant-Knight, W., Augustyn, M., Woods, R. W., Cabral, H., . . . Frank, D. A. (2008). Longitudinal association between infant disorganized attachment and childhood posttraumatic stress symptoms. *Development and Psychopathology, 20*(2), 493–508. https://doi.org/10.1017/S0954579408000643

Masten, A. S., & Cicchetti, D. (2010). Developmental cascades. *Development and Psychopathology, 22*(3), 491–495. https://doi.org/10.1017/S0954579410000222

Maughan, A., & Cicchetti, D. (2002). Impact of child maltreatment and inter-adult violence on children's emotion regulation abilities and socioemotional adjustment. *Child Development*, *73*(5), 1525–1542. http://dx.doi.org/10.1111/1467-8624.00488

McLaughlin, K. A., Peverill, M., Gold, A. L., Alves, S., & Sheridan, M. A. (2015). Child maltreatment and neural systems underlying emotion regulation. *Journal of the American Academy of Child & Adolescent Psychiatry*, *54*(9), 753–762. https://doi.org/10.1016/j.jaac.2015.06.010

McLaughlin, K. A., & Sheridan, M. A. (2016). Beyond cumulative risk: A dimensional approach to childhood adversity. *Current Directions in Psychological Science*, *25*(4), 239–245. https://doi.org/10.1177/0963721416655883

Pears, K. C., & Capaldi, D. M. (2001). Intergenerational transmission of abuse: A two-generational prospective study of an at-risk sample. *Child Abuse and Neglect*, *25*(11), 1439–1461. https://doi.org/10.1016/S0145-2134(01)00286-1

Pereira, J., Vickers, K., Atkinson, L., Gonzalez, A., Wekerle, C., & Levitan, R. (2012). Parenting stress mediates between maternal maltreatment history and maternal sensitivity in a community sample. *Child Abuse and Neglect*, *36*, 433–437. https://doi.org/10.1016/j.chiabu.2012.01.006

Piekarski, D. J., Johnson, C. M., Boivin, J. R., Thomas, A. W., Lin, W. C., Delevich, K., . . . Wilbrecht, L. (2016). Does puberty mark a transition in sensitive periods for plasticity in the associative neocortex? *Brain Research*, *1654*, 123–144. https://doi.org/10.1016/j.brainres.2016.08.042

Piko, B. F., & Balázs, M. A. (2012). Control or involvement? Relationship between authoritative parenting style and adolescent depressive symptomatology. *European Child and Adolescent Psychiatry*, *21*, 149–155. https://doi.org/10.1007/s00787-012-0246-0

Roth-Hanania, R., Davidov, M., & Zahn-Waxler, C. (2011). Empathy development from 8 to 16 months: Early signs of concern for others. *Infant Behavior and Development*, *34*(3), 447–458. https://doi.org/10.1016/j.infbeh.2011.04.007

Shanahan, L., Mchale, S. M., Crouter, A. C., & Osgood, D. W. (2007). Warmth with mothers and fathers from middle childhood to late adolescence: Within- and between-families comparisons. *Developmental Psychology*, *43*(3), 551–563. https://doi.org/10.1037/0012-1649.43.3.551

Shanahan, L., Mchale, S. M., Osgood, D. W., & Crouter, A. C. (2007). Conflict frequency with mothers and fathers from middle childhood to late adolescence: Within- and between-families comparisons. *Developmental Psychology*, *43*(3), 539–550. https://doi.org/10.1037/0012-1649.43.3.539

Sheridan, M. A., & McLaughlin, K. A. (2014). Dimensions of early experience and neural development: Deprivation and threat. *Trends in Cognitive Sciences*, *18*(11), 580–585. https://doi.org/10.1016/j.tics.2014.09.001

Shields, A., & Cicchetti, D. (2001). Parental maltreatment and emotion dysregulation as risk factors for bullying and victimization in middle childhood. *Journal of Clinical Child & Adolescent Psychology*, *30*(3), 349–363. https://doi.org/10.1207/S15374424JCCP3003_7

Simons, R. L., Simons, L. G., Harbin Burt, C., Drummund, H., Stewart, E., Brody, G. H., . . . Simons, R. (2006). Supportive parenting moderates the effect of discrimination upon anger, hostile view of relationships, and violence among African American boys. *Journal of Health and Social Behavior McLoyd*, *47*, 373–389.

Smyke, A.T., Zeanah, C.H., Fox, N.A., Nelson, C.A., & Guthrie, D. (2010). Placement in foster care enhances quality of attachment among young institutionalized children. *Child Development*, *81*(1), 212–223.

Sroufe, L.A. (2005). Attachment and development: A prospective, longitudinal study from birth to adulthood. *Attachment & Human Development*, *7*(4), 349–367. https://doi.org/10.1080/14616730500365928

Stronach, E.P., Toth, S.L., Rogosch, F., Oshri, A., Manly, J.T., & Cicchetti, D. (2011). Child maltreatment, attachment security, and internal representations of mother and mother-child relationships. *Child Maltreatment*, *16*(2), 137–145. https://doi.org/10.1177/1077559511398294

van Harmelen, A.-L., Gibson, J.L., St Clair, M.C., Owens, M., Brodbeck, J., Dunn, V., . . . Goodyer, I.M. (2016). Friendships and family support reduce subsequent depressive symptoms in at-risk adolescents. *PloS One*, *11*(5), e0153715. https://doi.org/10.1371/journal.pone.0153715

van Ijzendoorn, M.H., & Kroonenberg, P.M. (1988). Cross-cultural patterns of attachment: A meta-analysis of the strange situation. *Child Development*, *58*(1), 147–156. Retrieved from http://www.jstor.org/stable/1130396

van Ijzendoorn, M.H., Schuengel, C., & Bakermans-Kranenburg, M.J. (1999). Disorganized attachment in early childhood: Meta-analysis of precursors, concomitants, and sequelae. *Development and Psychopathology*, *11*(2), 225–249. https://doi.org/10.1017/S0954579499002035

van Noorden, T.H.J., Haselager, G.J.T., Cillessen, A.H.N., & Bukowski, W.M. (2014). Empathy and involvement in bullying in children and adolescents: A systematic review. *Journal of Youth and Adolescence*, *44*(3), 637–657. https://doi.org/10.1007/s10964-014-0135-6

Williford, A., Boulton, A.J., Forrest-Bank, S.S., Bender, K.A., Dieterich, W.A., & Jenson, J.M. (2016). The effect of bullying and victimization on cognitive empathy development during the transition to middle school. *Child and Youth Care Forum*, *45*(4), 525–541. https://doi.org/10.1007/s10566-015-9343-9

Zhang, A., Musu-Gillette, L., & Oudekerk, B.A. (2016). Indicators of school crime and safety: 2015 (NCES 2016–079/NCJ 249758). Washington, DC: National Center for Education Statistics, U.S. Department of Education and Bureau of Justic Statistics, Office of Justice Programs, U.S. Department of Justice. https://doi.org/10.1037/e541412012-001

CHAPTER 3

The Impact of Violence and Trauma on Health and Social Emotional Development

Krista Goldstine-Cole and Betsy McAlister Groves

This chapter examines the biological processes triggered by chronic stress and their effects on physical, mental and behavioral health. The first section, focused on the body's response to challenge and threat, considers the differences among positive, tolerable, and toxic stress. This is followed by an examination of scientific inquiry into the effects of trauma and chronic stress across the life span. It will conclude with a brief description of recent initiatives that offer reasons for hope.

Life experience doesn't just get under the skin. It is wired into the brain and remembered by the genome (Szyf, 2009). The environment, social interactions, and life experiences, particularly in the early years and during sensitive periods that occur intermittently into the 20s, unleash biological processes that shape brain development, genetic expression, and regulation of biochemicals. When interwoven with exposure to trauma, violence, and chronic family dysfunction, lifelong health is in the balance. Exposure to prolonged environmental and relational stress "promotes the development of high risk [health] conditions . . . including diabetes, depression, drug addiction and multiple forms of coronary heart disease"

(Meaney & Szyf, 2005, p. 104). However, while the effects of trauma and chronic stress are cumulative, and at times result in poor outcomes, adaptation is a universal process and is not a sign of damage (Lupien, McEwen, Gunnar, & Heim, 2009). Understanding the biology of trauma and chronic stress opens the door to new scientific inquiry, with significant influence on the development of community action, policy initiatives, and interventions at the individual, family, and institutional level.

Stress versus Chronic Stress

Although it does not always feel this way, stress can support learning and growth. For example, facing a new situation, such as the first day on a new job, generates stress, indicated by small increases in heart rate and hormone levels. Most people can cope with mild stressors, and occasional experiences of this kind build positive attributes such as resilience (Center on the Developing Child, n.d.). More pronounced stress, as with a personal loss or emergency, evokes a more powerful stress response. When intermittent and buffered by strong, healthy relationships, such stressors are uncomfortable, but tolerable. However, frequent or chronic instances of serious stress are not tolerable. Because of its deleterious effects on "learning, behavior and health across the lifespan," Harvard's Center on the Developing Child (n.d.) calls chronic stress "toxic stress."

Nature seeks homeostasis or balance, and at the biological level, stress is an exquisite balancing act. Without toxic stress, biochemicals excite and then calm the nervous system in quick succession when confronted by difficult or dangerous conditions. Alerted to potential threat, the autonomic nervous system, responsible for nonconscious bodily functions such as heartbeat, sounds a biochemical alarm that triggers a physical response, including an increase in blood pressure and heartbeat. This prepares the body for a short burst of physical activity, for example, running away. The HPA-axis, which controls production of many biochemicals, begins churning out high levels of steroid hormones known as glucocorticoids (GCs). GCs activate the amygdala, an area of the brain associated with fear. In essence, this blocks the capacity for critical thinking and revs up reactivity. Biology does not anticipate a protracted, epic battle with danger. Rather, these physiological mechanisms prepare the individual for a quick, decisive *fight*; a short but liberating *flight*; or a quiet, under-the-radar *freeze* response. Within a few minutes, the GCs that stimulated heart rate, sweat, and agitation at the beginning of the cycle switch their target to the parasympathetic nervous system, which is responsible for rest and calming. As quickly as the body prepared for (and perhaps executed) fight, flight, or freeze, it returns to its prestress state. The entire cycle takes less than half an hour (McEwen, 2005; Obradović, Busch, Stamperdahl, Alder, & Boyce, 2010).

In a system meant to balance and rebalance itself, both under- and overproduction of GCs can be harmful. Healthy levels of GCs regulate metabolism, inflammation, and immune system responses and are essential to well-being (Teicher, Anderson, Polcari, Anderson, & Navalta, 2002). When GCs are not produced, Addison's disease or primary adrenal insufficiency occurs, resulting in a range of blood-pressure-related and autoimmune conditions (Bancos, Hahner, Tomlinson, & Arlt, 2015). Low GCs, common in cases of child neglect, are associated with posttraumatic stress disorder (Lupien et al., 2009) and depression (Goff & Tottenham, 2014). Overproduction of GCs may result in a range of physical and mental health challenges, such as attention disorder or anxiety (Teicher et al., 2002).

Chronic stress occurs when GCs are continuously produced. Living in a war zone, famine, recurring community violence, and child abuse or neglect each presents ongoing threat that outstrips the cyclical capacity of the stress response system. Chronic production of stress hormones is unhealthy and potentially toxic for the nervous, cardiovascular, digestive, and metabolic systems. Importantly, early stress begets stress. Chronic stress in utero or in early life results in molecular changes that increase production of GCs at lower levels of provocation across the life span (Meaney et al., 1996).

Chronic stress in childhood and adolescence shapes the developing brain. As Teicher et al. (2002) note, "The brain is designed to be sculpted and modeled by experience" (p. 414). On the one hand, exposure to severe, stressful conditions produces the ability to anticipate and respond aggressively to danger, increasing the likelihood of survival in a threatening and stressful world. On the other, a nurturing and responsive environment produces the emotional stability and empathy prized in a more benevolent world of social relationships and creativity (Teicher et al., 2002). The following sections will highlight research that led to this understanding.

Learning from Animal Research

While recent developments in brain scanning technology have made it possible to look inside the brain, there are significant ethical and practical limitations to experimenting on humans. In fact, laboratory research on healthy, living neurons from humans was not achieved until 2017, when researchers partnered with brain surgeons to recover small amounts of healthy brain matter removed as part of surgical procedures to treat cancer and other disease (Hamilton, 2017). Therefore, much of what we know about the effects of stress on the development of the brain comes from animal research. Studies with rats and monkeys have demonstrated how cells and biological systems respond to chronic stress, and the results have helped scientists develop hypotheses they could test in humans using noninvasive and ethical methods, such as fMRI scans. Studies across mammals indicate that trauma and adversity can become hardwired into the brain.

All mammals have a similar brain architecture, a six-layer neocortex organized by functional regions, which are specialized areas that initiate and organize broad functions such as motor skills or language. Following a genetic blueprint, functional regions begin to form early in gestation. In succession, stem cells differentiate to become neurons, migrate to their designated functional region, and begin to develop axons, the branches that will eventually support networking among brain cells. Although this developmental process is driven by genes, biochemical disruptions, such as chronic stress in the mother, exposure to maternal drug use, or exposure to environmental toxins may alter the timing of events, thereby altering outcomes related to structure and function (Fox, Levitt, & Nelson, 2010; Szyf, 2009).

In one of the earliest mammal studies designed to measure the effects of stress on development, the psychologist Harry Harlow (1958) separated baby monkeys from their mothers. Some babies were offered a "substitute" mother, fashioned from wires and covered with cloth. Although these "mothers" were not lifelike, little monkeys still looked to them for protection and they would cling to the maternal stand-in when startled or frightened.

Persistent fear is an important feature of chronic stress across species, and it is also evident in poorly mothered rats. For rats, maternal care is expressed through grooming and licking their offspring, a highly variable trait across mothers. Some will lick frequently and with great vigor, while others lick far less. Meaney placed rats whose biological mothers were high grooming with low-grooming foster mothers and vice versa. Pups raised in a low-licking and grooming environment, whether by their biological mother or by a foster mother, showed signs of persistent fear, including strong startle reflex and failure to explore new spaces. The same behaviors were seen in their offspring. In contrast, rats raised by high-licking and grooming mothers or foster mothers did not have these signs of stress (Francis, Diorio, Liu, & Meaney, 1999; Meaney & Szyf, 2005).

Building on Harlow and Meaney's results, researchers hypothesized that GCs were related to the outcomes. To test this hypothesis, pregnant rats were injected with GCs or stressed in environmental ways. Observable changes to brain development, particularly in the hippocampus and amygdala regions of the brain, occurred in offspring when GCs were manipulated in these ways. Long-term consequences included learning impairments that worsened with age, anxiety and depression, and sensitivity to drug abuse (Lupien et al., 2009).

Stress, Trauma, and Brain Development in Children

In 2015, there were 683,000 substantiated cases of child abuse or neglect in the United States (Child Welfare Information Gateway, 2017). On any given day 428,000 American children are in foster care, removed from their home because the parent is unable or unwilling to care for them (Children's Rights.org n.d.). Domestic violence, parental substance abuse, and parental mental illness are often present alongside maltreatment, adding to the trauma and stress (Anda et al., 2006). Consistent with other mammals, children deprived of loving parental relations are at risk of cognitive, social, and behavioral difficulties. On average, maltreated children have lower test scores and grades and are more likely to repeat a grade than their nonmaltreated peers. They are referred to the office and suspended more often. In addition, they more frequently experience peer rejection and relationships with teachers who label them as "difficult" (Eckenrode, Laird, & Doris, 1993; Khan et al, 2015; Kinard, 2001; Kurtz, Gaudin, Wodarski, & Howing, 1993; Leiter, 2007; Myers & Pianta, 2008; Platt, Kadosh, & Lau, 2013; Rowe & Eckenrode, 1999; Toth & Cicchetti, 1996).

Past laboratory experiments and observational studies of maltreated children led scientists to hypothesize that overexposure to GCs due to intrafamily violence, deprivation, and dysfunction was shaping the development of specific regions of the brain responsible for learning, emotional regulation, and attachment and positive social relationships. In of particular, the existing science suggested that the amygdala and hippocampus would likely be affected by trauma and chronic stress. Over the past 25 years, results from study of these regions have, together with significant improvements to neuroimaging technology, allowed scientists to test, affirm, and expand these hypotheses.

The *amygdala* is part of the limbic system, the brain's emotional center. Development of the amygdala begins early, and it reaches adult size in females by age four (Andersen et al, 2008). This area of the brain is crucial to fear conditioning; the fight or flight response is triggered via the amygdala. Unlike other regions of the brain, which tend to lose mass to chronic stress, GCs stimulate neurons in the amygdala to grow branches that reach out to network with other neurons, thereby adding volume to this region (Pechtel, Lyons-Ruth, Anderson, & Teicher, 2014).

In addition, repeated exposure to GCs increases sensitivity to stress over time, creating a positive feedback loop: more stress results in more fear, which results in more stress. Beyond its role in the fear circuit of the brain, the amygdala is important to the formation and recall of memories involving emotion. It also regulates sexual behavior. Healthy amygdala function is essential to impulse control, including the regulation of impulsive violence (Lupien et al., 2009; Teicher et al., 2002, 2003).

As measured using scanning techniques, this region shows a significant increase in volume when exposed to chronic stress, a change that is lasting and nonreversible. Pechtel et al. (2014) found that exposure to maltreatment accounted for more than one-quarter of variation in amygdala volume. Stress effects on the amygdala are associated with posttraumatic stress disorder (PTSD), depression, and anxiety, as well as somatic conditions like headache and dizziness (Pechtel et al., 2014; Teicher, 2000; Teicher et al., 2003).

The *hippocampus* is also a part of the limbic system and is critical to attention and memory, as well as processes related to navigating time and space. The hippocampus is also responsible for pattern completion and recognition skills, critical in the process of learning to read (Gómez & Edgin, 2016). Stress effects on the hippocampus include memory problems, PTSD, panic disorder, depression, schizophrenia, and borderline personality disorder (Bremner et al., 1997; Teicher et al., 2002).

Like the amygdala, a child's hippocampus develops early, reaching many of its adult characteristics by 15 months of age (Gómez & Edgin, 2016); however, the hippocampus goes through iterative periods of pruning that make information processing more efficient (Andersen & Teicher, 2004; Teicher et al., 2002). The hippocampus is one of a few areas in the brain where new neurons are produced after birth (Bremner et al., 1997). This unique feature of the hippocampus helped to introduce a new and important theory in the study of brain development: sensitive periods (Andersen & Teicher, 2004).

Trauma and Sensitive Developmental Periods

Another line of inquiry that has received attention focuses on the developmental timing of the adversity. Are there periods in a child's life when he/she is more vulnerable to the impact of chronic stress? Recent brain research suggests that each functional region has a unique developmental trajectory. During sensitive periods, any exposure to a developmentally salient event has the power to shape that trajectory (Andersen, 2003). While the severity or frequency of stressors may shape the brain in non-sensitive periods, any level of exposure during a sensitive period is likely to have meaningful effects. As examples, Pechtel et al. (2014) found evidence of a sensitive period for the amygdala at age 10–11, replicating findings from Andersen et al. (2008), who found sensitivity to sexual abuse in this region at that age. Consistent with the hypothesis that functional regions may have more than one sensitive period, Andersen's team also found the amygdala to be sensitive to sexual abuse at ages 3–5.

Just as sensitive periods open a window of vulnerability to traumatic experience, they also open the possibility that positive experience will have profound effects (Andersen, 2003). Scientists following abandoned and institutionalized orphans in Romania have found that the timing of intervention has significant and lasting effects on development. The researchers, Nelson, Fox, and Zeanah (2007), were able to create a therapeutic foster care intervention and place children in treatment in a longitudinal, randomized control study. When the children were 4 and a half years old, these researchers found that those who entered foster care prior to 24 months of age fareed better on measures of cognitive, motor, and behavioral development than did same-age children who entered foster care when older than 24 months. While duration of deprivation (low levels of human contact in the orphanage) was strongly associated with low IQ, Fox, Almas, Degnan, Nelson, & Zeanah (2011) found that children placed in foster care prior to age 26 months were more likely to have typical IQ at age 8.

In a longitudinal study of more typical children, Luby, Belden, Harms, Tillman, & Barch (2016) found preschool to be a sensitive period for positive maternal support. Children were presented with a task that required significant impulse control (not opening a gift wrapped in brightly colored paper until all study-related paperwork was completed by the parent). Strong maternal support in navigating this task was associated with increased hippocampal volume, which persisted through puberty and into adolescence.

Scientists in a variety of fields, including psychology and neurobiology overwhelmingly agree that the first 1,000 days, or roughly, the first three years of life, are crucial to the healthy development of the human brain. Understanding of this body of science by policymakers has led to a number of initiatives throughout the United States. Broadly these policies fall into four categories: child health, strong families, positive learning experiences, and early childhood systems (Zero to Three, n.d.). One example of public investment that responds to the evidence of zero to three as a sensitive period is the federal Maternal, Infant and Early Childhood Home Visiting Program, a $372.4 million per year effort focused on prenatal care, breastfeeding, meeting early developmental milestones, and preventing child abuse and neglect (Health Resources & Services Administration [HRSA], n.d.).

Stress, Genes, and Biological Pathways to Health Outcomes

We now know that chronic stress, the ongoing secretion of steroid hormones known as GCs, profoundly influences how the brain develops. It also shapes which genes are expressed through processes known as epigenetics. Specifically, epigenetics modifies the genome without changing the gene sequence within DNA (Bagot & Meaney, 2010). Epigenetics likely undergirds a significant portion of trauma-related brain development (Fox et al., 2010) as well as contributes to other health risks associated with adverse childhood experiences.

At first, the idea of genes being turned on or off by experience may seem difficult to grasp, especially for anyone whose education in biology ended before the Human Genome Project or included a Mendelian explanation of dominant and recessive genes. The basic principles, however, are easy to observe by looking in the mirror. The eyeballs looking back from the mirror appear to be quite different from skin and hair, even though each cell in each of these features contains the same paired chromosomes and DNA sequence. Further, when a cell in the eyeball reproduces itself (cell replacement is ongoing), it does not (unless something has gone terribly astray) produce a cell that more properly belongs in the brain or the lung or the immune system. Rather, it clones itself with little, if any, variation.

The question of how cells with the same DNA can be both physically and functionally different from one another is not a new one. Until recently, it was believed that such differentiation occurred in utero, ceased after birth, and was permanent. However, the Human Genome Project, which began in 1990, made clear that the genome—an individual's complete set of chromosomes—is not "a static form of background information, but rather a dynamic and indeed modifiable force . . . constantly regulated by environmental signals" (Bagot & Meaney, 2010, p. 753). Laboratory experiments now suggest that epigenetic changes are ongoing and may be reversed (Szyf, 2009).

How is this explained? Essentially, while identical chromosomes and genes are present in each cell, not every gene is expressed in every cell. When a gene is expressed, it can be "read" by the cell and its directions followed, a process known as transcription. However, when methylation occurs—the covering of a gene through a chemical bonding process—the gene cannot be read and its directions are not followed. As a result, different cells—eyeballs, as opposed to skin—are differentiated by the genetic instructions they are following. Chronic stress may change which instructions cells have access to over the life span.

As with neurobiology, much of what we know about epigenetics comes from animal studies. For example, scientists have found that injecting pregnant rats with GCs altered the production of receptors in the HPA-axis associated with gene transcription in the offspring (Lupien et al., 2009). Alterations in just one transcription factor can change "the functional fate of cortical regions" of the brain (Fox et al., 2010, p. 32). Even small changes early in the formation of the brain can result in atypical networking among neurons, as the formation and regulation of synapses are premised largely on gene transcription. A synapse, the connection between two neurons, is formed by an axon, which sends messages from one neuron, and a dendrite, which receives messages for another neuron. Recent postmortem examination of people who died by suicide showed that specific genes related to dendrite production in the hippocampus were heavily methylated compared to controls who died by other causes (Szyf, McGowan, & Meaney, 2008). In other words, the genes associated with dendrite production in a stress-sensitive region of the brain were silenced in individuals who died by suicide. This discovery opens the door to the possibility that reduced hippocampal volume in traumatized individuals may be explained by this epigenetic mechanism (McEwen, 2007).

To summarize, epigenetics, which is deeply affected by chronic stress as well as environmental toxins (Szyf et al., 2008), affects not only brain development but also biologic processes associated with metabolism, energy and fatigue, regulation of stress, chronic pain, and eating behaviors (McEwan, 2007). Our understanding of epigenetics is being transformed with extensive research in this field; personalized medicine and cancer research are leading the way.

While stress may come in many forms, continuous production of GCs, the steroid hormones known as glucocorticoids, is pernicious. For children, such toxic stress is often triggered by trauma, including intrafamily or intracommunity violence and dysfunction. The biochemicals associated with chronic stress shape the brain and the epigenome.

While the chemical sculpting processes create a better fit between the individual and a "malevolent" world, these changes leave the individual vulnerable to a wide range of physical, mental, and behavioral health outcomes across the life span. The next section will explore common chronic stressors in childhood and their effects on lifelong health and functioning.

The Adverse Childhood Experiences Study

The Adverse Childhood Experiences (ACE) Study was undertaken in the 1990s to explore the relationship between health outcomes in adulthood and adverse childhood experience (Felitti et al., 1998). This landmark study, conducted in partnership between the U.S. Centers for Disease Control and Kaiser Permanente San Diego, a health maintenance organization, has transformed our understanding of the connections between childhood stressors and poor health in adults, and the enormous social and economic costs that are involved. This section will present an overview of the ACE Study, followed by several examples of the health findings. Finally, the study's limitations and its potential for use in the policy and practice realms will be explored.

Structure of the ACE Study

Between 1995 and 1997, over 17,000 adults seeking preventative healthcare at Kaiser Permanente's integrated health system in San Diego, California, were asked to complete a survey regarding the frequency and severity of various forms of child maltreatment and household dysfunction they may have experienced growing up. The aim of the study was to explore the possible links between childhood abuse and household stress, and adult health risk behavior and disease. During the first wave of data gathering, participants were asked about 7 categories of adverse experiences: childhood abuse (psychological abuse, physical abuse, and sexual abuse) and household dysfunction (violence against the mother, substance-abusing, mentally ill or suicidal household member, and incarceration of family any member; Felitti et al., 1998). During the second wave, physical and emotional neglect were added, along with parental discord as measured by divorce or separation, resulting in a list of 10 adverse childhood experiences (Dong et al., 2004; see Box 3.1). ACEs have been associated with a number of physical, mental, behavioral, and relational health outcomes across the life span.

Box 3.1 What Are the Adverse Childhood Experiences (ACEs)?

- Physical abuse
- Sexual abuse
- Emotional abuse
- Physical neglect
- Emotional neglect
- Depressed, suicidal, or mentally ill caregiver
- Alcoholic or substance-abusing family member
- Parental divorce or separation
- Witnessing domestic violence
- Incarcerated family member

(Anda et al., 2006; Felitti et al., 1998)

Prevalence of ACEs

The study found that two-thirds of the respondents had at least one adverse childhood experience (ACE); 87 percent of those with one ACE had at least one additional ACE; 10 percent had three ACEs; and 12.5 percent had four or more ACEs. In summary, it was rare that respondents experienced only one ACE. The most common experiences were physical abuse (28.3%) and exposure to household substance abuse (26.9%). The number of ACEs was strongly correlated with subsequent high-risk behaviors, such as smoking, drinking, or drug use (Dong et al., 2004). Through two decades of analyses that included medical records, prescriptions for medications, and death certificates (when relevant), it became clear that ACEs are correlated with a broad range of health outcomes, including heart, lung, and liver disease; cancer, diabetes, mental illness, and attempted suicide; alcohol, tobacco, and other drug use; multiple marriages/divorce; and high-risk sexual activity.

ACE Score, Risk, and the Dose-Response Relationship

The ACE score ranges from 0 to 10 and is the sum of the number of categories of ACEs experienced up to age 18. It is "a measure of cumulative exposure to traumatic stress during childhood" (Brown et al., 2007,

p. 961). As an example, experiencing physical abuse, regardless of the number of incidents, renders an ACE score of one. When physical abuse occurs alongside substance abuse and domestic violence, the ACE score is three.

Across analyses, researchers found that as the ACE score rises, the risk for a wide range of health outcomes increases in a stepwise fashion. For example, individuals who experienced one ACE are 10 percent more likely than those with no ACEs to suffer from obesity, while those with two or three ACEs are 40 percent more likely, and those with six or more ACEs are 60 percent more likely to be obese (Williamson, Thompson, Anda, Dietz, & Felitti, 2002). This dose-response relationship has been found between the ACE score and a broad range of physical, mental, behavioral, and relational outcomes. This finding has not only medical implications but social and economic implications as well. For example, the ACE Study found a graded dose-response relationship between absenteeism from work and serious financial problems (Anda et al., 2004) and between ACEs and disability from work (Anda & Brown, 2010). As the ACE score rises, the number of co-occurring health conditions experienced and medications prescribed also rises (Anda et al., 2007; Anda, Brown, Felitti, Dube, & Giles, 2008).

Independent Effects of ACEs on Health and Mental Health Outcomes

The ACE Study found evidence of a direct relationship between ACEs and various aspects of mental health. For example, there is a dose-response relationship between ACEs and depression and anxiety (Edwards, Holden, Felitti, & Anda, 2003), attempted suicide (Dube et al., 2001), and hallucinations (Whitfield, Dube, Felitti, & Anda, 2005). The ACE score is also associated with prescriptions for psychotropic medication. For example, those reporting one ACE are 1.3 times more likely to be prescribed antidepressants than those reporting no ACEs, while those with three ACEs are 1.8 times more likely, and those with five or more ACEs are 2.9 times as likely to be prescribed medication (Anda et al., 2007).

Cumulative Risks of ACEs on Health Outcomes

Many physical health disorders associated with ACEs are cumulative. As an illustration, consider smoking, which is a risk factor for a variety of heart, lung, and vascular diseases as well as cancer. Compared to those with no ACEs, those with five or more ACEs are 5.4 times more likely to smoke regularly by age 14; 3.1 times more likely to have smoked at least

100 cigarettes in their lifetime; 2.1 times more likely to currently smoke; and 2.8 times more likely to be a heavy smoker (more than 20 cigarettes a day). Thus, it is not surprising that the likelihood of experiencing chronic obstructive pulmonary disease (COPD), a progressive lung disease commonly associated with smoking, rises with the ACE score (Anda et al., 2008).

The High Costs of ACEs

High-ACE individuals utilize a disproportionate amount of health care in the United States, including office visits, emergency room visits (Chartier, Walker, & Naimark, 2010), and prescription drugs (Anda et al., 2008). On average, individuals with six or more ACEs die 20 years younger than those with no ACEs (60.6 years versus 79.1 years). Those with six or more ACEs are 1.7 times more likely to die before age 75 and 2.4 times more likely to die before age 65 compared to those with no ACEs. To date, 90 percent of deaths among ACE Study participants are due to the five leading causes of death in the United States—heart disease and stroke, cancer, disease of the nervous system and sensory organs, respiratory disease, and disease of the digestive system (Brown et al., 2009).

In addition to the direct health-related impacts, ACEs have staggering social costs. ACEs are associated with over half of illicit drug use, two-thirds of intravenous drug use, and two-thirds of addiction to drugs (Dube et al., 2003; Felitti, 2004). Half of incarceration in the United States is associated with drug use, possession, or distribution (Alexander, 2012). While no large-scale study of ACEs in prison currently exists, one study found that among incarcerated youth, only 2.8 percent report no ACEs while 50 percent report four or more (Baglivio et al., 2014). The cost of incarceration is approximately $80 billion per year (Schmitt, Warner, & Gupta, 2010).

Remaining Lines of Inquiry

The findings of the ACE Study are powerful. State governments, professional associations, and public-private partnerships are utilizing the ACE Study findings as a basis for policy and action (e.g., Health & Medicine Policy Research Group, n.d.). However, as in all studies, this one has limitations. Most notably, the ACE Study surveyed adults enrolled in a private health maintenance organization who were predominantly white, college educated, and middle income (Felitti et al., 1998); these demographics suggest caution in generalizing the findings to the broader population.

Efforts to apply the ACE Study in broader contexts and to address its limits have facilitated new lines of inquiry. Four examples are worth noting:

1. Does the focus on the accumulation of ACEs mask evidence of sensitive developmental periods, which, if better understood, might result in even more powerful action? Increasing evidence from neurobiology indicates that timing of adversity may be more important and powerful than the numbers of experiences for some outcomes (Lupien et al., 2009).
2. Are social conditions such as racism and discrimination as powerful or even more powerful determinants of health than ACEs? The ACE Study was designed to measure the effects of household dysfunction on physical, mental, behavioral, and relational health across the life span. As the study of trauma has expanded, the importance of social conditions, including exposure to racism and discrimination, economic hardship, and community violence, to health and healthy development has become clearer. Further inquiry is needed not only to understand the broader determinants of health but also to tailor interventions in a manner that makes best use of limited resources and produces the best results for young people.
3. How can we predict the specific outcomes for high-ACE individuals? The ACE Study findings make it clear that there is no singular path from a particular ACE score to a specific health outcome. The ACE Study was intended to describe health outcomes at the population level and not at the individual level. There is both merit and risk in attempting to utilize a study of health risk for individual prediction. Success on this front might result in prevention of illness. For example, if it could be predicted that an individual was most at risk of substance abuse, intervening early and preventing initial use of substances could save many lives. Nevertheless, it is difficult to take such an enterprise to scale. Both neurobiology and epigenetics suggest that a constellation of conditions above and beyond ACEs, including conditions in utero, age at the time of maltreatment, and exposures to toxins, is critical to ultimate outcomes.
4. Is it possible and/or feasible to screen for ACEs in health or other settings? With the large body of evidence linking adversity in childhood to lifelong health and mental health consequences, many are turning their attention to screening and early intervention as a form of prevention, garnering interest in a range of health settings, particularly pediatric practices. The American Academy of Pediatrics published a toolkit of papers for pediatricians in 2012 that includes a review of the ACE Study and its implication for pediatric practice, resources for parents, and a guide for pediatricians on talking with families about ACEs (American Academy of Pediatrics, 2012). While this guide recommends universal screening for child and adolescent exposure to trauma, there is a lack of consensus about how to screen in a way

that gathers accurate information and is not overly uncomfortable or intrusive to the parents who are answering the questions. Another approach that is being used in some practices is to screen for parental ACEs (Gillespie & Folger, 2017). This strategy links ACEs to parenting challenges, providing both education and support to parents.

Moving Forward: Reasons for Hope and Action

In the 20 years since the ACE Study results were first published, this body of research has had a significant impact on public policy, pediatric and adult health practices, and school reform (see Chapters 5 and 6 in Volume II). The Centers for Disease Control has established a website devoted to ACEs, with 86 journal articles reporting on findings from ACES data. The topics range from cancer to fetal death to workplace absenteeism—each using ACES data as its focal point. In addition to research, the ACE Study has influenced how community residents as well as governments act to solve high-cost social and health problems. For example, Washington State established a family, community, and state partnership to drive down the rates of child abuse and neglect, youth violence, youth substance abuse, and other major social problems by engaging communities to initiate research-informed, community-driven initiatives. Over 10,000 community members volunteered to learn about brain development and ACEs, collect and interpret data about the community, and initiate local efforts of their choosing intended to reduce the rates of ACEs and the physical, mental, and behavioral health problems that follow.

Over time, this partnership demonstrated increased community capacity, characterized by commitment to working and learning together, with attention to measurable results. Community capacity has been associated with reductions in intergenerational transmission of ACEs (Hall, Porter, Longhi, Becker-Green, & Dreyfus, 2012). Importantly, the capacity-building approach helps to disrupt intergenerational transmission of ACEs by supporting high-ACE community members in informing others and developing their own leadership and executive function (Porter, Martin, & Anda, 2016). Informed by these results, dozens of states, tribes, and cities are currently engaged in efforts to engage communities and build capacity in relationship to NEAR science (neuroscience, epigenetics, ACEs, and resilience). They include Philadelphia Urban ACE Study (Health Federation, n.d.), Children's Resilience Initiative in Walla Walla, Washington (Community Resilience Initiative, n.d.), and Building Strong Brains in Tennessee (Department of Children's Services, n.d.).

Some states have adopted a hybrid of research and community engagement. These states add ACEs questions to the Behavioral Risk Factor Surveillance System (BRFSS), a nationwide survey carried out each year at the state level. The results serve as a catalyst for public engagement and policy making. For example, Illinois has created the ACES Response Collaborative, a multiagency partnership that "strives to develop education, policies and responses to assist those who have experienced a high level of adversity, while simultaneously developing strategies to reduce the frequency and impact of ACEs as well as preventing their transmission to the next generation" (Health & Medicine Policy Research Group, n.d.).

While the Washington approach began with community engagement and the Illinois approach began with data collection, both promote a dual message: ACEs can have lifetime effects on a person's health and emotional well-being and resilience is real. Communities, policymakers, and service providers across the country are acting not only to prevent ACEs but to mitigate their effects as well; for example, analysis of BRFSS data collected 15 years after the establishment of Washington's partnership found that social supports—having a few people to rely on to meet emotional needs and provide help—made a significant difference in health and quality of life among high-ACE residents (Nurius, Logan-Greene, & Green, 2012). Increasingly, we are learning how to promote protective factors in children and families. (See Chapter 3 on resilience in Volume II of this book series.) The evidence suggests that each of us individually and all of us in community have the capacity to prevent ACEs, reduce intergenerational transmission, support high-ACE children and adults in healing, and develop protective factors for young people at risk of poor outcomes due to ACEs.

Conclusion

This chapter has focused on how life experience shapes the brain and the expression of genes and specifically how adverse childhood experiences impact physical, mental, behavioral, and relational health across the life span. These bodies of knowledge and research inform our understanding of the cumulative impact of trauma on well-being in children and adolescents. This knowledge can be used to better understand the complexities of young people's reactions to highly stressful events or environments and to mitigate the potential harms of their traumas. It can also be used to inform intervention at the individual or family level, at the service systems level, and at the policy level and to engage the community in making essential changes. The chapters that follow in this volume and in Volume II of this series will build upon this foundation by examining different types of trauma and interventions at multiple ecological levels.

References

Alexander, M. (2012). *The new Jim Crow: Mass incarceration in the age of colorblindness.* The New Press.

American Academy of Pediatrics. (2012). *Trauma guide.* Retrieved from www.aap.org/traumaguide

Anda, R., & Brown, D. (2010). Adverse Childhood Experiences and Population Health in Washington: The Face of a Chronic Public Health Disaster—Report for the Washington State Family Policy Council.

Anda, R. F., Brown, D. W., Dube, S. R., Bremner, J. D., Felitti, V. J., & Giles, W. H. (2008). Adverse childhood experiences and chronic obstructive pulmonary disease in adults. *American Journal of Preventive Medicine, 34*(5), 396–403.

Anda, R. F., Brown, D. W., Felitti, V. J., Bremner, J. D., Dube, S. R., & Giles, W. H. (2007). Adverse childhood experiences and prescribed psychotropic medications in adults. *American Journal of Preventive Medicine, 32*(5), 389–394.

Anda, R. F., Brown, D. W., Felitti, V. J., Dube, S. R., & Giles, W. H. (2008). Adverse childhood experiences and prescription drug use in a cohort study of adult HMO patients. *BMC Public Health, 8*(1), 198.

Anda, R. F., Felitti, V. J., Bremner, J. D., Walker, J. D., Whitfield, C. H., Perry, B. D., . . . Giles, W. H. (2006). The enduring effects of abuse and related adverse experiences in childhood. *European Archives of Psychiatry and Clinical Neuroscience, 256*(3), 174–186.

Anda, R. F., Fleisher, V. I., Felitti, V. J., Edwards, V. J., Whitfield, C. L., Dube, S. R., & Williamson, D. F. (2004). Childhood abuse, household dysfunction, and indicators of impaired adult worker performance. *The Permanente Journal, 8*(1), 30.

Andersen, S. L. (2003). Trajectories of brain development: Point of vulnerability or window of opportunity? *Neuroscience & Biobehavioral Reviews, 27*(1), 3–18.

Andersen, S. L., & Teicher, M. H. (2004). Delayed effects of early stress on hippocampal development. *Neuropsychopharmacology, 29*(11), 1988.

Andersen, S. L., Tomada, A., Vincow, E. S., Valente, E., Polcari, A., & Teicher, M. H. (2008). Preliminary evidence for sensitive periods in the effect of childhood sexual abuse on regional brain development. *The Journal of Neuropsychiatry and Clinical Neurosciences, 20*(3), 292–301.

Baglivio, M. T., Epps, N., Swartz, K., Huq, M., Sheer, A., & Hardt, N. S. (2014). The prevalence of adverse childhood experiences (ACE) in the lives of juvenile offenders. *OJJDP Journal of Juvenile Justice, 3,* 1–23.

Bagot, R. C., & Meaney, M. J. (2010). Epigenetics and the biological basis of gene × environment interactions. *Journal of the American Academy of Child & Adolescent Psychiatry*, 49(8), 752–771.

Bancos, I., Hahner, S., Tomlinson, J., & Arlt, W. (2015). Diagnosis and management of adrenal insufficiency. *The Lancet Diabetes & Endocrinology*, 3(3), 216–226.

Bremner, J. D., Randall, P., Vermetten, E., Staib, L., Bronen, R. A., Mazure, C., . . . Charney, D. S. (1997). Magnetic resonance imaging-based measurement of hippocampal volume in posttraumatic stress disorder related to childhood physical and sexual abuse—a preliminary report. *Biological Psychiatry*, *41*(1), 23–32.

Brown, D. W., Anda, R. F., Edwards, V. J., Felitti, V. J., Dube, S. R., & Giles, W. H. (2007). Adverse childhood experiences and childhood autobiographical memory disturbance. *Child Abuse & Neglect*, *31*(9), 961–969.

Brown, D. W., Anda, R. F., Tiemeier, H., Felitti, V. J., Edwards, V. J., Croft, J. B., & Giles, W. H. (2009). Adverse childhood experiences and the risk of premature mortality. *American Journal of Preventive Medicine*, *37*(5), 389–396.

Center on the Developing Child. (n.d.). *Key concepts: Toxic stress*. Retrieved from https://developingchild.harvard.edu/science/key-concepts/toxic-stress/

Chartier, M. J., Walker, J. R., & Naimark, B. (2010). Separate and cumulative effects of adverse childhood experiences in predicting adult health and health care utilization. *Child Abuse & Neglect*, *34*(6), 454–464.

Children's Rights (n.d.). *Foster care*. Retrieved from: http://www.childrensrights.org/newsroom/fact-sheets/foster-care/

Community Resilience Initiative. (n.d.). *We Are Children's Resilience Initiative*. Retrieved from https://resiliencetrumpsaces.org/about-us/we-are-cri/

Department of Children's Services, TN. (n.d.). *Building strong brains: Tennessee ACE Initiative*. Retrieved from https://www.tn.gov/tccy/ace/tccy-ace-building-strong-brains.html

Dong, M., Anda, R. F., Felitti, V. J., Dube, S. R., Williamson, D. F., Thompson, T. J., . . . Giles, W. H. (2004). The interrelatedness of multiple forms of childhood abuse, neglect, and household dysfunction. *Child Abuse & Neglect*, *28*(7), 771–784.

Dube, S. R., Anda, R. F., Felitti, V. J., Chapman, D. P., Williamson, D. F., & Giles, W. H. (2001). Childhood abuse, household dysfunction, and the risk of attempted suicide throughout the life span: Findings from the Adverse Childhood Experiences Study. *JAMA*, *286*(24), 3089–3096.

Dube, S. R., Felitti, V. J., Dong, M., Chapman, D. P., Giles, W. H., & Anda, R. F. (2003). Childhood abuse, neglect, and household dysfunction and the risk of illicit drug use: The adverse childhood experiences study. *Pediatrics*, 111(3), 564–72.

Eckenrode, J., Laird, M., & Doris, J. (1993). School performance and disciplinary problems among abused and neglected children. *Developmental Psychology*, *29*(1), 53.

Edwards, V.J., Holden, G.W., Felitti, V.J., & Anda, R.F. (2003). Relationship between multiple forms of childhood maltreatment and adult mental health in community respondents: Results from the adverse childhood experiences study. *American Journal of Psychiatry, 160*(8), 1453–1460.

Felitti, V. J. (2004). Kaiser Permanente Institutes of Preventive Medicine. *The Permanente Journal, 8*(1), 3.

Felitti, V.J., Anda, R.F., Nordenberg, D., Williamson, D.F., Spitz, A.M., Edwards, V., . . . Marks, J.S. (1998). Relationship of childhood abuse and household dysfunction to many of the leading causes of death in adults: The Adverse Childhood Experiences (ACE) Study. *American Journal of Preventive Medicine, 14*(4), 245–258.

Francis, D., Diorio, J., Liu, D., & Meaney, M.J. (1999). Nongenomic transmission across generations of maternal behavior and stress responses in the rat. *Science, 286*(5442), 1155–1158.

Fox, N.A., Almas, A.N., Degnan, K.A., Nelson, C.A., & Zeanah, C.H. (2011). The effects of severe psychosocial deprivation and foster care intervention on cognitive development at 8 years of age: Findings from the Bucharest Early Intervention Project. *Journal of Child Psychology and Psychiatry, 52*(9), 919–928.

Fox, S. E., Levitt, P., & Nelson, C. A., III (2010). How the timing and quality of early experiences influence the development of brain architecture. *Child Development, 81*(1), 28–40.

Gillespie, R.J., & Folger, A.T. (2017). Feasibility of assessing parental ACES in pediatric primary care: Implications for practice-based implementation. *Journal of Child & Adolescent Trauma, 10*(3), 249–256.

Goff, B., & Tottenham, N. (2015). Early-life adversity and adolescent depression: mechanisms involving the ventral striatum. *CNS Spectrums, 20*(4), 337–345.

Gómez, R.L., & Edgin, J.O. (2016). The extended trajectory of hippocampal development: Implications for early memory development and disorder. *Developmental Cognitive Neuroscience, 18*, 57–69.

Hall, J., Porter, L., Longhi, D., Becker-Green, J., & Dreyfus, S. (2012). Reducing adverse childhood experiences (ACE) by building community capacity: A summary of Washington Family Policy Council research findings. *Journal of Prevention & Intervention in the Community, 40*(4), 325–334.

Hamilton, J. (2017, October 25). Scientists and surgeons team up to create virtual human brain cells. *All Things Considered.* Retrieved from http://www.npr.org/sections/health-shots/2017/10/25/559819023/scientists-and-surgeons-team-up-to-create-models-of-living-human-brain-cells

Harlow, H.F. (1958). The nature of love. *American psychologist, 13*(12), 673.

Health & Medicine Policy Research Group. (n.d.). *Illinois ACE Response Initiative.* Retrieved from http://www.hmprg.org/Programs/IL+ACE+Response+Collaborative

Health Federation of Philadelphia. (n.d.). *The Philadelphia Urban ACE Study.* Retrieved from http://www.instituteforsafefamilies.org/philadelphia-urban-ace-study

HRSA. (n.d.). *Home visiting.* Retrieved from https://mchb.hrsa.gov/maternal-child-health-initiatives/home-visiting-overview

Khan, A., McCormack, H. C., Bolger, E. A., McGreenery, C. E., Vitaliano, G., Polcari, A., & Teicher, M. H. (2015). Childhood maltreatment, depression, and suicidal ideation: Critical importance of parental and peer emotional abuse during developmental sensitive periods in males and females. *Frontiers in Psychiatry, 6,* 42.

Kinard, E. M. (2001). Characteristics of maltreatment experience and academic functioning among maltreated children. *Violence and Victims, 16*(3), 323.

Kurtz, P. D., Gaudin, J. M., Jr., Wodarski, J. S., & Howing, P. T. (1993). Maltreatment and the school-aged child: School performance consequences. *Child Abuse & Neglect, 17*(5), 581–589.

Leiter, J. (2007). School performance trajectories after the advent of reported maltreatment. *Children and Youth Services Review, 29*(3), 363–382.

Luby, J. L., Belden, A., Harms, M. P., Tillman, R., & Barch, D. M. (2016). Preschool is a sensitive period for the influence of maternal support on the trajectory of hippocampal development. *Proceedings of the National Academy of Sciences, 113*(20), 5742–5747.

Lupien, S. J., McEwen, B. S., Gunnar, M. R., & Heim, C. (2009). Effects of stress throughout the lifespan on the brain, behaviour and cognition. *Nature Reviews Neuroscience, 10*(6), 434–445.

McEwen, B. S. (2005). Stressed or stressed out: What is the difference? *Journal of Psychiatry and Neuroscience, 30*(5), 315.

McEwen, B. S. (2007). Physiology and neurobiology of stress and adaptation: Central role of the brain. *Physiological Reviews, 87*(3), 873–904.

Meaney, M. J., Diorio, J., Francis, D., Widdowson, J., LaPlante, P., Caldji, C., . . . Plotsky, P. M. (1996). Early environmental regulation of forebrain glucocorticoid receptor gene expression: Implications for adrenocortical responses to stress. *Developmental Neuroscience, 18*(1–2), 61–72.

Meaney, M. J., & Szyf, M. (2005). Environmental programming of stress responses through DNA methylation: Life at the interface between a dynamic environment and a fixed genome. *Dialogues Clinical Neuroscience, 7*(2), 103–123.

Myers, S. S., & Pianta, R. C. (2008). Developmental commentary: Individual and contextual influences on student–teacher relationships and children's early problem behaviors. *Journal of Clinical Child & Adolescent Psychology, 37*(3), 600–608.

Nelson, C. A., Zeanah, C. H., Fox, N. A., Romer, D., & Walker, E. F. (2007). The effects of early deprivation on brain-behavioral development: The Bucharest Early Intervention Project. *Adolescent Psychopathology and the Developing Brain: Integrating Brain and Prevention Science,* 197–215.

Nurius, P. S., Logan-Greene, P., & Green, S. (2012). ACEs within a social disadvantage framework: Distinguishing unique, cumulative, and moderated contributions to adult mental health. *Journal of Prevention & Intervention in the Community, 40*(4), 278.

Obradović, J., Bush, N. R., Stamperdahl, J., Adler, N. E., & Boyce, W. T. (2010). Biological sensitivity to context: The interactive effects of stress reactivity and family adversity on socioemotional behavior and school readiness. *Child Development*, *81*(1), 270–289.

Pechtel, P., Lyons-Ruth, K., Anderson, C. M., & Teicher, M. H. (2014). Sensitive periods of amygdala development: The role of maltreatment in preadolescence. *Neuroimage*, *97*, 236–244.

Platt, B., Kadosh, K. C., & Lau, J. Y. (2013). The role of peer rejection in adolescent depression. *Depression and Anxiety*, *30*(9), 809–821.

Porter, L., Martin, K., & Anda, R. F. (2016). *Self-healing communities: A transformational process model for improving intergenerational health*. Princeton, NJ: Robert Woods Johnson Foundation.

Rowe, E., & Eckenrode, J. (1999). The timing of academic difficulties among maltreated and nonmaltreated children1. *Child Abuse & Neglect*, *23*(8), 813–832.

Schmitt, J., Warner, K., & Gupta, S. (2010). *The high budgetary cost of incarceration*. Washington, DC: Center for Economic and Policy Research.

Szyf, M. (2009). The early life environment and the epigenome. *Biochimica et Biophysica Acta*, *1790*(9), 878–885.

Szyf, M., McGowan, P., & Meaney, M. J. (2008). The social environment and the epigenome. *Environmental and Molecular Mutagenesis*, *49*(1), 46–60.

Teicher, M. H. (2000). Wounds that time won't heal: The neurobiology of child abuse. *Cerebrum*, *2*(4), 50–67.

Teicher, M. H., Andersen, S. L., Polcari, A., Anderson, C. M., & Navalta, C. P. (2002). Developmental neurobiology of childhood stress and trauma. *Psychiatric Clinics*, *25*(2), 397–426.

Teicher, M. H., Andersen, S. L., Polcari, A., Anderson, C. M., Navalta, C. P., & Kim, D. M. (2003). The neurobiological consequences of early stress and childhood maltreatment. *Neuroscience & Biobehavioral Reviews*, *27*(1), 33–44.

Toth, S. L., & Cicchetti, D. (1996). The impact of relatedness with mother on school functioning in maltreated children. *Journal of School Psychology*, *34*(3), 247–266.

U.S. Department of Healthy and Human Services, Administration for Children and Families, Administration on Children, Youth and Families, Children's Bureau. (2017). *Child Maltreatment 2015*. Retrieved from https://www.childwelfare.gov/catalog/

Whitfield, C. L., Dube, S. R., Felitti, V. J., & Anda, R. F. (2005). Adverse childhood experiences and hallucinations. *Child Abuse & Neglect*, *29*(7), 797–810.

Williamson, D. F., Thompson, T. J., Anda, R. F., Dietz, W. H., & Felitti, V. (2002). Body weight and obesity in adults and self-reported abuse in childhood. *International Journal of Obesity*, *26*(8), 1075.

Zero to Three. (n.d.) *Policy agenda*. Retrieved from https://www.zerotothree.org/policy-and-advocacy

CHAPTER 4

Principles of Trauma-Informed Therapy with Children and Adolescents

Rebecca Brown and Rebecca Hoffmann Frances

Children have an innate ability to learn from their experiences and develop ways to cope and heal in the face of adversity. Yet, exposure to trauma in childhood can also overwhelm a child's ability to thrive; chronic or repetitive exposure has the potential to cause long-term symptoms that can impede physical and emotional health and functioning throughout the life span. By offering children opportunities to heal in environments that are supportive and safe, trauma-exposed children can shed those symptoms and live happy and fulfilling lives. Using case vignettes, this chapter will review the principles of trauma-informed therapy for children and adolescents. The core components of trauma-specific treatment and examples of evidence-based trauma treatments will be discussed.

Evidence-Based Treatment for Child Trauma[1]

In the past 25 years, there has been increasing interest in the field of mental health in conducting rigorous research on psychotherapeutic interventions to establish their evidence base for efficacy. In short, this movement is focused on answering questions about what works in terms of therapy, thus empowering therapists and consumers with more knowledge and choice of interventions. The term "evidence-based practice" refers to the "judicious, explicit, and conscientious use of the evidence base to guide one's clinical practice" (Amaya-Jackson & DeRosa, 2007, p. 379; Ford & Courtois, 2013, p. 101). In mental health, evidence-based practices typically integrate systematic assessment, a clear articulation of treatment goals, specific intervention components, and ongoing monitoring and outcome assessments (Amaya-Jackson & DeRosa, 2007).

When using evidence-based practices with their clients, mental health therapists are asked to combine best available research and balance it with clinical reasoning. Therapists should do this while also considering individual client characteristics, family culture, and circumstances in order to arrive at the best individualized approach for the healing and recovery (Amaya-Jackson & DeRosa, 2007).

There is now a common language for rating the quality of the evaluations and evidence of success of interventions. In the health-care field, these interventions are generally referred to as evidence-based practices or evidence-based treatments. Several online registries of interventions provide information about interventions to the public. Some of the leading sources for learning about evidence for interventions and programs are listed here:

- National Registry of Evidence-Based Programs and Practices (NREPP): An evidence-based repository and review system managed by the Substance Abuse and Mental Health Services Administration (SAMHSA) designed to provide the public with reliable information on mental health and substance use interventions. Further information on NREPP can be found at nrepp.samhsa.gov/about.aspx.
- California Evidence-Based Clearinghouse for Child Welfare (CEBC): The California Department of Social Services (CDSS) established a registry of evidence-based child welfare practices as part of its mission toward improving the lives of children and families served within the child welfare system. The CEBC Program Registry provides information on both evidence-based and non-evidence-based child welfare–related practices to statewide agencies, counties, public and private organizations, and individuals. Further information about CEBC can be found at www.cebc4cw.org/.
- National Child Traumatic Stress Network (NCTSN): Established by Congress in 2000, the NCTSN funded through the SAMHSA brings a singular and comprehensive focus to childhood trauma. The NCTSN is a network of frontline providers, researchers, and families committed to collaborating to

raise the standard of care and increase access to services for children and families exposed to trauma. Further information about NCTSN can be found at www.nctsn.org.

Evidence-based trauma practices refer to research-based effective interventions and specific treatment models that have been found to alleviate the symptoms of trauma in children through rigorous scientific testing. These interventions typically have well-developed treatment manuals, training protocols for practitioners, and ongoing assessment of clinician practice fidelity (Shipman & Taussig, 2009). This rigorous training equips therapists with specific skills and directions for how to proceed with the therapeutic intervention. It also provides a standard of quality assurance for consumers.

The challenge, however, for clinicians, is balancing these established treatment protocols with an individual client's characteristics and circumstances. Therapists may be faced with the need to adapt their approaches while attempting to adhere to protocols in order to maintain evidence-based treatment fidelity. For example, many evidence-based child trauma treatments have a focus on consistent parent/caregiver involvement, which has proven invaluable in helping children heal and recover following trauma. However, therapists in community settings often find themselves treating children who may be experiencing frequent caregiver transitions, as in the case of children in the child welfare system or those being cared for by multiple family members. Other children have parents/caregivers who have their own challenges in engaging in treatment sessions, making it difficult for therapists to establish consistent contact. Whatever the reason, the required component of consistent parent/caregiver involvement in some of the evidence-based treatment models becomes challenging for practitioners as they attempt to maintain fidelity to a model and balance this with real-life barriers. While some evidence-based trauma treatments provide guidelines and recommendations for how to address such barriers, others rely on the therapist's ability to adapt the interventions to meet the child and family's individualized needs. To describe the situation more clearly, real-life practice settings can sometimes create challenges for therapists that are not found in the more controlled scientific test settings used to create an evidence base for a treatment intervention. Lisa Amaya-Jackson, an expert in the field of evidence-based treatment for childhood trauma, offers clinicians this advice when attempting to utilize an evidence-based treatment: "Adhere when possible, adapt when necessary, assess along the way" (Amaya-Jackson & DeRosa, 2007, p. 388).

Many treatments have now been validated to create a diverse pool of interventions that can be utilized to treat children exposed to traumatic events. The following discussion will highlight some of the core evidence-based practice principles found across interventions for treating trauma in children. The core principles will be explained. A case vignette will be presented to highlight the principle. This will be followed with a list of the leading evidence-based trauma treatments for children that utilize these principles. While these treatment approaches are distinct in the way that they deliver, address, and package these core principles, their use and inclusion of common tenets remain consistent across approaches.

Whether a therapist is using a manualized and validated evidence-based trauma treatment or relying on the use of evidence-based practice principles to treat childhood trauma, this specialized knowledge base is essential for high-quality treatment and recovery. Because of the many complexities regarding the psychological, developmental, and physiological impacts of childhood trauma exposure, the skills needed for treating these children require additional knowledge, study, and understanding beyond what is standard for general mental health practitioners. This is not unlike the medical field where specialties are common and require additional training and practice for optimum treatment outcomes. For example, an individual who has been diagnosed with cancer may have first sought out treatment from his or her primary care physician following initial symptoms and concerns. The primary care physician may even be the one who delivered the initial diagnosis. However, following diagnosis, this patient is likely going to seek treatment from an oncologist, because of their specialized training, understanding, and treatment of cancer. Families should consider a similar framework when seeking treatment for a child exposed to trauma. The medical community has historically accepted that there are certain diagnoses and conditions that require specialized care and training. The authors would argue this assertion as it applies to childhood trauma being one of those conditions that requires specialized clinical training in best practice principles or specific evidence-based trauma treatment to ensure optimum outcomes for the children and families seeking care for trauma-related concerns.

Another important consideration when assessing treatment interventions for children exposed to trauma is that the impacts of exposure reach far beyond the diagnosis of posttraumatic stress disorder (PTSD) in children and adolescents. Often, when people hear the word "trauma," they associate this experience with the diagnosis of PTSD. In fact, while rates of PTSD following exposure to trauma vary widely across studies and may be underrepresented in the research, it has been found that a relatively small percentage of infants and young children exposed to serious trauma actually develop PTSD (ZERO TO THREE, 2016). While a percentage of children who experience trauma will go on to meet diagnostic criteria for PTSD, there is a wide range of additional impacts and reactions that are common and well documented in the literature. For instance, many young children experience disruption in their attachment relationships and social-emotional functioning following trauma exposure, while depression and anxiety are common by-products of experiencing trauma in school-aged children and adolescents (Cohen, Mannarino, & Deblinger, 2006; Lieberman & Van Horn, 2008). It is likely because of this that many of the core principles in evidence-based trauma treatments aim to treat a range of common reactions and not simply those symptoms associated with PTSD.

Core Principles

A review of the literature reveals many attempts across experts to define the core components of evidence-based trauma treatment and establish treatment guidelines for PTSD (Cook et al., 2005; Forbes et al., 2010; Schnyder et al., 2015). While commonalities and themes exist, there is no consensus across publications and literature regarding the most effective therapeutic components for treating childhood trauma (Forbes et al., 2010). A great deal of the current literature on evidenced-based trauma treatment focuses on interventions designed to treat adults struggling with the symptoms of PTSD and associated mental health diagnoses; fewer resources outline the core components for the treatment of children and adolescents exposed to trauma. While the field recognizes a number of core components as critical to the treatment of childhood trauma, evidence-based practices vary on their inclusion and how they operationalize these components (Amaya-Jackson & DeRosa, 2007). Some of the most heavily relied-upon sources for the purpose of this discussion came from a framework developed by experts in the field of treating complex trauma in children and adolescents (Cook et al., 2005; Ford & Courtois, 2013). Complex trauma refers to children's exposure to "multiple traumatic events, often of an invasive, interpersonal nature, and the wide-ranging, long-term impacts of this exposure" (National Child Traumatic Stress Network (NCTSN), n.d. [retrieved from http://www.nctsn.org]). (See Chapter 14 in this volume.) Since many children and adolescents exposed to chronic violence could be classified as experiencing complex trauma, the authors will rely heavily on this framework to outline what they have found and believe to be the core principles of trauma-informed interventions for children. These principles represent common and overarching components and don't include the specific nuances of individual interventions that also help to promote healing and recovery. They also exclude those intervention principles delivered outside of the mental health context or across service systems and sectors.

The following six core principles of trauma-informed treatment have been chosen by the authors based on a review of the literature, their direct clinical experience treating children exposed to violence and trauma over the past decade, and their experience in the delivery and dissemination of multiple evidence-based child trauma treatments (see Box 4.1). The reader is asked to reflect upon each of these principles using both a developmental and a relational framework to consider how each principle may be applied to a specific child or a child's circumstances.

Box 4.1 Core Principles of Trauma-Informed Clinical Treatment for Children and Adolescents

1. Safety
2. Psychoeducation
3. Regulation
4. Parent/Caregiver support
5. Trauma processing
6. Instilling hope

A child's responses to stress and trauma are shaped by that child's age and developmental stage (Lieberman & Van Horn, 2008). Because all childhood trauma occurs in the context of a child's developmental stage and progress, the impact of the trauma on the multiple domains of child development (emotional, social, physical, cognitive) at any given point in time must be considered when assessing a child's responses to trauma and delivering an intervention.

Similarly, children's relationships with caring adults may have a significant impact on the reactions to traumatic events, as well as their responses, healing, and recovery. Research has well documented the importance of positive, safe, and stable caregiving relationships in creating healthy and secure children (National Scientific Council on the Developing Child, 2015). These early relationships act as the cornerstone for how children relate to others and navigate social relationships throughout the course of their development. Trauma and violence can disrupt these early attachment relationships in a multitude of ways, causing a range of negative impacts across functional domains that last well into adulthood (Osofsky, 2011).

Consequently, the repair and establishment of positive supportive relationships have been identified as one of the key protective factors in mitigating the harm of trauma on children (National Scientific Council on the Developing Child, 2015). Many of the leading evidence-based treatments for child trauma emphasize the inclusion of positive adult supports to optimize healing and recovery (Berkowitz, Stover, & Marans, 2011; Cohen et al., 2006; Lieberman & Van Horn, 2008). One can begin to understand therapeutic healing for any given child's trauma exposure through consideration of both the protective and injured relationships in the child's life, as well as how development may be influencing the child's responses.

Safety

Ensuring and creating safety for children is a driving principle at the core of any treatment for childhood trauma. The experience of a traumatic event undermines children's sense of protection and safety and often creates or magnifies children's fears about danger and risk (NCTSN, 2012a). Establishing a sense of safety is also one of the primary areas of intervention cited in the literature as critical in the immediate aftermath of trauma and includes strategies such as helping connect children to trusted adults and maintaining daily routines (Osofsky, 2011). In evidence-based trauma treatments, the extent to which safety is operationalized varies across modalities. However, it should always be a focal point of treatment and should include a focus on the installation and enhancement of both internal and environmental safety (Cook et al., 2005). There are multiple points of entry from which to accomplish physical safety, including regular assessment and intervention of a child's risk (to him/herself, to others, or by others), collaboration with the systems responsible for safety (i.e., child protection, law enforcement), and sometimes the explicit development of safety plans (Ford & Courtois, 2013). Increasing emotional safety, in and of itself, can be another complex goal of treatment. Two areas to consider, especially for young children exposed to trauma, are supporting parent-child relationships where children can rely on their parents to protect them and helping children regulate affect as a means to protect them from the internal danger of strong and unmodulated feelings (Lieberman & Van Horn, 2008). Ongoing or chronic danger in children's lives is a major and sometimes insurmountable barrier to creating long-lasting healing and change. Children who feel safe in their primary caregiving relationships, rely on the systems at hand to keep them safe, and learn not to fear their experiences of fear, anger, worry, sadness, and anxiety are often the ones who move forward from their traumatic experiences more quickly and with fewer negative impacts.

Jerome

Jerome was 12 years old when he began treatment after being sexually abused by his baseball coach for over a year. Jerome also lived in an unsafe neighborhood with gang activity, and he walked to school most days through this neighborhood. When Jerome finally told his mother about the abuse, she immediately reported it to the school and law enforcement. An investigation followed, and the coach was fired from his job. He was found guilty of a lesser charge and sentenced to multiple years on probation with time served. Safety was a core focus of Jerome's treatment in a variety of ways. First, it took Jerome's therapist, Tyler, a long time to create a sense of safety in their therapeutic relationship as Jerome struggled to trust males in positions of power or authority following his experience. Jerome actually preferred having his mother in all of his early treatment sessions as she remained his primary support and protector throughout his experience. Tyler highlighted the relationship with his mother as a primary source of support and as someone who believed in him and responded to keep him safe. Tyler also spoke regularly with Jerome about how he could build trust with Jerome and frequently asked him about his feelings of safety and comfort in the treatment room and during sessions. There were many times in their early individual sessions when Jerome would take a break during a session to check in with his mom who would sit right outside Tyler's office space. Eventually, Jerome came to trust Tyler enough that his mother waited in the waiting room instead of right outside the office door. Jerome shared with Tyler his increased worry and fear when walking to school. He said, "I used to feel fine about walking to school. I know it's not the safest neighborhood, but I never felt like I do now. Every day, I think he's going to come find me and every guy I see, I think he's going to hurt me." Tyler started by addressing Jerome's legitimate concerns for his physical safety. They created a plan for Jerome to walk to school with friends. His brother changed his schedule so he could be with Jerome on his way home from school. On days when neither was a possibility, Jerome took public transportation. Once Jerome's physical safety needs had been addressed, Tyler went on to discuss Jerome's fears about seeing his coach and the anxiety that resulted any time he saw something that reminded him of baseball. Through treatment, Jerome slowly began to focus on the reasons seeing his coach was unlikely (probation, the coach lived in another town, etc.) rather than on all the reasons he believed the coach might try to find him. They also talked about what Jerome could do if he ever did see his coach again. Having strategies to manage his fears and worries, his mother's and brother's support, and a plan he could rely on when feeling unsafe, all helped Jerome feel more secure in his environment and in his relationships. While safety risks were still present in the neighborhood and Tyler couldn't guarantee he wouldn't see his coach, Jerome felt empowered and safer at the end of therapy.

Psychoeducation

Psychoeducation refers to the provision of information about the common thoughts, feelings, and experiences that typically follow exposure to a traumatic event (NCTSN, n.d.). Children, adolescents, and their families will often experience a range of reactions, feelings, and responses following exposure to trauma. Learning about these responses helps children and families identify opportunities for assistance and support while simultaneously decreasing the stigma that is often associated with mental health symptoms and reactions. Sometimes, children seeking treatment have experienced reactions for years without understanding that their feelings and responses may be connected to their traumatic experience(s). Since the experience of trauma can be isolating, children are often left questioning themselves and the world around them as they try to make sense of these events. When children and their families hear about the reactions common to others who have experienced violence and trauma, they begin to understand that they are not alone in their experiences. Parents/caregivers begin to see their children as having expected or normative feelings and behaviors, when prior to learning about these common responses, they may have been labeling these behaviors or feelings as problematic or outside the norm (Cohen et al., 2006).

Psychoeducation about trauma and trauma responses helps children, adolescents, and their families identify, understand, and define problematic reactions for themselves as a first step toward addressing them. It becomes much easier to identify solutions to a problem when they are understood. Psychoeducation does just this. It helps children see that their reactions are not unique or abnormal and that others have experienced similar events. They learn to identify their own reactions, making them better able to identify the skills and supports necessary to decrease these reactions. As such, psychoeducation not only educates and decreases isolation but also empowers children and families to begin identifying their own solutions, reestablishing a sense of power or control that was likely lost during the trauma.

Hazel and Victoria

Victoria came to treatment with her three-year-old daughter, Hazel, after leaving an abusive relationship with Hazel's dad six months prior. Victoria had become worried about Hazel after she began having frequent temper tantrums that lasted 45 minutes. In addition, she hit other children at preschool and started pretending to strangle her mother during story time. Victoria was extremely distraught in the first session, believing that maybe her daughter was becoming like her ex-husband and may have "evil" in her. The therapist completed a thorough assessment over several sessions to gather Hazel's development and trauma history and explore Hazel and Victoria's attachment and relationship. Victoria struggled to focus throughout most of the assessment sessions, repeatedly expressing to the therapist her fears about her daughter's behavior. The therapist used the assessment sessions to provide Victoria with developmental guidance related to which behaviors may be consistent with that of other three-year-olds and which may be related to her witnessing domestic violence. The therapist explained how young children often display symptoms of aggression and reenact aspects of the traumatic events they have experienced. She also explained to Victoria that because Hazel does not yet have the words or cognitive capacity to express her feelings verbally, she communicates with her behavior. Hearing from the therapist that Hazel's reactions were consistent with other children who had been through similar experiences immediately relieved some of Victoria's fears and gave her a greater sense of tolerance and patience with Hazel when she became aggressive. It also helped decrease Victoria's overall anxiety about her daughter and provided greater space for her to focus during the remaining assessment sessions so they could move forward in treatment.

Regulation

A major focus of child trauma treatment is helping the child find ways to improve both behavioral and emotional regulation. The way in which this is therapeutically accomplished varies by treatment model, but each model includes interventions aimed at addressing the behavioral and emotional dysregulation that often results from repeated trauma exposure. When children experience early adversity, they can often experience dysregulation behaviorally, physiologically, and emotionally (Osofsky, 2011). Perhaps one of the most powerful therapeutic interventions a therapist can offer a child following trauma is to provide him or her the tools and supports necessary to improve impulse control and emotion management.

Behavioral regulation is achieved therapeutically through work with both the child and the parent/caregiver. Often, trauma disrupts children's abilities to manage their emotions and behaviors. They may be highly active, irritable, easily upset, hypervigilant, impulsive, angry, or withdrawn. In some models, especially those aimed at treating young children, behavioral regulation is accomplished through parent/caregiver behavior management training and helping parents/caregivers learn and practice positive parenting strategies found to be effective in shaping and responding to behavior. Clinicians will also work with parents/caregivers to try to understand the meaning underneath a particular behavior and explore those behaviors that may be a manifestation of trauma exposure (Lieberman & Van Horn, 2005). This helps parents/caregivers gain a greater understanding of what is causing certain behaviors so they can be better equipped to respond and manage them. As children get older and develop greater skills in behavioral regulation and impulse control, evidence-based treatment models begin to use interventions that directly help children better manage their own behavior. Many of the leading evidence-based trauma treatment models include cognitive behavioral frameworks, which help children understand the relationship between their thoughts, feelings, and behaviors (Cohen et al., 2006). Children begin to explore and understand the reasons why they are reacting, responding, or behaving in a certain way and identify antecedents to some of the behaviors that may be leading to negative consequences in their lives. The combination of addressing behavioral regulation with parents/caregivers along with working with the child can elicit significant clinical improvements in the behavioral domain (Ford & Courtois, 2013).

In addition to behavioral regulation, child trauma treatment models also help children build skills to regulate the intense affective experiences that often accompany trauma exposure. All evidence-based child trauma treatment interventions address emotion dysregulation in some way or another. This is accomplished through various techniques such as encouraging children to label and identify their feelings, teaching mindfulness and relaxation techniques, helping children accurately identify the feelings of others, identifying healthy ways to express emotion, and learning coping skills for managing intense or negative emotions (Cohen et al., 2006; Ford & Courtois, 2013). Further exploration into the connection between thoughts, feelings, and behaviors often occurs as clinicians work with children and their families around improving emotion regulation and managing dysregulation. For some children, addressing emotion regulation involves encouraging the expression of emotion, as some children exposed to trauma have difficulty even feeling emotions, and even more difficulty in identifying and expressing them.

Clinical interventions aimed at addressing emotion regulation often include parents/caregivers, in an effort to help them manage their own emotions and provide a positive model for their children. Parents/caregivers are encouraged to empathize with their children's affective states and help them identify tools and utilize skills to help during periods of intense emotion. The positive caregiving relationships in a child's life can therefore become the vehicle by which to accomplish improved emotion regulation through communication, connection, and support.

Kelsey

Kelsey is six years old and has recently been having difficulty at school. She gets angry easily at other children, sometimes for very minor things, and starts yelling and hitting. She has difficulty calming down and often leaves the classroom for at least half an hour. In one instance, a classmate was playing a game that involved sneaking up behind other children and yelling "boo" in their ears. When he did this to Kelsey, she turned around and punched the boy in the stomach. Kelsey was sent to the principal's office, where she paced for over an hour. She was unable to calm down enough to tell the principal what happened. Kelsey was referred to the school social worker who had training and experience in trauma treatment. She met with Kelsey's mother and learned that Kelsey had been exposed to domestic violence and physical abuse by her father from ages two to five. At that point, Kelsey's father was incarcerated. After learning this history, Kelsey's therapist realized that she may be struggling with identifying her emotions as a means of then regulating them. She was easily angered by classmates and was not able to express her anger in a healthy way. Kelsey's therapist helped her learn to identify when she was feeling angry. However, over time she learned about a range of emotions. Her therapist worked with Kelsey individually and also had her join a group with other children that taught her a variety of coping skills to be used in school when she felt angry. She worked with Kelsey's teacher and her mother to identify when Kelsey's anger may be escalating and guide her to use of coping skills prior to reacting to her anger. Over time, Kelsey's needs for leaving the classroom diminished significantly, and she experienced a major reduction in the number of times she acted on her anger inappropriately.

Parent/Caregiver Support

Parental and caregiver support has been emphasized and referenced repeatedly throughout this discussion as a key principle to the treatment of child trauma exposure and a core predictor of positive outcomes following trauma exposure. Most evidence-based trauma treatments emphasize the participation and involvement of parents/caregivers and/or include specific interventions for the parent/caregiver (Berkowitz et al., 2010; Cohen et al. 2006; Lieberman & Van Horn, 2008). The extent to which clinicians work directly with a parent/caregiver individually, as opposed to using a dyadic framework, varies across interventions, but the importance of the parent/caregiver can never be underestimated. This is true in models that address young children, school-aged children, and adolescents.

Parents/caregivers may be asked to learn and practice the same skills that their child is learning, as well as engage collaboratively with the therapist and the child to determine how interventions can be applied to a child's daily life. Clinicians are asked to engage parents/caregivers in therapeutic interventions and explore relational repair when damage to these relationships has occurred. These are often some of the most clinically complex and delicate navigations that occur between a therapist and a family throughout the course of treatment. In some models, the inclusion of the parent/caregiver in treatment and the focus of the parent–child relationship are the very core and foundation of every intervention delivered (Lieberman & Van Horn, 2005).

Alex and Melissa

Alex was 15 years old when he presented to an outpatient mental health clinic one month following the violent murder of his older brother. He was failing multiple classes in school due to an inability to concentrate or follow through on assignments and was experiencing nightmares and sleeplessness daily. His friends on the football team noticed that he was withdrawn, and he rarely showed emotion toward anything unless it was in anger or frustration when someone on the team made a mistake. Alex's mother, Melissa, often accompanied him to treatment and expressed frustration and sadness at her inability to help him cope with his loss. Through treatment, not only did Alex learn coping skills to manage his symptoms, but he and Melissa were also able to practice skills together, inadvertently increasing communication and connection between them. When talking about his feelings connected to the loss of his brother and the circumstances of his death, Alex remained hesitant to talk about his experience. With the support of a skilled therapist, Alex eventually revealed that he didn't feel like he could share his feelings openly because he needed to be strong for his family, and specifically, his mother. "She's just hurting so much. I don't want her to have to deal with my feelings too. I think it would break her and she's already about to break." The therapist encouraged Alex to identify and express his feelings connected to his trauma and also encouraged Alex to talk about his hesitancy to share his feelings with his mother. With some coaching, Alex told his mother that he believed showing his pain, sadness, and grief would be too much for her. Melissa, in turn, expressed her authentic desire to hear and understand his experience and explained how hearing his experience would in fact be healing for her, not harmful. Through a series of conversations between Alex and his mother, he learned to show his feelings and seek out his mother during times when he was struggling. As a result, he was better able to manage his symptoms, and his sleeping difficulties were resolved. Melissa also expressed extreme gratitude for the opportunity to provide support to her son while finding purpose following the loss of her oldest child. At the end of treatment, their relationship had strengthened beyond where it had been even before the traumatic loss, and Alex was healing with the support of Melissa.

Trauma Processing

At the core of many evidence-based child trauma treatments is the component of trauma processing: the opportunity for a child to discuss and make meaning of his or her trauma experience within a clinical context. In some treatment models, this is accomplished through the use of expressive or directed play; in others, it involves the creation of a narrative, and still others provide alternative storytelling interventions to help support children in the reexperiencing of events (Cohen et al., 2006; Lieberman & Van Horn, 2008). This retelling can place the events into the larger context of children's lives so that they can move forward with more accurate and helpful belief systems related to their past trauma (Cohen et al., 2006). Trauma processing accomplishes a number of therapeutic goals common in evidence-based trauma treatments. First, it exposes children to the very experiences and/or thoughts that are often creating fear reactions in their daily lives. Through reexperiencing and reexposure, the fear response closely connected to the memory of the events often diminishes over time as children learn that these memories can't actually harm them and that the intense feelings connected to these experiences can be managed. Second, processing trauma in a therapeutic setting and in the presence of a therapist provides children the opportunity to have a supportive person bear witness to what they experienced. This can decrease feelings of isolation and solitude connected to the trauma experiences of the past. Third, sharing these memories and details of trauma helps children make meaning of these experiences so that they can better fit them into the larger context of their lives. They are hopefully able to think about these experiences, not only from a place of fear, sadness, anger, and grief but also with a perspective of resilience, survival, and hope.

Sabine

Sabine is 14 years old and lives with her adoptive parents and younger sister. Sabine had a difficult childhood. Her birth mother was an alcoholic and used illicit drugs. She was rarely at home. Sabine had to raise herself and her younger sister. When her mother was home, she often had strangers over. At one time, one of the strangers sexually molested Sabine. When Sabine was 7, she was removed from her home. She and her sister were placed in foster care and then were adopted by their foster mother and father. Although Sabine is functioning well, she still has moments of deep sadness when she thinks about her childhood. Sabine is at the age where she is beginning to date. For her, this is both scary and uncomfortable. She avoids boys as much as she can, although she would like to fall in love and have a family someday.

With the support of her parents, she decided to go to therapy to discuss this sadness and these fears of dating. Her therapist noted that Sabine had only talked about her history peripherally and had not talked in detail about what happened to her. The goal of the therapy became focused on helping Sabine to develop skills to cope with difficult feelings that have resulted from her trauma history and then talk about her trauma memories of what happened to her. Sabine talked in detail about the neglect and the story of the molestation. Her therapist helped Sabine explore her belief that the abuse was her fault and that all relationships in her future would feel like the abuse. The therapist helped her see the impact these experiences had on her life and that these events were not her fault and they were only part of the story of her life, not the whole story. Through working with her therapist to shift her thinking around these beliefs, Sabine was able to release some of the pain she was holding about this past and fear about the future. She was also able to create a new belief, about herself as a survivor, rather than as a victim.

Instilling Hope

Experiencing trauma can shake the very safety and security that ideally should be a cornerstone of childhood. Children exposed to complex and chronic trauma often lack hope that the future can be any better than the past, while their reactions make it difficult to look positively into the future (Ford & Courtois, 2013). Children may be left with a foreshortened sense of future or hopelessness about the world around them or for the possibility of future love, safety, and security. While hope is an internal experience, it is also an outgrowth of the circumstances in which people live and many people who experience trauma can retain a sense of optimism, self-efficacy, and spiritual beliefs (Hobfoll et al., 2007). Hope is a hallmark of resiliency in that those who can retain a sense of hope and optimism in the face of significant adversity are likely to experience healing and recovery in the face of trauma. If therapists can find ways to offer hope and optimism to those children who have experienced the burdens of trauma, there is a greater likelihood of resolving some of the negative impacts resulting from these experiences.

Hope can be facilitated by a variety of interventions ranging from the individual level to group and community responses. For instance, studies have shown that cognitive behavioral strategies common across many evidence-based child trauma interventions can reduce an individual's distorted sense of personal responsibility for the trauma, one of the many things that can impede hope (Hobfoll et al., 2007). Other interventions, such as psychoeducation, help to instill hope through normalizing individual reactions and indicating that most people recover from traumatic stress reactions, thus promoting hope for returning to pretrauma functioning and finding relief from the distressing reactions and responses being experienced (Berkowitz et al., 2010). Instilling hope through evidence-based trauma interventions is paramount not only for the child exposed to trauma but also for the parents/caregivers. As parents/caregivers find hope in the possibility of healing and recovery for their child, this optimism can be projected from the parent/caregiver onto the child, thus increasing feelings of self-worth, belonging, and connection that can become the foundation of future resilience (Ginsberg, 2011).

Juan

Nine-year-old Juan has lived with his mom for the past five years. Prior to that, he lived with his mother and father. His parents separated after years of his father's abuse of his mother. Juan witnessed many instances where his mother feared for her life. Three weeks ago, Juan's father showed up at their home and violently assaulted his mother. He was arrested and remains incarcerated. Since the incident, Juan has felt very depressed and is missing a lot of school. He has not seen any of his friends and spends most of his time in his room. He recently got into a fight with his mother, and she said to Juan, "You are just like your father." A few hours following the argument, his mom approached Juan to apologize, and they decided to speak with someone about the recent events. Juan was connected to a therapist through his mother's victim-witness advocate. During the first few sessions, Juan and his mother answered many assessment questions. The answers on these assessments showed intense feelings of sadness and hopelessness about his life. He said that he hates where they live and that they have no money. He hates that he doesn't have a dad, and he fears that he acts like his dad when he gets angry. Juan's mother was surprised to hear that Juan felt this way, and she expressed similar concerns about the family's resources and lack of support. As Juan and his mother talked, they both identified Juan's neighbor, Peter, as a positive person in their life. With the help of the therapist, Juan and his mother developed a plan for Juan to spend more time with this neighbor. With Juan's permission, his mom spoke with Peter about Juan's history and current struggles, and Peter was more than willing to serve as a support. After two weeks, the therapist checked in with Juan and his mother and learned that Juan was spending a lot of time with Peter. Juan told the therapist that it was really helpful because Peter had told him he had experienced similar things as Juan and he just "gets" it. He and Juan played basketball after school and sometimes went to the movies. In a few short weeks, Juan appeared to be in a better mood—attending school regularly and getting together with his friends again. He now looks forward to spending time with Peter and argues less with his mother. Juan's mom asks him about this change in his personality in a therapy session, and he tells her that spending time with Peter has allowed him to see that he can be a different type of man than his father. Upon hearing this, Juan's mother provides Juan with a list of things that she sees as differences between him and his father and expresses a desire to also be a support for Juan's feelings. With symptoms mostly resolved and both Juan and his mother feeling hopeful about the future, they finish therapy.

Evidence-Based Trauma Treatments

As noted earlier in this chapter, the field of evidence-based trauma treatments has blossomed over the past 25 years. There are many treatment options for children who have experienced trauma that have been found to be highly effective. Practices and treatments that allow for flexibility are often the ones that are more effective over time, across age groups and trauma types. We list six examples of the more widely used and researched interventions next. These examples focus on different age groups, different systems, and different numbers of sessions. A more extensive list can be found in any of the online registries listed earlier in this chapter.

- **Trauma-Focused Cognitive Behavioral Therapy (TF-CBT):** TF-CBT is an intervention for children who are experiencing behavioral and/or emotional symptoms as a result of exposure to trauma (SAMHSA: National Registry of

Evidence-Based Programs and Practices, 2016). TF-CBT has the most extensive and empirical support for its efficacy in treating children exposed to trauma of all evidence-based child trauma treatments (Cohen, Mannarino, and Deblinger, 2012). TF-CBT has been found to be effective for many different types of trauma exposure (first utilized with sexual abuse but now with other types such as domestic violence, traumatic grief, and complex trauma). TF-CBT is a flexible and adaptive components-based model that emphasizes parent/caregiver involvement in treatment (Cohen et al., 2006). The model is hybrid in design, combining cognitive, behavioral, and family therapy, along with trauma interventions (Child Welfare Information Gateway, 2012a).

  - Age range: 3–21
  - Average treatment length: 12–25 sessions
  - Additional information: TF-CBT has been tested with diverse cultural groups, both in the United States and abroad. Modifications have been developed for military settings, residential treatment facilities, schools, and with children with developmental challenges.
  - Empirical evidence: TF-CBT has the strongest research evidence of any treatment model for children exposed to trauma. Multiple randomized control trials and replication studies have been conducted (NCTSN, 2012f).

- **Child-Parent Psychotherapy (CPP):** CPP is an intervention for young children and their parents/caregivers who have been exposed to at least one type of trauma and are experiencing behavior, attachment, or mental health concerns (National Resource Center for Permanency and Family Connections, 2013). It is a relationship- based intervention that is focused on the interactions and perceptions between the parent/caregiver and the child (Lieberman & Van Horn, 2005). CPP enhances child mental health by supporting the relationship between parent/caregiver and child and increasing parenting responsiveness, therefore strengthening the child's trust in being protected by that parent (Lieberman, Van Horn, & Ghosh Ippen, 2005).
  - Age range: 0–6
  - Average treatment length: 50 sessions
  - Additional information: CPP has been tested with diverse cultural groups. It is a flexible model and allows for the incorporation of cultural values and culture-related experiences.
  - Empirical evidence: CPP is one of the few empirically tested interventions for young children. There exist three randomized control trials with children exposed to trauma and additional studies that provide efficacy for the use of relationship-based models with at-risk samples (NCTSN, 2012c).

- **Child and Family Traumatic Stress Intervention (CFTSI):** CFTSI is a brief intervention for children and is designed to be implemented within the first 30–45 days after a traumatic event and/or disclosure of abuse (Childhood Violent Trauma Center: Yale Child Study Center, n.d.). The goal in the four to eight sessions of CFTSI is to increase social or familial support and enhance coping skills in order to prevent the likelihood of developing PTSD (NCTSN, 2012b). Care coordination and case management is also an integral part of this intervention in order to help reinstate stability in the immediate aftermath of trauma exposure.
    - Age range: 7–18 (young children treatment application: 3–7)
    - Average treatment length: Four sessions
    - Additional information: CFTSI can be used with children experiencing a wide range of trauma types. CFTSI has also been utilized with children from diverse cultural backgrounds and a wide range of income levels.
    - Empirical evidence: Research found that completers of CFTSI were 65 percent less likely than comparison youth to meet criteria for full PTSD at three month follow-up (Yale Childhood Violent Trauma Center, n.d.).
- **Parent-Child Interaction Therapy (PCIT):** PCIT is a family-focused intervention for children that have been exposed to abuse and/or neglect. PCIT utilizes coaching and conjoint treatment with child and caregiver through the entire course of treatment (Foote, Schuhmann, Jones, & Eyberg, 1998). PCIT has been found to be effective in decreasing behavior problems, increasing parental capacity, and enhancing the quality of the parent–child relationship through the use of two key components and a two-phase approach: (1) relationship enhancement and (2) compliance and discipline (Child Welfare Information Gateway, 2012b).
    - Age range: 2–12
    - Average treatment length: 12–20 sessions
    - Additional information: PCIT has been translated into Spanish and has been adapted for use in homes, groups, and for children with medical conditions, physically abusive families, and with Native American families.
    - Empirical evidence: PCIT has published case studies, randomized controlled trials, and studies that include some of the modifications listed previously (NCTSN, 2012e).
- **Trauma Systems Therapy (TST):** TST is both a clinical model and an organizational model, which provides a framework for organizing a multidisciplinary team of providers to coordinate individual and system interventions.

A team of providers comes together to address the needs of traumatized youth in the child's social environment. It is designed to be delivered in both office- and community-based settings.

- Age range: 5–21
- Average treatment length: Varies by level of severity and phases of treatment. Typically seven to nine months
- Additional information: TST has been widely used with diverse cultural groups, including refugees and recent immigrants. It has also been implemented in both urban and rural settings. It is designed to meet the needs of a "trauma system," whereas a system is not able to help a traumatized child regulate survival states resulting from trauma. In this intervention, the social context includes family, school, and neighborhood.
- Empirical evidence: Outcomes of studies on TST have found a decrease in the use of seclusion and physical restraint, decrease in levels of functional impairment, and improvement in foster care placement stability (NCTSN, 2012g).

- **Cognitive Behavioral Intervention for Trauma in Schools (CBITS):** CBITS is a school-based program designed to be flexibly implemented to meet the needs and address barriers of the population being served. It is a skills-based child group intervention aimed at relieving symptoms often associated with children exposed to trauma, including depression, anxiety, and PTSD.

    - Age range: 10–15
    - Average treatment length: 10 sessions
    - Additional information: CBITS is designed for underserved ethnic minority students and has also been delivered to newly immigrated students from diverse cultural backgrounds. It has also been used with children from a wide range of income levels and has also been conducted in Spanish.
    - Empirical evidence: A randomized controlled study of CBITS found greater improvements in PTSD and depressive symptoms than comparison group, and improvements were also found at both three- and six-month follow-ups (NCTSN, 2012d).

As mentioned earlier, there are many other evidence-based or evidence-informed treatment models that exist for children exposed to trauma. These six happen to include the core principles already outlined and the interventions highlighted in the vignettes. They also exemplify the variety of elements that exist between practices aimed at helping children of all ages heal from trauma.

Conclusion

This chapter defines evidence-based clinical trauma interventions and describes the strengths and challenges of implementing and using these interventions. It summarizes the common principles of treatment that are shared by these interventions and provides a list of the more commonly used interventions. The importance of utilizing research and evidence to guide the care of children seeking mental health treatment for trauma-related concerns cannot be overemphasized, but neither can the importance of unconditional positive regard, compassion, and bearing witness to a child's "truth." On one hand, there is the utilization of science to promote healing and recovery for childhood trauma, and on the other, there is the "art" of connection and empathy in working with children exposed.

Trauma treatment can be described as a dance, requiring therapists to seamlessly anticipate a client's next step and read when they need to lead the dance versus when they should follow. In talking with highly trained, effective, and experienced child trauma therapists, these are the principles that therapists struggle to put into words as they reflect on the magic of trauma work with children and adolescents. Some of this magic comes from the therapist, but most of it stems from the child's capacity to survive and thrive, like the ingredients to an elixir that comes together and begins to rebuild that which was lost during trauma. These intangible qualities of meaningful and healing relationships are challenging to capture in any discussion of core principles and evidence-based practice, but they may be at the very foundation of these highly effective trauma treatments and one of the keys to true recovery for childhood trauma exposure.

Note

1. For the purposes of this chapter, the authors will use the term "child trauma" to include children and adolescents. The authors will also use the term "child trauma" to include both violent and nonviolent traumatic events. All vignettes included in this chapter are fictional. The stories resemble characteristics of cases treated by the authors but are not representative of any actual child or family.

References

Amaya-Jackson, L., & DeRosa, R. R. (2007). Treatment considerations for clinicians in applying evidence-based practice to complex presentations in child trauma. *Journal of Traumatic Stress, 70*(4), 379–390.

Berkowitz, S.J., Stover, C.S., & Marans, S.R. (2011). The child and family traumatic stress intervention: Secondary prevention for youth at risk of developing PTSD. *Journal of Child Psychology and Psychiatry, 52*(6), 676–685.

Child Welfare Information Gateway. (2012a). *Issue brief: Trauma-focused cognitive behavioral therapy for children affected by sexual abuse or trauma*. Children's Bureau/ACYF. Retrieved from http://www.childwelfare.gov/pubs/trauma

Child Welfare Information Gateway. (2012b). *Issue brief: Parent–child interaction therapy with at-risk children*. Children's Bureau/ACYF. Retrieved from http://www.childwelfare.gov/pubs/trauma

Cohen, J.A., Mannarino, A.P., & Deblinger, E. (2006). *Treating trauma and traumatic grief in children and adolescents*. New York, NY: The Guilford Press.

Cohen, J.A., Mannarino, A.P., & Deblinger, E. (Eds.). (2012). *Trauma focused CBT for children and adolescents*. New York, NY: The Guilford Press.

Cook, A., Spinazzola, J., Ford, J., Lanktree, C., Blaustein, M., Cloitre, M., . . . van der Kolk, B. (2005). Complex trauma in children and adolescents. *Psychiatric Annals, 35*(5), 390–398.

Foote, R.C., Schuhmann, E.M., Jones, M.L., & Eyberg, S.M. (1998). Parent–child interaction therapy: A guide for clinicians. *Clinical Child Psychiatry and Psychology, 3*(3), 361–373.

Forbes, D., Creamer, M., Bisson, J.I., Cohen, J.A., Crow, B.E., Foa, E.B., . . . Ursano, R.J. (2010). A guide to guidelines for the treatment of PTSD and related conditions. *Journal of Traumatic Stress, 23*(5), 537–552.

Ford, J.D., & Courtois, C.A. (Eds.). (2013). *Treating complex traumatic stress disorders in children and adolescents*. New York, NY: The Guilford Press.

Ginsberg, K.R. (2011). *Building resilience in children and teens*. Elk Grove Village, IL: American Academy of Pediatrics.

Hobfoll, S.E., Watson, P., Bell, C.C., Bryant, R.A., Brymer, M.J., Friedman, M.J., . . . Ursano, R.J. (2007). Five essential elements of immediate and mid-term mass trauma intervention: Empirical evidence. *Psychiatry, 70*(4), 283–315.

Lieberman, A.F., & Van Horn, P. (2005). *Don't hit my mommy*. Washington, DC: ZERO TO THREE.

Lieberman, A.F., & Van Horn, P. (2008). *Psychotherapy with infants and young children*. New York, NY: The Guilford Press.

Lieberman, A. F., Van Horn, P., Ghosh Ippen, C. (2005). Toward evidence-based treatment: Child-parent psychotherapy with preschoolers exposed to marital violence. *Journal of the American Academy of Child and Adolescent Psychiatry, 44*(12), 1241–1248.

National Child Traumatic Stress Network. (2012a). *The 12 core concepts: Concepts for understanding traumatic stress responses in children and families*. Retrieved from http://www.nctsn.org/resources/audiences/parents-caregivers/what-is-cts/12-core-concepts

National Child Traumatic Stress Network. (2012b). *Trauma informed interventions: Child and family traumatic stress intervention*. Retrieved from www.nctsn.org/resources/topics/treatments-that-work/promising-practices

National Child Traumatic Stress Network. (2012c). *Trauma informed interventions: Child parent psychotherapy.* Retrieved from www.nctsn.org/resources/topics/treatments-that-work/promising-practices

National Child Traumatic Stress Network. (2012d). *Trauma informed interventions: Cognitive behavioral intervention for trauma in schools.* Retrieved from www.nctsn.org/resources/topics/treatments-that-work/promising-practices

National Child Traumatic Stress Network. (2012e). *Trauma informed interventions: Parent child interaction therapy.* Retrieved from www.nctsn.org/resources/topics/treatments-that-work/promising-practices

National Child Traumatic Stress Network. (2012f). *Trauma informed interventions: Trauma focused cognitive behavioral therapy.* Retrieved from www.nctsn.org/resources/topics/treatments-that-work/promising-practices

National Child Traumatic Stress Network. (2012g). *Trauma informed interventions: Trauma systems therapy.* Retrieved from www.nctsn.org/resources/topics/treatments-that-work/promising-practices

National Child Traumatic Stress Network. (n.d.) *Early recovery services.* Retrieved from http://www.nctsn.org/resources/early-recovery-services

National Resource Center for Permanency and Family Connections: Silberman School of Social Work at Hunter College. (2013). *Child-parent psychotherapy.* Retrieved from http://www.nrcpfc.org/about-us.html

National Scientific Council on the Developing Child. (2015). *Supportive relationships and active skill-building strengthen the foundations of resilience: Working paper No. 13.* Retrieved from www.developingchild.harvard.edu

Osofsky, J. D. (Ed.). (2011). *Clinical work with traumatized young children.* New York, NY: The Guilford Press.

Schnyder, U., Ehlers, A., Elbert, T., Foa, E. B., Gersons, B. P. R., Resick, P. A., . . . Cloitre, M. (2015). Psychotherapies for PTSD: What do they have in common? *European Journal of Psychotraumatology, 6,* 281–286.

Shipman, K., and Taussig, H. (2009). Mental health treatment of child abuse and neglect: The promise of evidence-based practice. *Pediatrics Clinics of North America, 56,* 417–428.

Substance Abuse Mental Health Services Administration National Registry of Evidence-based Programs and Practices. (2016). *Trauma-focused cognitive behavioral therapy.* Retrieved from http://nrepp.samhsa.gov/ProgramProfile.aspx?id=96

Yale Childhood Violent Trauma Center. (n.d.). *Child and family traumatic stress intervention.* Retrieved from https://medicine.yale.edu/childstudycenter/cvtc/programs/cftsi/

ZERO TO THREE. (2016). *DC: 0–5.* Washington, DC: Zero to Three.

CHAPTER 5

When Home Is Not Safe

Violence within Families

Betsy McAlister Groves

This chapter focuses on traumatic experiences within the family: child maltreatment, which includes child abuse and neglect, and intimate partner violence (IPV). It is estimated that 1 in 25 children in the United States are victims of child abuse and/or neglect (U.S. Department of Health & Human Services, Administration for Children and Families, 2015). As many as 15 million children witness domestic violence each year (McDonald, Jouriles, Ramisetty-Mikler, Caetano, & Green, 2006). Child maltreatment and exposure to IPV commonly occur in the same families (Hamby, Finkelhor, Turner, & Ormrod, 2010; McDonald et al., 2006). In a nationwide telephone survey of children's exposure to violence, 1 in 4 children were exposed to at least one form of violence (exposure to IPV, abuse by parents or siblings) during their lifetimes (Hamby, Finkelhor, Turner, & Ormrod, 2011). Children's experiences as victims or witnesses of family violence are associated with a range of adverse physical and emotional health consequences (Graham-Bermann & Perkins, 2010). Victims of violence face both immediate safety and health risks, and longer-term impacts on health and emotional functioning. Victims of violence and abuse may intersect with multiple facets of the health and legal systems: child protective services; law enforcement; and civil, criminal, juvenile, and/or family courts. Pediatric and adult health practitioners may be able to offer access to safety and protection by screening for family violence and by referring families for services as needed.

The chapter begins with an overview of child maltreatment and exposure to IPV, providing definitions and case examples. Then, information is presented on the prevalence and impact on child functioning. The next part focuses on identification of children who are at risk and on clinical interventions. Although children of all ages are affected by child maltreatment and exposure to IPV, this chapter will focus on younger children, age six and younger. As the statistics in the next section will demonstrate, this age group is represented disproportionately in the reports of prevalence for both child maltreatment and exposure to IPV. Exposure to IPV in the early years poses a heightened risk for children's development (Stover, Ippen, Liang, Briggs, & Berkowitz, 2017). Accumulating research has shown that the developing brain is most vulnerable to chronic stress and trauma in early life (National Scientific Council on the Developing Child, 2014). Unfortunately, while young children are disproportionately exposed to traumatic stressors in general, they are underrepresented in the literature on child trauma (Lieberman, Chu, Van Horn, & Harris, 2011).

Definitions

The terms "child maltreatment," "family violence," and "intimate partner violence" are used throughout this chapter. "Child maltreatment" includes both child abuse and child neglect. "Family violence" describes violence between family members. For the purposes of this chapter, two forms of family violence will be highlighted—child maltreatment and IPV, as well as the phenomenon of a child's exposure to IPV. These types of violence are defined as follows:

Child maltreatment: The general term that encompasses both child abuse and child neglect:

- **Child abuse**: Physical abuse is generally defined as "any non-accidental physical injury to the child" and can include striking, kicking, burning, or biting the child; sexual abuse; or any other action that results in a physical impairment of the child (Child Welfare Information Gateway, 2016).
- **Child neglect**: Failure by a caregiver, either deliberately or through negligence or inability, to take those actions necessary to provide a child with minimally adequate food, clothing, shelter, medical care,

supervision, emotional stability and growth, or other essential care; provided, however, that such inability is not due solely to inadequate economic resources or solely to the existence of a handicapping condition (Child Welfare Information Gateway, 2016).

"Intimate partner violence (IPV)" (also called domestic violence) is defined as "a pattern of abusive behavior in any relationship that is used by one partner to gain or maintain power and control over another intimate partner. Domestic violence can be physical, sexual, emotional, economic, or psychological actions or threats that influence another person" (U.S. Department of Justice, 2017).

- **Victim of IPV**: For pronouns that refer to victims of IPV, this chapter will use "she" or "her." Data on victims of domestic violence affirm that the majority of victims are women. The majority of nonfatal domestic violence assault victims are women and the majority of IPV homicide victims are women. Women sustain more serious injuries from domestic violence assaults. However, these data should not minimize the fact that there are also male victims of domestic violence. There are also limitations with data reporting due to the prevailing assumption of heterosexual relationships. There are less data describing violence in same-sex relationships, perhaps reflecting the reluctance of victims to seek help. In summary, gendered pronouns limit the full scope of recognizing who victims and perpetrators are.
- **Child exposure to IPV**: "Child exposure" refers to a wide range of experiences for children whose parents are being abused physically, sexually, or emotionally by an intimate partner. This term includes the child who observes his or her parents being harmed, threatened, or murdered; who overhears this behavior from another part of the home; or who is exposed to the short- or long-term physical or emotional aftermath of the abuse without hearing or seeing a specific aggressive act. Children exposed to IPV may see their parents' bruises or other visible injuries or bear witness to the emotional consequences of violence, such as fear or intimidation without having directly witnessed violent acts.

Parent/caregiver: This chapter will use the term "parent" in its broader context, referring to the significant and consistent adult providers in a child's life. While these are most often the biological or adoptive parents, they also can be extended family members or other adults in the home.

Child Protection Services (CPS): The generic name for the governmental agency in each state that is responsible for protecting children, including receiving and responding to reports of suspected child maltreatment, and maintaining a system of foster care placements for children who are legally removed from their parents/caregiver's home.

Case Examples

The following two cases provide examples of violence within the home, both the child's experiences of the violence and the system's responses. They will be referred to throughout the chapter.

Bobby: Age Five Years

Bobby, age 5, is the only child of Janna, age 20, and Raul, age 24. The family became involved with their state's CPS when Bobby disclosed to his kindergarten teacher that the bruises on his arm were from his father hitting him with a shoe. After interviewing each member of the family, CPS opened a case on behalf of Bobby, and a caseworker was assigned for regular visits. In the course of getting to know more about Bobby and the family, the caseworker contacted the child-care center for a report on Bobby. His teacher described him as a fearful and anxious child who was often aggressive with others. The worker also discovered that Janna, Bobby's mother, was a victim of Raul's abuse, which had been intermittent since Bobby's birth. As part of the CPS service plan, Raul was mandated to attend a group for perpetrators of abuse. Approximately three months after the case was opened by CPS, the local police, acting on a tip about drug dealing activity, raided their home, searching for drugs and arresting Bobby's father for drug possession and distribution. Because there were allegations of Janna's participation in the drug dealing, she was also detained and taken into custody. A CPS worker was summoned to the home, and Bobby was put into the custody of CPS. He was placed with a family friend for four days, at which time his mother was cleared of all charges. He was reunited with her after the fourth day of separation. As part of the plan for custody being returned to the mother, CPS required that Janna and Bobby have no contact with Raul (who was incarcerated) and that Bobby be seen in counseling. In the first session, Janna expressed concerns to the therapist about Bobby's aggressive behavior, reporting that he kicked the dog, tried to hit his mother, and had disrupted sleep, with nightmares.

Keisha: Age 2.5 Years

Keisha is a 2.5-year-old girl who was in her mother Sonya's arms when Sonya was assaulted by her boyfriend who lived with them. By Sonya's report, she picked up Keisha and fled the house after an argument that escalated. He pursued them and attacked Sonya from behind. Keisha, who was in her mother's arms, saw the boyfriend stab her mother. Sonya was knocked to the ground but did not lose consciousness. Keisha was physically unharmed but witnessed the entire incident. Sonya summoned help from a passerby who saw what happened. The police and the emergency medical technicians (EMTs) arrived within moments. Sonya called a neighbor who came to get Keisha and was then taken to the hospital. The police called CPS who sent an emergency on-call social worker to the scene. She was able to talk to Sonya by telephone, learning that Sonya's mother lived nearby and could provide temporary care of Keisha. After several telephone calls, including a background check of Keisha's grandmother, CPS approved this arrangement, and Keisha was picked up by her grandmother within three hours of the incident. Keisha was separated from her mother for two days while Sonya recovered in the hospital from the assault. She did not want Keisha to visit her at the hospital because she worried that the experience would be upsetting for Keisha. While Sonya was in the hospital, she was visited by a staff member of the hospital-based domestic violence program. They provided assistance in seeking a protective order against the boyfriend. Sonya later learned that he had fled the state and returned to his home in the Dominican Republic.

According to her mother, Keisha seemed subdued when Sonya returned home. She wanted to stay near her at all times. She screamed in protest about going to her daycare program the next day. She had trouble sleeping at night. She cried when she heard a car siren; she startled at loud noises. She asked repeatedly about her mother's "boo-boos." Her mother worried about the changes in her behavior and wondered if what she saw could have a lasting effect on Keisha. She decided to call her pediatrician at the local community health center, who suggested that she bring her in for a visit. The pediatrician asked about Keisha, and Sonya described her sleep difficulties, clinginess, and "baby-like" behavior. Sonya said that prior to the assault, Keisha was developing normally and did not have any of these symptoms. The doctor talked with Sonya about how young children might react to such frightening events, mentioning that sleep problems and clinginess are common reactions to very scary events. He asked if she was interested in talking to a counselor to get some advice about how to help Keisha. She agreed, and the referral was made to a local program that provided trauma-focused counseling for young children and their families. CPS made a follow-up visit and decided that no further services were needed, and then they closed the case.

The stories of Bobby and Keisha are stories about complex emotional, social, and legal problems. They are also stories about the special vulnerability of very young children to traumatic events in their environment, especially when they involve the people on whom they depend the most—their parents. Their stories (with some details changed for confidentiality) are two of hundreds of stories that the Child Witness to Violence Project at Boston Medical Center has heard from families over the past 25 years. This chapter will incorporate research on this subject and the clinical findings from the program to describe the impact of domestic violence and child abuse on children and to discuss interventions.

As the stories of Bobby and Keisha illustrate, families who experience violence in the home are often involved in multiple systems: the law enforcement/legal system, the child protection system, the health system, and the school or childcare system. Bobby's family was involved with CPS, batterer's intervention program, child care, and family and criminal courts. Keisha's family was involved with CPS, family court, and child care. Families often experience further stress by their involvement in multiple systems, especially if there is poor communication among the service providers.

The Scope of the Problem

In its 2015 annual report on prevalence rates, the U.S. Children's Bureau reported that an estimated 683,000 children were victims of abuse and neglect nationwide, a rate of 9.2 victims per 1,000 children in the population. Children in the age group of birth to one year had the highest rate of victimization at 24.2 per 1,000 children of the same age group in the national population (Child Welfare Information Gateway, 2015).

Statistics from the National Coalition against Domestic Violence (NCADV, 2015) reveal the scope of the problem of domestic violence in the United States. One woman is fatally shot by a spouse, ex-spouse, or dating partner every 14 hours. One in 3 women and 1 in 4 men have been victims of some form of physical violence by an intimate partner within their lifetime (NCADV). These and other statistics remind us that while most victims of domestic violence are women, and they also account for the majority of those who are most seriously injured, men, also, can be victims. In some relationships, the violence is bidirectional.

The most recent national telephone survey of children and adolescents age 17 years and younger, the National Survey of Children Exposed to Violence, gathered data from a representative sample of 4,549 individuals. In asking about exposure to domestic violence, 1 in 15 children reported exposure to domestic violence within the past year (Hamby et al., 2011). While this provides a useful (and alarming) picture of the prevalence of exposure to domestic violence, it likely misses young children. For all children under the age of 9, the interviewers spoke with parents to obtain their reports of their children's exposure to violence. It is plausible that parents minimized or failed to report domestic violence or child maltreatment—either because of concerns about having their children removed from their care or, in the cases of IPV, because they assumed that their young children were less aware of the violence. Young children are disproportionately represented in samples of children who are exposed to domestic violence. One study on police responses to domestic violence calls in five large metropolitan areas found a disproportionate representation of young children in those homes, with an average of 45 percent of children being under the age of 6 (Fantuzzo & Fusco, 2007). A second study focused on data from 8,446 children and youth receiving trauma-focused mental health services in the United States. The age of onset for exposure to domestic violence was before age 2 for 30 percent of their sample and before age 7 for an additional 26 percent (Stover et al., 2017).

The Impact of Exposure to Family Violence on Children

Children of all ages are impacted by exposure to violence in the home. The more chronic the abuse, the more severe are the symptoms. Chronic exposure may affect the child's developing brain, and the impact may have lifetime consequences. The first three years of life are a critical period for human brain development (Garner et al., 2012). Research has greatly expanded our understanding of the impact of chronic or toxic stress on the developing child's brain (Shonkoff et al., 2012; Teicher et al., 2003). The Adverse Childhood Experiences Study makes the case for the long-term health consequences of significant stress or adversity in childhood, by linking chronic adult disease and early death to stressors in childhood (Felitti et al., 1998). This research is summarized in Chapter 2 of this volume.

Altered neuroendocrine stress response is one important mechanism linking exposure to family violence and poor physical health. When a child feels nervous or scared, the body generates a "fight or flight" response. From a biological perspective, this is how the body responds to threat and prepares to escape. Both the central nervous system and the endocrine (hormonal) system are activated, leading to changes in the body, such as increased heart rate and respiration and increased blood glucose. Although these changes are adaptive in the short term, repeated activation of this stress response results in pathological changes in neurological and hormonal systems (Kertes, Gunnar, Madsen, & Long, 2008; Shonkoff, Boyce, & McEwen, 2009). These pathological changes then impact later immune and inflammatory functions and increase risk for a host of health problems. Thus, a child's traumatic experiences of child maltreatment and IPV can lead to a range of health risks over the course of a lifetime (Brown et al., 2009; Shonkoff et al., 2009).

Child maltreatment and child exposure to IPV, even in cases in which children are not abused themselves, predict poor health (Rogosch, Dackis, & Cicchetti, 2011). Compared to children admitted to the hospital for accidental injuries, maltreated children are more likely to suffer from severe injury, to be admitted to an intensive care unit, and to die as a result of their injuries. Specific childhood physical health outcomes that have been associated with child abuse or IPV exposure include asthma, failure to thrive, developmental delay, and increased number of somatic complaints (Bair-Merritt, Blackstone, & Feudtner, 2006; Scarborough, Lloyd, & Barth, 2009). Asthma is a particularly good example of an inflammatory health condition that is significantly impacted by childhood stress (Chen, Chim, Strunk, & Miller, 2007). Children exposed to domestic violence have a twofold greater risk of developing asthma than children who are not exposed (Suglia, Enlow, Kullowatz, & Wright, 2009). This increased risk most likely occurs because altered stress physiology magnifies the body's response to allergens and irritants, leading to increased airway hyperreactivity and, ultimately, a diagnosis of asthma.

Child behaviors or psychological symptoms vary by age (see Table 5.1.). Child maltreatment is associated with a wide range of emotional problems, including internalizing and externalizing behaviors and high-risk behaviors, like substance abuse, multiple sexual partners, and increased risk of depression in adolescence (Gilbert et al., 2009). By young adulthood, there is also increased risk for suicide (Gilbert et al., 2009). For children exposed to any form of family violence, the risk of posttraumatic stress disorder (PTSD) is increased, with the typical symptoms of hyperarousal; hypervigilance; sleep disturbances; nightmares; difficulties with concentration; impulsive, aggressive, or reckless behavior; and numbing or withdrawal (American Psychiatric Association, 2013). As of 2013, the diagnosis of preschool posttraumatic stress disorder has been officially recognized, validating years of research on the responses of very young children to significant stress or trauma (American Psychiatric Association, 2013). This diagnosis takes young age into account, acknowledging limitations in language development and the young child's nearly exclusive dependence on caregivers for protection. If we consider the behaviors shown by Keisha and Bobby, we see that they are consistent with the clusters of symptoms that are associated with preschool posttraumatic stress disorder: sleep disturbance, hyperarousal, increased aggression, intrusive thoughts, and fear of being separated from a parent (see Table 5.1).

One of the most interesting findings from this large body of research on the trauma responses of very young children concerned the particular intensity of exposure to IPV for children under the age of four. This study focused on a group of children who were in state custody because of

Table 5.1 Symptoms/Behaviors Associated with Child Exposure to Domestic Violence by Age

Ages Birth to 5	Ages 6 to 11	Ages 12 to 18
• Sleep and/or eating disruptions • Withdrawal/lack of responsiveness • Intense/pronounced separation anxiety • Inconsolable crying • Developmental regression, loss of acquired skills • Intense anxiety, worries, and/or new fears • Increased aggression and/or impulsive behavior	• Nightmares, sleep disruptions • Aggression and difficulty with peer relationships in school • Difficulty with concentration and task completion in school • Withdrawal and/or emotional numbing • School avoidance and/or truancy	• Antisocial behavior • School failure • Impulsive and/or reckless behavior • School truancy • Substance abuse • Running away • Involvement in violent or abusive dating relationships • Depression • Anxiety • Withdrawal

Source: National Child Traumatic Stress Network: http://nctsn.org/content/ages-and-developmental-stages-symptoms-exposure

severe abuse or neglect (Scheeringa & Zeanah, 1995). Since this was a population with well-documented histories of severe trauma, the researchers viewed this as an opportunity to learn more about the symptoms and behaviors of these children and to determine if their responses were similar to the trauma responses of older children and adolescents. As they expected, the observed behaviors and symptoms were quite similar to those of older children. The unexpected finding, however, was about the power of exposure to domestic violence as a predictor of PTSD in very young children. In comprehensive chart reviews, documenting the kinds of traumatic events these children had experienced, they found that exposure to domestic violence was a stronger predictor of trauma symptoms than actual physical abuse. In other words, being a bystander to actual or threatened violence against a parent was more psychologically toxic than being a direct victim of the abuse.

Researchers have explored the specifics of a child's exposure to IPV in the home, addressing questions of the child's proximity to the violence and the risk of injury or longer-term consequences. One such study looked at a sample of 507 families with 1,012 children who had been exposed to domestic violence (Gewirtz & Medhanie, 2009). These families were identified by police after they responded to an incident of domestic violence and were referred to a counseling program that provided acute clinical and advocacy services. Researchers were able to analyze specific information about the nature of the violence from police reports and clinical data on children that was collected by clinicians at the counseling program. Half of the children in this sample were under the age of seven. Eighty-three percent of the incidents involved physical aggression; 57 percent of the children directly witnessed the violence; 16 percent were present in the home but were not direct witnesses; and 12 percent were directly involved by calling the police, attempting to prevent the assault or being physically injured. Age was associated with the child's response to the violence: for both boys and girls, older age was positively associated with direct involvement in the violence. Consistent with children's development, it is logical that older children would feel more responsible and capable of directly intervening.

Research and clinical experience with young children who live with family violence make the case for the particular risks that they face. Young children lack the developmental and cognitive abilities to keep themselves safe. They cannot understand the danger and mayhem around them, and they are unable to make decisions about how to protect themselves. Young children depend exclusively on their parents for physical and psychological safety. Several studies of a young child's awareness of perceived threats in early childhood have been linked to adjustment problems in three to seven year old children (Miller, 2015).

Young children carry these experiences and expectations with them as they enter preschool or kindergarten and learn to negotiate social relationships. They are unsure whether these environments are safe, and they do not trust that adults can take care of them. They often expect danger, a stance that may not help them in the outside world. Behavioral and emotional dysregulation is commonly shown through aggressive behaviors. In fact, the most frequent referral complaint voiced by parents who sought services for children at the Child Witness to Violence Project and other similar programs was concern about their child's aggression, short temper, or impulsive behavior. Other children respond with increased anxiety about any separation from a parent, and with irregular sleeping and eating patterns. Children also learn early and powerful lessons about the use of violence in interpersonal relationships. Violence is an acceptable way to relieve stress and exert one's will. It can also be confused with expressions of love and intimacy.

Given what is known about the impact of living with violence in the home, both Bobby and Keisha are at risk. Bobby has been exposed to prior violence, possibly since birth. His teacher described him as a fearful and aggressive child. Although he was reunited with his mother, he experienced a frightening episode where police raided his home and the sudden separation from both parents. Keisha witnessed the traumatic injury of her mother, at the hands of her father. She too was separated from her parent at the moment of the traumatic experience. She has fewer words to talk about what happened, but her behavior has changed notably, communicating fear, confusion, and worries about safety. At her young age, she has little capacity to understand what happened. However, she was acutely aware of her mother's injury and the ensuing disruption in their lives.

IPV and Its Impact on Parenting

Young children, by virtue of age and developmental stage, look to their parents or caregivers for cues. They depend on them to make sense of the world and to protect them. Homes in which there is maltreatment or chronic domestic violence are not safe havens. Children learn early lessons about the vulnerability of both parents: when a parent is the terrified victim or the terrorizing aggressor, children have no refuge. Both Bobby and Keisha experienced terrifying moments when neither parent could protect them.

A parent's capacity to support or buffer children's responses to stressful events is an essential element of parenting young children (Lieberman & Knorr, 2007). The parents' physical and mental health status, in turn, has a significant impact on their parenting capacity. Numerous studies reflect the physical and psychological impact of IPV on its adult victims with increased rates of injury, higher health costs, and higher rates of PTSD, depression, and substance abuse in victims (Dillon, Hussain, Loxton, & Rahman, 2013).

The symptoms of withdrawal and numbing that are among the common cluster of symptoms associated with PTSD may compromise a parent's ability to be attentive to her child or to accurately assess safety and danger in the child's environment (Groves, 2002). If we consider Bobby and Keisha's situations from their mothers' perspectives, they were both closely involved, as bystander and direct victim of significant trauma. In those cases, a parent may need intervention on her own, as she attempts to manage the aftermath of extremely stressful events.

Resilience and Protective Factors That Mitigate Children's Exposure to Family Violence

Despite the accumulation of research that affirms the toxic nature of family violence on children, there are also reports on the ways that children show resilience. Afifi and MacMillan (2011) conducted a literature search on several databases to review studies of resilience in populations of maltreated children and adolescents. Consistent with studies of resilience in the context of other childhood risks, several factors were identified: a stable family environment, supportive relationships, relatedness to a caregiver, and social skills. When looking specifically at child exposure to IPV, many children appear to withstand the impact of exposure to domestic violence and maintain equilibrium. A study, conducted by Graham-Bermann, Gruber, Howell, and Girz (2009), describes various contextual factors in families that are associated with children's resilience. This study evaluated the social and emotional profiles of 219 children between the ages of 6 and 12 who had witnessed varying levels of domestic violence. Based on a battery of child measures, child adjustment, and beliefs, the children were divided into four adjustment profiles: severe adjustment problems, children who were struggling, children with depression only, and resilient children. Graham-Bermann et al. (2009) also assessed levels of violence, parenting skills, family cohesion, and maternal mental health. Twenty-four percent of the children had severe adjustment problems and 20 percent were resilient; the remainder fell in between. When looking at protective factors, Graham-Bermann found the factors most strongly associated with resilience were children having fewer exposures to violence and mothers having better mental health and parenting skills. Another study of protective factors that contributed to a decrease in PTSD symptoms in children found that teaching children self-regulation skills and intervention to decrease parental stress were associated with a decrease in child PTSD symptoms (Schultz et al., 2013). Together, these studies suggest several important strategies for interventions that will bolster protective factors in children and families: addressing the parents' mental health issues, providing parenting support and training, providing preventive or proactive strategies that reduce or prevent child exposure to domestic violence, and teaching children self-regulation and emotion-control strategies.

Identifying Children Affected by Family Violence

As research and clinical data have amply shown, child maltreatment and exposure to domestic violence carry a host of short- and long-term risks for the healthy development of children. Both forms of abuse are complicated and rooted in the larger social context of violence, gender roles, poverty, and economic inequality. Successful solutions require the efforts of multiple systems (Turner et al., 2017). It is important to note that Bobby and Keisha's maltreatment and exposure to IPV were brought to the attention of a childcare provider (Bobby) and a pediatrician (Keisha). Using these trusted relationships with professionals who knew the families, Bobby and Keisha's mothers were able to disclose the abuse, thus beginning a process of seeking help to address the problem.

In addition to being significant social problems, child abuse and neglect and domestic violence are legal problems. All 50 states have laws specifically defining child abuse and IPV; states can prosecute child abusers and perpetrators of domestic violence (National Council on Juvenile and Family Court Judges, 2013). The Violence against Women Act, initially enacted in 1996, is an example of powerful and far-reaching legislation that defined violence in the home as a crime and provided federal funding for services in every state for victims of domestic violence. Prevention efforts have included large-scale endeavors to educate women about their rights and about resources that are available (see websites for the National Coalition against Domestic Violence and Futures without Violence). Batterer's intervention programs now exist in every state, and most states have standards to certify these programs. While program evaluation outcomes are mixed, there is consensus about modest gains and evidence shows that the dose of counseling for abusers is important: those who participate longer have lower rates of reoffending (Groves, 2012). Schools and other youth-oriented services have adopted programs that promote discussion and education about healthy relationships. These programs often address adolescent social norms and views of gender-based behavior.

The logical and essential first step to addressing the adverse impacts of child maltreatment and exposure to IPV is to identify the children who are impacted as early in life as possible. However, this is not an easy task. Despite the existence of national child abuse prevention efforts, such as Healthy Families American and Prevent Child Abuse America, and the widespread outreach of national domestic violence coalitions, such as the National Coalition against Domestic Violence and Futures without Violence, that offer outreach and education, violence in the home often remains hidden. There is stigma and shame associated with disclosing the abuse. Parents or caregivers worry that their children will be removed from their homes. Perpetrators of domestic violence may threaten their partner with harm or revenge if she tells anyone or seeks help. The victim may fear that if she talks about the abuse, she may be reported to child protective services. Parents may worry about becoming involved with the police. Abusers may threaten that if their partner leaves, they will lose custody of their child. In some families, religion or marriage vows discourage separation or divorce. For many victims, it is not possible, financially, to leave the relationship. Other parents worry that leaving with the children may be harder and more disruptive for the children than staying. The decision to leave is rarely an easy one.

It is, therefore, essential that agencies and systems serving families and children provide information about family violence and that, when appropriate, they find ways to ask about or screen for family violence. For young children, childcare and preschool settings, Early Intervention and Head Start, are logical and important settings to offer information and resources for families affected by child maltreatment or domestic violence (Campbell et al., 2016). In many of these programs, intake forms and questionnaires contain questions about safety in the home: whether a parent feels unsafe in the parent relationship or general questions about how conflict is managed. Information, along with hotline information about parental stress or IPV, is available in the centers; workshops are offered about negotiating family conflict or healthy parenting. Teachers are also trained to recognize signs of child abuse or neglect and to be familiar with the protocol for reporting suspected abuse or neglect. In Bobby's case, the teacher received a clear verbal report from the child. In her center, the protocol was for the teacher to notify the center director, who, in turn, notified CPS. A worker came to the center and saw the child before going to the home to interview the parents. In many instances, the child does not directly report the abuse but shows worrisome behavior or has unusual marks or bruises. A child may come to school hungry or without a coat. Each instance requires careful assessment and planning by staff about whether to notify CPS and how to talk with the parents and the child about their concerns.

The Role of Pediatric Health Systems

Perhaps the system that is best equipped to provide screening and parent education about child maltreatment or exposure to IPV is the pediatric health system. Proponents of early identification of abuse point out that health-care providers are the only professionals to see virtually all children at some point. Rates for children under age six are the highest because of their required visit schedule (American Academy of Pediatrics, 2017). The pediatric health setting thus provides a critical opportunity for family screening for a number of social and health risks—including child abuse and exposure to IPV—and for linkage with services to help with the problem. Pediatric staff are mandated reporters, required by law to report suspected child abuse or neglect. In most states, providers are not required to report IPV to CPS, unless there is a specific concern about child risk or injury. However, asking about abuse is essential in providing early identification and intervention.

In its 2010 policy statement, the American Academy of Pediatrics affirmed the position that "intimate partner violence is a pediatric problem" (Thackeray, Hibbard, & Dowd, 2010) and encouraged pediatricians to ask about IPV in the home. Increasingly, pediatric practices are incorporating a range of screening instruments into their routine care. The screenings are often done universally with all families. These questionnaires may track the social and physical development of the child, ask about unmet family needs, such as housing, food, or transportation, and also ask about stressors in the family: substance abuse, family violence, or other stressors (Garg et al., 2007). The questionnaires not only provide opportunities for parents to talk with their providers about problems but also communicate important messages about the broader determinants of health and well-being that are within the purview of the pediatric visit (see Chapter 5 in Volume II of this series, "Trauma-Informed Care in the Pediatric Primary Care Setting").

Clinical Interventions for Children Affected by Family Violence

This section will provide an overview of mental health interventions for young children affected by family violence. Effective interventions frequently involve a larger network of service providers, with clinical intervention being only one component of the services provided. There may have been police involvement with the family. CPS may be actively involved with the child; there may be a restraining order in effect, limiting the abusing parent's access to the family home or visits with the child. Custody and general access to the child are often contentious issues that end up being heard in family court. The essential first step for every responding system is to address basic safety issues for the child and family. When systems can work together effectively, there is great potential to help each member of the family (see Chapter 9 in Volume II, "Judicial Perspective on Violence and Trauma within the Family").

Trauma-focused clinical treatment for children under the age of six generally involves active participation by the nonabusing parent or caregiver. The goal is to support the parent in helping the child to recover from the traumatic experience. At these young ages, children need the ongoing support and protection from a parent who understands what they have been through and can be seen by the child as a protective person. The most widely used interventions for this age group are Child Parent Psychotherapy (CPP) (Lieberman, Ghosh Ippen, & Van Horn, 2015) for children from birth to age 6, Trauma-Focused Cognitive Behavioral Therapy, for children ages 3 and older (Cohen, Mannarino, & Deblinger, 2012), and Parent Child Interaction Therapy (PCIT); (Chaffin et al., 2004), a therapy model with live coaching sessions with the parent/caregiver and the child, for children ages 2–12. Another evidence-based intervention, Attachment and Biobehavioral Catch-up (ABC) (Bernard et al., 2012) is a 10-session home-based intervention specifically developed for young children (under 24 months of age) with histories of abuse and neglect, with a focus on supporting foster parents of these children. These models of treatment share common goals of restoring safety, providing support and education to the parent, helping children regulate their trauma-related symptoms, and helping the parent and the child be able to process the traumatic experience. However, they differ in their approach and the number of sessions that are recommended.

Family Violence and the Role of Culture

Regardless of which intervention is chosen, the clinician should consider the family's culture as an important dimension of treatment. Culture shapes practices and beliefs associated with child-rearing, discipline, roles within families, and gender roles. Culture also impacts definitions of what constitutes abusive behavior and how one seeks help for family problems. The clinician should be sensitive to the wide range of help-seeking practices across cultures. In some traditions, talking about family problems with a stranger is not only unhelpful but also inappropriate. Psychotherapy, as it is practiced in the United States, is not viewed as being helpful. Since it is not possible for a therapist to have knowledge of all cultures, he or she can be actively and respectfully curious about practices and family relationships in other cultures. They can ask the family or seek a consultation from others within that culture. The time and interest a clinician takes to seek an understanding of experiences within a cultural context is often rewarded with the trust of the parent and a stronger therapeutic relationship.

Treatment for Bobby and Keisha

Both children and their mothers were seen by mental health clinicians who were trained in Child Parent Psychotherapy (CPP): Bobby for nine months and Keisha for three months. Weekly sessions usually involved the child and parent in the room together.

Keisha

Sonya and Keisha began counseling about three weeks after the abusive event. Sonya met with the CPP clinician twice before Keisha joined the sessions. The clinician explained CPP to the mother, suggesting that the goals for counseling were for Sonya to better understand Keisha's reactions and for both of them to have a place to "talk," through play, about what had happened. The clinician asked about Keisha's general development, medical history, and history of prior traumatic experiences for both Keisha and Sonya. None were reported. Keisha was in child care and she enjoyed it. She had a close relationship with her grandmother who lived nearby and spent time each week with her. Sonya related that the violent incident with her boyfriend stemmed from her announcement that she wanted him to move out of the house. There had been escalating tension between them although no prior abusive incidents. She described that she became frightened during the discussion as his anger escalated, and he began to threaten her. She picked up Keisha and left the house. She said that she was terribly upset and guilty for having put her daughter in such a dangerous situation, having no idea that the argument would end in this way. She had first hoped that Keisha, at her young age, would forget about it, but now she expressed worry about how this would affect her. She explicitly asked for help in making sure that she would be OK. The clinician provided information about typical responses of young children to frightening events in their environment. She asked about whether Sonya was worried that her boyfriend might return or threaten her in some other way. Sonya said that he had left the country and she did not fear for her safety. Over the next two sessions, they discussed the importance of routines for young children, and Sonya decided to spend extra time each night with bedtime preparations, hoping to be able to read her a story each night. By the third session, Keisha's sleep disruptions had diminished. However, she continued to have trouble with the transition from home to child care in the morning and to talk about her mother's "boo-boos." In the third session, Keisha and her mother explored the toys in the office and engaged in play with small dolls in the dollhouse. Sonya was engaged with her daughter in the play, and Keisha clearly enjoyed playing with her mother. In the fifth session, Keisha picked up a doll and commented on a "boo-boo." Sonya got the doctor's kit and together they tended to the doll. This theme of "fixing" the doll was replayed several times over the next sessions, and Sonya asked the clinician if this could have anything to do with what had happened. This provided an opportunity for the clinician to suggest that perhaps Sonya might talk about that with Keisha. In the next sessions, the theme of the dolls being hurt was revisited and Keisha asked directly about "Mommy's boo-boos." This provided a direct opportunity for response, with Sonya asking if she remembered when Mommy got hurt. Keisha nodded. Sonya replied, saying that she was OK now and that "this won't happen again." Keisha crawled into her mother's lap and sat for a few minutes. This moment of resolution was possibly as comforting for Sonya as it was for Keisha. Sonya expressed relief and felt reassured that they both had been able to move beyond the immediate distress and impact of the traumatic experience. Within a few more sessions, Sonya felt that Keisha was "her old self again," and the counseling sessions ended.

With this family, there were several protective factors at work—the relationship, the family, and the larger community. There was a solid attachment between the mother and the child. Keisha had strengths: she was verbal and she appeared to have an even and flexible temperament. There was no prior history of trauma in Keisha's life. She had a strong relationship with her grandmother. Sonya was a keen observer of her daughter's behavior. She was strongly motivated to seek help, first from her pediatrician and then from the therapist. With prompt intervention and support, Keisha, like many young children, was able to "bounce back" after this experience.

Bobby

In the initial session with Bobby's mother, Janna, the clinician explained the counseling approach and obtained background information. She asked Janna what her hopes were for the counseling. Janna replied that she wanted to know if Bobby had been affected by the police coming to the house and taking them away. She expressed concern that he would think about the things he had witnessed and she did not want those things to affect him later in life. In addition to the recent police raid and the separation from mother and father, she disclosed a history of domestic violence. She recalled that Bobby had witnessed some of the violence, in particular, an incident that took place in their car. Bobby was sitting in the back seat and saw his father hit his mother. She tried to hide her injury from him. She remembered that he was very quiet, saying nothing, and that he did not want to look at her.

The therapist obtained permission from the mother to have ongoing contact with the CPS worker and also to contact the childcare center where Bobby was enrolled. She learned that Department of Children and Families planned to close the case in six weeks, if all went well. Bobby's childcare teacher said that before the incident that resulted in Bobby's temporary removal from home, he did well in the classroom, and she did not have behavioral concerns about him. She reported that he sometimes came to school tired and often took long naps. Since he had returned to the classroom, she noted changes in behavior. He needed more attention from her, and he seemed anxious at times, asking when he could go home, and being wary if someone new came in the classroom.

Early in the joint sessions with Bobby and Janna, Bobby began to use the police dolls in his play. He would seek them out each week and create various scenes with them. The scenes always revolved around themes of danger and aggression. In some scenes, the police would go into the dollhouse and throw furniture around. In others, they would take the baby dolls and throw them or push them off the table. He would do this repetitively, as his mother sat beside him and watched. He invited her to play with him and she refused. She later commented to the therapist that she did not like to see him playing that way. It seemed as though she was avoiding the play altogether. Bobby, however, was quite ready to communicate what he had seen. For many sessions, she sat in the chair silently as he played. One day, after a session in which Bobby put a small animal in the oven of the play stove and announced triumphantly that he was dead, his mother spoke sharply to him, "He is NOT dead. You shouldn't play that kind of game." Bobby ignored her and stated again that the doll was dead. At that point the mother began to cry.

In follow-up with the mother alone, Janna cried through much of the session as she began to talk about how difficult it was for her to see Bobby's play because it made her realize that he remembered everything and that he knew more than she thought he did. Despite her stated goal for the treatment—that he be able to talk about what had happened so that she could better understand how he was affected—it was painful for her to realize how much he remembered. It seemed "too big" to talk about, and of course that was the message that Bobby was getting. The traumatic experience had driven a wedge in their relationship, and both were suffering. The therapist began to wonder with Janna about what it might be like to talk with Bobby about the experience. What did she want to say to him? Janna commented, "If I tell the story, I will fall apart and that will be bad for Bobby." Initially, she could not imagine what to say, but over time, she began to actively seek the therapist's help in talking with Bobby. Together, they developed a plan for how to talk with Bobby about his experience.

In the session, Janna asked Bobby if he wanted to talk about what happened when the police came to their house. Bobby's expression changed; he looked away and then said "yes." The mother sat on the floor with him and asked him if he remembered when the police came. He nodded his head. She then asked if he remembered when the police took him and his mother. Bobby got a large police car from the toy shelf. He and his mother put three doll figures in the car: a little boy, a female figure, and a police officer. He said, "They took us in their car. Then when we got out of the car, they said, 'I am going to keep you.'" Janna's expression changed at that point, and she asked, "That's what they said to you?" Bobby did not answer. He took the police car and said, "The boy is going to drive now," and at that point, he stopped playing. It seemed clear to the mother and the therapist that Bobby was reliving the experience from his perspective and that the moment of separation from his mother had been overwhelming. At that point, the mother leaned over to hug him and said, "That won't happen again." After that session, Bobby's play with the police dolls diminished. Perhaps more importantly, Janna felt considerable relief from having been able to revisit the traumatic event with him. In this case, it was not the child's inability to talk about the trauma but the parent's inability to acknowledge it that created the wedge in their relationship.

In both cases, we see how trauma can derail a child's behavior and functioning. Age, developmental phase, and prior history of trauma are important variables in understanding how these children responded behaviorally and how they made meaning of their experiences. We also see how closely the child and parents' experiences and emotional reactions are intertwined. Keisha is younger than Bobby and has, as far as we know, not experienced repeated traumatic stressors. Bobby, at age five, has experienced direct abuse, exposure to IPV, and a traumatic separation from both parents. He has more cognitive ability to anticipate danger and to be fearful of harm to himself or his mother, and he has language with which to communicate his fears. Because of his multiple exposures, there is concern about his vulnerability and future challenges he may face.

Both children and their parents benefited from the therapy. Their trauma-related symptoms had abated. In both cases, the mothers' concern, perspective, and participation in the therapy were essential to the children being able to move forward in a positive way. The children were able, in their developmentally appropriate manner, to communicate their experiences and to benefit from the emotional presence and reassurance of their parent.

Conclusion and Lessons Learned

This chapter focuses on violence and abuse within families, which is the most widespread form of violence in our country and the least disclosed or discussed. Although beyond the scope of this chapter, we must consider the larger societal backdrop with its persistent environmental stressors of poverty, structural inequality, and isolation. In these contexts, families live with ongoing stressors, increasing the likelihood of child maltreatment and IPV, which may co-occur in families. Research and clinical experience have given us valuable information about identification and intervention, emphasizing several key lessons. First, the burdens of child maltreatment and exposure to IPV fall disproportionately on very young children who are both the most vulnerable and the least likely to be able to ask for help. The consequences of this abuse may last throughout the life span, with significant physical and mental health impacts. Second, early identification of family violence becomes an essential form of prevention of later health and behavioral adversities in children. Supporting key child-serving systems, especially early care and education and pediatric primary care settings, to screen for family violence is essential. Third, children and families are best helped when the legal, medical, child protection, and mental health systems can work together to increase safety and stability. Fourth, there are a number of evidence-based interventions that can help children and families. These may range from parenting programs to trauma-focused interventions for children and adults to treatment for adults who are abusive. Interventions should consider the family's culture, and they should leverage the resilience and protective factors that are present in most families. Fifth, working at the macro level to address the broad societal stressors that families encounter should be a shared endeavor for all who work on behalf of children and families.

References

Afifi, T. O., & MacMillan, H. L. (2011). Resilience following child maltreatment: A review of protective factors. *The Canadian Journal of Psychiatry*, *56*(5), 266–272.

American Academy of Pediatrics. (2017). *AAP schedule of well-child care visits.* Retrieved from https://www.healthychildren.org/English/family-life/health-management/Pages/Well-Child-Care-A-Check-Up-for-Success.aspx

American Psychiatric Association. (2013). *Diagnostic and statistical manual of mental disorders, Fifth Edition: DSM-5.* Arlington, VA: American Psychiatric Association.

Bair-Merritt, M. H., Blackstone, M., & Feudtner, C. (2006). Physical health outcomes of childhood exposure to intimate partner violence: a systematic review. *Pediatrics*, *117*(2), e278–e290.

Bernard, K., Dozier, M., Bick, J., Lewis-Morrarty, E., Lindhiem, O., & Carlson, E. (2012). Enhancing attachment organization among maltreated children: Results of a randomized clinical trial. *Child development*, *83*(2), 623–636. doi:10.1111/j.1467–8624.2011.01712.x

Brown, D. W., Anda, R. F., Tiemeier, H., Felitti, V. J., Edwards, V. J., Croft, J. B., & Giles, W. H. (2009). Adverse childhood experiences and the risk of premature mortality. *American Journal of Preventive Medicine*, *37*(5), 389–396.

Campbell, C., Roberts, Y., Synder, F., Papp, J., Strambler, M., & Crusto, C. (2016). The assessment of early trauma exposure on social-emotional health of young children. *Children and Youth Services Review*, *71*, 308–314.

Campos, J.J., Hiatt, S., Ramsay, D., Henderson, C., & Svejda, M. (1978). The emergence of fear on the visual cliff. *The Development of Affect, 1*, 149–182.

Chaffin, M., Silovsky, J. F., Funderburk, B., Valle, L. A., Brestan, E. V., Balachova, T., . . . Bonner, B. L. (2004). Parent–child interaction therapy with physically abusive parents: Efficacy for reducing future abuse reports. *Journal of Consulting and Clinical Psychology, 72*(3), 500–510.

Chen, E., Chim, L. S., Strunk, R. C., & Miller, G. E. (2007). The role of the social environment in children and adolescents with asthma. *American Journal of Respiratory and Critical Care Medicine, 176*(7), 644–649.

Child Welfare Information Gateway. (2015). *Child maltreatment information*. https://www.childwelfare.gov/pubPDFs/canstats.pdf

Child Welfare Information Gateway. (2016). *Definitions of child abuse and neglect*. https://www.childwelfare.gov/pubPDFs/define.pdf

Cohen, J. A., Mannarino, A. P., & Deblinger, E. (Eds.). (2012). *Trauma-focused CBT for children and adolescents: Treatment applications*. New York, NY: Guilford Press.

Dillon, G., Hussain, R., Loxton, D., & Rahman, S. (2013). Mental and physical health and intimate partner violence against women: A review of the literature. *International Journal of Family Medicine, 2013*, 313909–313924.

Fantuzzo, J. W., & Fusco, R. A. (2007). Children's direct exposure to types of domestic violence crime: A population-based investigation. *Journal of Family Violence, 22*(7), 543–552. doi: 10.1007/s10896007–9105-z

Felitti, V. J., Anda, R. F., Nordenberg, D., Williamson, D. F., Spitz, A. M., Edwards, V., . . . Marks, J. S. (1998). Relationship of childhood abuse and household dysfunction to many of the leading causes of death in adults: The Adverse Childhood Experiences (ACE) Study. *American Journal of Preventive Medicine, 14*(4), 245–258.

Garg, A., Butz, A. M., Dworkin, P. H., Lewis, R. A., Thompson, R. E., & Serwint, J. R. (2007). Improving the management of family psychosocial problems at low-income children's well-child care visits: The WE CARE Project. *Pediatrics, 120*(3), 547–558.

Garner, A. S., Shonkoff, J. P., Siegel, B. S., Dobbins, M. I., Earls, M. F., McGuinn, L., . . . Committee on Early Childhood, Adoption, and Dependent Care. (2012). Early childhood adversity, toxic stress, and the role of the pediatrician: translating developmental science into lifelong health. *Pediatrics, 129*(1), e224–e231. doi:10.1542/peds.2011–2662

Gewirtz, A. H., & Medhanie, M. (2009). Proximity and risk in children's witnessing of intimate partner violence incidents. In R. Gefner, Dawn Griffin, & James Lewis III (Eds.), *Children exposed to violence: Current issues, interventions and research* (pp. 64–79). New York, NY: Routledge Press.

Gilbert, R., Widom, C. S., Browne, K., Fergusson, D., Webb, E., & Janson, S. (2009). Burden and consequences of child maltreatment in high-income countries. *The Lancet, 373*(9657), 68–81.

Graham-Bermann, S. A., Gruber, G., Howell, K. H., & Girz, L. (2009). Factors discriminating among profiles of resilience and psychopathology in children exposed to intimate partner violence (IPV). *Child abuse & neglect*, *33*(9), 648–660.

Graham-Bermann, S. A., & Perkins, S. (2010). Effects of early exposure and lifetime exposure to intimate partner violence (IPV) on child adjustment. *Violence and Victims*, *25*(4), 427–439.

Groves, B. M. (2002). *Children who see too much: Lessons from the child witness to violence project*. Boston, MA: Beacon Press.

Groves, B. M. (2012). What works in child welfare: Prevention and treatment of family violence. In P. A. Curtis & G. Alexander (Eds.), *What works in child welfare*. Washington, DC: Child Welfare League of America.

Hamby, S., Finkelhor, D., Turner, H., & Ormrod, R. (2010). The overlap of witnessing partner violence with child maltreatment and other victimizations in a nationally representative survey of youth. *Child Abuse & Neglect*, *34*(10), 734–741.

Hamby, S., Finkelhor, D., Turner, H., & Ormond, R. (2011). *Children's exposure to intimate partner violence and other family violence*. Retrieved from www.ncjrs.gov/pdffiles1/ojjdp/232272.pdf

Kertes, D. A., Gunnar, M. R., Madsen, N. J., & Long, J. D. (2008). Early deprivation and home basal cortisol levels: A study of internationally adopted children. *Development and Psychopathology*, *20*(2), 473–491.

Lieberman, A. F., Chu, A., Van Horn, P., & Harris, W. W. (2011). Trauma in early childhood: Empirical evidence and clinical implications. *Development and Psychopathology*, *23*(2), 397–410. doi:10.1017/S0954579411000137

Lieberman, A. F., Ghosh Ippen, C., & Van Horn, P. (2015). *Don't hit my mommy: A manual for Child Parent Psychotherapy with young witnesses of family violence* (2nd ed.). Washington, DC: Zero to Three Press.

Lieberman, A. F., & Knorr, K. (2007). The impact of trauma: A development framework for infancy and early childhood. *Psychiatric Annals*, *37*(6), 416–422.

McDonald, R., Jouriles, E. N., Ramisetty-Mikler, S., Caetano, R., & Green, C. E. (2006). Estimating the number of American children living in partner-violent families. *Journal of Family Psychology*, *20*(1), 137–142.

Miller, L. E. (2015). Perceived threat in childhood: A review of research and implication for children living in violent households. *Trauma, Violence & Abuse*, *16*(2), 153–168.

National Coalition against Domestic Violence. (2015). *Domestic violence national statistics*. Retrieved from https://ncadv.org

National Council of Juvenile and Family Court Judges. (2013). *State laws*. Retrieved from https://www.ncjfcj.org/our-work/state-laws

National Scientific Council on the Developing Child (2014) Retrieved from https://developingchild.harvard.edu/science/national-scientific-council-on-the-developing-child/

Rogosch, F. A., Dackis, M. N., & Cicchetti, D. (2011). Child maltreatment and allostatic load: Consequences for physical and mental health in children from low-income families. *Development and Psychopathology*, 23(4), 1107–1124.

Scarborough, E. C., Lloyd, R., & Barth, P. (2009). Maltreated infants and toddlers: Predictors of developmental delay. *Journal of Developmental Behavioral Pediatrics, 30*(6), 489–498.

Scheeringa, M., & Zeanah, C. (1995). Symptom expression and trauma variables in children under 48 months of age. *Infant Mental Health Journal, 16*, 259–270.

Schultz, D., Jaycox, L. H., Hickman, L. J., Setodji, C., Kofner, A., Harris, R., & Barnes, D. (2013). The relationship between protective factors and outcomes for children exposed to violence. *Violence and Victims, 28*(4), 697–714.

Shonkoff, J. P., Boyce, W. T., & McEwen, B. S. (2009). Neuroscience, molecular biology, and the childhood roots of health disparities: Building a new framework for health promotion and disease prevention. *Journal of the American Medical Association, 301*(21), 2252–2259. doi:10.1001/jama.2009.754

Shonkoff, J. P., Garner, A. S., The Committee on Early Childhood, Adoption, and Dependent Care and Section on Developmental and Behavioral Pediatrics, Siegel, BS, Dobbins MI, Earls. M.F., Mcguinn, L, Pascoe J., Wood D. L. (2012). The lifelong effects of early childhood adversity and toxic stress. *Pediatrics, 129*(1), e232–e246.

Stover, C. S., Ippen, C. G., Liang, L., Briggs, E. C., & Berkowitz, S. J. (2017). An examination of partner violence, poly-exposure, and mental health functioning in a sample of clinically-referred youth. *Psychology of Violence*. doi: 10.1037/vio0000131

Suglia, S. F., Enlow, M. B., Kullowatz, A., & Wright, R. J. (2009). Maternal intimate partner violence and increased asthma incidence in children: Buffering effects of supportive caregiving. *Archives of Pediatrics & Adolescent Medicine, 163*(3), 244–250.

Teicher, M. H., Andersen, S. L., Polcari, A., Anderson, C. M., Navalta, C. P., & Kim, D. M. (2003). The neurobiological consequences of early stress and childhood maltreatment. *Neuroscience & Biobehavioral Reviews, 27*(1), 33–44.

Thackeray, J. D., Hibbard, R., Dowd, M. D., Committee on Child Abuse and Neglect, & Committee on Injury, Violence, and Poison Prevention. (2010). Intimate partner violence: The role of the pediatrician. *Pediatrics, 125*(5), 1094–1100. doi: 10.1542/peds.2010–0451

Turner, W., Broad, J., Drinkwater, J., Firth, A., Hester, M., Stanley, N., Szilassy, E., & Feder, G. (2017). Interventions to improve the response of professionals to children exposed to domestic violence and abuse: A systematic review. *Child Abuse Review*, 26, 19–39.

U.S. Department of Health & Human Services, Administration for Children and Families, Administration on Children, Youth and Families, Children's Bureau. (2015). *Child maltreatment*. Retrieved from http://www.acf.hhs.gov/programs/cb/research-data-technology/statistics-research/child-maltreatment

U.S. Department of Justice, Office of Violence against Women. (2017). *Domestic violence*. Retrieved from https://www.justice.gov/ovw/domestic-violence

CHAPTER 6

Navigating the Vortex of Community Violence

Applying the STRONG Families Treatment Approach for Gang-Involved Youth

Jaleel Abdul-Adil and Liza M. Suarez

Recent research suggests that an epidemic of interpersonal violence is rampant among contemporary youth and communities in the United States. For example, almost 60 percent of adolescents have witnessed a community assault during their lifetime, and almost half of the population has been personally victimized or has directly witnessed violence during the past year (Finkelhor, Turner, Shattuck, & Hamby, 2015). This chapter will focus on the segment of contemporary youth who are most vulnerable to community violence—urban adolescents of color. It will summarize the challenges youth experience and provide an example of an integrated treatment program for urban adolescents and their families at risk for violent victimization and/or perpetration of community violence.

Urban Adolescents Exposed to Community Violence

According to the National Child Traumatic Stress Network (NCTSN, 2013), "community violence" can be defined as:

> Exposure to intentional acts of interpersonal violence committed in public areas by individuals who are not intimately related to the victim. Common types of community violence that affect youth include individual and group conflicts (e.g., bullying, fights among gangs and other groups, shootings in public areas such as schools and communities, civil wars in foreign countries or "war-like" conditions in U.S. cities, spontaneous or terrorist attacks, etc.).

This definition is consistent with contemporary scholars (Dahlberg & Krug, 2002; Voisin & Berringer, 2015) who consider community violence exposure to comprise being a witness and/or target in a violent incident (e.g., robberies, muggings, gang-related deaths, or homicides) that occurs outside the home between unrelated individuals who may or may not know each other.

Urban adolescents of color (e.g., racial/ethnic minorities who live in large metropolitan areas with high population densities and low infrastructure resources) have particularly elevated risks for chronic community violence exposure and subsequent adverse emotional, behavioral, academic, and substance abuse outcomes (Cooley-Strickland et al., 2009). The 2012 Bureau of Justice Statistics indicated that African American adolescents who reside in racially segregated, high-density populated, and underresourced urban areas are twice as likely to be victims of serious violent crimes as other youth (Truman, Langton, & Planty, 2013). A recent study of low-income urban adolescents (95% minorities) reported higher rates and varied types of community violence exposure such as "being chased by gangs or other people, witnessing someone carrying or holding a gun or knife, and knowing someone who was picked up, arrested, or taken away by the police" (Taylor et al., 2016).

Gang Involvement: Boon, Bane, and beyond "the Box"

While all components of community violence are considered destructive, gang violence is a particularly complex and pervasive phenomenon among urban youth, especially for low-income racial and ethnic minorities. Given the aforementioned tendencies toward tough guise stances and functionally aggressive behaviors, urban adolescents are primed to join or affiliate with neighborhood street gangs that successfully facilitate attaining vital goals of social status, self-protection, and economic sustenance. Gang-based identification or affiliation as a means of surviving certain gang-proliferated neighborhoods can be so important that even "good kids" associate with "deviant" gang-involved peers as a "resilience" strategy in high-risk neighborhoods (Patton & Roth, 2016). These gang-involved adolescents, however, also encounter increased risk for further violence exposure and activity due to increased antisocial behaviors, disrupted prosocial peer relationships, and fixed antisocial peer networks (Kerig, Chaplo, Bennett, & Modrowski, 2016).

Gang violence is not limited to urban ethnic minority communities. Although much of the mainstream media attention and discourse on street gangs is focused on impoverished youth of color, youth of *all* cultures and races continue to be involved with, and at risk for, gang violence. Whether formally involved in newer multiracial gangs, historically white ethnic gangs or other groups that receive less attention (e.g., biker gangs, Irish and Italian gangs, Asian gangs), youth their exposure or involvement with gang violence has become a national problem that requires a collective solution that is beyond "the box" of simplistic analyses, premature conclusions, and reactionary responses.

Adverse Impacts of Community Violence Exposure

Exposure to community violence is associated with adverse impacts across the age span of children and adolescents. First, early exposure to community violence increases the psychosocial risks for young children. Studies have shown that witnessing violence at an early age (three to five years old) can place youth at risk for developing behavior problems (Shahinfar, Fox, & Leavitt, 2000). Younger adolescents are more likely to develop internalizing symptoms (fearfulness, social withdrawal, somatic complaints) following violence exposure compared to older adolescents (Schwab-Stone et al., 1999). Researchers suggest that as youth get older, they habituate or become desensitized to violence due to repeated exposure (Fitzpatrick & Boldizar, 1993), while younger children or those who are not exposed as frequently may experience a sustained fear response. Additionally, caregivers can also suffer the negative impacts of violence exposure and other stressors that impair their ability to appropriately support the high needs of violence-exposed youth and prevent negative emotional and behavioral outcomes (Aisenberg & Ell, 2005; Linares et al., 2001).

Although exposure to community violence at any age increases risks for negative outcomes, adolescence is a particularly vulnerable period in which environmental stressors and community violence can increase difficulties in developmental trajectories. Youth endure a number of transitional and stressful life experiences during this developmental period that substantially increases the range of both internalizing and externalizing symptoms, including delinquency and depression (Chen, Voisin, & Jacobson, 2016; Finkelhor, Turner, Shattuck, & Hamby, 2013; Goldner, Gross, Richards, & Ragsdale, 2015; Liu, Bolland, Dick, Mustanski, & Kertes, 2015). For example, adolescents are typically vulnerable to mental health problems, antisocial behavior, school failure, illegal drug use, and health risks (Mahalik et al., 2013). They also experience an increased number of violent incidents as perpetrators and/or victims (Loeber & Farrington, 2012), violent crime (Finkelhor, Turner, Shattuck, Hamby, & Kristen, 2015), and access to illegal weapons (Webster, Meyers, & Buggs, 2014) compared to younger children and adults. In fact, homicide is one of the top five causes of adolescent death in the United States (David-Ferdon & Simon, 2014). Recent studies suggest that stressful life events, racial discrimination, and violence exposure directly influence adolescents' internalizing problems (e.g., depression, anxiety, somatic problems), and these relationships are mediated in part by youth's externalizing behaviors (e.g., physical aggression, disobeying rules, cheating, stealing, destruction of property; Liu, Mustanski, Dick, Bolland, & Kertes, 2016).

Urban Minority Male Adolescents: In the Bull's-Eye?

Adolescent community violence exposure is higher for impoverished urban racial/ethnic minorities, especially young males (Bushman et al., 2016). While concerns about urban minority females remain salient and deserve attention (Kennedy, A. C., Bybee, & Greeson, 2014; Richards et al., 2015; Tisak, Tisak, Baker, & Graupensperger, 2016), the particular challenges for minority males exposed to, and involved with, community violence include disproportionately higher rates of aggression (Gaylord-Harden, Zakaryan, Bernard, & Pekoc, 2015), polyvictimization (Elsaesser & Voisin, 2015), and juvenile justice system involvement (Voisin, Kim, Takahashi, Morotta, & Bocanegra, 2016), as well as horrific recent incidents of unarmed minority males being killed by police (Dow, 2016; Geller, Fagan, Tyler, & Link, 2014; Moore, Robinson, & Adedoyin, 2016; Reid, 2015). The fatal consequences of these chronic community violence risks are clearly reflected in the fact that *homicide* is the leading cause of death for all African Americans between ages 15–34. Almost half

(40%) of African American males in this age group who died were murdered compared to just 3 percent of European American males (Centers for Disease Control and Prevention, 2013).

The disturbing and devastating trends of death and imprisonment among minority males have prompted urgent calls for solutions across diverse sectors of the society ranging from the White House (e.g., President Obama's 2014 "My Brother's Keeper" initiative) to specialized academic journals (Watkins, Patton, & Miller, 2016) to community-based grassroots activism (e.g., "Black Lives Matter"). Clearly, clinicians, providers, and other professionals should seek this growing effort to understand and address the distinct and disproportionate rates of community violence and related adverse outcomes that impact minority males.

Self-Protective or Sabotaging Responses?

Community violence exposure undermines the goals of positive youth development for adolescents. Adolescents exposed to community violence are more likely to engage in a cycle of violent actions as a means of protection or retaliation when interacting with peers who participate in high degrees of interpersonal violence (Taylor et al., 2016). Some adolescents may even receive implicit or explicit support from parents and caretakers for using aggressive and retaliatory responses when confronted with community violence situations that encourage assertive protection but encumber physical risks (Thomas, Caldwell, Assari, Jagers, & Flay, 2016). Moreover, adolescents in the United States are exposed to a societal context where aggression and violence are criticized in mainstream discussions of morals and values but celebrated in multiple activities of role models and national celebrations (e.g., historical recognition of military leaders, media glorification of gangster imagery). These types of proviolence messages and actions at the family and society levels can appear to "justify" similar proviolence messages and actions at the individual level by adolescents, especially those who prioritize self-protection, favorable adult feedback, peer social status, and material acquisition as markers of successful development.

The impact of these adolescents' adverse experiences is often underestimated or misunderstood by parents and providers because youth often present increasing followed by declining rates of psychological symptoms over time (Taylor et al., 2016). Several studies describe a trajectory of symptoms in adolescents who are exposed to community violence that begins with externalizing behaviors/symptoms. Over time, these adolescents experience more internalizing symptoms/behaviors, which are harder to detect because they are masked by aggression or delinquent behaviors. This "mask" is necessary to maintain their "tough" guise as a means of gaining or maintaining status, safety, and other rewards among their peers (Gaylord-Harden, So, Bai, Henry, & Tolan, 2016; Kennedy, T. M. & Ceballo, 2016). Consequently, these adolescents may have maladaptive or "pathological" self-protective strategies that actually sabotage their attempt to avoid being victims of community violence.

Traumatic Events and Stressors

Given the high levels of community and gang violence exposure among urban youth, traumatic stress is an important framework for developing responsive prevention and intervention programs for urban youth exposed to community violence. According to the NCTSN (2003), a *traumatic event* involves personally experiencing and/or witnessing an imminent threat to physical integrity, serious injury to yourself, or serious injury or death to someone else. Following a potentially traumatic event, NCTSN identifies *child traumatic stress* as a condition where children and adolescents are exposed to a traumatic event, and this exposure overwhelms their ability to cope with what they have experienced.

Recent research has confirmed links between chronic community violence exposure and subsequent posttraumatic stress symptoms (Hunt, Martens, & Belcher, 2011; Smith & Patton, 2016), including traumatic grief and loss resulting from peer homicides (Smith, J. R., 2015; Smith, S. S., 2014). Consistent with notions of cumulative effects and polyvictimization models of community violence exposure, current studies suggest that youth who experience a higher number and broader range of violence-related experiences will end up with more severe and complex psychosocial symptoms (Kennedy, A. C. et al., 2014). For example Violence-related trauma can prompt subsequent delinquent behaviors resulting in additional trauma and/or juvenile justice recidivism (Stimmel, Cruise, Ford, & Weiss, 2014). In addition, many of these youth whose violence-driven trajectories result in juvenile detention placements report high levels of community violence exposure that is associated with posttraumatic stress symptoms and severe emotional and behavioral problems (Stimmel et al., 2014).

Linkages between community violence exposure and traumatic stress symptomatology are common for low-income urban minority youth who often endure chronic and pervasive stress from surrounding community violence. Recent studies illustrate that urban African American adolescents who are exposed to chronic and multiple types of community violence face increasing risks of posttraumatic stress symptoms (Post et al., 2014) as well as delinquency and depression (Fowler, Tompsett, Braciszewski, Jacques-Tiura, & Baltes, 2009; Goldner et al., 2015). Moreover, gang-involved violence among minorities has been shown to have traumatizing effects for *both* the perpetrator and the victim. Researchers studying "harm as harm or 'perpetration-induced trauma' have found that inflicting harm on others is associated with post-traumatic stress symptoms" (Beresford & Wood, 2016; Kerig et al., 2016).

The concept of *historical trauma* that characterizes the collective experiences of institutionalized racism, discrimination, and oppression in the African American community has garnered increasing recognition (Danzer, Rieger, Schubmehl, & Cort, 2016; West, 2016). This historical trauma includes (a) brutal chattel slavery (physical/sexual violence, economic exploitation, etc.); (b) psychosocial conditioning for self-hatred (e.g., anti-black); (c) legalized racial discrimination (e.g., constitutional disenfranchisement until 1870, Jim Crow segregation); and (d) continued civil rights struggles (e.g., racism, hate crimes, inferior school structures, disproportionate mass incarceration rates). These historical trauma dynamics have helped shape the current structural inequalities of poverty, insufficient resources, and other socioeconomic stressors that help spark or sustain community violence in low-income urban African American neighborhoods.

Finally, distinct *ongoing* traumatizing stressors for impoverished urban adolescents of color, such as the intrusive, intense, and violent interactions between youth of color and the police (Geller et al., 2014), only underscore the need for incorporating a "trauma-informed" lens into services that support low-income adolescents of color. For example, the recent community protests against police brutality, racial profiling, and other unjust institutional practices under the "Black Lives Matter" movement illustrate a need for more trauma-informed policies and practices that effectively acknowledge, address, and respond to both historic roots and ongoing conditions of oppression in the African American community.

STRONG Families: Integrated Trauma-Informed Treatment

Given the urgent need to address the multiple stressors affecting low-income African American urban adolescents who are exposed to community violence and who present with severe behavior problems, the Urban Youth Trauma Center (UYTC) established the STRONG Families (SF) program (Abdul-Adil et al., 2013, 2014). Cofounded by Drs. Jaleel Abdul-Adil and Liza Suarez through funding from the Substance Abuse and Mental Health Services Administration (SAMHSA), UYTC is a Treatment Service Adaptation Center in the NCTSN. UYTC designs, disseminates, and evaluates both public health prevention programs and mental health intervention programs as a means of providing comprehensive, integrated, and coordinated care for multiproblem, high-risk youth affected by community violence and related traumatic stress.

As one of the UYTC mental health interventions, the SF program provides an integrated trauma-informed treatment for addressing urban adolescent problems related to community violence exposure and severe externalizing problems, including gang involvement. The SF program uses a manualized family systems therapy approach that addresses individual youth needs and interpersonal interactions within the contributing family context (e.g., parent/caretaker interactions with youth, family roles and rules for adults and children, extended family influences, intergenerational behavior expectations and impacts). Using this systemic method, the SF program seeks to incorporate client strengths while restructuring negative interpersonal interactions within a clinical treatment model that is designed for urban youth, especially from low-income communities of color. In particular, the SF program seeks to serve these youth and families through trauma-informed treatment strategies arranged according to the following topics modules: (1) youth and family engagement, (2) case conceptualization and assessment, (3) cognitive-affective-behavioral restructuring, (4) caretaker–adolescent interaction, (5) disruptive behavior disorder management, (6) youth trauma narrative, (7) traumatic grief, and (8) posttrauma meaning and posttreatment planning.

These SF strategies are implemented through a sequential components approach where each module consists of four to five sessions for covering an identified set of skills within each weekly therapy session and subsequent between-session "homework." While the SF manual offers this comprehensive structure, the modules are also implemented through a flexible fidelity framework where assigned clinicians can use their clinical expertise and creativity to tailor the manual content, sequence, pace, and review (e.g., "practice") to the individual needs, emphases, and requests of each youth and family. The SF strategies are launched through a multiple family group to provide an introductory overview and orientation to program topics that will be covered in the subsequent individual family therapy sessions. The initial goal is to increase subsequent family engagement and collaboration through the duration of this therapeutic program.

The remainder of this chapter will focus on briefly summarizing and illustrating the clinical applications of the main components of the SF program using a hypothetical composite of actual cases who will be referred to by the pseudonym "Maurice." These summaries and illustrations of the SF program will provide tangible examples of using a manualized trauma-informed treatment approach with low-income urban adolescents of color who struggle with psychosocial issues related to community violence exposure and traumatic stress.

Case Example: Maurice

"Maurice" is a 16-year-old African American male who has lived in a large urban metropolitan neighborhood in low-income housing projects for his entire life with his biological father and mother, 13-year-old sister, and 8-year-old brother. His father was involved with gangs during adolescence and early adulthood for key reasons of protection, peers (friends who grew up together joined a gang together to continue this same "bond"), and prosperity ("fast money," access to successful material acquisitions of cars, clothes, jewelry, etc., that also boosted social status and influence). Maurice's father spent two years in jail on drug distribution charges and has been on parole (successfully) for the past year. His mother has had periodic battles with substance abuse. Both parents used alcohol, but Maurice's mother also used marijuana to self-medicate for depression before seeking her own professional help. Neither parent attended college, but both graduated with high school diplomas.

Maurice has struggled with the legacy of his family—especially his father—as well as the violence and lack of resources in his neighborhood. When he was five years old, he was with his father when he was targeted in an unsuccessful drive-by shooting. This traumatic incident in early childhood left Maurice acutely aware of the safety threats in his neighborhood and hypervigilant to real or imagined threats in the environment. Maurice had been under pressure through challenges, threats, and warnings from neighborhood youth—mainly males—about joining a gang since early adolescence. He was often viewed as an "affiliated" person by other neighborhood youth and officially joined the main gang in his neighborhood after a few altercations with gang members from a rival neighborhood while traveling back and forth to school.

He has knowledge of, and implicit access to, his father's gun in his house for protection. He also has access to his gang members' arsenal of handguns if needed, and he struggles about if and when to respond to rival gang members' threats with verbal or physical retaliation—including the use of weapons.

Although they have had periods of separation, Maurice's parents currently live together with him and his two younger siblings. These periods of separation led to relationship struggles that persisted into adolescence, as Maurice resented his mother for making him stay with father during one of the parental separations while also resenting his father for always comparing him to his brother and saying he wasn't good enough. Given these resentments, Maurice had a very hard time respecting and listening to his dad when he was being reprimanded for his behavior at home or at school.

Despite these ongoing family stressors, Maurice was attending Al-Anon in support of his parents' sobriety and had begun to participate in an after-school recreational program that became available in his neighborhood. One day, he was walking home with two friends and witnessed his best friend being shot and killed by gang members from a different neighborhood. Maurice ran away and called 911 to request help. A police officer arrived on the scene first, and he made the initial police report. Immediately after the incident, the police began questioning the three boys in an accusatory rather than inquiring manner, and this further angered and upset Maurice. He began to distrust and resent social institutions in general, including hospitals and clinics where clinical services are provided because he viewed them as part of the same "system."

Maurice was struck with grief. Despite growing up together, his best friend had managed to avoid joining any gangs. The loss of his friend and subsequent challenges he experienced had a tremendously negative impact on his life. While he was already having trouble at school (getting detention for talking back, arriving late), his problems now intensified. He had trouble sleeping, with frequent nightmares and intrusive memories of the event. His anger intensified, as did his mistrust, hypervigilance, and growing concerns for his own safety. His grades dropped severely, he did not spend much time at home, and he began using marijuana sporadically. This led to increased conflict at home, where time spent in the same room with his family almost always led to heated arguments. His parents were very concerned about his behavior at home, verbalizations of anger, and desire for revenge. These concerns led them to search for supportive treatment.

Maurice's father was instrumental in convincing his son to seek services. He pleaded with Maurice, saying that he didn't want him to end up in the "school-to-prison" pipeline where he drops out, gets put into juvenile detention, or is killed. Maurice agreed to attend. However, he refused to accept his father's pleas for leaving the gang because his father's street credibility provided added social status and perceived protection for Maurice. Father's "do as I say, not as I do" approach with intimidation to compel Maurice to comply was not having much success.

Although he was guarded when he arrived to the therapy appointment, Maurice stated that he was willing to discuss the traumatic loss of his best friend. He acknowledged that emotional vulnerability was extremely difficult for both son and father. The therapist quickly noticed that sometimes father's attempted advice to his son was met with resentment and arguments that led to mutual withdrawal and it upset mother as well.

Youth and Family Engagement: Motivation without Mandates

The SF program emphasizes cultural context and collaborative processes as a means of engaging urban youth and families across all program modules and activities. Unlike most mainstream clinical services that use generic approaches to engage urban youth and families of color, the SF program embraces the distinct components and strengths of an individual family's cultural context to convey mutual respect and cultivate clinician–client collaboration. This type of respectful and collaborative approach is especially important for successfully engaging low-income urban youth and families of color who often perceive disrespect or feel disillusioned when seeking clinical services due to typical barriers of institutional mistrust (e.g., stigma, skepticism), clinician–family goal misalignment (e.g., disagreement over what is "the" problem), and participation logistics (e.g., transportation, child care, inconsistent session attendance). In addition, this culturally sensitive approach can facilitate overcoming client perceptions about racial or ethnic "mismatches" by providing the clinician with clinical techniques derived from strengths-oriented affirmations of the clients' lived experiences and choices—which is particularly important in serving historically oppressed and marginalized communities.

After the initial assessment with Maurice and his family, the clinical team identified specific strengths and assets for the family and its members. Despite the frequent and heated arguments between them, they noted that Maurice's caregivers were deeply concerned about his well-being and that this concern was at the root of most disagreements. Both parents had experienced early life challenges, which resulted in poor choices as young adults, but they had achieved sobriety and involved Maurice in the Al-Anon supportive services as an attempt to prevent him from following a similar path. Since his release from prison, the father had stayed away from participation in gang activities and drug distribution. However, growing up in that environment had altered Maurice's expectations for his own behavior. While Maurice did not want to engage in "senseless" violence, he viewed gang involvement as necessary for assuring his own safety and that of his friends and loved ones. His ideas for what was right and fair were influenced by his peer affiliations. While the recent loss of his friend fueled a strong desire for revenge, he was contending with a newfound inclination to honor his memory by striving to be a better person. As the clinical team formulated treatment goals with the family, it was very important to reflect the different points of views and life experiences of each family member. Given Maurice's implicit and explicit mistrust of social institutions, the clinical team took great care to destigmatize treatment participation and validate past negative experiences with service providers and people in positions of authority.

Case Conceptualization and Assessment: Learn before Leaping—to Treatment

The SF program module Treatment Planning, Assessment and Engagement employs a biopsychosocial model of conceptualization, assessment, and treatment planning that is based on an ecological framework. The SF program conceptualizes the appropriate causes and proposed intervention responses regarding the adolescent's presenting problems by using a combination of qualitative (e.g., intake interview, session observations, clinical impressions) and quantitative (empirical measures of strengths and challenges in current psychosocial functioning) data to formalize case conceptualization and treatment planning. This type of comprehensive and client-focused case conceptualization decreases the probability of inaccurate diagnosis (and subsequent ineffective treatment)—especially with complicated co-occurring trauma and behavioral problems including gang involvement—while increasing the likelihood of family responsiveness, compliance, and motivation for treatment.

Following completion of the initial assessment and a battery of assessment measures of behavioral, emotional, family, and community functioning, Maurice met diagnostic criteria for posttraumatic stress disorder and oppositional defiant disorder. As expected, Maurice and his parents reported high levels of community violence exposure. The family was impacted by increased levels of parenting stress and impaired communication. His caregivers brought Maurice to treatment due to the worsening of his oppositional behavior, school challenges, and to prevent escalation in gang involvement given his desire for avenging his friend's murder. Maurice reported being bothered by intrusive thoughts and sleep difficulties and showed interest in talking about what happened to his friend. While the family has its share of challenges and stressors, they were willing to participate in ongoing treatment.

The most urgent priority at the start of treatment was to guide Maurice and his family in navigating options for maximizing safety to and from school. By identifying safety as a shared goal, it facilitated discussions about participation in gang activities and addressed concerns for Maurice's behavior in the school and community while at the same time acknowledging his own distress and concerns for repeated violence. The family participated in the process of identifying existing supports and challenges, which were deemed useful in addressing the identified goals.

Cognitive-Affective-Behavioral Restructuring: Rethinking Reactions

The SF program module Affective Expression, Modulation, and Cognitive Coping uses a cognitive-affective-behavioral approach to address ideas, emotions, and behaviors in youth and his/her family related to community violence and traumatic stress. This cognitive-behavioral-affective approach involves replacing problematic patterns in youth such as intrusive negative thoughts, disturbing emotions, and self-destructive or socially reprehensible actions by teaching youth to adopt positive sets of adaptive cognition, emotional regulation, and prosocial behavior. This holistic shift of personality and practice occurs with the support of the caretaker/parent who attends treatment sessions. This reinforces the protective parent role and the healing dynamic that can reshape youth characteristics from negative reactions to prosocial coping in response to community violence and traumatic response.

Maurice could acknowledge some of his distress and identify negative thoughts such as jumping to conclusions—"I know they are going to yell at me"; emotional reasoning—"the teacher makes me so mad, that proves I am being treated unfairly"; or discounting the positive—"the coach telling me I did a good job doesn't count because that's his job." However, in self-report measures and during the individual portion of the intake assessment, he had a difficult time discussing his feelings in front of his parents. With the therapist's guidance, both parents shared their own examples, and this provided a model to help Maurice become more comfortable acknowledging feelings and thoughts that went beyond anger and mistrust. Using the tools available within the SF program, family members developed a shared language to acknowledge distress, triggers, and trauma reminders, for example, "Are you 'ticked off' right now?"; "What words 'set you off'?"; "What brings back bad memories?" They were also able to identify similarities and differences in their emotional responses and thought patterns and select more prosocial alternatives to cope with distress, for example, "We see that the same way"; "Your way and my way are both okay"; "Can we talk about this without screaming at each other?"; and "Let's take a break—we're just fighting not talking."

Caretaker-Adolescent Communication: From Coercion to Collaboration

The SF program module Family Communication uses a family systems model of assessing, managing, and reformulating daily interactions between youth and caretakers. This module addresses the consistent and repetitive patterns of interaction that are considered the family "structure." The family is supported to change the overt and implicit "rules" governing youth–caretaker interactions from maladaptive and toxic interactions to healthy and mutually supportive interactions geared toward prosocial youth development and family harmony.

At the root of the family arguments was Maurice's complaint of a "double standard" in their expectations for his behavior in light of his father's history as an adolescent and young adult. The family interactions began to take a positive turn when members reached an agreement about ground rules and behavioral expectations for all family members, which acknowledged the progress not only for Maurice but his mother and father as well. Sessions emphasized an increased understanding of their shared experience of trauma and community violence. The family practiced active listening skills and using "I" statements in neutral situations and then applied them when discussing topics that were emotionally loaded for all. They also used family problem-solving exercises to increase positive family interactions.

Disruptive Behavior Disorder Management: Directing the Defiance

The SF program module Addressing Disruptive Behavior Stemming from Trauma uses a trauma-informed behavior management approach that is appropriate for adolescent developmental levels by addressing issues such as chronic defiance, severe delinquency, emotional explosiveness, and gang involvement through a healing lens. The emphasis is on "what happened to you" and "how this is affecting you" rather than relying on an increasing and ultimately detrimental series of escalating punishments. This trauma-focused tactic of rallying the youth and family to collaboratively construct different ways of understanding and addressing community violence–involved behavior problems is a refreshing and necessary alternative to typically rigid narratives that can alienate (and even exacerbate) the adolescent's antisocial activities.

For a behavioral management plan to be successful, it was important to gain a better understanding of how Maurice's behaviors were connected to internal and external triggers. Through in-session exercises and weekly self-report measures, it became evident that many arguments at home and behavioral difficulties at school were tied to situations where Maurice felt threatened (raised voices, being criticized). Additionally, time spent away from the house was linked to a desire to avoid reminders of his loss. The family also identified additional reasons underlying the misbehavior, including wanting attention, desire for more power, or wanting to get even. Maurice's parents practiced providing praise and encouragement, and the family engaged in behavior management strategies, including tracking desired behavior (showing up to school and home on time, being respectful) and providing positive reinforcement (permission to go on special outings, television and video game privileges).

Youth Trauma Narrative: Healing the Wounds

The SF program module Trauma Narrative uses a story-telling approach with youth to articulate and explore the traumatic experience that is primarily responsible for the problems of disruptive behavior and traumatic stress. Although many youth may have experienced multiple and ongoing traumatic events, the SF program works with them to identify the traumatic experience during their lifetime (e.g., seeing or being shot in a gang conflict) that is directly related to their current behavior and trauma symptoms. While some clients may initially be unwilling or unable to discuss the most dramatic traumatic events in their lives, the preceding SF modules lay the groundwork to provide the necessary prerequisites and preparations for constructing the trauma narrative as a story. The youth's trauma narrative helps the client to integrate memories, experiences, and ramifications of the traumatic experience into a coherent and holistic story at a client-focused pace that permits positive meaning making and healing for both the youth and his or her family.

For Maurice, the traumatic event that caused the most distress was witnessing the murder of his best friend. In addition, witnessing his father getting shot at when he was five years old had a substantial impact on Maurice's behavior and views about the world. For these reasons, a trauma narrative was also formed around this event. Processing this early trauma helped Maurice face the (previously unacknowledged) distress surrounding this experience. Additionally, he could identify ways in which it shaped the way he viewed the world as a dangerous place, and the gang affiliation as necessary for survival. His father was able to express his own feelings about the shooting, noting that this event marked a turning point in his life because he realized that his family was in danger as a result of his gang affiliation. The similarities and the contrast between Maurice and his father's reaction to the incident were useful in identifying prosocial life goals for both Maurice and his father.

Youth Traumatic Grief

The SF program module Traumatic Grief uses a similar approach that is adopted in the trauma narrative but with a specific focus on traumatic loss. These youths may have severe and prolonged reactions to the loss of a family member or significant person (e.g., close friend, adult mentor, fellow gang member) in their life. Youth who experience sudden and violent loss or separation from family members, peers, or other important people due to death, imprisonment, or child protection removal are particularly primed for traumatic grief treatment as a means of helping them to avoid destructive responses, such as depression, anger, or retaliation, that complicate co-occurring behavior and trauma problems. Instead, the focus is on adopting productive emotional processing strategies (e.g., positive memories, commemorative rituals) that enable healthy resolution.

Helping Maurice deal with his friend's murder involved going over the details of the shooting and helping him manage the distress associated with these memories. Maurice described in more depth his anger about the loss, what he felt to be an inadequate response from the ambulance and the police, and how this affected the way he interacted with teachers and other adults. In addition, Maurice was encouraged to talk about his thoughts and feelings toward death in general, and his relationship with his friend in particular, and how these have influenced his behaviors prior to and after the loss. When asked to describe his relationship with his best friend, Maurice broke down as he remembered a time that they had gotten into an argument. He felt very guilty about not formally working it out with his friend. He was also able to recall positive memories and reasons why their friendship was unique. Maurice's greatest struggle was his desire to try to "make things right" through retaliation. To address these challenges, Maurice's father was able to share similar experiences he had in his life, and together with mother they discussed the never-ending cycle of violence.

Posttrauma Meaning and Posttreatment Planning: Moving Forward

The SF program module Moving Forward employs a treatment termination process that celebrates client accomplishments while preparing for possible future challenges. Youth and families who reach the conclusion of the SF program have successfully achieved the program milestones of managing behavioral and traumatic challenges in a competent and prosocial manner on both individual and family levels. Consequently, these youth and families deserve and appreciate recognition for navigating a challenging route from disorder to wellness. The SF program recognizes the chronic and recurrent nature of behavior problems and community violence exposure among peers and in neighborhoods of low-income urban ethnic minority youth. In terminating with families, clinicians openly and proactively discuss prevention of regressive behaviors during possible future risky situations.

After discussing Maurice's trauma narrative, both Maurice and his father were struck by the realization of how traumatic experiences and the way they are interpreted can have such an impact on the choices people make. The shooting that led father to begin to "change his ways" was one of the driving forces behind Maurice's affiliation with gang involved peers. This led them to be able to view the trauma in a new light, each noting that they had an opportunity to choose an alternative path. When asked what advice he would give to other youth in similar situations, Maurice was able to come up with many alternatives that were actually useful for him to follow. The therapist guided the family in identifying individual and family strengths as well as ways to address possible challenges that may arise in the future. An ongoing theme that was brought up by the family was the many challenges that African American males face in their community, and their desire to be part of bigger efforts to make things better.

Conclusion

Contemporary youth, especially those adolescents of color who reside in low-income urban settings, face acute conditions of chronic community violence that often contribute to elevated rates of conduct problems and traumatic stress. The subset of these urban minority youth who become formally involved in, or informally affiliated with, street gangs faces additional pitfalls from intensified violence (e.g., weapons, homicide) and criminal behavior (e.g., drug trade, retaliatory homicide, disproportionate and mass minority incarceration) in reaction to the pervasive poverty and community violence. Trauma-informed treatment programs, such as SF, which integrates treatment techniques for community violence and traumatic stress in a manner that is tailored to the views and values of urban ethnic minority families, provide a promising option for supporting prosocial youth development in high-risk minority adolescents. While community violence remains a complicated and chronic phenomenon in their lives, urban youth and families of color may at least increase the likelihood of transcending traumatic community violence with practical program options of trauma-informed treatment.

References

Abdul-Adil, J., Farmer, D., Suarez, L., Gibson, L., Cojocaru, S., Williams, M., & Ford, H. (2014). *Strengths for trauma resilience—Overcoming n' growing (STRONG) families: Family systems therapy treatment manual for community violence exposure* (2nd ed.). Chicago, IL: University of Illinois at Chicago, Department of Psychiatry.

Abdul-Adil, J., Jackson, J., Schellinger, K., Sterrett, E., Farmer, D., & Suarez, L. (2013). *Strengths for trauma resilience—Overcoming n' growing (STRONG) families: Psycho-educational multiple family group treatment manual*. Chicago, IL: University of Illinois at Chicago, Department of Psychiatry.

Aisenberg, E., & Ell, K. (2005). Contextualizing community violence and its effects: An ecological model of parent–child interdependent coping. *Journal of Interpersonal Violence, 20*, 855–871. doi:10.1177/0886260505276833

Beresford, H., & Wood, J. (2016). Patients or perpetrators? The effects of trauma exposure on gang members' mental health: a review of the literature. *Journal of Criminological Research, Policy and Practice*, 2(2), 148–159.

Bushman, B. J., Newman, K., Calvert, S. L., Downey, G., Dredze, M., Gottfredson, M., & Romer, D. (2016). Youth violence: What we know and what we need to know. *American Psychologist*, *71*(1), 17.

Centers for Disease Control and Prevention. (2013). *Leading causes of death by age group, Black Males-United States, 2013*. Retrieved from https://www.cdc.gov/healthequity/lcod/index.htm

Chen, P., Voisin, D. R., & Jacobson, K. C. (2016). Community violence exposure and adolescent delinquency: Examining a spectrum of promotive factors. *Youth & Society, 48*(1), 33–57.

Cooley-Strickland, M., Quille, T. J., Griffin, R. S., Stuart, E. A., Bradshaw, C. P., & Furr-Holden, D. (2009). Community violence and youth: Affect, behavior, substance use, and academics. *Clinical Child and Family Psychology Review*, *12*(2), 127–156.

Dahlberg L. L., & Krug, E. G. (2002). Violence: A global public health problem. In E. Krug, L. L. Dahlberg, J. A. Mercy, & R. Lozano (Eds.), *World report on violence and health* (pp. 1–56). Geneva, Switzerland: World Health Organization.

Danzer, G., Rieger, S. M., Schubmehl, S., & Cort, D. (2016). White psychologists and African Americans' historical trauma: Implications for practice. *Journal of Aggression, Maltreatment & Trauma*, *25*(4), 351–370.

David-Ferdon, C., & Simon, T. R. (2014). *Preventing youth violence: Opportunities for action*. Atlanta, GA: National Center for Injury Prevention and Control, Centers for Disease Control and Prevention.

Dow, D. M. (2016). The deadly challenges of raising African American boys navigating the controlling image of the "thug." *Gender & Society*, *30*(2), 161–188.

Elsaesser, C. M., & Voisin, D. R. (2015). Correlates of polyvictimization among African American youth an exploratory study. *Journal of Interpersonal Violence*, *30*(17), 3022–3042.

Finkelhor, D., Turner, H. A., Shattuck, A., & Hamby, S. L. (2013). Violence, crime, and abuse exposure in a national sample of children and youth: An update. *JAMA Pediatrics, 167*(7), 614–621. doi:10.1001/jamapediatrics.2013.42

Finkelhor, D., Turner, H. A., Shattuck, A., & Hamby, S. L. (2015). Prevalence of childhood exposure to violence, crime, and abuse: Results from the National Survey of Children's Exposure to Violence. *JAMA Pediatrics, 169*(8), 746–754.

Finkelhor, D., Turner, H.A., Shattuck, A., Hamby, S.L. & Kristen, K. (2015). *Children's exposure to violence, crime, and abuse: An update*. Washington, DC: U.S. Department of Justice, Office of Justice Programs, Office of Juvenile Justice and Delinquency Prevention.

Fitzpatrick, K.M., & Boldizar, J.P. (1993). The prevalence of depression among low-income African American youth. *Journal of Consulting and Clinical Psychology, 61*, 528–531.

Fowler, P.J., Tompsett, C.J., Braciszewski, J.M., Jacques-Tiura, A.J., & Baltes, B.B. (2009). Community violence: A meta-analysis on the effect of exposure and mental health outcomes of children and adolescents. *Development and Psychopathology*, *21*(1), 227–259.

Gaylord-Harden, N.K., So, S., Bai, G.J., Henry, D.B., & Tolan, P.H. (2016). Examining the pathologic adaptation model of community violence exposure in male adolescents of color. *Journal of Clinical Child & Adolescent Psychology*, *46*(1), 125–135.

Gaylord-Harden, N.K., Zakaryan, A., Bernard, D., & Pekoc, S. (2015). Community-level victimization and aggressive behavior in African-American male adolescents: A profile analysis. *Journal of Community Psychology, 43*(4), 502–519.

Geller, A., Fagan, J., Tyler, T., & Link, B.G. (2014). Aggressive policing and the mental health of young urban men. *American Journal of Public Health, 104*(12), 2321–2327.

Goldner, J., Gross, I.M., Richards, M.H., & Ragsdale, B.L. (2015). The relation of severity and type of community violence exposure to emotional distress and problem behaviors among urban African American adolescents. *Violence and Victims*, *30*(3), 432–449.

Hunt, K.L., Martens, P.M., & Belcher, H.M. (2011). Risky business: Trauma exposure and rate of posttraumatic stress disorder in African American children and adolescents. *Journal of Traumatic Stress*, *24*(3), 365–369.

Kennedy, A.C., Bybee, D., & Greeson, M.R. (2014). Examining cumulative victimization, community violence exposure, and stigma as contributors to PTSD symptoms among high-risk young women. *American Journal of Orthopsychiatry*, *84*(3), 284.

Kennedy, T.M., & Ceballo, R. (2016). Emotionally numb: Desensitization to community violence exposure among urban youth. *Developmental Psychology*, *52*(5), 778.

Kerig, P.K., Chaplo, S.D., Bennett, D.C., & Modrowski, C.A. (2016). "Harm as harm": Gang membership, perpetration trauma, and posttraumatic stress symptoms among youth in the juvenile justice system. *Criminal Justice and Behavior*, *43*(5), 635–652.

Linares, L.O., Heeren, T., Bronfman, E., Zuckerman, B., Augustyn, M., & Tronick, E. (2001). A meditational model for the impact of exposure to community violence on early child behavior problems. *Child Development, 72*, 639–652.

Liu, J., Bolland, J. M., Dick, D., Mustanski, B., & Kertes, D. A. (2015). Effect of environmental risk and externalizing comorbidity on internalizing problems among economically disadvantaged African American youth. *Journal of Research on Adolescence, 26*(3), 552–566. doi: 10.1111/jora.12213

Liu, J., Mustanski, B., Dick, D., Bolland, J., & Kertes, D. A. (2016). Risk and protective factors for comorbid internalizing and externalizing problems among economically disadvantaged African American youth. *Development and Psychopathology, 29*(3), 1043–1056.

Loeber, R., & Farrington, D. P. (Eds.). (2012). *From juvenile delinquency to adult crime: Criminal careers, justice policy and prevention*. New York, NY: Oxford University Press.

Mahalik, J. R., Levine Coley, R., McPherran Lombardi, C., Doyle Lynch, A., Markowitz, A. J., & Jaffee, S. R. (2013). Changes in health risk behaviors for males and females from early adolescence through early adulthood. *Health Psychology, 32*(6), 685.

Moore, S. E., Robinson, M. A., & Adedoyin, A. C. (2016). Introduction to the special issue on police shooting of unarmed African American males: Implications for the individual, the family, and the community. *Journal of Human Behavior in the Social Environment, 26*(3–4), 247–250.

National Child Traumatic Stress Network. (2003). *What is child traumatic stress?* Retrieved from http://www.nctsnet.org/sites/default/files/assets/pdfs/what_is_child_traumatic_stress_0.pdf

National Child Traumatic Stress Network. (2013). *Community violence*. Retrieved from http://www.nctsn.org/trauma-types/community-violence

Patton, D. U., & Roth, B. J. (2016). Good kids with ties to "deviant" peers: Network strategies used by African American and Latino young men in violent neighborhoods. *Children and Youth Services Review, 66*, 123–130.

Post, M., Hanten, G., Li, X., Schmidt, A. T., Avci, G., Wilde, E. A., & McCauley, S. R. (2014). Dimensions of trauma and specific symptoms of complex posttraumatic stress disorder in inner-city youth: A preliminary study. *Violence and Victims, 29*(2), 262–279.

Reid, R. (2015). Reflections on Ferguson. *The American Journal of Psychiatry, 172*, 223–224.

Richards, M. H., Romero, E., Zakaryan, A., Carey, D., Deane, K., Quimby, D., . . . Burns, M. (2015). Assessing urban African American youths' exposure to community violence through a daily sampling method. *Psychology of Violence, 5*(3), 275.

Schwab-Stone, M., Chen, C., Greenberger, E., Silver, D., Lichtman, J., & Voyce, C. (1999). No safe haven II: The effects of violence exposure on urban youth. *Journal of the American Academy of Child & Adolescent Psychiatry, 38*, 359–367.

Shahinfar, A., Fox, N., & Leavitt, L. (2000). Preschool children's exposure to violence: Relation of behavior problems to parent and child reports. *American Journal of Orthopsychiatry, 70*, 115–125.

Smith, J. R. (2015). Unequal burdens of loss: Examining the frequency and timing of homicide deaths experienced by young Black men across the life course. *American Journal of Public Health, 105*(S3), S483–S490.

Smith, J.R., & Patton, D.U. (2016). Posttraumatic stress symptoms in context: Examining trauma responses to violent exposures and homicide death among Black males in urban neighborhoods. *American Journal of Orthopsychiatry, 86*(2), 212.

Smith, S.S. (2014). Traumatic loss in low-income communities of color. *Focus (San Francisco, Calif.), 31*, 32–34.

Stimmel, M.A., Cruise, K.R., Ford, J.D., & Weiss, R.A. (2014). Trauma exposure, posttraumatic stress disorder symptomatology, and aggression in male juvenile offenders. *Psychological Trauma: Theory, Research, Practice, and Policy*, *6*(2), 184.

Taylor, J.J., Grant, K.E., Zulauf, C.A., Fowler, P.J., Meyerson, D.A., & Irsheid, S. (2016). Exposure to community violence and the trajectory of internalizing and externalizing symptoms in a sample of low-income urban youth. *Journal of Clinical Child & Adolescent Psychology*, 1–15.

Thomas, A., Caldwell, C.H., Assari, S., Jagers, R.J., & Flay, B. (2016). You do what you see how witnessing physical violence is linked to violent behavior among male African American adolescents. *The Journal of Men's Studies, 24*(2), 185–207.

Tisak, M.S., Tisak, J., Baker, E.R., & Graupensperger, S.A. (2016). Relations among victimization, witnessing, and perpetration of aggression impact of gender among youth offenders. *Journal of Interpersonal Violence*, 1–23.

Truman, J., Langton, L., & Planty, M. (2013). *Bureau of Justice Statistics bulletin: Criminal victimization, 2012*. Retrieved from https://www.bjs.gov/content/pub/pdf/cv12.pdf

Voisin, D.R., & Berringer, K.R. (2015). Interventions targeting exposure to community violence sequelae among youth: A commentary. *Clinical Social Work Journal*, *43*(1), 98–108.

Voisin, D.R., Kim, D., Takahashi, L., Morotta, P., & Bocanegra, K. (2016). Involvement in the juvenile justice system for African American adolescents: Examining associations with behavioral health problems. *Journal of Social Service Research*, *43*(1), 129–140.

Watkins, D.C., Patton, D.U., & Miller, R.J. (2016). Introduction to the special issue on the intersections of race, gender, and class in the wake of a national crisis: The state of black boys and men post-Ferguson. *The Journal of Men's Studies, 24*(2), 119–129.

Webster, D.W., Meyers, J.S., & Buggs, M.S. (2014). Youth acquisition and carrying of firearms in the United States: Patterns, consequences, and strategies for prevention. In *Proceedings of means of violence workshop, forum of global violence prevention, Institutes of Medicine of the National Academies*. Washington, DC.

West, C.M. (2016). Living in a web of trauma: An ecological examination of violence among African Americans. In C.C. Cuevas & C.M. Rennison (Eds.), *The Wiley-Blackwell handbook on the psychology of violence* (pp. 649–665). Chicester, UK: John Wiley.

CHAPTER 7

Child Sexual Abuse

Michele M. Many

Definition of Child Sexual Abuse

Child sexual abuse (CSA) is a form of child maltreatment. In the United States, the first nationally recognized and uniform definitions of forms of child maltreatment were developed as part of the Child Abuse Prevention and Treatment Act (CAPTA; originally enacted in 1974 and amended numerous times with the most recent reauthorization completed in 2010). The definitions developed for CAPTA provided language used as the framework for child welfare laws and for many state criminal statutes. In the 2010 revision, CAPTA defined CSA as:

> The employment, use, persuasion, inducement, enticement, or coercion of any child to engage in, or assist any other person to engage in, any sexually explicit conduct or simulation of such conduct for the purpose of producing a visual depiction of such conduct; or the rape, and in cases of caretaker or interfamilial relationships, statutory rape, molestation, prostitution, or other form of sexual exploitation of children, or incest with children. (U.S. Code: Title 42, Chapter 67, Subchapter I, § 5106g)

State civil and criminal laws defining CSA were modeled on this definition and generally vary little from state to state. The primary differences relate to the age at which an adolescent is considered competent to legally consent to sexual activity. This is determined by each state. The age of consent currently ranges from 15 to 18 years of age.

Those who provide supportive advocacy and clinical services to survivors of sexual abuse generally employ simpler definitions of sexual abuse. One goal of these agencies is educating the public about sexual abuse; therefore, the use of more accessible language is essential to that purpose. For example, the definition of CSA provided by the National Child Traumatic Stress Network (NCTSN) is as follows:

> Child sexual abuse is any interaction between a child and an adult (or another child) in which the child is used for the sexual stimulation of the perpetrator or an observer. Sexual abuse can include both touching and non-touching behaviors. Non-touching behaviors can include voyeurism (trying to look at a child's naked body), exhibitionism, or exposing the child to pornography. (n.d.)

The American Professional Society on the Abuse of Children (APSAC) provides another, even simpler definition: "Sexual abuse involves any sexual activity with a child below the legal age of consent" (Berliner, 2011, p. 215).

Research

The study of CSA presents several challenges to researchers. Those who study CSA are presented with a broad spectrum of behaviors that are considered sexually abusive, types of abusers, and methods abusers employ. There are varying impacts and outcomes based on the kind of sexual abuse (i.e., violent/forced versus grooming/persuasion), the age of the victim and the circumstances in which the abuse occurs, as well as the relationship of victim to abuser, and the cultural and social beliefs, biases, and rules about gender roles and sexual behavior that surround the abuser and the abused. As a result, most studies focus on a specific subgroup of offender, victim or crime characteristics.

Additionally, while evidence of physical abuse and neglect is generally observable and can be documented, objective evidence of CSA often proves more elusive. Most CSA occurs in private with no witnesses, meaning that the child victim is the only witness who can testify to his or her own abuse. There are often no physical signs of CSA. Most CSA involves fondling, which is not likely to cause physical injury. Even CSA that involves penetration often leaves no long-term physical signs or injuries. In their 2002 study, Heger, Ticson, Velasquez, and Bernier reviewed the records of 2,384 children who presented for medical examination as part of their forensic evaluation due to suspicion of CSA. They found that "even with a history of severe abuse such as vaginal or anal penetration, the rate of abnormal medical findings is only 5.5%" (pp. 645–646). Further, several forms of CSA (i.e., exposing the child to pornography, exhibitionism, and voyeurism) do not involve physical contact with the child. There are relatively few cases of CSA where other corroborating evidence (i.e., photographs or videos, STDs, or a witness) is found (Myers, 2011; Walsh, Jones, Cross, & Lippert, 2010). Therefore, timely and convincing disclosure of CSA by the child is a critical factor in determining whether most cases of CSA are discovered, reported, and prosecuted. As Myers (2011) states, "In the majority of sexual abuse trials, the child testifies and the outcome of the case rises or falls on the child's shoulders" (p. 388).

Prevalence

A recent review of the literature identified the likely national prevalence rate of *contact* sexual abuse of children to be 1 in 7 girls and 1 in 25 boys (Townsend & Rheingold, 2013). However, this statistic underestimates the actual prevalence for a number of reasons. The challenges to identifying an accurate prevalence rate relate to the secrecy that characterizes most CSA, and to the shame both victims and their families often experience. Challenges include problems around the disclosure of CSA by the victim, reporting by the person to whom the disclosure is made, and the missing data of very young victims who may not be identified as having been sexually abused. We will explore these challenges in this chapter.

Disclosure

Research has established that timely and convincing disclosure by the child greatly increases the likelihood that the case will be reported, investigated, that charges will be filed and that the prosecution of the abuser will result in a conviction (Myers, 2011). However, disclosures of CSA by child victims are often delayed, partial, or never made at all, and recantation is common (Finkelhor, Hotaling, Lewis, & Smith, 1990; Paine & Hansen, 2002; Smith et al., 2000).

In fact, many survivors have neither denied nor recanted disclosed abuse; they simply never told anyone about it (Lyon & Ahern, 2011). In one survey of 3,400 adults, of those who endorsed a history of contact sexual abuse in childhood, 74 percent of women and 78 percent of men reported they had never disclosed the abuse to anyone during their childhood (Laumann, Gagnon, Michael, & Michaels, 1994). School-aged children and adolescents may be induced by the offender through the use of bribes, positive attention and affection, or other rewards, and teens may interpret the abuse as consensual; thus, both may believe that they are complicit in the sexual activity as equal partners. These victims may be afraid to disclose the abuse due to their mistaken sense of being culpable in the activity (Lanning, 2002). Since the majority of sexual abuse occurs after a process of "grooming," is often done in concert with fun activities (i.e., positive attention, affection, access to desirable games and toys), and is commonly perpetrated by a known and trusted older child or adult, victims may feel conflicted about reporting the abuse. Since abusers are frequently family members or are known to and trusted by the child's parents, the child may worry about the impact of disclosure on their family members (Crisma, Bascelli, Paci, & Romito, 2004; Goodman-Brown, Edelstein, Goodman, Jones, & Gordon, 2003; Lyon, Ahern, Malloy, & Quas, 2010). Indeed, abusers often take advantage of these feelings, telling the child that loved ones would be upset if the child told or that the abuser would go to jail (Malloy, Lyon, & Quas, 2007; Schaeffer, Leventhal, & Asnes, 2011).

Disclosed But Not Reported

In those cases where children do disclose their abuse, many do not tell an adult. One study found that, of those who disclosed the abuse during their childhood, 40 percent disclosed to a peer or sibling who had never told an adult (Broman-Fulks et al., 2007). Even in those cases where a child disclosed the abuse to an adult, a number reported that the abuse never was brought to the attention of the authorities (Smith et al., 2000). Reasons adults may fail to report the abuse to authorities are numerous. Both caregivers and noncaregivers alike may feel they might have misunderstood what the child told them, or that the child had confused nonabusive touch with abusive touch, or they may feel unsure whether the child was telling the truth. When the abuser is a family member, a respected community member, or a trusted friend of the family, the adult to whom the abuse was disclosed may feel especially conflicted and fear the repercussions of reporting. If the family is undocumented, is part of a socially or culturally isolated group, has suffered historical trauma related to governmental agencies, or otherwise has learned to mistrust authorities, they may fear that reporting the abuse could be dangerous to the family. Fontes and Plummer (2010) observed, "In minority cultures, the act of sharing personal matters with people from outside the inner circle may be seen as leading to unwanted and threatening attention that might jeopardize family and community integrity" (pp. 505–506). In cases where a child discloses to a nonfamily member (teacher, friend's parent, counselor), the adult may not know how to report or may fear repercussions for making the report (Kenny, 2004).

Younger Victims

In addition, an unknown percentage of CSA cases involve infants and toddlers who lack the verbal skills to communicate what has happened to them. Since most known cases of CSA involve fondling, such abuse can easily go undetected in this younger population. In those cases where some physical indicators of CSA are present, they may not rise to the level of conclusive evidence, and in the absence of a clear verbal disclosure, these cases are often deemed inconclusive or "invalid" even if the caregiver reports concerns.

CSA Characteristics

The research does give us some notion of what is commonly seen in cases of CSA. Girls are more likely to be sexually abused than boys. Perpetrators are most often known and trusted by the family or may be a family member. Older children or teenagers are perpetrators in up to 40 percent of cases of CSA. Contrary to popular notions, stranger-perpetrated sexual assault on minors only occurs in approximately 4 percent of cases (Finkelhor & Shattuck, 2012). Most sexual abuse occurs in the home of the child or of the perpetrator. Risk factors include living with a stepparent or a single parent, living in a rural area, having a parent who is unemployed, and living in a low socioeconomic status household (Snyder, 2000). These last data must be viewed cautiously. Certainly poverty and single parenthood can leave children vulnerable to abuse due to the increased stress on the family and the lack of supportive resources available to the caregiver. It must also be considered that abused children from wealthier, intact families may be less likely to come to the attention of authorities due to the resources available to those families.

Additional risk factors include passive, quiet, lonely children and disabled children. These children are much more likely to be receptive to the attention, affection, and time a perpetrator will shower them with as part of the grooming process. Passive or quiet children are also less likely to disclose the abuse to others. Also, some perpetrators may target troubled youth, knowing that, should the youth disclose the sexual abuse, the perpetrator can use the child's troubled past to call the disclosure into question (Elliott, Browne, & Kilcoyne, 1995).

CSA can have serious and enduring negative sequelae. Many survivors display behavior problems including aggression and noncompliance during their childhood and adolescence (Douglas & Finkelhor, 2005). Survivors are at higher risk for anxiety, depression, and suicidality as well as substance abuse and increased risk-taking behaviors than are nonabused children (Briere & Elliott, 2003; Finkelhor, Ormrod, Turner, & Hamby, 2012). As the Adverse Childhood Experiences study identified, CSA has a catalyzing effect when combined with other adverse experiences, markedly increasing survivors' vulnerability to short- and long-term emotional, psychological, and physical/medical problems (Felitti et al., 1998).

Case Description

Becca Price is a six-year-old, African American female child. She lived with her mother, Mrs. Angela Price. Mrs. Price was a widow. Becca's father had been in the military but was killed in action when Becca was two years old. When Sgt. Price died, Mrs. Price moved in with her mother (called "Grandma" by Becca), who helped her with Becca. Mrs. Price had no other family living in the state. Her own father had left the family many years ago and had never been part of Mrs. Price's life.

Since her husband's death, Mrs. Price had maintained a good relationship with her in-laws, especially Becca's paternal grandmother, "Nana" Price who also was widowed, and who doted on Becca. Both of the grandmothers had also grown close, often spending time together. Nana had two additional sons besides Sgt. Price—one who lived out of state with his wife and children and 30-year-old Lenny, a bachelor who lived near his mother and helped care for her. Lenny was a teacher in a middle school, and he coached little league in his free time. Lenny was currently involved in a long-term dating relationship with a woman who also worked as a teacher in the school where Lenny taught. Mrs. Angela Price had never warmed up to Lenny, but she respected him for how he looked after his mother. Mrs. Price had a few friends but generally was too busy working and raising Becca to spend much time socializing.

Impact of CSA: Developmental Perspective

Over the past few months, Mrs. Price noticed that Becca seemed different. Once an outgoing child, Becca progressively had grown more withdrawn and quiet. Becca had become demanding at times as well. She now wanted to bathe and dress herself and became angry if Mrs. Price entered the room or offered to help her while she dressed or bathed. Mrs. Price regarded this as Becca wanting to show she could do things for herself, so she went along with Becca's demands. Yet when they were around other people, Becca clung to Mrs. Price like she used to when she was a baby. Mrs. Price was very confused and troubled about this change in her child, but when she asked Becca if she was okay, if something was bothering her, Becca would shake her head and would stop talking. Becca also periodically complained that it hurt when she urinated. Mrs. Price told Becca she would have to look at that area to see if it was okay. Becca did not want her to do so but finally allowed Mrs. Price to look. There did seem to be some redness around the vaginal opening, so Mrs. Price brought Becca to her pediatrician the next day. The doctor thought the irritation around Becca's genitals may have been caused by poor toileting hygiene. This sounded reasonable to Mrs. Price. Since Becca had insisted on bathing herself, she likely wasn't cleaning herself adequately, and this was the result. The rash went away after a few days but came back. Mrs. Price insisted that Becca let her help with bathing again, and she also talked with Becca about wiping well after using the bathroom, but the rash kept coming back. One day, Becca was playing with her dolls as Mrs. Price sat nearby watching television. Mrs. Price noticed that Becca had placed an adult male doll facedown at the crotch area of the little girl doll. Mrs. Price asked: "What are you doing? Why are the dolls like that?" Becca didn't look up but said, "That's a game Uncle Len Len plays with me." Mrs. Price peppered Becca with questions about this "game," but Becca shut down and would not answer. Mrs. Price talked to her mother, who thought Mrs. Price must have misunderstood what she saw and what Becca said. It wasn't possible that Lenny would do such a thing. Her mother said, "He's a good man. He's got a good job and a girlfriend. He takes care of his mother. He's not some child molester." Mrs. Price was not reassured by her mother's comments, and immediately called the pediatrician, who advised her to bring Becca to the emergency room for a medical exam. The pediatrician also said Mrs. Price should call the police and tell them what Becca had said to her. Mrs. Price asked if that was necessary and shouldn't she let the doctors at the ER look at Becca first. She would hate to bring the police into the matter if it were a misunderstanding. Becca's doctor explained that Becca's play, her statement, and her chronic episodes of irritation around her genitals were concerning, and as a mandated reporter, he felt it was necessary to report. Sensing Mrs. Price's hesitance to be the person to call the police on her brother-in-law, the doctor offered to make the report for Mrs. Price. Mrs. Price agreed with this plan. Mrs. Price brought Becca to the emergency room at the local Children's Hospital where she met a detective from the local police department. While Becca was examined, Mrs. Price told the detective what Becca had said and about what she had done with the dolls. Once Becca's medical examination was completed, the ER doctor met with Mrs. Price and the detective. He said that he could find no physical signs that Becca had been sexually abused. Mrs. Price was relieved and apologized for calling the detective out on a false alarm. The doctor explained that there seldom are any physical signs of sexual abuse because many kinds of CSA involve fondling or other kinds of sexual touch that do not injure the child physically. The doctor referred Becca for a forensic interview to try to determine if abuse had occurred or not. The detective then met with Becca and Mrs. Price together. Mrs. Price asked Becca to tell the detective what she had told Mrs. Price about her uncle and the game. Becca hesitated and then said reluctantly, "Uncle Len Len plays a game with me. I don't like it. It hurts." But when she noticed that her mother had started crying, Becca stopped talking and would not say any more. The detective thanked Becca for talking to her. An appointment for the forensic interview was set at the local Child Advocacy Center for the following morning. The detective gave Mrs. Price directions to the Advocacy Center and discussed how Mrs. Price might talk to Becca to explain where they were going. She urged Mrs. Price to ask Becca no further questions about Lenny and the game until the interview was completed.

The interview took place the following morning in a house that looked like a cozy home. Becca and Mrs. Price met the interviewer who took time to show Becca the room where they would talk together and the nearby room where her mom would be waiting for her until she finished. Becca liked the animal stickers all over the walls of the interview room, and she liked that the lady who interviewed her had brought Play-Doh to play with while they talked. During the interview, the lady asked Becca a lot of questions about her family, her school, and her favorite toys. Then they talked about the game. When the interviewer asked Becca to tell her about the game, Becca whispered it in her ear so that Uncle Len Len didn't hear her. Becca told the interviewer that Uncle Len Len played a game with her sometimes. She said that the game involved Uncle Len Len kissing her pee pee (vaginal area) and that sometimes he "puts a stick in there . . . it hurts." Becca could not describe the stick because she never saw it but only felt it. It felt hard and it hurt. Becca said it happened more than one time, but she could not say how many times. She did remember that the last time they played the game was at a party at her Nana's house, but she did not remember what the party was celebrating. She said there were balloons and music and a lot of food, but no cake. She recalled it was hot that day and that they ate at picnic tables in the yard. Uncle Len Len was wearing brown shorts and a green shirt. Becca said Nana didn't know about the game because Uncle Len Len said it was a secret and made Becca promise not to tell anyone. Becca was afraid now because she had told. She was worried she would get in trouble and also worried that Uncle Len Len would get in trouble. She liked her uncle, but she did not like the game.

Once the interview was completed, Mrs. Price was advised that there were indications that Becca had been sexually abused by Lenny. The detective told Mrs. Price that as part of the investigation, Lenny and his mother would be interviewed. Mrs. Price felt both anger at Lenny and worry about how the investigation would affect the family, especially the relationship between Becca and her Nana, whom Becca adored. Mrs. Price had hoped it was all a mistake—that she had misunderstood what Becca said and that everything could go back to normal. Mrs. Price could not bear to think that Becca had been abused. How could she have not known this was happening to Becca? Why didn't Becca tell her? The staff at the Advocacy Center told Mrs. Price that children often delay in telling about abuse, and many don't ever tell anyone. They said that Becca and Mrs. Price would benefit from seeing a trauma therapist who had experience helping families where sexual abuse may have taken place. They gave Mrs. Price a referral to a therapist to assess whether Becca would benefit from treatment and to provide Mrs. Price with psychoeducation on how CSA affects children and their families.

Key Clinical Issues

Sexual abuse presents differently depending on the age of the child, the type of abuse, the relationship of the perpetrator to the child, cultural norms, and overall family functioning. For example, a child with a prior trauma history is likely to be more negatively affected by the added trauma of CSA than a child for whom the CSA is a single-incident event with no other trauma history (Turner, Finkelhor, & Ormrod, 2006). In this case, Becca was fortunate to be part of a well-functioning family system. While Becca did suffer the death of her father when she was two years old, because Sgt. Price had been deployed for much of her life, including at the time of his death, she experienced his loss more through her attunement to her mother's grief process. An additional protective factor was Mrs. Price's immediate and supportive response to Becca's disclosure, despite her understandable hopes that it was a misunderstanding. Many children do not experience such a quick and supportive response, and the lack or delay of such a response increases the chance that the abuse will continue and that the child will suffer long-term and more severe social and psychological problems (Everson, Hunter, Runyon, Edelsohn, & Coulter, 1989; Leifer, Shapiro, & Kassem, 1993).

Nonoffending caregivers of CSA survivors are themselves deeply affected by the abuse. In most cases the offender is known and trusted, sometimes an immediate family member. Nonoffending caregivers can experience waves of anger, denial, dismay, and feelings of betrayal. Parents who do report abuse navigate legal, medical, and mental health systems that can be bewildering and overwhelming. These parents benefit enormously from having supportive guidance through these systems and psychoeducation regarding CSA and its impact on children and their families. Additional education about red flags that indicate the need for more in-depth treatment of the survivor and the possible long-term sequelae of the abuse is also very helpful.

Presenting Problem

Children who have been sexually abused may present with a number of symptoms. However, no behavioral symptom or cluster of symptoms is considered to be diagnostic of sexual abuse. Many symptoms seen in survivors of CSA are also common among children suffering other kinds of trauma. Additionally, a subset of children appears to emerge from CSA without any long-term negative effects. However, we cannot predict which children will react with such resilience.

Some symptoms commonly seen in cases of CSA include marked changes in behavior, fearfulness, depression, anxiety, regression, clinginess, irritability, acting-out, outbursts, dissociation, controlling behaviors, precocious sexual behaviors or knowledge, increased risk-taking behaviors, and flashbacks. In younger children flashbacks can present as nightmares or as reenactment in the form of posttraumatic play, which is characterized by a repetitive and joyless replaying of a scene of trauma without resolution. An example of posttraumatic play was seen in Becca's doll play. Younger children will present with more clinging, fearfulness, or acting-out and controlling behaviors. Adolescents will more often engage in social withdrawal, depression, eating disorders, and risk-taking behaviors, including substance use and abuse. Younger children may exhibit more distress when contact with the perpetrator is likely to occur or has recently happened. However, they may engage in posttraumatic play when away from the perpetrator as they attempt to make sense of their abuse experiences.

Cultural Considerations

Culture plays a significant role in CSA impact, disclosure, recantation, reporting, treatment, and prosecution. While some beliefs, practices, and norms are culture-specific, many exist in multiple ethnic and cultural groups. They can be impacted by legal status, social status, level of acculturation, personal trauma history, and other factors. Therefore, it may be more helpful to look at these dynamics in terms of values and beliefs that may be important to assess when working with a family. Fontes and Plummer (2010) described cultural concepts that may play a role in creating vulnerability to CSA. These include the impact of values related to taboos, modesty, virginity, the status of females, as well as honor/respect. They note that in cultures where the subject of sexuality is a taboo, it is very difficult to disclose CSA. If the child does disclose, a female child may be judged as having dirty thoughts or of being immodest. A male child who discloses having been sexually abused within a culture with strict gender role definitions may find his own sexuality questioned. In some cultures, if a sexual assault occurs, the female often feels that she brought it on herself. Many cultures place a high value on virginity, so even in cases where sexual abuse has not involved penetration, the girl is seen as "damaged" irreparably. Fontes and Plummer (2010) noted, "The girl's value does not rest solely on her actual virginity, but also on her 'honor' or her reputation. The notion that girls are less valuable as brides if they are not virgins inhibits disclosure of sexual assaults in numerous countries throughout the world and in numerous ethnic communities in the United States" (p. 500).

When the survivor is part of an ethnic and/or cultural minority, disclosure and reporting of CSA may be discouraged due to concerns about the impact on the larger group. "A child's refusal to disclose may even be conceptualized as a highly adaptive trait—that of protecting one's community from hostile outsiders" (Fontes & Plummer, 2010, p. 501). It is important to keep in mind that minority cultures have often suffered historical and current racism, especially when dealing with larger systems like hospitals, law enforcement, and child protection. As Pence (2011) stated, "In some societies, cooperation with government agencies, including police, is dangerous" (p. 329). Therefore, those who work with these families must practice cultural humility; that is, they must maintain awareness of their own biases and be open to learning from clients about their experience. Above all it is important to understand that cultures and ethnicities are not monolithic and that beliefs and practices vary from region to region, subgroup to subgroup, and even family to family. Therefore, the therapist should make no global assumptions about the client's culture. Rather, it is important that the therapist sensitively ask the nonoffending caregiver to help him or her gain insight into how the caregiver and his or her family perceive and understand what the child has experienced and the concerns it evokes within the family.

Methods Children/Caregiver(s) Use to Seek Help

In the case example, Becca revealed the abuse unintentionally to her mother via her doll play, which prompted Mrs. Price to ask the questions that led to Becca's verbal disclosure. Mrs. Price reached out to Becca's pediatrician who responded supportively, giving her clear and accurate guidance on how to proceed while also urging her to report her concerns to the police. In cases where parents do not have a regular pediatrician, they may not have a trusted professional available to help guide them. Often when CSA is suspected, parents seek guidance from family members or a trusted friend about their concerns and how they should proceed. Some parents may mistrust the authorities and seek to deal with the suspected abuse through informal systems. Sadly, some caregivers respond punitively when children disclose CSA. They blame the child or accuse the child of making up the allegation leaving the child to fend for himself or herself.

General Principles of Intervention

There are several aspects of treating CSA that are consistently addressed in evidence-based interventions for CSA: (1) improving parental support/response; (2) addressing cognitive distortions the child and caregiver may have related to the abuse, the abuser, and themselves; (3) helping the child integrate the trauma, usually via development of a narrative; (4) remediating any sexualized behavior the child may engage in as a result of premature sexualization; and (5) reducing the risk that the child will be revictimized. These are issues that commonly arise in the treatment of CSA and that are most likely to improve the child's functioning if addressed adequately and proactively (Pollio, Deblinger, & Runyon, 2011).

Currently, the preferred intervention for CSA is Trauma-Focused Cognitive Behavioral Therapy (TF-CBT). This is a 12- to 25-session treatment model for CSA survivors aged 3–21 years old. Like many other evidence-based treatments (EBTs) for trauma, it includes development of a trauma narrative, parental psychoeducation and support, and parental participation in the child's treatment. Other evidence-based intervention models used specifically for CSA survivors are (1) Risk Reduction through Family Therapy (RRFT), which is a family therapy model for use with boys and girls, ages 13–18 years old and (2) Skills Training in Affective and Interpersonal Regulation/Narrative Story Telling (STAIR/NST), which is an individual/group intervention designed for girls ages 12–21 years old. Since TF-CBT is so widely used, it will be explored more fully as an example of an EBT to treat CSA.

Assessment

Mrs. Price met with the therapist referred to her. The therapist began the assessment with an interview with Mrs. Price and, later with both Mrs. Price and Becca. The therapist asked Mrs. Price to describe how she learned about the abuse and what they had experienced during the ER visit, medical exam, and forensic interview and since the initial disclosure. Time was taken to learn about how Mrs. Price viewed the abuse and Becca's disclosure, and the family's cultural beliefs or norms were also explored. Mrs. Price completed several psychological and trauma measures that assessed Becca's level of traumatization, current symptoms, and sexualized behaviors if present and also evaluated Mrs. Price's current functioning. Measures would be repeated periodically to assess the effectiveness of the intervention and to inform any adaptations needed to support Becca's needs.

Authorizations were obtained from Mrs. Price to speak with the collateral sources (i.e., Child Advocacy Center) involved in the case in order to gather information related to Becca's abuse. Additionally, the therapist asked if there would be a child protection or criminal case going forward and what the status of the case was currently. Knowing this allowed the therapist to support Mrs. Price and Becca through the process.

Given Becca's age, the therapist assessed Becca's ability to describe and express her feelings. Younger children (under six years of age) are still developing the ability to describe even the most mundane experiences in a coherent narrative. Since most treatment for CSA involves the development of a narrative of their abuse, this task can be adapted for younger children or those whose expressive language capacity is limited to include nonverbal methods. In these cases, the therapist might encourage the child to play out a narrative of the trauma using dolls or puppets or to show the narrative using a series of drawings. With younger children time will be spent on helping the child develop an adequate vocabulary to enable affective expression. A similar assessment would take place with any survivor who had communication difficulties (i.e., developmentally delayed survivors or those with other speech disorders).

The Treatment Process

Once this information was gathered, the therapist met with Mrs. Price and Becca to discuss the format of TF-CBT and answer any questions they might have. TF-CBT follows a format with eight components including psychoeducation (about the impact of CSA) and parenting skills, relaxation techniques, expressing and managing feelings, addressing any cognitive distortions, developing and processing the trauma narrative, mastery of trauma reminders, parent–child sessions, and enhancing safety. It should be noted that trauma survivors in general, and sexual assault survivors particularly, often experience difficulty talking about the abuse. Many trauma survivors avoid talking or thinking about it altogether in an attempt to escape the feelings it brings up (avoidance), or they may describe the trauma in a detached manner (numbing) but be unable to identify how they felt or what they were thinking during those experiences. CSA survivors' trauma experience differs in that there is a dynamic of secrecy that is central to most CSA cases. The abuser explicitly or implicitly imposes a rule of silence about the abuse, either through persuasion/grooming ("This is our secret game.") or through threat of harm ("If you tell anyone I will kill your dog." or "You will get in trouble/go to jail.").

Addressing Avoidance

During the first treatment session, the therapist provided Mrs. Price and Becca psychoeducation regarding avoidance as a common response to trauma. She explained that Becca experienced an overwhelming threat to her safety, during which she felt unable to defend herself or to escape. Having survived that experience, Becca would never want to feel that way again. The therapist explained that therapy asks Becca to remember what happened with Uncle Len Len and she might have strong feelings when remembering. The therapist reassured Becca and Mrs. Price that she would make sure the feelings did not get too strong and that they would learn things to do that would make the big feelings smaller. By talking about it in advance and normalizing Becca's feelings, the intensity of their avoidance was eased. To help Becca with these feelings, the therapist taught Becca and her mother relaxation techniques like deep breathing, progressive muscle relaxation, and yoga poses at each session that Becca could use to feel better when she needed to do so. Mrs. Price was encouraged to practice the techniques between sessions. Learning these skills early in treatment, before strong feelings are evoked, gives the child and caregiver time to practice them and to test them in mildly stressful situations. By doing so, the family develops confidence, both in their ability to implement the skills and in the coping skills' effectiveness in decreasing their anxiety symptoms to more tolerable levels.

Addressing Cognitive Distortions

When the investigation began, Mrs. Price's in-laws cut off all communication with Becca and Mrs. Price. Mrs. Price's mother was heartbroken, since she had enjoyed a friendship with Becca's Nana before the abuse came to light. Several times she asked Mrs. Price if she was sure that she had not made a mistake about what Becca said. Once Mrs. Price found her mother chastising Becca for "telling a lie on your Uncle Lenny. He could go to jail because of that lie." Mrs. Price and her mother had words about it, and her mother did not do it again, but after that Becca began saying that she had lied and that she didn't want Uncle Len Len to go to jail. With all the disruption to the family and all the pain she saw Becca feeling from being unable to see her Nana and uncle, Mrs. Price had gone through waves of doubt: Was it all a terrible mistake? But then she remembered the dolls and Becca's statement to the detective at the hospital. She told Becca she knew it wasn't a lie and that grandma shouldn't have chastised her. Mrs. Price said to Becca, "No matter what, you should always tell the truth, even if folks get upset. I know you told the truth, and I'm proud of you. It was so brave." During the next therapy session, Becca stated that Uncle Len Len was going to jail "because I told about the game." The therapist addressed this cognitive distortion by stating that Lenny got into trouble because he had broken the law by touching Becca in a way that grown-ups are not allowed to touch children, not because Becca had told her mother about it. The therapist praised Mrs. Price for having responded supportively to Becca when this incident happened.

As mentioned earlier, shame plays a large role in CSA not only for the victims but also for the nonoffending parents who often experience waves of guilt that their child was abused, that they did not see it sooner as well as doubt and denial regarding the abuse. The parent needs a great deal of support through their waves of doubt so that they can be the consistent support that their child needs them to be. These doubts are understandable when we consider how globally disruptive and damaging the discovery of sexual abuse of one's child by a relative or friend is to a family as well as to one's confidence in one's own judgment.

At this age children who have been abused by a family member may express a desire to see the abuser or even love for the abuser. This is due to children's belief that the offender can simply stop abusing them. The child remembers and misses the fun and affectionate side of the abuser; they just want them not to touch them sexually. This can cause the nonoffending parent to doubt that the abuse took place, which could place the child at risk again. The therapist would educate Mrs. Price about children's magical thinking and how best to support Becca. The therapist would also explain to Becca that the offender could not simply stop touching them, so they cannot see the adult because it would not be safe. Conversely, some offenders may threaten the child to ensure that the child did not disclose the abuse to others. Children may have strong feelings of fear or the misperception (common in younger children) that the offender is all-powerful and knows what they are saying and thinking. The child may fear that the offender will break into their home and hurt them or a loved one. By checking in with the child on a regular basis, the therapist gives them the opportunity to express and address these fears if they are present.

Trauma Narrative

Development of a trauma narrative is the central component of TF-CBT. Traumatic memories are fragmented and disjointed due to the way the brain encodes experiences when under extreme stress. The memories of the thoughts, feelings, and actions a person experienced are not integrated in traumatic memories as they are in nontraumatic memories (van der Kolk, 2014). The goal of the narrative development is to help the survivor reintegrate these fragments through development of the trauma narrative. The narrative weaves together the disconnected threads of thoughts, actions, and emotions into a coherent memory of the traumatic experience. The narrative is generally developed with the survivor in his or her individual sessions rather than with the parent. (Exceptions could be made in cases with younger children who would benefit from the immediate support and coregulation that having their caregiver in the room would offer.)

Becca developed her narrative of Uncle Len Len's abuse through a series of drawings made over a number of individual sessions. Becca and the therapist then spent several more sessions looking at each drawing and identifying what Becca remembered thinking and feeling when the part of her experience shown in the drawing was happening. These were written in where Becca thought they should go using the marker, pen, or crayon Becca chose for each remembered thought or feeling. When she finished, Becca looked at the array of pictures and nodded her approval. The therapist and Becca then went through the drawings as Becca told the whole story of that experience from beginning to end. Becca was now ready to present her story to Mrs. Price. At the next joint parent–child session, Becca showed Mrs. Price each drawing and described what it depicted, what Becca was thinking and feeling at that time. Mrs. Price (who had been prepared in advance by the therapist for this session) listened intently, and when the story was finished, she hugged Becca and said she was proud of her. Mrs. Price thanked Becca for telling her the story of what Uncle Len Len had done to her. Mrs. Price affirmed that she would do her best to protect Becca from now on.

Enhancing Safety and Looking to the Future

CSA disrupts and blurs adult–child roles and personal boundaries. Most child survivors benefit from reestablishing healthy boundaries, and they may engage in sexualized play and behaviors. Parents often need clear guidance on how to respond supportively and also protectively so that the child does not risk acting out on other children or being revictimized. In Becca's case, Mrs. Price called the therapist before their session in a panic. Mrs. Price said that Becca had started "playing with her privates" while watching TV with Mrs. Price and Grandma. Grandma saw it first and had yelled at Becca to stop, saying, "That's nasty. Don't ever let me catch you doing that again!" Becca had looked startled and ran from the room. The next evening Mrs. Price found Becca masturbating again as she bathed. The therapist reassured Mrs. Price that masturbation was not unusual for a child of Becca's age, but it may have been triggered or intensified by the abuse, and it was concerning that she had masturbated in a public area of the house when Mom and Grandma were present. The therapist and Mrs. Price discussed how to talk to Becca about the activity and set appropriate limits on it. At the next parent–child session, the therapist and Mrs. Price talked with Becca about this behavior and worked together to identify rules for private parts. Once they had agreed on a list of rules, a copy was given to Mrs. Price to review with Becca between sessions.

In general, personal boundaries are defined and reinforced over a number of sessions through educating the child in the accurate names for their private parts, developing rules related to sharing private parts, discussing "ok" and "not ok" touching, and talking about good secrets (like a surprise birthday party) and bad secrets (Lenny's game).

The remaining sessions were focused on further enhancing Becca's safety. In each session they reviewed the rules for private parts, touching, and secrets, and they talked about what Becca should do if anyone wanted to play a game like Uncle Len Len did. Becca made a list of trusted people she could talk to if she ever felt confused or uncomfortable with something she was asked to do or allow someone else to do. Becca and the therapist role-played how that might look. In an individual session with Mrs. Price, the therapist would discuss how Becca's trauma might reemerge in the form of depressive or anxiety symptoms in the future.

Ongoing Therapeutic Issues

Impact of Prosecuting the Offender on the Child

For many children prosecution can powerfully communicate that the offender is culpable for the abuse, not the child. This is important since many survivors feel partly or wholly responsible for the abuse and for the difficulties that others undergo once the abuse is disclosed. However, for some child survivors, prosecution of the offender can be a double-edged sword. If they are fond of the offender, especially when that person is a family member or close friend of the family, the child in many cases will not want to see them get in trouble or be punished. At times prosecution can increase tension and conflict within the family in cases where family members do not believe the child. When faced with the upheaval and upset associated with the family's discovery of their abuse, children often mistakenly connect the family's upset to their own disclosure of the abuse, not to the abuse itself. When she was seven years old, Maya Angelou disclosed to her family that her mother's boyfriend had sexually abused her. Soon after he was found killed, likely by male family members. Ms. Angelou said in an interview, "I thought my voice had killed him, and so it was better not to speak. I thought that if I spoke, my words could kill anybody" (Hamilton, 2012). Ms. Angelou was selectively mute for the next five years. This extreme example highlights the child victim's capacity for "owning" the culpability for the abuse, including feeling responsible for the consequences imposed on the abuser.

Another area of concern related to child responses to prosecution relates to "compliant victims" (Lanning, 2002). These are often older children who feel they are able to consent to sexual activity and who view themselves as being in a relationship with the offender. When the abuse is discovered, these children and teenagers may feel overwhelming guilt, shame, and even anger about the prosecution of the offender due to the child's belief that the offender truly cares about them. Care must be taken to understand how the child perceives the offender and the abuse. Based on a clear understanding of this situation, the therapist should tailor the intervention to address these cognitive distortions, advocate for the child's emotional well-being, and educate and empower the caregiver to be a source of consistent support and safety for the child through this process.

In some cases the child may be called upon to testify about his or her abuse. Court procedures and the laws that govern them were developed for adult witnesses and can be overwhelming, confusing, and intimidating to children. Facing the offender in court while talking to a roomful of strangers about the abuse they endured adds to the stress the child experiences and can retraumatize the child. While some accommodations may be made to reduce these stressors (i.e., emotional support service dogs, remote closed-circuit video testimony, or positioning the questioning attorney away from the defendant), such accommodations cannot fully mitigate the distress child witnesses endure. It should be noted that despite these challenges, some children receive excellent and sensitive preparation and support and emerge from the experience feeling empowered and validated.

The therapist must be attuned to each child's unique experience of abuse—how they think about the abuse, their feelings about and for the abuser, and their sense of their own role and/or culpability for the abuse, and from this information, develop a sense of how the child would cope with being involved in the prosecution of the offender. The therapist should be prepared to advocate for the child's emotional well-being related to the investigation and prosecution of his or her abuse case.

Becca's Case

Although Becca had made a clear disclosure in her forensic interview, she was judged to be too young to testify in court, and no corroborating evidence was found, with the exception of her doll play and the changes in her behavior. As the weeks passed, it remained unclear whether there would be an arrest made. The therapist continued to check in with the Child Advocacy Center and the detective so that she could adapt treatment to include any needed additional support related to arrest of the offender and/or a trial. Ultimately, the district attorney did not accept the case. Mrs. Price was heartbroken. She called the therapist to ask for a supportive session. When they met, Mrs. Price was furious and exhausted. She was relieved now that the Price family had wanted nothing to do with her and Becca since the investigation began. They had not seen the Prices since, and that meant that it was unlikely that Becca would ever see Lenny again. Mrs. Price said she felt like their lives had been turned upside down, that even her own mother still questioned whether the abuse had happened at all, and now she and Becca would not get the chance to have the abuse proven in court. The therapist asked Mrs. Price to think of the people who did believe Becca: Mrs. Price listed herself first, then the detective and the doctor from the ER, Becca's pediatrician, the forensic interviewer, the therapist, Becca's school, and Mrs. Price's friend from work, who had become a source of great support throughout this ordeal. The therapist said, "Looks like Becca's got a lot of folks who believe her and who were there for her when she needed it." Mrs. Price nodded and smiled. Mrs. Price and the therapist talked about how much better Becca was doing in school and at home. The therapist congratulated Mrs. Price on all she had done to protect Becca by seeing and responding to her hints about the abuse, believing her when few others did, reporting the abuse to the authorities, and bringing Becca to therapy. By doing so, Mrs. Price and Becca had developed skills and tools to increase Becca's safety and to integrate this experience and continue with her life.

Lessons Learned and Key Points

This was a challenging case but is typical of cases in this age range. Prosecution of the offender is very important to prevent the offender from victimizing other children. However, from a behavioral health perspective, the most important outcome for a child who has endured CSA is establishing and maintaining a safe environment with a supportive caregiver, successful integration of the trauma, remediation of any symptoms related to the abuse, reestablishment of clear and appropriate adult–child boundaries and roles, and a return to a normal developmental trajectory. The therapist should be vigilant in maintaining allegiance to these goals.

In Becca's case, these goals were met. Therapists working in this field, especially those working with younger children, understand the importance of supporting the non-offending caregiver through this process. When provided accurate information, emotional support and the safe space in which they can explore their own powerful and sometimes conflicted feelings, the caregiver is empowered to be the same kind of resource to and safe space for their child. The therapist is an essential component in this process, but if treatment goes as it should, the child will "graduate" from treatment and move on with his or her lives. Therefore, supporting and empowering the caregiver as the healing relationship for the child ensures the child will have ongoing support once formal therapy ends.

Conclusion

A therapist who treats cases of CSA should be trained in EBTs for this population, and he or she should be knowledgeable about the dynamics that can present in CSA cases. The therapist should have a good understanding of his or her own role and responsibilities (clinical, ethical, and legal), as well as the roles and responsibilities of other professionals who may be working with the family. The therapist should monitor the clinical, legal, and ethical challenges and requirements presented by the case. It is most helpful to have trusted supervision or peer consultation as a resource to aid the therapist in navigating the "gray areas" and challenges that can arise. Additionally, the therapist should stay up to date on the current literature in the field and maintain relevant trainings annually to stay up to date with best practices.

While it is beyond the scope of this chapter to address the many complicating factors that can arise in CSA cases (e.g., CSA in the context of divorce/separation), there are excellent resources available through such groups as APSAC and the National Child Advocacy Center that can provide the therapist with information on the latest research and best practices and professional standards related to treating this challenging population.

Finally, the therapist must be able to monitor their own emotional well-being, maintain self-care practices, and be able to set limits when they note signs of vicarious trauma or secondary traumatic stress related to their work. Trauma work is very demanding both professionally and personally. If the therapist does not manage the stress of the work adequately and is not able to set limits appropriately, he or she is at high risk for burnout. This can express itself through the therapist leaving the field or through the therapist becoming cynical and emotionally detached. In either case, the children are ill-served, so it is of the utmost importance that therapists in this field consider appropriate self-care to be part of their professional responsibilities and that the agencies in which they work support personal and professional wellness practices. Ultimately, the goal of behavioral health support for survivors of CSA is reduction of distress and improved functioning both for the child and for the supportive caregiver who will help the child sustain the gains made in therapy. Training, supervision/consultation, self-care practices, and adherence to best practices in their own field will empower the therapist to help the child survivor and his or her caregiver achieve these twin goals.

References

American Professional Society on the Abuse of Children. (2016, April). *APSAC position paper on allegations of child maltreatment and intimate partner violence in divorce/parental relationship dissolution*. Retrieved from http://www.apsac.org

Berliner, L. (2011). Child sexual abuse: Definitions, prevalence, and consequences. In J. E. B. Myers (Ed.), *The APSAC handbook on child maltreatment* (3rd ed., pp. 215–232). Los Angeles, CA: Sage.

Briere, J., & Elliott, D. M. (2003). Prevalence and psychological sequelae of self-reported childhood physical and sexual abuse in a general population sample of men and women. *Child Abuse & Neglect, 27*(10), 1205–1222.

Broman-Fulks, J. J., Ruggiero, K. J., Hanson, R. F., Smith, D. W., Resnick, H. S., Kilpatrick, D. G., & Saunders, B. E. (2007). Sexual assault disclosure in relation to adolescent mental health: Results from the National Survey of Adolescents. *Journal of Clinical Child and Adolescent Psychology, 36*, 260–266.

Crisma, M., Bascelli, E., Paci, D., & Romito, P. (2004). Adolescents who experienced sexual abuse: Fears, needs and impediments to disclosure. *Child Abuse & Neglect, 28*(10), 1035–1048.

Douglas, E., & Finkelhor, D. (2005). *Childhood sexual abuse fact sheet: Crimes against children center, University of New Hampshire*. Retrieved from http://www.unh.edu/ccrc/factsheet/pdf/CSA-FS20.pdf

Elliott, M., Browne, K., & Kilcoyne, J. (1995). Child sexual abuse prevention: What offenders tell us. *Child Abuse & Neglect, 5*, 579–594.

Everson, M. D., Hunter, W. M., Runyon, D. K., Edelsohn, G. A., & Coulter, M. L. (1989). Maternal support following disclosure of incest. *American Journal of Orthopsychiatry, 59*(2), 197–207.

Felitti, V. J., Anda, R. F., Nordenberg, D., Williamson, D. F., Spitz, A. M., Edwards, V., . . . Marks, J. S. (1998). Relationship of childhood abuse and household dysfunction to many of the leading causes of death in adults: The adverse childhood experiences (ACE) study. *American Journal of Preventative Medicine, 14*, 245–258.

Finkelhor, D., Hotaling, G., Lewis, I. A., & Smith, C. (1990). Sexual abuse in a national survey of adult men and women: Prevalence, characteristics, and risk factors. *Child Abuse & Neglect, 14*, 19–28.

Finkelhor, D., Ormrod, R., Turner, H. A., & Hamby, S. L. (2012). Child and youth victimization known to police, school, and medical authorities in a national sample of children and youth. *Juvenile Justice Bulletin*, No. NCJ 235394. Retrieved from https://www.ojjdp.gov/Publications/PubResults.asp?sei=94

Finkelhor, D., & Shattuck, A. (2012). Characteristics of crimes against juveniles. Durham, NC: Crimes against Children Research Center.

Fontes, L. A., & Plummer, C. (2010). Cultural issues in disclosures of child sexual abuse. *Journal of Child Sexual Abuse, 19*, 491–518.

Goodman-Brown, T. B., Edelstein, R. S., Goodman, G. S., Jones, D. P. H., & Gordon, D. S. (2003). Why children tell: A model of children's disclosure of abuse. *Child Abuse & Neglect, 27*, 525–540.

Hamilton, D. (2012). Saluting a living legend: Maya Angelou. *The Voice*. Retrieved from http://www.voice-online.co.uk/article/saluting-living-legend-maya-angelou

Heger, A., Ticson, L., Velasquez, O., & Bernier, R. (2002). Children referred for possible sexual abuse: Medical findings in 2384 children. *Child Abuse & Neglect, 26*(6), 645–659.

Kenny, M. C. (2004). Teachers' attitudes toward and knowledge of child maltreatment. *Child Abuse & Neglect, 28*, 1311–1319.

Lanning, K. V. (2002). Law enforcement's perspective on the compliant child victim. *APSAC Advisor, 14*(2), 4–9.

Laumann, E. O., Gagnon, J. H., Michael, R. T., & Michaels, S. (1994). *The social organization of sexuality: Sexual practices in the United States*. Chicago, IL: University of Chicago Press.

Leifer, M., Shapiro, J. P., & Kassem, L. (1993). The impact of maternal history and behavior upon foster placement and adjustment in sexually abused girls. *Child Abuse & Neglect, 17*, 755–766.

Lyon, T. D. & Ahern, E. C. (2011). Disclosure of child sexual abuse. In J. E. B. Myers (Ed.), *APSAC handbook on child maltreatment* (3rd ed., pp. 233–252). Thousand Oaks, CA: Sage Publications, Inc.

Lyon, T. D., Ahern, E. C., Malloy, L. C., & Quas, J. A. (2010). Children's reasoning about disclosing adult transgressions: Effects of maltreatment, child age, and adult identity. *Child Development, 81*(6), 1714–1728.

Malloy, L. C., Lyon, T. D., & Quas, J. A. (2007). Filial dependency and recantation of child sexual abuse allegations. *Journal of the American Academy of Child and Adolescent Psychiatry, 46*(2), 162–170.

Myers, J. E. B. (2011). Proving child maltreatment in court. In J. E. B. Myers (Ed.), *APSAC handbook on child maltreatment* (3rd ed., pp. 377–397). Thousand Oaks, CA: Sage Publications, Inc.

National Child Traumatic Stress Network. (n.d.). *Child sexual abuse*. Retrieved from http://www.nctsn.org/trauma-types/sexual-abuse

Paine, M. L., & Hansen, D. J. (2002). Factors influencing children to self-disclose sexual abuse. *Clinical Psychology Review, 22*, 271–295.

Pence, D. M. (2011). Child abuse and neglect investigation. In J. E. B. Myers (Ed.), *APSAC handbook on child maltreatment* (3rd ed., pp. 325–335). Thousand Oaks, CA: Sage Publications, Inc.

Pollio, E., Deblinger, E., & Runyon, M. K. (2011). Mental health treatment for the effects of child sexual abuse. In J. E. B. Myers (Ed.), *APSAC handbook on child maltreatment*, (3rd ed., pp. 215–232). Thousand Oaks, CA: Sage Publications, Inc.

Schaeffer, P., Leventhal, J. M., & Asnes, A. G. (2011). Children's disclosures of sexual abuse: Learning from direct inquiry. *Child Abuse & Neglect, 35*(5), 343–352.

Smith, D. W., Letourneau, E. J., Saunders, B. E., Kilpatrick, D. G., Resnick, H. S., & Best, C. L. (2000). Delay in disclosure of childhood rape: Results from a national survey. *Child Abuse & Neglect, 24,* 273–287.

Snyder, H. N. (2000). *Sexual assault of young children as reported to law enforcement: Victim, incident, and offender characteristics.* Retrieved from https://www.bjs.gov/content/pub/pdf/saycrle.pdf

Townsend, C., & Rheingold, A. A. (2013). *Estimating a child sexual abuse prevalence rate for practitioners: A review of child sexual abuse prevalence studies.* Retrieved from http://www.D2L.org/1in10

Turner, H., Finkelhor, D., & Ormrod, R. (2006). The effect of lifetime victimization on the mental health of children and adolescents. *Social Science & Medicine, 62*(1), 13–27.

U.S. Code: Title 42, Chapter 67, Subchapter I, § 5106g; *Child Abuse Prevention and Treatment Act (CAPTA).* Retrieved from https://www.law.cornell.edu/uscode/text/42/5106g

Van der Kolk, B. (2014). *The body keeps the score.* New York, NY: Penguin Books.

Walsh, W. A., Jones, L. M., Cross, T. P., & Lippert, T. (2010). Prosecuting child sexual abuse. *Crime and Delinquency, 56*(3), 436–454.

CHAPTER 8

Adolescent Suicide

James McCauley and Lawrence (Larry) Berkowitz

Adolescent suicide is heart wrenching and unfathomable. It is hard to imagine a teenager getting into such a dark place that he or she decides there is no way out of the pain and misery other than to die at his or her own hands. The impact of a teen suicide death can be devastating to family, friends, and the community. Loss survivors are often plagued with trying to understand why their loved one did not reach out for help and instead ended their life. They search for what they could have said or done differently to prevent this tragic loss of life. Rhode Island psychologist, author, and educator John Jordan calls this the "tyranny of hindsight" (Jordan & Baugher, 2016, p. 137). Survivors seek a root cause: "He killed himself because he was bullied"; "She killed herself because her boyfriend broke up with her"; "He couldn't tolerate the academic stress and just snapped and killed himself." The search often leads to blaming and scapegoating. Although a particular incident may be the tipping point, adolescent suicide is always more complicated. In most suicide deaths, there are underlying vulnerabilities: examples of those vulnerabilities include depression, anxiety, substance abuse, and struggles with sexual identity.

In this chapter, we will review the prevalence and demographics of adolescent suicide, delineate risk factors and warning signs, identify ways to engage a suicidal adolescent, introduce possible action plans and treatment approaches for helping adolescents struggling with thoughts of suicide, and discuss how best to respond to a community after an adolescent dies by suicide.

Demographics Related to Adolescent Suicide and Related Behaviors

Suicide is the second leading cause of death among those ages 10–24 in the United States (National Vital Statistics System, Centers for Disease Control and Prevention [CDC]). In 2014 (the most recent year of available data), of the 42,773 suicide deaths in the United States, 5,507 were in the 10- to 24-year-old age group: 7 percent were 14 years or younger (CDC, Data & Statistics Fatal Injury Report, 2014). Similar to trends seen in adults, adolescent male suicide rates are triple the rates of females, while the rate of attempts was two times greater for females than males in the 15–19 age range.

According to the Youth Risk Behavior Surveillance Survey (YRBSS), a survey conducted in middle and high schools, 17.7 percent of U.S. high school students said they "seriously considered" suicide. Of the students responding to the YRBSS, 14.6 percent said that they had made a plan for how they might attempt suicide while 8.6 percent of the students indicated they had made a suicide attempt (CDC, 2015). There are marked differences in the demographics of youth suicide by race. While white youth accounted for 84 percent of suicide deaths among youth ages 10–19 in 2014, American Indian/Alaskan Native youth had the highest suicide rates in that age group, 9.34 per 100,000, followed by white youth at 5.93. The rate among Asian American/Pacific Islander youth was 3.14 while the African American youth suicide rate was 3.14, with females having generally lower rates in all categories (CDC, Fatal Injury Reports, n.d.).

Case Example: Anne

Anne is a white, 16-year-old high school junior in a middle-class community with high academic expectations. In the past two months, she has been screened for suicidal ideation and suicidal behaviors three times in the local hospital emergency department. On the first two occasions, she was screened and sent home with a recommendation for follow-up care at the local mental health outpatient clinic. The last time, she was hospitalized for five days after she overdosed on pain pills she found in the family medicine chest.

Although she has a long history of cutting and self-mutilation, upon admission to the hospital, the admitting physician also observed that Anne had very recently carved "DEAD" into her arm with a knife. Anne reports that her cutting, depression, anxiety, and suicidal ideation have increased following the suicide death of her friend, Megan, two months earlier. Anne reports she never really liked school. She struggles academically and "doesn't know how to make friends." She told the hospital staff that she has been thinking about suicide since she was in the second grade. She feels hopeless about ever feeling better and her suicidality is chronic. She states, "One day I will do it for sure." She also posted on Instagram she was closing her account because she was going to kill herself.

In understanding background factors that may contribute to adolescent suicidal ideation and suicidality, it is important to consider Anne's earlier development and trauma history. She was placed in foster care when she was 18 months old after she and her two older siblings were removed from their birth parents who both struggled with substance use disorders. She and her siblings were adopted by her current family when she was 4 years old. Anne reports that she knows her family loves her and wants to help her, but it's "just too late." She states that her family would be better off if she were "out of the picture."

During the previous school year, Anne and Megan had a sexual relationship, but recently Anne described the relationship as "we were just good friends and now I have no friends." Anne feels very disconnected from school but acknowledges that she was part of an active group of students who successfully advocated for a Gay-Straight Alliance at her school. She also loves music and thinks if she ever did feel better, she would like to study music. She feels "invisible" to most of her teachers and classmates except for her art teacher who is "the only one who gets her."

Understanding Adolescent Suicide

Profound developmental changes occur during adolescence. Children gain 50 percent of their adult body weight. Puberty results in rapid physical changes that can feel overwhelming and frightening. Teenagers experience extreme changes in their brain development, and all this occurs as they expand their journey into the adult world. During this time, adolescents become more independent from parents, seek out jobs and careers, enter romantic relationships, and learn how to make friends (McNeely & Blanchard, 2009). Changes in the brain and changes in how the adolescent views the world lead to more self-blame in response to challenging social interactions (Spirito & Esposito-Smythers, 2006). For a teenager struggling with a mental illness, identity issues, or life conflicts, the challenges can feel overwhelming and contribute to the notion that suicide would be a viable solution to the psychic pain they are experiencing.

Anne's history of childhood trauma, her disconnect from school, her suicidal ideation, the cutting behavior, and the death of her close friend to suicide are factors that place Anne at a high risk for suicide. She also has little sense of connectedness to others, feels "invisible," and is convinced that she would not be missed if she were dead.

Anne's pain is "crushing" and the idea of suicide is appealing because she would no longer be in pain. As is true for so many suicidal adolescents, thinking about or attempting suicide may be more of an attempt to escape intense psychological pain rather than a wish to be dead. Many people experience intense physical or psychological pain but imagine the pain will be short-lived or hold hope they can eventually find a solution or make accommodations (Klonsky & May, 2015). But for Anne, it is difficult to imagine a life with connections to others, strong avocational interests, and a worthy career. These factors coupled with Anne's intense pain result in her wish to be dead (Klonsky & May, 2015).

An often-heard myth about suicide is that it is "selfish" or an act of revenge. In fact, the suicidal person, as we see in the case example of Anne, imagines that he or she is a burden on his or her family and friends. Anne states that her family would be better off if she were "out of the picture." Despite knowing they love her and are supportive of her sexual orientation, Anne feels she has caused them undue hardship and her death would be a relief to them. Of course, nothing could be further from the truth. Their hearts would be broken and their grief would likely remain forever.

The Leap from Suicidal Ideation to Attempt

Most adolescents who experience suicidal ideation do not go on to attempt or complete suicide. Humans are biologically "wired" to avoid pain, injury, and death. It takes extraordinary processes to move from thinking about death to enacting a suicide (Klonsky & May, 2015). So how does a person move from thinking about suicide to acting on those thoughts? Thomas Joiner argues that only those suicidal people who have been exposed to intense psychological and/or physical pain have acquired the capability to kill themselves (Joiner, 2010). Adolescents such as Anne who have been exposed to the trauma of early loss and neglect, nonsuicidal self-injury such as cutting and self-mutilation, and loss of a friend to suicide and who are experiencing intense psychological pain find it easier to follow through and attempt suicide.

Risk and Protective Factors

Anne's case highlights some of the risk and protective factors related to suicide that we consider when working with adolescents and young adults. In general, there is a long list of risk factors associated with suicide that include demographics, personality characteristics, and other factors that have been shown to have correlations with suicide. On the other hand, activities and characteristics that promote suicide prevention and enhance resilience are called "protective factors."

Suicidal behavior results from a "perfect storm" or confluence of factors rather than a single factor. It is the cumulative effect of risk factors and lack of protective factors that explain an increased risk of suicidal thoughts (Orpinas & Horne, 2015). Moreover, in the same way that risk factors for heart disease (smoking, genetics, etc.) do not mean a cardiac event is imminent, risk factors for suicide do not necessarily mean that a suicide is pending. Many youth will have a combination of these factors but never consider suicide. It does, however, suggest that we must be watchful and consider screening youth who have some of these factors. We will identify some of the risk and protective factors specific to adolescents in order to provide more understanding of Anne's situation.

Childhood trauma is a particularly important factor to consider related to suicide risk and youth. Most notable are the findings of a study on adverse childhood experiences—research known in the field as the "ACEs" study (see Chapter 3 in this volume for detailed information). The ACEs studies found consistent, strong associations between early adverse events and later health complications that could lead to early death. One of the health risks was a suicide attempt, with the risk of suicide attempt increasing from 2- to 5-fold for any one of the adverse childhood experiences. For every increase by one of an ACE score, the risk of a suicide attempt increased by 60 percent, and if there were four or more adverse experiences in childhood, an individual was 12.4 times more likely to attempt suicide than was someone who had no adverse childhood experiences (Felitti et al., 1998). An ACE score of 7 increased suicide risk for those under age 18 by 51-fold. According to an analysis by Dube et al. (2001), suicides in childhood or adolescence would be reduced by 80 percent if there were no exposure to those early events. "Estimates of adjusted risk factors are of a magnitude that is rarely observed in epidemiology and public health data" (Dube et al., 2001, p. 2,095).

Another risk for suicide in adolescence is minority sexual identity status (CDC, 2015). Forty-three percent of youth who identify as gay, lesbian, or bisexual or report they were "not sure" of their sexual identity report that they thought of, planned, or attempted suicide as compared to 15 percent of high school youth who identify as heterosexual/ straight.

The Suicide Prevention Resource Center has concluded that "the elevated risk of suicide attempts among LGB adolescents is a consequence of the psychosocial stressors associated with being lesbian, gay, or bisexual, including gender nonconformity, victimization, lack of support, dropping out of school, family problems, suicide attempts by acquaintances, homelessness, substance abuse, and psychiatric disorders. While heterosexual adolescents also experience these stressors, they are more prevalent among LGB adolescents" (Suicide Prevention Resource Center, 2008, p. 20). While LGB youth, in general, appear to be at higher risk of suicide, some are even more so, that is, those who have run away, are homeless, and are in foster care or juvenile justice systems. Similarly, a report by the Gay Lesbian and Straight Education Network (GLSEN) noted that 76 percent of transgender students and 53 percent of LGB youth report feeling unsafe at school. A review of the nascent literature on gender identity/expression and suicidal thoughts and behaviors has varied outcomes, finding ranges from 38 to 83 percent of transgender individuals (youth and adults) reporting suicidal ideation and up to one-third reporting having made a suicide attempt (and often, multiple attempts; Testa & Hendricks, 2015). For Anne, while her experience of having a sexual relationship with a same-sex friend is not of itself what causes increased risk, the associated issues such as internalized oppression, stigma, minority status stress, and potential for victimization may increase risk. Counter to the risk factors, Anne's advocacy for a Gay-Straight Alliance in her school and having parents who support her sexual identity may mitigate the risk of suicidal behavior.

Bullying is another risk factor that has received much attention in the media. Many people may not know that risk for suicidal behaviors is found not only among victims of bullying but also among perpetrators of bullying, as well as for individuals where there is a mixed experience—both victim and bully. Twenty to 30 percent of youth are involved in bullying in some capacity, and cyberbullying rates vary by reports from 10 to 35 percent for those who are victims and 5–20 percent for those who are perpetrators (Holt, 2015). Nickerson and Torchia (2015) reviewed increasing evidence that bullying others is associated with depression, thoughts of suicide, and suicide attempts. The highest rates of suicidal behavior associated with bullying were found in bully victims, with suicidal ideation reported by 60 percent of the bully victims and suicidal behaviors reported by 44 percent (Espelage & Holt, 2013).

A recent, robust meta-analysis of research on the topic of the relationship between substance use disorders and suicidal behavior in adolescents confirms a strong association between substance use and suicide (Pompili et al., 2012). Among the findings highlighted in this analysis, it was reported that there is a threefold increase in the risk of repeat suicide attempts in adolescents who have a diagnosis of alcohol abuse and a fourfold increased risk of a repeat attempt in the 12 months following a suicide attempt among adolescents with a diagnosis of illicit drug abuse. Adolescents who die by suicide and those who make attempts show increased rates of alcohol use and intoxication at the time of the attempt. As with other risk factors, it is difficult to determine to what degree alcohol contributes to increased risk and how much it is related to co-occurring risk factors typically associated with alcohol and drug use, such as increased stress, legal and discipline problems, conflict, trauma, and depression. Fortunately, Anne did not report a history of substance use; however, it would be important to inquire further about this issue when meeting with her.

Several mental health diagnoses are associated with suicide. When interviewed about her thoughts of suicide, Anne clearly described experiences of depression and anxiety. Depression is often identified as the leading behavioral health condition associated with suicide. The 2015 National Survey on Drug Use and Health (National Institute on Mental Health, 2015) estimates that 12.5 percent of adolescents ages 12–17 in the United States had at least one major depressive episode in the preceding year, while the 2015 YRBSS of high school students found 30 percent of students supported a statement indicating they had "felt so sad or hopeless for 2+ weeks that they stopped doing some usual activity"—one of the criteria for major depression. Indeed, most studies find an association between depression and other affective disorders (e.g., anxiety) and suicide.

In their research specific to adolescents and suicide, Matthew Nock and his team identified several conditions, such as attention deficit hyperactivity disorder, conduct disorders, eating disorders, and intermittent explosive disorder, as conditions that predict which adolescents who have thoughts of suicide may go on to make an attempt (Nock et al., 2013). This is consistent with data from a large-scale study of adults in the United States that found that depression predicts thoughts of suicide but does not adequately predict those who will go on to attempt suicide. Conditions that are characterized by anxiety, agitation, and problems in impulse control (substance use disorders, bipolar disorder, etc.) predict those individuals who may go on to make an attempt (Nock, Hwang, Sampson, & Kessler, 2010).

The Nock study found that one-third of those 18 and younger who died of suicide had a crisis on the same day as their death. As people aged beyond adolescence, they were less likely to have experienced a crisis on the same day as their death. For an adolescent such as Anne who has numerous risk factors, we need to pay particular attention to a stressor or crisis that occurs, (e.g., a relationship breakup, fight with friends or parents, school suspension) and check with her to see if the crisis may have triggered an increase in thoughts of or plans for suicide.

Anne's exposure to the suicide loss of a significant friend elevated her risk of suicide. The issues of exposure and "contagion" have captured the attention of many who study suicide and adolescents. Some of the evidence for this notion of contagion, that one suicide influences a subsequent suicide, comes from studies of the effects of reports of suicide in media on suicide rates. There is significant statistical evidence that both stories about suicide in the mass media and fictional accounts increase rates of suicide, especially among younger, vulnerable individuals (Gould, Jamieson, & Romer, 2003). Similarly, exposure to the suicide death of a peer is thought to account for a small percentage (2–5%) of adolescent suicide deaths (Gould, Wallenstein, & Kleinman, 1990). A large-scale report from Canada demonstrated that adolescents who are exposed to a death by suicide experience elevated risk of suicidal ideation and behaviors up to two years after the death of a peer (Swanson & Coleman, 2013). Other data have shown that adolescents who had a friend or family member who had attempted suicide were three times more likely to make an attempt than adolescents who did not know someone who had made an attempt (Cutler, Glaeser, & Norberg, 2001). The concept of behavioral contagion has been explained in several ways. One possible mechanism is the result of social modeling (de Leo & Heller, 2008; Insel & Gould, 2008)—where the behavior of one person influences another, vulnerable individual. Alternately, it may be the result of extreme empathy (Pompili, 2015), where an individual blurs the lines between self and other and imagines doing the same thing that another has done. We have heard adolescents or family members describe ruminative thinking about the suicide of a friend or family member, where the person imagines, often in vivid detail, the emotional state and physical actions of the person who died, thus continually reexposing himself or herself to traumatic details of the death. Others refer to the concept that people with similar characteristics tend to cluster together or affiliate with one another; thus, there may be a greater likelihood of adverse behaviors within a group (Cheng, Li, & Caine, 2014; Joiner, 2003). The possibility must be considered that a combination of Anne's previous attempts and her friend's recent death by suicide might have reinforced for her that suicide was a compelling "tool" in her "toolbox" of problem-solving strategies.

As with all areas of psychological functioning, understanding the role of race, culture, and ethnicity is essential to understanding risk and protective factors related to suicidality. At the beginning of this chapter, we mentioned racial and cultural differences in suicide rates. Numbers alone cannot tell a full story about racial and ethnic differences. In their comprehensive article on culture related to youth and suicide attempts and deaths, Goldston et al. (2008) identify multiple, overarching areas to understanding prevention and treatment issues in a cultural context. Areas to consider include the acculturation process, the role of the family, understanding collectivism versus individualism, cultural mistrust of mental health systems and associated stigma that may lead to avoidance of help seeking, religion and spirituality, and different manifestations of distress.

As we weigh factors that contribute to and mitigate risk of suicide, it is important to attend to the contribution of protective factors for adolescents. Unfortunately, protective factors have not been studied as extensively as have risk factors, but we know that having a sense of connectedness with peers, family, community, and social institutions may be the most important protective factor for a struggling adolescent (U.S. Department of Health and Human Services, 2012). Moreover, availability of health and mental health services in a community contributes to protective factors as does ensuring continuity of care for a young person who is in crisis. Schools that create a climate where vulnerable teens feel safe, supported, and valued and where counselors and human service professionals help adolescents improve problem-solving skills, build friendships, increase their competence in the academic and social arena, and become more fully engaged in school and community activities are all strong protective factors (Miller, 2011). Moral and religious objections to suicide also tend to protect against suicide (U.S. Department of Health and Human Services, 2012). Included among the protective factors is a list of items that comes from the "Reasons for Living Inventory" (Linehan, Goodstein, Nielsen, & Chiles, 1983) and adapted for use with adolescents in the Brief Reasons for Living Inventory for Adolescents (Osman et al., 1996). This inventory includes the following items: a sense of responsibility to family, fear of suicide, moral objections, fear of social disapproval, and having a belief in being able to work out problems. These are all important factors when considering risk specific to an individual as well as when constructing more broad-based prevention programs and treatment planning.

Warning Signs of Adolescent Suicide and Communication of Intent

When describing risk factors, we used the analogy of understanding risk factors for heart disease—those factors that potentially increase the likelihood of an adverse event occurring. We may think of warning signs of suicide in the same way. Warning signs of a heart attack (chest pain, shortness of breath, etc.) portend an event may be imminent. The three warning signs foretelling the highest possibility of a suicide attempt include suicidal communication, preparing and/or rehearsing a plan, and seeking access to/recent use of lethal means (Department of Veteran Affairs and the Department of Defense, 2013). Anne's actions are chilling examples of these warning signs: she has stated "One day I will do it for sure"; she has closed her Instagram account because she was "planning to kill myself"; and she recently accumulated and swallowed a large number of pills.

Box 8.1 Suicide Warning Signs and Risk Factors for Youth

The American Association of Suicidology has compiled a list of signs of potential suicide crises in adolescents:

1. Feelings of hopelessness
2. Anxiety, agitation, trouble sleeping, or sleeping all the time
3. Expressions of having no reason for living; no sense of purpose in life
4. Feelings of being trapped—no way out
5. Withdrawal from friends, family, and community
6. Rage, uncontrolled anger, expressions of wanting or seeking revenge
7. Reckless behavior or more risky activities, seemingly without thinking
8. Dramatic mood changes
9. Giving away prized possessions

(American Association of Suicidology, n.d.)

Studies indicate that 50–70 percent of people communicate intent prior to making a suicide attempt or dying by suicide (Coombs, Miller, Herlihy, Lee, & Morrison, 1992; Robins, Seymour, Kayes, Wilkinson, & Murphy, 1959). Their communication may be as direct as Anne's: "I have been thinking about suicide since I was in the second grade," or the communication may be coded or behavioral rather than a direct threat, for example, Anne carving "DEAD" into her arm.

Talking with the Suicidal Adolescent

Anne reports that her prior experiences with therapy have been "worthless." She says her first therapist "tried too hard to cheer her up" and her second therapist "got scared" when she was honest about how she really felt and sent her to the hospital.

It is not uncommon for mental health clinicians and others in the helping professions to acknowledge their fear of working with a suicidal adolescent (Joiner, Van Orden, Witte, & Rudd, 2009). A professional who is not aware of and able to manage his or her emotional reactions to being with a teen in the middle of an acute crisis could indirectly or directly convey that he or she doesn't want to hear how much pain the adolescent is experiencing or that suicide is on his or her mind. When it comes to interacting with adults, adolescents have "radar for authenticity" and will get the message or see the body language of the adult that conveys they shouldn't talk about their pain and suicidal thinking.

Teens are afraid that adults will overreact and worry that they will end up in the hospital or transferred out of school. The adult's goal may be to prevent a death and not get blamed while the adolescent's goal is just to find a way to eliminate his or her intense psychological pain (Jobes & Ballard, 2011). This discrepancy may result in the adolescent feeling that adults are not at all helpful and in this vulnerable state they are likely to withdraw and keep their inner thoughts private (Michel et al., n.d.).

In order to engage a skeptical and desperate adolescent like Anne, a supportive adult will need to manage her or his own anxiety and understand that the adolescent may be engaging in these harmful behaviors because they "make sense" and they function as a coping strategy.

Adults who are comfortable with a suicidal adolescent will be able to ask directly about suicide: "Are you thinking of killing yourself?" or, "Have you thought about suicide?" As a first step it may be okay to ask about suicide indirectly: "Do you wish you were dead?"; "Do you think about hurting yourself?" but we always want to make sure there is no confusion, so following up and asking directly about suicide is an important part of the conversation.

Suicidal ideation and behaviors are often fluid states and may subside or increase over time; therefore, it is important to ask again when there are any changes or transitions. Such changes might include increases in suicidal behaviors, changes in treatment or medicines, discharge from the hospital, changes in milieu status, or upcoming vacations.

A common myth about suicide is that asking an adolescent if he or she is thinking about suicide may plant the idea of suicide. On the contrary, most adolescents who are asked answer honestly and are relieved that someone finally understands how much pain they are experiencing.

Supporting an Adolescent in a Suicidal Crisis

Adolescents who are considering suicide often describe feeling overwhelmed and experiencing "tunnel vision"; they can't think of any way out of their painful situation other than to kill themselves. The task for professional school staff and family members is to help the young person manage the crisis and stabilize his or her situation until they can focus on long-term solutions.

Safety Planning

Hospital emergency rooms and crisis teams have traditionally asked suicidal clients to sign a contract after their initial assessment was complete stating that they would not kill themselves. In most cases, this is not helpful to the adolescent in crisis and does not afford the mental health clinician or hospital any legal protection. There is no research evidence these contracts work and they often provide a false sense of security. A "no suicide contract" only asks the adolescent to stay alive without providing support or strategies about how to remain safe (Stanley & Brown, 2012).

One of the most effective tools for helping an adolescent manage his or her suicidal crisis is a comprehensive and collaborative safety plan (Brown, Wenzel, & Rudd, 2011; Stanley & Brown, 2012). A safety plan is a hierarchically arranged list of coping strategies for use during the suicidal crisis or when suicidal urges are prominent. It is a brief, easy-to-read document developed jointly by the adolescent and the mental health clinician, school staff, or other members of a support team. Ideally, it will be written in the adolescent's own words and perhaps even in his or her own handwriting. Using this hierarchical safety plan to support Anne in her current suicidal crisis might look similar to this:

A safety plan for Anne

1. **Recognize the warning signs that a suicidal crisis is imminent**: "When I start to cut"; "I start thinking about joining Megan"; "I oversleep and miss school."

2. **Coping strategies that I can use by myself**: "Taking a hot shower"; "Going for a walk"; "Using the Virtual Hope Box App on my phone"; "Listening to and playing music."
3. **People I can socialize with**: "The kids in the Gay Straight Alliance"; "My brother, Keith"; "Play music together with Jody."
4. **People who can support me**: "My Mom and Dad"; "My art teacher"; "My friend, Mike, from my hospital therapy group"; "TrevorSpace" (a social networking site for GLBTQ youth at www.trevorspace.org).
5. **Professionals who can support me**: "My therapist" (add phone number); "My psychiatrist" (add phone number); "the Emergency Services Team" (with phone number); "the National Suicide Prevention Hotline: 1–800–273-TALK"; "the Trevor Lifeline—866–488–7386, www.thetrevorproject.org."
6. **Removing any lethal means**: There are no guns in the house. "I will ask my mom to hold my medicines and give them to me once a day."

With a safety plan that is now jointly developed and in Anne's own words, her clinician and Anne must have a conversation about what barriers might keep her from using the plan. Where will she keep it so it's always visible? Does it make sense to take a picture of the plan and keep it on her phone? When changes occur in Anne's life, it will be important to update the plan to reflect her new situation. It is extremely helpful that Anne has included her family in her safety plan as they can play a key role in supporting her through this crisis and can be a valuable resource to Anne's treatment team.

Treatment

Effective treatment begins with the premise that a person considering suicide is trying to solve a problem of intense, psychological pain. While any approach must begin with establishing safety, it should also focus on efforts to help the adolescent decrease and/or tolerate the intense pain they experience. One framework for treatment that we find useful is articulated by Biglan, Flay, Embry, and Sandler (2012) who identify three overarching actions in keeping adolescents safe and increasing their hopefulness:

1. Minimize toxic conditions, whether biological, interpersonal, or ecological.
2. Teach the adolescent skills that will increase their empathy and concern for the welfare of others.

3. Promote psychological flexibility, which includes adapting to changing circumstances, developing problem-solving skills, promoting executive functions, and being more mindful.

Following these principles with Anne might lead us to question what is going on in her school or home environment that is making life more challenging. Is she being bullied because of her sexual orientation? Is she being adequately treated for her underlying depression or anxiety (decreasing toxic influences)? Can we encourage her to build on her advocacy with the Gay-Straight Alliance at school? Turn her grief and sadness at losing a friend by suicide into advocacy for suicide prevention (prosociality)? Can we help her learn mindfulness skills and distress tolerance skills to withstand emotional storms rather than resorting to cutting or planning suicide (psychological flexibility)?

We noted earlier the importance of demonstrating empathy and a sincere desire to partner with the young person in trying to ameliorate the problems they experience (Michel & Jobes, 2011). This same approach guides effective treatment as we consider the adolescent the expert in understanding his or her experience and he or she must be given the opportunity to explain the narrative of his or her experience. The adult's role is to listen with empathy and curiosity and to work collaboratively with the teen to find ways to relieve the pain, develop strategies for effectively coping with harmful thoughts, and then build a life worth living. This is an essential approach to working with someone like Anne.

Another approach that provides a helpful framework for conducting treatment with a person experiencing suicidal thoughts and behaviors is the Collaborative Assessment and Management of Suicide (CAMS; Jobes, 2016). CAMS establishes that once suicidal thoughts and behaviors are present, they must become the primary focus of treatment. Assessment and treatment are structured and problem focused, where the clinician and teen collaborate to find ways of managing thoughts and plans for suicide in ways that should decrease risk. The adolescent is then able to work with the clinician to better react to the issues that led to their crisis. The CAMS approach is described as having features that are "promising practices" in the U.S. National Registry of Evidence-Based Practices and Programs.

There are several additional approaches to treatment that have solid evidence of effectiveness. Cognitive behavior therapy (CBT) is a general category of psychotherapy that is frequently applied to those with suicidal thoughts and behaviors (Rudd, Joiner, & Rajab, 2001). CBT is based on the premise that our thoughts cause our feelings and behaviors. It is an educational model where people unlearn their unwanted reactions. CBT interventions often include tools and strategies such as use of a Hope Kit/box or the smartphone application listed in Anne's safety plan, called "Virtual Hopebox." "Coping cards," relapse prevention strategies, and guided imagery might also be incorporated into CBT treatment. A specific, highly structured CBT program called Cognitive Therapy for Suicidal Patients (Wenzel, Brown, & Beck, 2009) has also demonstrated good outcomes.

An extension of CBT, dialectical behavioral therapy (DBT), helps people diagnosed with borderline personality disorder learn to manage emotional distress and to manage suicidal crises. This complex and multifaceted treatment has been used successfully with people having a wide range of diagnoses and specifically with adolescents (Miller, A. L., Rathus, & Linehan, 2007).

Other therapies that have evidence for their effectiveness include attachment-based family therapy (Diamond, Diamond, & Levy, 2014), motivational interviewing (Miller, W. R. & Rollnick, 2012), which was first developed as a tool for helping people with substance use disorders make changes, and Multisystemic Therapy with Psychiatric Supports (MST-Psychiatric; National Registry of Evidence Based Programs, n.d.). MST, which is applied in the home, school, or community service settings, was found to decrease repeat suicide attempts.

Pharmacotherapy may play an important role in treating someone who is thinking about, planned, or has attempted suicide, by treating an underlying disorder. In fact, medication treatment along with some form of psychotherapy is often the recommended treatment approach. Antidepressant medications known as SSRIs (Selective Serotonin Reuptake Inhibitors) are often frontline medications for treating underlying depression and/or anxiety disorders. Lithium has been particularly effective in reducing risk for those with bipolar disorder (Baldessarini et al., 2006), and Clozapine has demonstrated positive outcomes related to suicide for those individuals who have schizophrenia and may be at high risk (Hennen & Baldessarini, 2005).

Postvention: Providing Support and Stability in the Aftermath of an Adolescent Suicide Death

The impact of adolescent suicide deaths has far-reaching consequences. On average 60–80 people report being intimately and directly impacted by a teen's suicide death (Berman, 2011). Grieving friends and classmates are at significant risk for developing depression, posttraumatic stress disorder, and suicidal ideation. As noted earlier, in the 15- to 24-year-old age group, there is worry about the possibility of suicide contagion, what people generally think of when they talk about "copycat" suicides (Gould et al., 1990). A teen suicide death can cause the school environment to feel unstable and diminish learning. Friends and family members of those impacted by a suicide death typically experience intense emotional reactions.

The behavioral health services provided in the immediate aftermath of a suicide death in a school, agency, or community are referred to as suicide postvention. The primary goals of suicide postvention in a school setting are to (1) facilitate healthy grieving; (2) stabilize the school environment so students can get back to learning and teachers can get back to teaching and; (3) reduce the likelihood of contagion (Underwood & Dunne-Maxim, 1997). Acknowledging and commemorating a student's death by suicide is a difficult balancing act. A student's suicide death should be recognized but not glorified. The response from the school leadership should include a narrative for supporting all students and provide the necessary resources for students who are grieving and/or at risk. As we referenced in the introduction, after a suicide death, everyone impacted searches for the reason why their friend/loved one died. The weeks and months following the suicide death become a "teachable moment" (Berkowitz, McCauley, Schuurman, & Jordan, 2010), and suicide loss survivors of all ages are open and interested in learning about suicide and how additional deaths can be prevented.

Bereavement after suicide loss can be a traumatic event. While it was noted earlier that trauma could be a risk factor for suicide, experiencing the suicide loss of a friend or family member may also be experienced as traumatic. Grief following suicide is similar to the distress of death following other traumatic events such as auto accidents and homicides and typically causes far more distress than natural causes of death (Jordan & McIntosh, 2011). Those impacted may have been exposed to the scene of the death, or they may have heard vivid details of death. For this reason, the reactions friends and families experience often mirror the global reactions we see after any traumatic event.

Shame, stigma, and blame often follow suicide grief. In one community we supported after four adolescents died by suicide in an 18-month period, shame and blame rocked the community and parents were terrified their child might be the next to die. Comments included students saying "This school is cursed" and "I can't wait to get out of this hell hole." One community leader announced, "This town needs to stop killing kids." The shame residents felt was palpable: "I go out of my way to avoid telling people where I am from." Ultimately, this very courageous community took responsibility for building a powerful and comprehensive suicide prevention coalition that built protective factors and reduced community risk factors so the stigma for depression, suicide, and help seeking was greatly reduced. Simultaneously, access to mental health services was greatly increased. The local high school began a transformation into a safe and supportive environment, an effort collaboratively generated by students, staff, and community members.

A narrative of hope and healing. Messages that underplay the complicated nature of suicide, such as "he killed himself because of a bad break-up," can convey a narrative to teens that if something goes wrong in life, they can always consider suicide as an option. One of the major tasks for schools and communities after a suicide death is to shape the narrative to a message of hope and healing. It is important for adults to reassure teens at risk that suicidal feelings are temporary, that connections to others and treatment lead to feeling better, and that asking for help is a sign of strength, not weakness. Students as well as teachers should learn risk factors and warning signs of suicide and know that talk of suicide, whether in person or online, should always be taken seriously. Any student in pain should have access to high-quality mental health resources in school and in the community and be in an environment where no one must suffer alone. And schools, media, and communities should routinely provide examples of individuals who have learned to manage life's challenges and who have gone on to live meaningful lives.

Communities can play a major role in reducing the risks of adolescent suicide by removing barriers to health and mental health services and by campaigning to reduce the stigma of mental illness, suicide, and help-seeking behavior. The movements to promote safe, supportive, trauma-sensitive schools are upstream prevention approaches that can build prosociality and social cohesion for all students regardless of race, ethnicity, religion, sexual orientation, or disability. Such a comprehensive approach would go a long way to not just reducing the likelihood of adolescent suicide but to addressing other social ills as well.

Conclusion: "Holding the Hope" for Anne

Anne's recovery will be a long, arduous journey. Her early childhood trauma and chronic history of depression and suicidal behaviors have contributed to her sense of despair and isolation. A collaborative safety plan should stabilize Anne until she can engage in a trusting relationship with a counselor who can listen to her full story. She will need a supportive network of family, friends, and teachers. It is hopeful that Anne has a supportive family that accepts her sexuality, has a supportive school with a Gay-Straight Alliance, and has a passion for music. Individual and family treatment will help her learn strategies to manage emotional distress, find ways to build a life she feels is meaningful and worth living, and find peers and adults with whom she can feel connected and valued. Most people who survive a suicide attempt go on to live a full life (Harvard, T.H. Chan School of Public Health, n.d.; Miller, M., Lippmann, Azrael, & Hemenway, 2007), and an increasing number of those attempt survivors find meaning in becoming an important part of the suicide prevention community by sharing their personal stories of hope and healing. Together, family, school, mental health professionals, and supportive peers become a powerful team in helping Anne develop a narrative of hope for a positive future.

It is our hope that by understanding the perplexing and painful phenomenon of adolescent suicide, we can provide timely and effective interventions, reduce the stigma, and make it easier for caring adults to support the adolescent who is looking to escape his or her overwhelming emotional pain by ending his or her own life. Although there are many risk factors prominent in adolescent suicide, the increased risk associated with childhood trauma is particularly noteworthy. The preponderance of evidence for children who have been abused or neglected being at high risk is inflamed by their habituation to pain, making it easier for a desperate adolescent to make the leap from thinking about suicide to following through with a suicide attempt. But regardless of the risk factors or combination of risk factors, adolescent suicide is always complicated.

There is still much that we do not know about suicidal behavior, particularly what combination of risk factors will predict who will go on to make a suicide attempt (Nock, Borges, & Ono, 2012). We also need increased knowledge about why the exposure of an adolescent to the suicide of someone they know increases the risk of depression, PTSD, or suicide attempts. There is an urgent need for research that can tell us how we may become better at combining risk factors in a way that predicts those at highest risk. We also need research to help us develop new, objective measures of risk and what leads young people to move from thoughts about suicide to action (Glenn & Nock, 2014). What we do know is that an adolescent in crisis will benefit from a supportive adult who will listen, without judgment, in an environment that is safe and inclusive with treatment that is collaborative and authentically hopeful.

References

American Association of Suicidology. (n.d.). *Warning signs and risk factors*. Retrieved from http://www.suicidology.org/ncpys/warning-signs-risk-factors

Baldessarini, R.J., Tondo, L., Davis, P., Pompili, M., Goodwin, F.K., & Hennen, J. (2006). Decreased risk of suicides and attempts during long-term lithium treatment: A meta-analytic review. *Bipolar Disorders, 8*, 625–639. doi:10.1111/j.1399–5618.2006.00344.x

Berkowitz, L., McCauley, J., Schuurman, D.L. & Jordan, J.R. (2011). Organizational postvention after suicide death. In J.R. Jordan & J.L. McIntosh (Eds.), *Grief after suicide: Understanding the consequences and caring for the survivors* (pp. 157–178). New York, NY: Routledge (Taylor & Francis Group).

Berman, A. (2011). Estimating the population of survivors of suicide: Seeking an evidence base. *Suicide and Life-Threatening Behavior, 41*(1), 110–116.

Biglan, A., Flay, B., Embry, D., & Sandler, I. (2012). The critical role of nurturing environments for promoting human well-being. *American Psychologist, 67*(4), 257–271. doi:10.1037/a0026796

Brown, G., Wenzel, A., & Rudd, D. (2011). Cognitive therapy for suicidal patients. In K. Michel & D. Jobes (Eds.), *Building a therapeutic alliance with the suicidal patient* (pp. 273–291). Washington, DC: American Psychological Association.

Centers for Disease Control and Prevention (CDC) (n.d.). *Fatal Injury Reports, National, Regional and State, 1981–2016*. Retrieved from https://webappa.cdc.gov/sasweb/ncipc/mortrate.html

Centers for Disease Control and Prevention (CDC). (2014). *Data & statistics fatal injury report for 2014*. Retrieved from https://webappa.cdc.gov/sasweb/ncipc/mortrate10_us.html

Centers for Disease Control. (2015). *Youth Risk Behavior Surveillance System (YRBSS)*. Retrieved from www.cdc.gov/HealthyYouth/yrbs/index.htm

Cheng, Q., Li, H., & Caine, E.D. (2014). Suicide contagion: A systematic review of definitions and research utility. *PLoS ONE, 9*(9), e108724. http://dx.doi.org/10.1371/journal.pone.0108724

Coombs, D.W., Miller, H.L., Herlihy, C., Lee, J.M., & Morrison, D.P. (1992). Presuicide attempt communications between parasuicides and consulted caregivers. *Suicide and Life Threatening Behaviors, 22*(3), 289–302.

Cutler, D.M., Glaeser, E.L., & Norberg, K.E. (2001). Explaining the rise in youth suicide. In J. Gruber (Ed.), *Risky behavior among youths: An economic analysis* (pp. 219–270). Chicago, IL: University of Chicago Press.

de Leo, D., & Heller, T. (2008). Social modeling in the transmission of suicidality. *Crisis: International Journal of Crisis Intervention and Suicide Prevention, 29*, 11–19.

Department of Veteran Affairs and the Department of Defense (VA/ DoD). (2013). *Clinical practice guidelines for assessment and management of patients at risk for suicide*. Washington, DC: Veterans Health Administration.

Diamond, G.S., Diamond, G.M., & Levy, S.A. (2014). *Attachment-based family therapy for depressed adolescents*. Washington, DC: American Psychological Association.

Dube, S. R., Anda, R. F., Felitit, V. J., Chapman, P., Williamson, D. F., & Giles, W. H. (2001). Childhood abuse, household dysfunction and the risk of attempted suicide throughout the lifespan: Findings from the Adverse Childhood Experiences Study. *Journal of the American Medical Association, 286*(24), 3089–3096.

Espelage, D. L., & Holt, M. K. (2013). Suicidal ideation and school bullying experiences after controlling for depression and delinquency. *Journal of Adolescent Health, 53*(1), S27–S31.

Felitti, V. J., Anda, R. F., Nordenberg, D., Williamson, D. F., Spitz, A. M., Edwards, V., . . . Marks, J. S. (1998). Relationship of childhood abuse and household dysfunction to many of the leading causes of death in adults: The Adverse Childhood Experiences (ACE) Study. *American Journal of Preventive Medicine, 14*(4), 245–258.

Glenn, C. & Nock, M. (2014). Improving the short-term prediction of suicidal behavior. *American Journal of Preventive Medicine, 47*, 176–180.

Goldston, D. B., Molock, S. D., Whitbeck, L. B., Murakami, J. L., Zayas, L. H., & Hall, G. C. N. (2008). Cultural considerations in adolescent suicide prevention and psychosocial treatment. *American Psychologist, 63*(1), 14–31.

Gould, M., Jamieson, P., & Romer, E. (2003). Media contagion and suicide among the young. *The American Behavioral Scientist, 46*(9), 1269–1284.

Gould, M., Wallenstein, S., & Kleinman, M. (1990). Time-space clustering of teenage suicide. *American Journal of Epidemiology, 131*(1), 71–78.

Harvard, T. H. Chan School of Public Health. (n.d.). *Attempters longterm survival.* Retrieved from www.hsph.harvard.edu/means-matter/means-matter/survival/

Hennen, J., & Baldessarini, R. J. (2005). Suicidal risk during treatment with clozapine: A meta-analysis. *Schizophrenia Research, 73*, 139–145.

Holt, M. K. (2015). Suicidal risk as a function of bullying and other victimization exposures. In P. Goldbulm, D. L. Espelage, J. Chu, & B. Bongar (Eds.), *Youth suicide and bullying: Challenges and strategies for prevention and intervention* (pp. 31–38). Oxford, England: Oxford University Press.

Insel, B. J., & Gould, M. S. (2008). Impact of modeling on adolescent suicidal behavior. *Psychiatric Clinics of North America, 31*, 293–316.

Jobes, D. (2016). *Managing suicidal risk: A collaborative approach.* New York, NY: The Guilford Press.

Jobes, D., & Ballard, E. (2011). The therapist and the suicidal patient. In K. Michel & D. A. Jobes (Eds.), *Building a therapeutic alliance with the suicidal patient* (pp. 51–61). Washington, DC: American Psychological Association.

Joiner, T. E. (2003). Contagion of suicidal symptoms as a function of assortative relating and shared relationship stress in college roommates. *Journal of Adolescence, 26*, 495–504. doi:10.1016/s0140–1971(02)00133–1.

Joiner, T. E. (2010). *Myths about suicide.* Cambridge, MA: Harvard University Press.

Joiner, T., Van Orden, K., Witte, T., & Rudd, D. (2009). *The interpersonal theory of suicide: Guidance for working with suicidal clients.* Washington, DC: American Psychological Association.

Jordan, J.R., & Baugher, R. (2016). *After suicide loss: Coping with your grief* (2nd ed.). Newcastle, WA: Robert Baugher.

Jordan, J.L. & McIntosh, J.L. (2011). Is suicide bereavement different? A framework for re-thinking the question. In J.R. Jordan & J.L. McIntosh (Eds.), *Grief after suicide: Understanding the consequences and caring for the survivors* (pp. 19–42). New York, NY: Routledge (Taylor & Francis Group).

Klonsky, D.E., & May, A.M. (2015). The three-step theory (3ST): A new theory of suicide rooted in the "Ideation-to-action" framework. *International Journal of Cognitive Therapy, 8*(2), 114–129.

Linehan, M.M., Goodstein, J. L., Nielsen, S. L., & Chiles, John A. (1983). Reasons for staying alive when you are thinking of killing yourself: The reasons for living inventory. *Journal of Consulting and Clinical Psychology, 51*(2), 276–286.

McNeely, C., & Blanchard, J. (2009). *The teen years explained: A guide to healthy adolescent development*. Baltimore, MD: Center for Adolescent Health, Johns Hopkins Bloomberg School of Public Health.

Michel, K., & Jobes, D. (Eds.). (2011). *Building a therapeutic alliance with the suicidal patient*. Washington, DC: American Psychological Association.

Michel, K., Jobes, D., Leenaars, A.A., Maltsberger, J.T., Dey, P., Valach, L., & Young, R. (n.d.). *Meeting the suicidal person*. Retrieved from http://www.aeschiconference.unibe.ch/pdf/Guidelines.pdf

Miller, D. (2011). *Child and adolescent suicidal behavior: School-based prevention, assessment, and intervention*. New York, NY: The Guilford Press.

Miller, A.L., Rathus, J.H., & Linehan, M.M. (2007). *Dialectical behavior therapy with suicidal adolescents*. New York, NY: Guilford Press.

Miller, M., Lippmann, S.J., Azrael, D., & Hemenway, D. (2007). Household firearm ownership and rates of suicide across the 50 U.S. states. *Journal of Trauma, 61*, 1029–1035.

Miller, W.R., & Rollnick, S. (2012). *Motivational interviewing: Helping people change* (3rd ed.). New York, NY: The Guilford Press.

National Institute on Mental Health. (2015). *National Survey on Drug Use and Health (NSDUH)*. Retrieved from https://www.nimh.nih.gov/health/statistics/prevalence/major-depression-among-adolescents.shtml

National Registry of Evidence Based Practices. (n.d.). *Multisystemic therapy with psychiatric supports*. Retrieved from http://legacy.nreppadmin.net/ViewIntervention.aspx?id=17

Nickerson, A.B., & Torchia, T.O. (2015). Bullying and mental health. In P. Goldbulm, D.L. Espelage, J. Chu, & B. Bongar (Eds.), *Youth suicide and bullying: Challenges and strategies for prevention and intervention* (pp. 39–49). Oxford, England: Oxford University Press.

Nock, M.K., Borges, G., & Ono, Y. (2012). Conclusions and future directions. In M.K. Nock, G. Borges, & Y. Ono. (Eds.), *Suicide: Global perspectives from the WHO world mental health surveys* (pp. 222–225). Cambridge, England: Cambridge University Press.

Nock, M.K., Green, J.G., Hwang, I., McLaughlin, K.A., Sampson, N.A., & Kessler, R.C. (2013). Prevalence, correlates, and treatment of lifetime suicidal behavior among adolescents: results from the national comorbidity survey replication adolescent supplement. *Archives of General Psychiatry, 70*(3), 300–310.

Nock, M. K., Hwang, I., Sampson, N. A., & Kessler, R. C. (2010). Mental disorders, comorbidity and suicidal behavior: Results from the National Comorbidity Survey Replication. *Molecular Psychiatry, 15*, 868–876. doi:10.1038/mp.2009.29

Orpinas, P., & Horne, A. M. (2015). Suicidal ideation and bullying: An ecological examination of community impact. In P. Goldbulm, D. L. Espelage, J. Chu, & B. Bongar (Eds.), *Youth suicide and bullying: Challenges and strategies for prevention and intervention* (pp. 50–62). Oxford, England: Oxford University Press.

Osman, A., Kopper, B., Barrios, F., Osman, J., Besett, T., & Linehan, M. (1996). The brief Reasons for Living Inventory for adolescents (BRFL-A). *Journal of Abnormal Child Psychology, 24*(4), 433–443.

Pompili, M. (2015). Our empathic brain and suicidal individuals. *Crisis, 36*(4), 227–230. doi:10.1027/0227–5910/a000327

Pompili, M., Serafini, G., Innamorati, M. Biondi, M., Siracusano A., DiGiannantonio, M., . . . Möeller- Leimkühler, A. M. (2012). Substance abuse and suicide risk among adolescents. *European Archives of Psychiatry and Clinical Neuroscience, 262*, 469–485. doi:10.1007/s00406-012-0292-0

Robins, E., Seymour, G., Kayes, J., Wilkinson, R., & Murphy, G. (1959). The communication of suicidal intent: A study of 134 consecutive cases of successful (completed) suicide. *The American Journal of Psychiatry, 115*(8), 724–733.

Rudd, D. M., Joiner, T., & Rajab, M. H. (2001). *Treating suicidal behavior: An effective, time-limited approach*. New York, NY: The Guilford Press.

Spirito, A., & Esposito-Smythers, C. (2006). Attempted and completed suicide in adolescence. *Annual Review of Clinical Psychology, 2*, 237–266. doi:10.1146/annurev.clinpsy.2.022305.095323

Stanley, B., & Brown, G. K. (2012). Safety planning intervention: A brief intervention to mitigate suicide risk. *Cognitive and Behavioral Practice, 19*(2), 256–264. https://doi.org/10.1016/j.cbpra.2011.01.001

Suicide Prevention Resource Center. (2008). Suicide risk and prevention for lesbian, gay, bisexual, and transgender youth. Newton, MA: Education Development Center, Inc.

Swanson, S. A., & Coleman, I. (2013). Association between exposure to suicide and suicidality outcomes in youth. *Canadian Medical Association Journal, 185*, 870–877.

Testa, R. J., and Hendricks, M. L. (2015). Suicide risk among transgender and gender-nonconforming youth. In P. Goldbulm, D. L. Espelage, J. Chu, & B. Bongar (Eds.), *Youth suicide and bullying: Challenges and strategies for prevention and intervention* (pp. 121–133). Oxford, England: Oxford University Press.

Underwood, M. M, & Dunne-Maxim, K. (1997). *Managing sudden traumatic loss in the schools*. Piscataway, NJ: University Behavioral HealthCare.

U.S. Department of Health and Human Services, Office of the Surgeon General and National Action Alliance for Suicide Prevention. (2012). *2012 National strategy for suicide prevention: Goals and objectives for action*. Washington, DC: U.S. Department of Health and Human Services.

Wenzel, A., Brown, G. K., & Beck, A. T. (2009). *Cognitive therapy for suicidal patients: Scientific and clinical applications*. Washington, DC: American Psychological Association.

CHAPTER 9

The Impact of Parental Military Deployment on Children

Abigail H. Gewirtz and Na Zhang

This chapter focuses on the impact on children of exposure to a parent's deployment. In these cases, children themselves are not typically directly exposed to the traumatic stressor (combat/war zone) but instead are exposed to the stressors related to extended separation from a parent, the anxiety associated with a parent being in harm's way, and, when that parent returns, possible exposure to parental combat stress symptoms (including posttraumatic stress disorder [PTSD], as well as other "invisible" injuries such as traumatic brain and physical injuries).

In 2015, it was estimated by the U.S. Department of Defense that the total number of active duty members was over 1.3 million, comprising the larger portion of the military force, whereas the total number of personnel in the reserve component (i.e., National Guard and Reserves) was over 1.1 million.[1] Including active duty and reserve component family members brings the military population to 2.8 million, including spouses, children, and adult dependents. In 2015, the number of military children was estimated to be 1.76 million (U.S. Department of Defense, 2015). Overall, 41.2 percent of military personnel reported having children in

2015, up from 39.9 percent in 2000. Military-dependent children are mostly young: 37.5 percent are between 0 and 5 years of age, 31.3 percent are 6–11 years of age, 24.2 percent are 12–18 years of age, and just 7.0 percent are between 19 and 22 years of age (U.S. Department of Defense, 2015). More than 2 million children have been affected by the deployment of a parent to the conflicts in Iraq and Afghanistan since 2001 (Chartrand, Frank, White, & Shope, 2008).

Impact of Deployment and Combat Stress on Children

Military children are just as resilient as their civilian peers (Park, 2011). However, much recent evidence suggests that a parent's deployment to war increases risk for child behavioral and emotional challenges. Moreover, an increasing body of research has focused on the impact of parents' PTSD on their children's adjustment and functioning. Earlier research suggested that parental PTSD might increase risk for childhood PTSD, likely through genetic vulnerabilities as well as gene–environment interactions (e.g., Cicchetti & Rogosch, 2001; Van Ijzendoorn, Bakermans-Kranenburg, & Sagi-Schwartz, 2003; Yehuda, Halligan, & Bierer, 2001). However, in the broader realm of developmental research on families under stress, research has long identified parenting as a crucial mediator of the impact of stressful events, processes, or contexts on children. Family stress models (e.g., Caspi, Bolger, & Eckenrode, 1987; Conger et al., 1992, 2002) have demonstrated that stressors, including poverty, parental psychopathology, and divorce, negatively affect children by impairing parenting. In turn, impaired parenting detrimentally affects children's adjustment.

A parent's wartime deployment constitutes a stressful family context. In this context, the stressors include parental absence for extended periods of time, as well as the readjustment to the "new normal" after a parent returns, with the cycle of deployment often repeating. For families in which a parent has been injured, exposure to a parent's physical or psychological injury can be very stressful. Parents with PTSD, for example, may withdraw from their children for fear of experiencing a traumatic reminder in the child's presence and becoming aggressive or violent. Traumatic brain injuries (TBIs)—even mild TBIs—can cause impulsivity, a lack of inhibition, and aggressive behavior that can be frightening to children. Spouses may suffer from secondary or vicarious traumatic stress, so focused on treading carefully around their partner that they themselves display avoidant behaviors (Davis, Hanson, Zamir, Gewirtz, & DeGarmo, 2015; Snyder et al., 2016).

In the sections to follow, we review what is known about the impact of deployment on children across developmental stages. We then discuss the specific stressors related to a parent's wartime injury and/or mental health problems, focusing specifically on PTSD. Finally, we review the literature showing how parenting might serve as a key mechanism through which deployment stress affects children's adjustment. Using a case example, we illustrate the impact of deployment and related stressors on child adjustment and the avenues for intervention when needed.

For very young children, separation from primary caregivers due to deployment may disrupt the crucial attachment bonds between parent and child. Children who were born during a deployment, or who were just infants when their fathers were deployed, may be strangers to those fathers upon their return. Two studies that examined the records of hundreds of thousands of birth to eight-year-old children of active duty military personnel during 2006–2007 showed parental deployment to be associated with increased pediatrician clinic visits (Eide, Gorman, & Hisle-Gorman, 2010; Gorman, Eide, & Hisle-Gorman, 2010). Specifically, among children aged three to eight years, mental and behavioral health visits to clinics increased by 11 percent in children whose parents had been deployed, behavioral disorders increased 19 percent, and stress disorders increased 18 percent (Gorman et al., 2010). Among younger children (birth to age two), overall increases of 7 percent for outpatient visits and 8 percent for well-child visits were observed when parents were deployed (Eide et al., 2010).

The Impact of Deployment on Children across Developmental Stages

For school-aged children and adolescents, the impact of the deployment may manifest over an extended period of time that does not end when the deployed parent returns home. Developmentally, normative levels of anxiety peak at around the age of 10 (Cohen et al., 1993). Younger school-aged children have greater access to news media than preschool children but still do not have the cognitive capacity for abstract thinking. After 9/11 it was well documented, for example, how school-aged children watching the Twin Towers fall over and over again on the news thought that new attacks were happening over many days and were happening geographically close to them regardless of where they lived. Children of deployed parents may watch with alarm any news report of attacks on U.S. service members and worry when their deployed parent doesn't phone them when scheduled. An added challenge for reserve component families (i.e., those in the National Guard or Reserves) is their relative isolation among civilian communities who know very little about military life. We have heard stories of well-meaning school counselors moving children into less challenging classes when their performance suffers, not understanding that this is a temporary adjustment to a difficult situation. Civilian peers may not understand how life changes for children whose parents have been deployed. Younger children sometimes report their friends asking them "Did your dad kill anybody when he was in Iraq?" or "Aren't you worried your dad is going to get shot and killed?"

A medical records study conducted between 2007 and 2009 of more than 350,000 children aged 9–17 years compared psychiatric hospitalization rates and lengths of stay between children of civilian families versus children exposed to an active duty parent's deployment to Operation Enduring Freedom (Afghanistan; OEF) or Operation Iraqi Freedom (Iraq; OIF; Millegan, Engel, Liu, & Dinneen, 2013). Youth with a deployed parent (about one-third of the sample) had a psychiatric hospitalization rate of 0.71 percent compared with 0.65 percent among youth whose parent(s) were not deployed. Adjusting for variables such as child gender, age, and past psychiatric history, psychiatric hospitalization following a parent's deployment increased by 10 percent compared with youth whose parents were not deployed during the same timeframe, though hospital length of stay between the two groups was not significantly different.

Results of an interview study with teachers, counselors, and administrative staff at military installation schools indicated that children experience heightened anxiety related to parental deployment, stress related to increased responsibilities at home, and difficulties in coping with poor mental health of some nondeployed parents (Chandra, Martin, Hawkins, & Richardson, 2010).

Children and adolescents may also be angry with their parent(s) for leaving on deployment. "Aren't I more important than the army?" is a common theme expressed by children. Monitoring and supervision are crucial ways in which parents prevent adolescent delinquent behavior, such as truancy, drug use, or petty criminal behavior. When a parent is gone, however, and the other parent is struggling to keep the house and family together, youth may spend more time unsupervised and at risk for externalizing behavior problems. Indeed, data from the California Healthy Kids Survey, a statewide survey of school-aged youth, show that children whose parents have been deployed reported more drug use and related risk behaviors than military youth whose parents were not deployed or civilian youth (Benbenishty, Roziner, & Astor, 2015).

Self-reported average rates of alcohol use across three survey time points (2008, 2011, 2013) were 9 percent greater for youth in deployed families than for youth in civilian families and nondeployed military families; their average rates of having carried a weapon were 80 percent greater than children in civilian families and double the rate for children in nondeployed military families. Finally, youth in deployed families expressed suicidal ideation at rates 34 percent greater than civilian children and four times the rate of children of nondeployed military families (MacDermid Wadsworth, Bailey, & Coppola, 2016).

Caution is necessary when interpreting these findings, as biases may occur due to methodological limitations (e.g., self-report, school-related variations). Nonetheless, existing data appear to demonstrate that parental wartime deployment is associated with increased risk for child and adolescent emotional and behavioral problems. These problems may be exacerbated when a parent returns from deployment with an injury.

Parental Injury Following Deployment

The injury of a parent during deployment can have profound effects for the service member and the entire family. Initial information about the deployed parent's injury may be incomplete or inaccurate, which often leads to greater levels of anxiety in children and nondeployed spouses (Cozza, Chun, & Polo, 2005). Nondeployed spouses may visit the injured service members at military hospitals, typically far away from their homes. Consequently, children may be left behind at home with other adults while worrying about parents. Parents may not be transparent with their children about what happened—either to "protect" children or because they may not know what to say, further compounding children's worries. In some cases, children are brought along to the military hospital to visit the injured parent, potentially disrupting school and daily life routines and increasing anxiety. Particularly with severe physical injuries (e.g., loss of a limb), the process of adapting to the "new normal" is often accompanied by a sense of loss and grief for both the service member and his or her partner, which may challenge parents' effective caregiving for their children (Cozza et al., 2005). How parents cope with these adjustments will index, to a certain degree, how children will respond. For example, children whose at-home parent prepares them for their injured parent's homecoming by discussing and addressing their fears, questions, and concerns will likely show improved adjustment compared with those who have had no such preparation.

TBI is a relatively common injury of the recent conflicts. A survey of Iraq and Afghanistan veterans reported a rate of 12 percent for mild TBI using a brief screening questionnaire (Schneiderman, Braver, & Kang,

2008). Another study used a clinician-interview approach, and 22.8 percent of the sample of Iraq combat veterans were identified with TBIs (the majority was mild; Terrio et al., 2009). The high rates of TBI are primarily due to the proliferation of improvised explosive devices (IEDs) as well as medical advances that save the lives of individuals who would, in prior conflicts, have likely not survived their severe injuries. Depending on the level of injury (mild, moderate, and severe), patients with TBI may suffer from a variety of symptoms and different degrees of symptom severity. Typical physical symptoms consist of physical pain, headaches, breathing problems, sensory disabilities (hearing, vision), motor disabilities, and/or coma. Psychologically, TBI is highly comorbid with PTSD, as well as with depression, anxiety, chronic pain, and substance abuse or dependence. Each of the psychological symptoms poses increased risk for suicidality. Recently, researchers have studied a sample of military personnel who were referred to an outpatient TBI clinic and found that depression, PTSD, insomnia, and loss of consciousness were associated with suicidality outcomes (Bryan, Clemans, Hernandez, & Rudd, 2013).

There is little research on the adjustment of children who live with a veteran suffering from TBI as a result of combat-related trauma (Cozza, 2016). In general, children of parents with TBI may feel a sense of loss and grief because their parent no longer appears to be the same person—as a consequence of TBI symptoms. Even when the injury is mild, parents can exhibit impulsivity and disinhibition, which may increase the risk for abuse and violence in a home. Withdrawal behaviors are also common in these parents; children may perceive a psychological absence. Finally, depression, substance abuse, or suicidality can significantly affect children's healthy socioemotional development.

Impact of Deployed Parents' Mental Health Challenges on Children's Adjustment

Reintegration may also be more challenging for children and families when parents return from deployment suffering from posttraumatic stress (PTSD) and related disorders. Studies of Vietnam War veterans as well as service members and veterans of the recent conflicts suggest that PTSD has a significant negative influence on children's adjustment (Lambert, Holzer, & Hasbun, 2014) and that the influence is greater than that of combat exposure (Gewirtz, DeGarmo, & Zamir, 2017). This may in part be due to experiential avoidance (i.e., attempts to escape unwanted feelings, being physically present but appearing emotionally absent; sometimes called the "thousand-yard stare"), a core symptom of PTSD, which may be particularly disruptive for family functioning and children's adjustment (Brockman et al., 2016; Snyder et al., 2016).

Some recent research on adult PTSD has focused on "moral injury": symptoms that follow a person's participation in or witnessing of violence committed by others, killing others, failing to prevent killing, losing a buddy in combat while surviving oneself, or betrayal. Moral injury appears to be associated with difficulties in functioning across multiple domains, as well as increased suicidal ideation (Litz et al., 2009). Moral injury of a deployed parent may be transmitted to children, such as when information about war and violence communicated by a deployed parent conflicts with a youth's moral beliefs or when wartime acts against children are at the core of the moral injury (Nash & Litz, 2013). For example, Bill was a father of two who struggled with moral injury following a deployment to Afghanistan in which he and his unit were engaged in a firefight with children who fired upon them. Bill was haunted by the experience of killing a child and suffered from PTSD. When he returned home, he found it extremely difficult to parent his own children, as they triggered reminders of the traumatic memories of his war experiences and reminded him of the life he had taken. Only after addressing the moral injury in therapy did Bill feel able to return to the family home and take an active role in parenting.

Effects of Nondeployed Parental Mental Health Challenges on Children's Adjustment

Civilian spouses of deployed service members are at increased risk for mental health problems such as depression and anxiety (e.g., O'Toole, Outram, Catts, & Pierse, 2010). Renshaw et al. (2011) surveyed 190 wives of male service members with probable PTSD and found that 23.7 percent of the civilian spouses endorsed symptoms consistent with a PTSD diagnosis. Almost 90 percent reported at least one PTSD symptom. Of these spouses, 24.7 percent attributed their symptoms in part to their husbands' military experiences, and 12.9 percent reported that their sole trauma was their husbands' military experience. While returned service members' PTSD may play a role in contributing to their spouses' PTSD symptoms (i.e., secondary traumatic stress), the psychological distress experienced by the spouses could be a result of family process in general and *not necessarily* attributable to the service member's deployment experiences (Renshaw et al., 2011; Sheppard, Weil Malatras, & Israel, 2010). Psychological distress could reasonably be related to the combination of worry about the service member's deployment or reintegration, increased responsibilities at home as a sole caregiver of multiple children, or greater level of child externalizing behaviors while the other parent is deployed. Lester et al. (2010) found that at-home civilian parents' mental health symptoms strongly predicted children's internalizing and externalizing symptoms even after controlling for length of time that spouses were deployed.

The Importance of Parenting in Influencing Child Adjustment after Deployment

A large body of civilian research has demonstrated *parenting* to be a key mechanism through which stressful family experiences negatively impact children's adjustment (e.g., Conger et al., 2002; Simons et al., 2016). Our recent study of military families exposed to a parent's deployment has documented this same phenomenon (Gewirtz et al., 2017). Deployment likely increases psychological stress of the at-home parent and the deployed parent, impairing parenting by increasing parents' irritability with children, reducing follow-through and consistency, and raising the likelihood that parents will be preoccupied with concerns about deployment, the deployed parent, and/or, in the case of the deployed individual, memories and thoughts of war.

Two studies have demonstrated increased risk for child maltreatment during deployments, likely a result of increased stress for the at-home caregiver (Gibbs, Martin, Kupper, & Johnson, 2007; Rentz et al., 2007). Gibbs et al. (2007) examined records of 1,771 enlisted military families who experienced at least one combat deployment between September 2001 and December 2004, finding the rate of child maltreatment (predominantly neglect) during soldier deployments to be 42 percent higher than when a parent was not deployed. Rentz et al. (2007) followed military and civilian families through 2000–2003 and described patterns of child maltreatment rates. Prior to 9/11, military rates of child maltreatment were, in fact, lower than civilian controls, but by the end of 2002 and the onset of the war in Afghanistan, child maltreatment rates among military families had almost doubled. By the end of 2003, the rates of child maltreatment in military families went beyond the civilian rate. Over the study period, the rates of child maltreatment in civilian families were stable.

Maltreatment is an extreme example of *coercive parenting*, instances in which a parent uses aversive, negatively reinforcing, or escalating behavior to stop a conflict with a child. A typical example might be a frustrated parent shouting at a child to complete his or her homework. When the child refuses, the conflict escalates with both partners shouting. The conflict is terminated when the parent, shouting, threatens to ground the child for a week. Patterson (1982, 2005) identified coercion as a key *mechanism* through which parenting adversely affects children's adjustment. Parents under stress demonstrate higher rates of coercive interactions and lower rates of positive interactions with their children (Patterson, Capaldi, & Bank, 1991), and, over time, children learn to interact using coercive techniques, which elevate risk for externalizing problems. For example, Patterson and colleagues found that the intensity and frequency of coercive interactions predicted substance use and arrest rates three years later (Patterson et al., 1991).

Patterson's social interaction learning model also identifies positive parenting practices that can buffer children from stressful contexts. These include contingent positive reinforcement for prosocial behaviors, effective problem solving, good monitoring and supervision of children, warm caregiving/positive involvement, and effective nonphysical discipline. Both positive and coercive parenting contribute unique variance to child adjustment (Forgatch & DeGarmo, 1999).

Despite the risks summarized in the discussion so far, most families facing deployment and/or combat injury are resilient and resourceful in coping with deployment (Park, 2011). Many parents, for example, are intentional in the way they explain and discuss a parent's deployment in service of the country. Families display pride in their service, which likely contributes to the fact that children of military parents are far more likely than their civilian peers to enlist in the military (Gewirtz & Youssef, 2016). During and after deployment, parents actively look for resources and participate in programs to improve their parenting and their families' functioning (Doty, Rudi, Pinna, Hanson, & Gewirtz, 2016; Pinna, Hanson, Zhang, & Gewirtz, 2017).

Case Presentation: Sam Smith

Sam is a 10-year-old girl living in a small town in a midwestern state. She has twin siblings, age 5. Her parents both joined the Army National Guard when they were 19 years old and have renewed their contracts twice, for a total of 15 years of service thus far. Sam's father, Dave, and her mother, Dawn, are both 34 years old and were high school sweethearts. In his civilian job, Dave worked as an auto mechanic for a local garage. Dawn is an elementary school teacher. They live in a town with few National Guard families and do their monthly weekend drill training with units that are based about 70–100 miles from their home.

Dawn deployed within the United States in service of OEF (the war in Afghanistan) before their children were born, and Dave was deployed twice to Iraq and once to Afghanistan in a National Guard combat unit. Dave was injured after exposure to an IED in his third deployment; he was diagnosed with a mild TBI and also suffers from hearing loss. Dave also was diagnosed with PTSD from his combat exposure. Sam has twin siblings, James and Joyce, aged 5. Sam's mom was pregnant with her during her dad's first deployment; he returned when she was 2 months old. She was 3 at the second deployment, and her dad's third deployment occurred during Sam's first-grade year, when she was 6–7 years old.

Dave witnessed combat in his first two deployments. Although he escaped injury, he saw several of his buddies injured and killed. Dawn reports that after his first deployment, Dave returned somewhat changed. He was more withdrawn than she had expected given their new baby. He seemed scared to hold the baby and would often retreat to the sofa, staying awake late into the night watching war movies or playing on his Nintendo. When Dawn asked him about his experiences in Iraq, Dave demurred, saying he didn't want to taint Dawn or their new baby with the things he had seen and done. After about a year, things seemed to settle down. As baby Sam became a toddler and seemed less fragile, Dave became a more engaged dad. He loved to take her to daycare and enjoyed playing ball with her. Dave seemed to have a short fuse, which was surprising to Dawn as he had always seemed laid back; things had rarely bothered him. She learned when not to bug him, when he seemed to be brooding, or when he had the "thousand-yard stare" on his face. Eventually, life seemed to return to normal.

Dave and his brigade team were surprised to be deployed for the second time, less than three years after the first deployment. This second deployment to Iraq was difficult, occurring at the height of the surge of 2007–2008. The soldiers and their families were told that it would be a 16-month deployment—longer than average for the army. However, shortly before they were due to return home, the unit received word that their deployment was to be extended for another 6 months. Families and service members were devastated and angry; they had had anticipated that their loved ones would be home for Christmas.

The deployment itself was difficult. Although Dave mostly worked inside the "wire" (i.e., inside the U.S. military compound) in Baghdad, going outside, their patrols were routinely attacked. Roadside bombs were commonplace, and Dave knew several soldiers who were killed and injured. Dave finally returned home, after 22 months, and Dawn became pregnant with twins soon after. Dave attended prenatal classes with Dawn, which helped him to feel more confident as a new father. Along with his experience with Sam, who was now a preschooler, Dave felt more competent and shared care of the twins with Dawn, getting up at nights, holding one twin while the other nursed, and helping to put them back to sleep.

Dave volunteered for his third deployment, much to Dawn's irritation and concern. With three children at home, Dawn and Dave debated whether to renew their National Guard contracts. Dawn was opposed to it, but Dave, now a sergeant, did not want to let his soldiers down. When he told Dawn he was considering redeploying, he said that he felt his soldiers needed him.

The twins were two and Sam was seven when Dave deployed to Afghanistan, in a valley outpost that was vulnerable to sniper activity. Conditions were poor, and morale was low. When they moved about the valley, the soldiers expected to be ambushed or to roll over an IED at any time. Dawn and the children worried a lot about Dave. Dawn tried hard not to share her concerns with the kids, but well-meaning adults at church and school asked them often about their dad's deployment. More often than not, the kids slept with Dawn in her bed.

One day, on routine patrol, Dave's Humvee rolled over an IED; two soldiers were killed, and Dave and three others were injured. He was knocked unconscious and was pulled out of the vehicle by a buddy. Fortunately, back-up was close by, and the injured were helicoptered to a field hospital and later to Landstuhl Regional Medical Center in Germany, where Dawn met him and accompanied him back to Walter Reed Army Medical Center in Washington, D.C. He remained at Walter Reed for two months before returning home. Dave doesn't remember much about the incident except what others have told him.

Once he was home, Dawn tried to reassure the kids that all was now well. She did her best to help the children and Dave adjust to the family's "new normal." Dave's physical recovery was remarkable, but the TBI caused him severe and chronic headaches. He was sensitive to light and noise and found it difficult to drive. Dave was diagnosed with PTSD. He slept separately from Dawn for a number of months after returning home, as his nightmares would frighten her, and he worried he might hurt her in his sleep. He erupted into angry outbursts, particularly when the children became noisy or cried. Though he was often physically present at home, the thousand-yard stare was a sign to Dawn and the kids that he was psychologically absent. He was unable to resume his work as an auto mechanic. For six months after he arrived home, he stayed around the house all day, playing video games in his sweatpants. His doctors had cleared him to find work, but Dave couldn't find the motivation to look for work. Dawn explained that he needed to find work because they were running out of money; she was finding it impossible to do the household chores, watch the kids, and keep down a full-time job. Dawn begged Dave to go with her to therapy, for the sake of the kids.

Impact of Deployment and Father's Injuries on Sam's Functioning

Sam's parents recall that she was a happy, laid-back baby, easy to put to sleep, sociable, and curious about the world. As a toddler, she developed a close relationship with her father, and Dave enjoyed spending time with her. When she was three, he redeployed, and this deployment was hard on Sam. Dave and Dawn had together decided to explain that daddy had a very important job protecting the country and that job meant that he had to go far away. Sam often asked her mom questions about where her father was and when (and then, if) he was coming home. Dawn and Dave worked to ensure that Sam would stay in touch with her dad. Dave would Skype every week with Dawn and Sam; he sent letters and small gifts to Sam, and he had prerecorded himself reading her favorite books. Seeing dad on video reading to her became Sam's favorite bedtime routine. Dawn bought a "flat daddy" of Dave (a life-size cardboard cutout of him), and Sam took it to preschool to show her classmates and to explain why he was away. Sam was considered a well-behaved child in preschool, if somewhat anxious. She sometimes had nightmares, although not often, and she created a nighttime routine that involved Mom going through the house to make sure there were no monsters lurking in the closets and that all the doors were locked.

After Dad returned from his second deployment, Sam seemed to adjust well. She reveled in the birth of her twin siblings. She took pride in being the older sister and loved to help her parents with feeding, changing, and playing. Sam's transition to kindergarten was made easier by the fact that Mom taught sixth grade in her school. She knew the school well and felt at home there. She had a few close friends and was a very compliant child.

When Dave left for his third deployment, Sam, now age seven, appeared more worried than before, understanding more of the danger her father was in. At school, kids would ask her whether her dad was "killing the bad guys." Concerned adults would ask her when she last heard from her father. Sam could see that her mom was also very stressed, and Dawn often looked as if she had been crying or was about to cry. Sam thought that maybe if she stayed at home instead of going to school, she would be able to care for her mom and help with her siblings. She would often complain of headaches or stomachaches or say she was feeling feverish.

When Dave was injured in Afghanistan, Dawn called her mother, who came to stay with the children, while she flew out to Germany to be with him. When Dave was flown back to Walter Reed Army Medical Center, Dawn returned home but visited Dave for extended periods every month. Grandma stayed with the children throughout this period. Sam was a "perfect child" according to Grandma, helping her grandma with the cooking, cleaning, and child care. She had a hard time sleeping, however, and Dawn's mom worried that Sam had "grown up too fast." When Mom and Dad returned home, Sam was overjoyed but very anxious. She rarely ventured out of the house except for school. She turned down playdates, declined to play after-school sports, and said she would rather spend the summer at home than go to day camp. Sam appeared anxious in her dad's presence.

Dad was more irritable than he ever had been; he would yell at the kids if the phone rang or if there were another unexpected noise. Other times he often sat alone, playing video games or staring off into space. Sam wanted to help her dad, although he would be mean to her if she didn't do exactly as he asked. Dawn appeared tired and very stressed and wrapped up in keeping her job and the household together. The younger kids tried to avoid Dad, though they got into shouting matches with him quite frequently. Twice, Dawn had to intervene to stop Dad from hitting the kids after an argument.

Family-Based Interventions to Support Children after Deployment

Given the data showing that deployment and its sequelae—such as PTSD—pose risks for parenting and children's adjustment, preventive interventions focused on boosting *parenting* are indicated for this population of stressed families. Evidence-based parent training programs help parents to be their children's best teachers, improving children's emotional and behavioral functioning (Forgatch & Gewirtz, in press; Forgatch, Patterson, & Gewirtz, 2013). One such intervention, After Deployment, Adaptive Parenting Tools or ADAPT, is the first evidence-based parent training program specifically developed for deployed military families with children ages 4–13 (Gewirtz, Erbes, Polusny, Forgatch, & Degarmo, 2011; Gewirtz, Pinna, Hanson, & Brockberg, 2014). ADAPT helps parents to be their children's best teachers by providing parenting tools that parents try out in group, individual, telehealth, or online self-directed sessions (Gewirtz & Youssef, 2016). ADAPT is a military family adaptation of the Parent Management Training-Oregon/PMTO Model (Patterson, 2005), a family of parent training interventions that are grounded in the social interaction learning model described earlier and that have been shown to improve not only parenting practices but also multiple family outcomes, including child adjustment, maternal depression, and standard of living (Patterson, Forgatch, & Degarmo, 2010). Data from a randomized controlled trial of the ADAPT group program with 336 National Guard and Reserve families demonstrated that the program improved parenting, leading to improvements in children's adjustment one year after the intervention (Gewirtz, DeGarmo, & Zamir, 2016). The ADAPT program also improved parents' self-efficacy in parenting, which in turn reduced PTSD, depression, and suicidality in parents a year after the intervention (Gewirtz, DeGarmo, & Zamir, 2017).

Dawn and Dave were referred to ADAPT. They participated in the ADAPT program via telehealth format, as they lived too far away to attend in person. They met via online video conference with their coach once a week for 14 weeks. The program targets key positive parenting practices, helping parents to form a united front in parenting. Dawn and Dave articulated their parenting values and set parenting goals. They learned behavioral tools (e.g., teaching new behaviors to children, contingent positive reinforcement, discipline, problem solving, monitoring). They also learned how to respond to their children's worries and how to communicate as a family to address and preempt conflicts. Dave particularly benefited from the emotion regulation tools, such as mindfulness exercises, which required him to take a few minutes each day to notice the world around him and to be more present with his children. Both reported that the program helped them to learn to parent as partners rather than as adversaries whom the children could line up, one against the another. By practicing between sessions, Dawn and Dave were able to see and enjoy successes and troubleshoot with their coach. They reported feeling more competent as parents—especially Dave—and enjoying being with their children. Dave reported having concrete skills that he could apply when he "just didn't know what to do with the kids." Dawn reported feeling less anxious about the kids—and that the children themselves seemed to be less worried. The younger children appeared to be less oppositional and defiant, and Sam reported feeling less anxious.

Dave also agreed to go to therapy together with his wife. Their therapist, who provided cognitive-behavioral couple therapy for PTSD (Monson et al., 2012), also referred Dave for telephone case management at the VA hospital. The case manager helped Dave to apply for disability and to find a job working in outreach at a local vet center.

Conclusions: Lessons Learned

Military families are resilient, but deployment is a family stressor that can challenge children's—and parents'—adjustment. Whether or not a parent suffers from injuries or other sequelae of deployment, children may find it hard to adjust to both the deployment and the reintegration process. Supports and services are available but harder to find for reserve component families, who may live far from military resources. Relatively few prevention and intervention programs have been proven effective in strengthening adjustment and buffering the stress of deployment. One such program, ADAPT (Gewirtz, Pinna, et al., 2014), provides parents with parenting tools to strengthen both their co-parenting relationship and their children's as well as their own adjustment.

Much is yet to be learned about children's resilience following a parent's deployment (see, e.g., MacDermid Wadsworth et al., 2016), as well as what interventions best support these children. In particular, while most parents who deploy are fathers, a growing minority of deployed parents are mothers, and almost nothing is known about the impact of a mother's deployment on child adjustment (Gewirtz, McMorris, Hanson, & Davis, 2014; Gewirtz & Youssef, 2016). Finally, yet to be understood is the long-term impact of deployment on children and families as children develop into adults, who, more likely than not, will become the next generation of service members.

Note

1. The U.S. military is comprised of the active duty (i.e., those who serve full-time) and the reserve component (i.e., those who serve occasionally). The reserve component includes members of the National Guard (Army and Air Guard; these are state militias that may be called to active duty by the president, such as during war) and the Reserves (Army, Air, Navy, Marines, and Coast Guard), who may also be called as needed. Since 9/11/2001 the military has relied in an unprecedented way on the National Guard, deploying these service members to a far greater extent than in prior conflicts.

References

Benbenishty, R., Roziner, I., & Astor, R. A. (2015). Substance abuse and other adverse outcomes for military-connected youth in California: Results from a large-scale normative population survey. *JAMA Pediatrics, 169*(10), 922–928.

Brockman, C., Snyder, J., Gewirtz, A., Gird, S. R., Quattlebaum, J., Schmidt, N., . . . DeGarmo, D. (2016). Relationship of service members' deployment trauma, PTSD symptoms, and experiential avoidance to postdeployment family reengagement. *Journal of Family Psychology*, *30*, 52–62.

Bryan, C. J., Clemans, T. A., Hernandez, A. M., & Rudd, M. D. (2013). Loss of consciousness, depression, posttraumatic stress disorder, and suicide risk among deployed military personnel with mild traumatic brain injury. *The Journal of Head Trauma Rehabilitation*, *28*, 13–20.

Caspi, A., Bolger, N., & Eckenrode, J. (1987). Linking person and context in the daily stress process. *Journal of Personality and Social Psychology*, *52*, 184–195.

Chandra, A., Martin, L. T., Hawkins, S. A., & Richardson, A. (2010). The impact of parental deployment on child social and emotional functioning: perspectives of school staff. *Journal of Adolescent Health*, *46*, 218–223.

Chartrand, M. M., Frank, D. A., White, L. F., & Shope, T. R. (2008). Effect of parents' wartime deployment on the behavior of young children in military families. *Archives of Pediatrics & Adolescent Medicine*, *162*, 1009–1014.

Cicchetti, D., & Rogosch, F.A. (2001). The impact of child maltreatment and psychopathology on neuroendocrine functioning. *Development and Psychopathology, 13*, 783–804.

Cohen, P., Cohen, J., Kasen, S., Velez, C.N., Hartmark, C., Johnson, J., . . . Streuning, E.L. (1993). An epidemiological study of disorders in late childhood and adolescence—I. Age- and gender-specific prevalence. *Journal of Child Psychology and Psychiatry, 34*, 851–867.

Conger, R.D., Conger, K.J., Elder, G.H., Jr., Lorenz, F.O., Simons, R.L., & Whitbeck, L.B. (1992). A family process model of economic hardship and adjustment of early adolescent boys. *Child Development, 63*, 526–541.

Conger, R.D., Wallace, L.E., Sun, Y., Simons, R.L., McLoyd, V.C., & Brody, G.H. (2002). Economic pressure in African American families: A replication and extension of the family stress model. *Developmental Psychology, 38*, 179–193.

Cozza, S.J. (2016). Parenting in military families faced with combat-related injury, illness, or death. In A.H. Gewirtz & A.M. Youssef (Eds.), *Parenting and children's resilience in military families* (pp. 151–173). Switzerland: Springer International Publishing.

Cozza, S.J., Chun, R.S., & Polo, J.A. (2005). Military families and children during operation Iraqi freedom. *The Psychiatric Quarterly, 76*, 371–378.

Davis, L., Hanson, S.K., Zamir, O., Gewirtz, A.H., & DeGarmo, D.S. (2015). Associations of contextual risk and protective factors with fathers' parenting practices in the postdeployment environment. *Psychological Services, 12*, 250–260.

Doty, J.L., Rudi, J.H., Pinna, K.L.M., Hanson, S.K., & Gewirtz, A.H. (2016). If you build it, will they come? Patterns of internet-based and face-to-face participation in a parenting program for military families. *Journal of Medical Internet Research, 18*, e169.

Eide, M., Gorman, G., & Hisle-Gorman, E. (2010). Effects of parental military deployment on pediatric outpatient and well-child visit rates. *Pediatrics, 126*, 22–27.

Forgatch, M.S., & DeGarmo, D.S. (1999). Parenting through change: An effective prevention program for single mothers. *Journal of Consulting and Clinical Psychology, 67*, 711–724.

Forgatch, M.S., & Gewirtz, A.H. (in press). Evolution of Parent Management Training-Oregon Model: A dynamic model of an empirically supported intervention. In J.R. Weisz & A.E. Kazdin (Eds.), *Evidence-based psychotherapies for children and adolescents*. New York, NY: Guilford Press.

Forgatch, M.S., Patterson, G.R., & Gewirtz, A.H. (2013). Looking forward: The promise of widespread implementation of parent training programs. *Perspectives on Psychological Science, 8*, 682–694.

Gewirtz, A.H., DeGarmo, D.S., & Zamir, O. (2016). Effects of a military parenting program on parental distress and suicidal ideation: After deployment adaptive parenting tools. *Suicide & Life-Threatening Behavior, 46*(Suppl 1), S23–S31. Retrieved from https://doi.org/10.1111/sltb.12255

Gewirtz, A. H., DeGarmo, D. S., & Zamir, O. (2017). After Deployment, Adaptive Parenting Tools: One year outcomes of an evidence-based parenting program for military families. *Prevention Science*. Advance online publication. doi:10.1007/s11121-017-0839-4

Gewirtz, A. H., Erbes, C. R., Polusny, M. A., Forgatch, M. S., & Degarmo, D. S. (2011). Helping military families through the deployment process: Strategies to support parenting. *Professional Psychology, Research and Practice, 42*, 56–62.

Gewirtz, A. H., McMorris, B. J., Hanson, S., & Davis, L. (2014). Family adjustment of deployed and non-deployed mothers in families with a parent deployed to Iraq or Afghanistan. *Professional Psychology, Research and Practice, 45*, 465–477.

Gewirtz, A. H., Pinna, K. L. M., Hanson, S. K., & Brockberg, D. (2014). Promoting parenting to support reintegrating military families: after deployment, adaptive parenting tools. *Psychological Services, 11*, 31–40.

Gewirtz, A. H., & Youssef, A. (2016). Parenting and children's resilience in military families. In A. H. Gewirtz & A. Youssef (Eds.), *Parenting and children's resilience in military families. Risk and resilience in military and veteran families* (pp. 1–9). Cham, Switzerland: Springer.

Gibbs, D. A., Martin, S. L., Kupper, L. L., & Johnson, R. E. (2007). Child maltreatment in enlisted soldiers families during combat-related deployments. *Journal of the American Medical Association, 298*, 528–535.

Gorman, G. H., Eide, M., & Hisle-Gorman, E. (2010). Wartime military deployment and increased pediatric mental and behavioral health complaints. *Pediatrics, 126*, 1058–1066.

Lambert, J. E., Holzer, J., & Hasbun, A. (2014). Association between parents' PTSD severity and children's psychological distress: a meta-analysis. *Journal of Traumatic Stress, 27*, 9–17.

Lester, P., Peterson, K., Reeves, J., Knauss, L., Glover, D., Mogil, C., . . . Beardslee, W. (2010). The long war and parental combat deployment: Effects on military children and at-home spouses. *Journal of the American Academy of Child and Adolescent Psychiatry, 49*, 310–320.

Litz, B. T., Stein, N., Delaney, E., Lebowitz, L., Nash, W. P., Silva, C., & Maguen, S. (2009). Moral injury and moral repair in war veterans: A preliminary model and intervention strategy. *Clinical Psychology Review, 29*, 695–706.

MacDermid Wadsworth, S., Bailey, K. M., & Coppola, E. C. (2016). U.S. military children and the wartime deployments of family members. *Child Development Perspectives, 11*(1), 23–28. https://doi.org/10.1111/cdep.12210

Millegan, J., Engel, C., Liu, X., & Dinneen, M. (2013). Parental Iraq/Afghanistan deployment and child psychiatric hospitalization in the US military. *General Hospital Psychiatry, 35*, 556–560.

Monson, C.M., Fredman, S.J., Macdonald, A., Pukay-Martin, N.D., Resick, P.A., & Schnurr, P.P. (2012). Effect of cognitive-behavioral couple therapy for PTSD: A randomized controlled trial. *JAMA*, *308*, 700–709.

Nash, W.P., & Litz, B.T. (2013). Moral injury: A mechanism for war-related psychological trauma in military family members. *Clinical Child and Family Psychology Review*, *16*, 365–375.

O'Toole, B.I., Outram, S., Catts, S.V., & Pierse, K.R. (2010). The mental health of partners of Australian Vietnam veterans three decades after the war and its relation to veteran military service, combat, and PTSD. *Journal of Nervous and Mental Disease*, *198*, 841–845.

Park, N. (2011). Military children and families. *American Psychologist*, *66*, 65–72.

Patterson, G.R. (1982). *Coercive family process*. Eugene, OR: Castalia Publishing Company.

Patterson, G.R. (2005). The next generation of PMTO models. *The Behavior Therapist/AABT*, *28*(2), 25–32.

Patterson, G.R., Capaldi, D., & Bank, L. (1991). An early starter model for predicting delinquency. In D. Pepler & R.K. Rubin (Eds.), *The development and treatment of childhood aggression*. Hillsdale, NJ: Lawrence Erlbaum Associates.

Patterson, G.R., Forgatch, M.S., & Degarmo, D.S. (2010). Cascading effects following intervention. *Development and Psychopathology*, *22*, 949–970.

Pinna, K.L.M., Hanson, S., Zhang, N., & Gewirtz, A.H. (2017). Fostering resilience in National Guard and Reserve families: A contextual adaptation of an evidence-based parenting program. *American Journal of Orthopsychiatry*, *87*, 185–193.

Renshaw, K.D., Allen, E.S., Rhoades, G.K., Blais, R.K., Markman, H.J., & Stanley, S.M. (2011). Distress in spouses of service members with symptoms of combat-related PTSD: Secondary traumatic stress or general psychological distress? *Journal of Family Psychology*, *25*, 461–469.

Rentz, E.D., Marshall, S.W., Loomis, D., Casteel, C., Martin, S.L., & Gibbs, D.A. (2007). Effect of deployment on the occurrence of child maltreatment in military and nonmilitary families. *American Journal of Epidemiology*, *165*, 1199–1206.

Schneiderman, A.I., Braver, E.R., & Kang, H.K. (2008). Understanding sequelae of injury mechanisms and mild traumatic brain injury incurred during the conflicts in Iraq and Afghanistan: Persistent postconcussive symptoms and posttraumatic stress disorder. *American Journal of Epidemiology*, *167*, 1446–1452.

Sheppard, S.C., Weil Malatras, J., & Israel, A.C. (2010). The impact of deployment on U.S. military families. *American Psychologist*, *65*, 599–609.

Simons, L.G., Wickrama, K.A.S., Lee, T.K., Landers-Potts, M., Cutrona, C., & Conger, R.D. (2016). Testing family stress and family investment explanations for conduct problems among African American adolescents. *Family Relations*, *78*, 498–515.

Snyder, J., Gewirtz, A., Schrepferman, L., Gird, S. R., Quattlebaum, J., Pauldine, M. R., . . . Hayes, C. (2016). Parent–child relationship quality and family transmission of parent posttraumatic stress disorder symptoms and child externalizing and internalizing symptoms following fathers' exposure to combat trauma. *Development and Psychopathology*, *28*, 947–969.

Terrio, H., Brenner, L. A., Ivins, B. J., Cho, J. M., Helmick, K., Schwab, K., . . . Warden, D. (2009). Traumatic brain injury screening: preliminary findings in a US Army Brigade Combat Team. *The Journal of Head Trauma Rehabilitation*, *24*, 14–23.

U.S. Department of Defense. (2015). *2014 demographics: Profile of the military community*. Retrieved from http://download.militaryonesource.mil/12038/MOS/Reports/2014-Demographics-Report.pdf

Van Ijzendoorn, M. H., Bakermans-Kranenburg, M. J., & Sagi-Schwartz, A. (2003). Are children of Holocaust survivors less well-adapted? A meta-analytic investigation of secondary traumatization. *Journal of Traumatic Stress*, *16*, 459–469.

Yehuda, R., Halligan, S. L., & Bierer, L. M. (2001). Relationship of parental trauma exposure and PTSD to PTSD, depressive and anxiety disorders in offspring. *Journal of Psychiatric Research*, *35*, 261–270.

CHAPTER 10

The Psychosocial Impact of War on Children and Families

Emma Cardeli, Saida Abdi, and B. Heidi Ellis

Millions of children worldwide have been affected by war and conflict. In the early millennium, wartime events were estimated to have left 12 million children destitute, 6 million severely injured and/or disabled, and 2 million dead (UNICEF, 1996, 2011). An additional 300,000 children were presumed to be serving as child soldiers in over 30 conflicts across the globe (Machel, 1996; Wexler, Branski, & Kerem, 2006). With the present conflicts in Syria and Iraq, an additional 14 million children have been affected by wartime violence, 2 million of which are living in areas of Syria cut off from humanitarian assistance (UNICEF, 2015). This chapter examines the psychosocial impact of war on children and families and includes a case vignette to highlight mental health challenges and treatment needs unique to this population. Developmental and cultural considerations are explored, and recommendations for best practices in intervention with children and families exposed to war are provided.

The effects of war on children and families can vary based on a number of factors. This includes proximity to conflict zones, the frequency and duration of exposures, the availability of life-sustaining resources (e.g., access to food, water, shelter, and protection from disease), and the degree to which conflict disrupts family, social, and community infrastructures (Morgos, Worden, & Gupta, 2008; Neugebauer et al., 2009).

Wartime events can assert their deleterious effects through direct physical and/or visual impact, media exposure, and various forms of interpersonal hardships (e.g., the wounding and killing of loved ones, separation from caregivers, loss of peer networks, widespread emotional distress, and the interruption of routinized family, school, and community activities; Shaw, 2003). The impact of war further depends on a child's individual capacities, such as his or her developmental stage, ability to elicit support from caretaking adults in the social environment, and capacity to engage in meaning making around the trauma (Barenbaum, Ruchkin, & Schwab-Stone, 2004; Lustig et al., 2004). Despite the profound and diverse ways in which children are affected by war, relatively few studies have examined the effects of war on youth specifically.

War and conflict not only expose children to widespread and severe violence but also disrupt basic family and community infrastructure critical to their healthy development. Basic health care and nutrition, access to education, and the structure of families, homes, and neighborhoods may all be disrupted in the presence of war. While such system disruption affects anyone, children—who are navigating critical developmental milestones—may be particularly affected. The multiple adversities and losses of war may furthermore interact in complex ways that challenge children's health and development. Loss of home, or displacement, as faced by refugees and internally displaced persons (IDPs), can affect social and emotional development in addition to physical health and well-being. Displacement challenges healthy identity development, heightens a youth's vulnerability to malnourishment (Ajdukovic & Dean, 1998), and is associated with particularly high rates of trauma exposure (Kuterovac, Dyregrov, & Stuvland, 1994). It is also related to heightened psychological distress (Barenbaum et al., 2004; Smith, Perrin, Yule, Hacam, & Stuvland, 2002), perhaps due, in part, to these multiple stressors. Youth exposed to war must contend with significant trauma and loss within a context of disrupted social and community systems, all of which can place undue strain on the developmental process (Joshi & O'Donnell, 2003).

Children are more susceptible than adults to certain risks associated with war-like situations (UNICEF, 2005b) and can even be the primary targets of violence (UNICEF, 1996). For example, children are exceedingly vulnerable to landmines, abandoned weapons, and other explosive remnants of war as they tend to be curious about unfamiliar, novel objects and they are less likely than adults to comprehend signs marking minefields. This risk is compounded in settings where youth typically shoulder familial responsibilities (i.e., fetching water or herding animals) that require traversing large tracts of land alone (UNICEF, 2005a). Indeed,

75 percent of injuries incurred from landmines in rural areas of Somalia were suffered by children between the ages of 5 and 15 (International Committee of the Red Cross, 1994).

Even after moving out of conflict zones, many challenges remain. The conditions in refugee and IDP camps are often quite poor. Inadequate shelters, overcrowding, unsanitary conditions, and diseases are common. Food and drinking water can be scarce and of poor quality, resulting in chronic malnutrition and dehydration (Cronin et al., 2008). Education is an additional struggle for children, as many experience significant educational lapses due, in part, to poor infrastructure and lack of resources available to refugee schools (Kirk & Winthrop, 2007). In addition, there is a risk of further exposure to violence while living in camps in part because assisting aid organizations are often unable to provide the necessary staffing to keep camps safe (Iaccino, 2014).

Some children exposed to war and conflict are granted refugee status and are consequently resettled in another country. Although resettlement often brings with it a sense of hope and safety, it nonetheless raises new challenges, such as economic deprivation, discrimination, acculturative stress, and isolation (Ellis, Lincoln, et al., 2010). Indeed, research shows that postresettlement stressors, acculturative stress, and perceived discrimination are predictive of mental health symptoms, even after accounting for trauma exposure (Ellis, Macdonald, Lincoln, & Cabral, 2008).

The following case vignette provides an example of the kinds of stressors that young refugees encounter. Fathia, an adolescent Somali refugee, has been exposed to war in her country of origin, sent to a refugee camp in another country, and resettled in a third county, the United States. Fathia's experiences provide examples of the unique mental health challenges for children of war and for their families. This case will also highlight developmental and cultural considerations critical to treatment.

Case Example: Fathia

Fathia is a 13-year-old girl who was born in Somalia amid civil war. She has seen suffering and experienced a great deal of stress and loss, both during the time she lived in Somalia and also during her journey out of war and into resettlement. Fathia is Somali Bantu—an ethnic group that has been marginalized and oppressed within Somalia—and is the second oldest of five children. By the age of seven, many of Fathia's relatives had been killed, including her father. During one particularly brutal attack on their village, Fathia's mother, Ilhan, decided to flee with her children to a refugee camp in Kenya. While en route, Fathia was separated from her family and held by a rebel group for several days during which she was repeatedly physically assaulted. Her back is still covered in scars from the beatings. She reunited with her mother and siblings at a refugee camp a few weeks later, having been left behind by the rebel group who deemed her too weak to be of any utility. Although Fathia felt relieved upon arrival, fear and uncertainty soon overwhelmed her. Food and water were scarce, disposal of waste was unsanitary, living quarters were cramped and vulnerable to collapse, and numerous refugees at the camp had fallen ill with cholera. Furthermore, the camp where Fathia and her family were living was often attacked by bandits during the night who robbed them of their meager rations and raped and kidnapped women and girls. Often, Fathia and her family would be alerted to the fact that they were under attack by the screams of those who were being assaulted. The family would then grab whatever they could and hide in the woods until these screams had stopped, signaling that the attacks were over.

At the age of 11, Fathia and her family received approval from the U.S. Embassy for resettlement in the United States. Upon entry to the United States, the family arrived in Minnesota but moved to an urban area in New England shortly thereafter to join distant cousins. Once in New England, she and her family moved several times due to the high cost of housing, making it hard for Fathia to settle into a school routine. She eventually enrolled in a middle school with a large number of Somali students, all of whom had previously lived in refugee camps scattered throughout East Africa. Despite the large Somali student body, the school personnel had no prior experience serving refugee children and families and were unaware of the extent of trauma and loss that Fathia carried with her.

At the time of her enrollment, Fathia presented as a quiet girl with few friends, if any. At school, she isolated herself from her peers, particularly during large group activities, and generally seemed overwhelmed by the hustle and bustle of the school hallways. Despite her interest in academics, Fathia frequently begged her mother, Ilhan, to let her stay home from school. Ilhan, frightened by the desperation in her daughter's voice, permitted Fathia to stay home some days. Although Ilhan cared greatly about her daughter's education, she worried that something bad was happening to Fathia at school and was unsure of how to express these concerns to school personnel. Because Fathia took the bus to school, Ilhan did not know where her daughter's school was located. She also did not speak English. The school had no resources for interpreters, creating further barriers to Ilhan's access to and participation in her daughter's educational experiences.

Fathia frequently tried to leave school. Without any explanation, she would quickly and intentionally pack her things, put her backpack on, and rush toward the exit, despite the fact that her teacher was watching. Each time, school personnel, including administration and security staff, surrounded her in order to stop her from leaving. This approach never worked, as Fathia only seemed to grow angrier when surrounded. She would scream out for help and aggress against any security staff who tried to physically calm her down. Attempts by school personnel to talk to Fathia about why she didn't want to attend school failed. Fathia could not describe what about school upset her. She would shut down whenever she was reminded of the importance of staying in school and getting an education. School staff were stumped by Fathia's constant attempts to leave, especially since it was clear that she could not get home by foot.

Finally, the school contacted an ethnic-based community organization in the New England area, whose staff included "culture brokers."[1] The school requested the services of a culture broker, and a Somali Bantu staff member was assigned to the case. Upon speaking to Fathia in her own language, the culture broker discovered that Fathia experienced a physical assault while her family was fleeing the war. Fathia described how noisy and frenetic movement in her school environment reminded her of the chaos and noise that preceded her assault by the rebel group and the attacks in the refugee camp. When the kids in her classroom were all talking and moving about, she would feel overcome by a sense of imminent danger, thus the overwhelming need to escape and find her family. In this regard, Fathia portrayed her efforts to leave school as driven by a fear of physical attack and subsequent familial loss.

Psychological Impact of War

Fathia's behaviors are consistent with symptoms of posttraumatic stress and are typical of the kinds of psychological distress shown by many children exposed to war. The psychological impact can be devastating, yet it is largely underresearched (Attanayake et al., 2009). Available studies have examined the prevalence of certain trauma exposures among children exposed to war (Dyregrov, Gjestad, & Raundalen, 2002; Karam et al., 2008) in addition to the differential effects of these exposures (Layne et al., 2010; Macksoud & Aber, 1996). For example, an investigation of the psychosocial effects of guerrilla-style warfare on displaced children in Southern Darfur reported that youth ages 6–17 endorsed an average of 8.94 of 16 assessed war experiences (Morgos et al., 2008). The most frequently experienced war exposures included being forcibly removed from one's home (98%), experiencing a home invasion (95%), witnessing homes burned (94%), and hiding to protect oneself from rape or death (90%). Furthermore, the majority of interviewees endorsed fear of starvation (75%) and the witnessing of family members being tortured/experiencing torture themselves (75%). Half of children revealed that they had lost one or more sibling to death and 25 percent reported the loss of one or both parents, while 50 percent of youth endorsed being threatened with death. Of note, the strongest predictors of posttraumatic stress symptoms in order of strength were as follows: (1) abduction, (2) hiding to protect oneself, (3) being raped, (4) forced to hurt or kill family members, and (5) seeing someone burned alive. Being raped and hiding to protect oneself were predictive of depressive symptoms as well, in addition to witnessing the rape of others, death of a parent(s), and being forced to fight.

Given the high rates of trauma exposure common to this population, it is unsurprising that war-exposed youth from a variety of countries have been found to demonstrate an elevated risk of psychological distress, particularly symptoms of posttraumatic stress (Lavi & Solomon, 2005; Thabet, Abed, & Vostanis, 2002). These symptoms include hypervigilance, intrusive thoughts related to past traumatic event(s), and avoidance of trauma reminders—all of which were evidenced by Fathia in the above case vignette. Coexisting disorders are also common, including depression, anxiety, bereavement-related disorders, or externalizing disorders characterized by behavioral dysregulation (e.g., aggression or impulsivity; Betancourt, McBain, Newnham, & Brennan, 2014; Kinzie, Cheng, Tsai, & Riley, 2006).

The story of Fathia illustrates the struggles of a young girl who continues to be haunted by horrific events that transpired many years ago in her country of origin. Although long-term outcomes of war exposure can vary, studies have shown that children exposed to war can remain symptomatic many years after the conflict has ended (Sack, Him, & Dickason, 1999). Individual, family, and contextual factors are often associated with mental health outcomes among refugee children and adolescents like Fathia (Ellis et al., 2008).

While many refugee youth have experienced traumatic exposure before and during migration, other aspects of stress that accompany the resettlement process are also critical to understanding current psychosocial support needs. Research suggests that for some youth, the stressors encountered in resettlement, such as social isolation, are important predictors of mental health problems (Miller et al., 2002). For example, in a sample of Bosnian refugees, the strongest predictor of depressive symptoms was social isolation; past trauma history did not predict depressive symptoms (Miller et al., 2002). In addition, experiences of discrimination, which may contribute to a sense of social isolation or rejection, have been identified as important predictors of both posttraumatic stress disorder (PTSD) and depression among adolescent Somali refugees resettled in North America (Ellis, Macdonald, et al., 2010; Ellis et al., 2008).

The Impact of War on Children: Developmental Considerations

Though only 14 years of age, it is clear from the vignette in this chapter that Fathia has experienced a tremendous amount of loss and trauma. At the age of seven, Fathia experienced a particularly horrific event—separation from her family followed by repeated physical assaults—leaving scars on her back that serve as a continual reminder of the physical abuse she endured while held by a rebel group in Somalia. Studies have reported on the greater vulnerability of children between the ages of five and nine to war exposure (e.g., Kuterovac-Jagodić, 2003), suggesting that youth within this age group have a growing ability to recognize and process events but lack an integrated identity and sophisticated defense mechanisms (Barenbaum et al., 2004).

Young children are assumed to be more susceptible than adolescents to the impact of traumatic events due to their limited cognitive capacities for remembering, processing, and coping with trauma (Schneider, 2000). However, there is a competing belief that this reduced capacity to fully grasp the potential prolonged impact of war exposure on well-being might protect young children against negative outcomes (Masten & Narayan, 2012). Indeed, cognitive maturity brings greater awareness of betrayals, loss, and the scope of devastation as well as a heightened understanding of the stigma that can come with surviving war atrocities such as rape or involvement in combat (Betancourt et al., 2014).

Studies examining how age effects the development of PTSD have produced contradictory results (Derluyn, Broekaert, Schuyten, & De Temmerman, 2004; Thabet, Abed, & Vostanis, 2004), likely due to regional differences in the context for war (Morgos et al., 2008). Although older children typically report a greater number of war exposures (e.g., Masten & Narayan, 2012; Morgos et al., 2008), this does not preclude young children from the psychological effects of wartime violence. In fact, even infants and toddlers exposed to war can develop PTSD (Feldman & Vengrober, 2011) though subtle differences in symptom presentation are often apparent (see Scheeringa, Zeanah, Myers, & Putnam, 2003). For example, results of a study of Israeli, early childhood-aged youth living near the Gaza Strip highlighted the tendency of preschool-age children to exhibit nonspecific behavioral problems, mood lability, and developmental regression in response to war exposure rather than traditional posttraumatic stress symptoms (Feldman & Vengrober, 2011).

The extent to which development impacts symptom presentation has also been explored in older age groups exposed to war and conflict. For instance, Dyregrov et al. (2002) noted that youth ages 10–13 living in

Iraq during the Gulf War endorsed more avoidance symptoms than any other age cohort interviewed. Additional posttraumatic stress symptoms reported with greater frequency among older children include somatic and reexperiencing symptoms, feelings of isolation, and fear that the traumatic event(s) will reoccur (Morgos et al., 2008). Older children and adolescents have also been found to report significantly higher levels of grief than younger ones (Morgos et al., 2008), which is suggestive of developmental differences in children's understanding of the finality of death and/or their ability to articulate grief (Raphael, 1983; Wooding & Raphael, 2004).

Cultural Considerations for Working with Children and Families Affected by War

In considering appropriate mental health services for children and adolescents exposed to war, the culture and belief systems of the family must be considered. Culturally sensitive practice requires having a basic fund of knowledge about the specific cultural group in need of services. This includes their country of origin's history, cultural norms and traditions, and, in the case of refugees or IDPs, reasons for fleeing (Delgado, Jones, & Rohani, 2005). It is also critical to be aware of culturally specific explanations and expressions of mental illness (Bolton et al., 2007; Morgos et al., 2008), in addition to the potential role of local, traditional practitioners in healing (Brach & Fraserirector, 2000).

An individual's narrative of his or her distress is often imbued with culturally relevant terminology and symbolism (see Bolton et al., 2007). For example, in their investigation of the psychosocial effects of war experiences among displaced children in Southern Darfur, Morgos et al. (2008) noted that participants described the severity of their depressive symptoms through storytelling and local idioms rather than using quantitative language (i.e., "less than once a month" or "always"). This phenomenon is captured in the following anecdotes from the study:

> One child answered, "I cry as much as the rain falls in the rainy season and soaks the fields and as fast as the blood flows in my body." This answer was his attempt to explain the "depth" of his tears rather than "frequency" as intended by the instrument. When asked about how much he cries, [another] child answered "just like the morning dew" indicating the frequency as well as severity of his tears. (p. 46)

Fathia's story emphasizes her struggle with posttraumatic stress, as evidenced by symptoms of hypervigilance, intrusive thoughts related to past traumatic event(s), and avoidance of trauma reminders, all typical symptoms associated with PTSD. However, there are notable cultural differences in prevalence rates of PTSD, suggesting that it is not a universal disorder (Attanayake et al., 2009). Culture can also impact responses to grief and loss (Dyregrov et al., 2002), particularly in societies where idealization of the dead is common (Nader, 1997) or where "forgetting" is utilized as a primary coping strategy (Dyregrov et al., 2002).

It is for these reasons that several authors caution against the assumption that PTSD is the sole diagnosis appropriate for children exposed to war, or more broadly, that Western diagnostic entities universally capture the essence of human response to adversity (Kinzie et al., 2006; Summerfield, 2000). The reframing of reasonable distress in the face of extreme adversity as a psychological disturbance also has the potential to inadvertently disregard individual strengths and priorities (Summerfield, 2000). Consequently, a culturally sensitive treatment approach involves attending to the specific social or cultural context in order to distinguish dysfunctional responses from normative ones within that culture (Kirmayer & Young, 1999).

As underscored by Bracken, Giller, and Summerfield (1995), coping strategies are ultimately determined by social, cultural, and political factors. It is essential, therefore, that practitioners with cultural backgrounds divergent from the population in need work with culturally informed caregivers/providers (culture brokers) who can provide insight into trauma exposure and idioms of distress (Laor & Wolmer, 2002). These types of cross-cultural partnerships are often critical to care, as evidenced by Fathia's story. Consultation with the Somali culture broker was essential to the school developing an accurate understanding of Fathia's difficulties and needs. The involvement of a culture broker allowed Fathia to communicate her distress in her own language, rather than struggling to find the words in English to describe what was upsetting her. Furthermore, Fathia felt as though the culture broker could understand where her fears were coming from, because the culture broker herself was a Somali refugee who had similarly fled from the civil war in Somalia. Without this external support, Fathia's behavior could have easily been misinterpreted as school refusal, or worse, as disinterest in learning, both of which have negative implications for Fathia obtaining the help she so desperately needed.

The culture broker also understood that Fathia's ethnicity as Somali Bantu added an additional layer of complexity with important implications for intervention planning. The Somali Bantu have been marginalized and oppressed within Somalia. This history of marginalization in conjunction with a legacy of disempowerment in social, political, and economic arenas may lead to a mistrust of service providers who represent a more empowered, Somali majority group (Hundley & Lambie, 2007). Indeed, issues of power and distrust may affect services at the individual or familial level, challenging the development of a therapeutic alliance, or at the programmatic/community level, resulting in lower rates of engagement.

Fathia's case is thus an example of the extent to which attending to issues of power and hierarchy are critical to the provision of culturally sensitive services for war-exposed children and their families (see Summerfield, 2000). Although school personnel were trying to help, surrounding her when she attempted to exit only frightened her more and caused her to feel as though school staff were asserting their control over her. Fathia felt coerced and misunderstood by staff members who repeatedly asked her why she didn't want to go to school or would lecture her on the importance of attending school for her own career development. Each time, she would disengage from these conversations, feeling as though the school assumed she didn't care about her education.

The involvement of service providers and/or culture brokers from these specific ethnic groups may also help with family engagement. For instance, in the case of Fathia who was Somali Bantu, her family might be more open to engaging in services with Somalis who are ethnically similar due to their history of marginalization by other Somali ethnic groups. In addition, having a coethnic culture broker can reduce linguistic barriers and can enhance engagement.

In summary, awareness of and sensitivity to context are critical in the provision of effective mental health services to children and families exposed to war. Recognition of cultural differences within social support systems is especially important, as these differences can greatly impact service engagement (see Ehntholt, Smith, & Yule, 2005) and directly inform intervention strategies (Schwab-Stone, Ruchkin, Vermeiren, & Leckman, 2001). Finally, treatment approaches that cultivate trust not only between service providers and the child/family but also between practitioners and the whole community may be better accepted.

Patterns of and Barriers to Help Seeking among Children and Families

Despite elevated levels of distress, relatively few children exposed to war obtain mental health services. Among refugee children and adolescents in particular, as many as 92 percent of those in need do not access mental health services (Birman et al., 2005; Ellis, Lincoln, et al., 2010).

Although access rates are likely to vary by specific ethnic group and other demographic characteristics, these generally low rates suggest that attention to service access and utilization in addition to modes of help seeking is needed.

Help seeking is driven by internal, external, demographic, socioeconomic, and cultural factors (Al-Krenawi, Graham, Al-Bedah, Kadri, & Sehwail, 2009). Culture is particularly relevant to service utilization and is believed to permeate the entire help-seeking pathway, from problem identification to actual help seeking (Cauce et al., 2002). In Arab society, for example, lower rates of help seeking among adolescents are largely explained by fear of stigma and reluctance to share family issues with strangers. The fear of status loss and discrimination can be a significant barrier to seeking out formal sources of support (Ahmead, Rahhal, & Baker, 2010; Leshem, Haj-Yahia, & Guterman, 2015). In many cultures, mental illness is considered a taboo topic and is not openly discussed (Scuglik, Alarcón, Lapeyre, Williams, & Logan, 2007). For instance, a study of teenage Palestinians living in the West Bank or East Jerusalem revealed that a primary barrier of help seeking for this group was not wanting others to find out about their distress (Leshem et al., 2015).

In cultures characterized by a collective social system, the family is often seen as the primary resource for help and coping (Al-Krenawi & Graham, 2003). Family problems are regarded as issues that concern the family alone, without involvement from external supports (Kulwicki, Aswad, Carmona, & Ballout, 2010). Obligations, needs, aspirations, and social ties of the family as a unit are believed to supersede the needs of the individual (Haj-Yahia, 2005), just as the success or failure of one family member is perceived as belonging to the entire family rather than to the individual (Haj-Yahia, 2005). In a study examining patterns of help seeking among Palestinian adolescents after exposure to community violence, almost half of teenagers interviewed reported that they sought informal help primarily through family members and friends to cope with their distress (Leshem et al., 2015). In Fathia's country of origin, Somalia, support is often sought through informal networks (e.g., family, friends, and neighbors) or faith-based leaders. However, losses associated with war and resettlement can greatly disrupt those networks, leaving families like Fathia's feeling isolated and alone.

Little is known about the extent to which parents of youth exposed to war look beyond their informal networks for help when their children are struggling (De Anstiss, Ziaian, Procter, Warland, & Baghurst, 2009). When Fathia said that she didn't want to attend school, her mother immediately worried that her daughter was unsafe there—an assumption largely shaped by her own trauma history and experience. For Fathia's mother, Ilhan, obtaining access to support systems outside of her informal networks felt nearly impossible due to countless, systemic barriers common to the refugee experience. Ilhan did not speak English. She didn't know where her daughter's school was located. The school did not offer the services of an interpreter upon enrollment to ensure that she had information about the school location and programming. Transportation and childcare barriers further limited Ilhan's ability to connect with support. As a result, Ilhan felt she could do little other than keep her daughter home from school and wait for Fathia's teachers to come to her if something was wrong.

When outside help is accessed for refugee children, referrals are more likely to be initiated by practitioners than by parents or caregivers themselves (Nadeau & Measham, 2006). Schools and social service agencies have a particularly important role to play in connecting youth to resources and bridging care, given their high level of contact with refugee children, which speaks to the need for close collaboration between divergent service sectors (De Anstiss et al., 2009; Howard & Hodes, 2000). At the service system level, perhaps the most critical explanation for low service use concerns the global failure of Western mental health-care systems to recognize and respond to the needs of ethnically diverse populations (Summerfield, 2001). As a result, attempts to communicate distress can be unrecognized, ignored, or misunderstood. This is particularly relevant to Fathia's case, as her attempts to pack her bags and exit school in front of peers and staff were initially perceived as a behavioral problem by school personnel.

Intervention with War-Exposed Children and Youth: Treatment Considerations

Five broad intervention principles/components have been proposed for treating individuals with recent exposure to extensive trauma and mass violence: fostering a sense of safety, calming, self- and collective efficacy, connectedness, and hope (Hobfoll et al., 2007). In this regard, intervention with war-affected groups prioritizes protecting, supporting, and restoring the most fundamental adaptive systems believed to cultivate resilience (see Masten, 2001, 2011). For youth in particular, this includes reestablishing natural protective systems as well as normal routines of school and play (Masten & Narayan, 2012).

Masten and Narayan (2012) caution against using practices that have little evidentiary support, are developmentally or culturally inappropriate, and/or disrupt or challenge naturally occurring resilience and recovery processes. Research has shown little support for interventions implemented in the immediate aftermath of war, beyond those that involve disseminating concrete information, providing for basic needs (e.g., water, food, shelter, medicine, or money), and maintaining or restoring social support networks (Bonanno, Brewin, Kaniasty, & La Greca, 2010). Rather, psychological intervention delivered at least several months after exposure has proven more effective (e.g., Karam et al., 2008).

In recent years, researchers and practitioners alike have begun to question the cross-cultural applicability and utility of trauma treatment focused primarily on extinguishing symptoms of PTSD (Summerfield, 1999). There is now more focus on fostering strength, capacity, and resilience among war-affected individuals and communities (Papadopoulos, 2007). For refugees, this includes understanding challenges within the resettlement environment and rectifying these challenges when possible. In addition, emphasis has been placed on utilizing interventions that recognize cultural differences in meaning and distress and that nurture culture-specific methods of coping and responding to adversity (Dossa, 2010; Von Peter, 2008). Similarly, relationship-based and narrative therapy approaches that align well with more collectivistic[2] and oral traditions have garnered evidentiary support (Bolton et al., 2007; Meffert et al., 2014).

In working with children exposed to war, the largest body of evidence has been in the evaluation of school-based programs (Ehntholt & Yule, 2006; Ellis et al., 2013). Some of these programs focus on the use of arts-based therapies (Rousseau, Lacroix, Bagilishya, & Heusch, 2003), providing a developmentally appropriate medium through which to safely express and resolve trauma and adjustment-related concerns. Some refugee mental health programs have also focused on addressing social and environmental stressors that youth can encounter with resettlement, such as family conflict, unstable living conditions, and financial stressors (e.g., Ellis et al., 2013).

Trauma Systems Therapy for Refugees (TST-R) is an example of one such program, providing school-based, skill-building groups that focus on increasing one's capacity for self-regulation in addition to reducing acculturative stress. TST-R also encourages parent and community outreach by focusing on providing psychoeducation and decreasing stigma in addition to providing more intensive, individualized trauma treatment for youth with significant mental health needs. In this regard, TST-R is a multitiered treatment model that includes interventions targeting both the individual child and child's social environment. Programs such as this represent essential multilayered responses that recognize not only the importance of addressing trauma but also the need to address the resettlement challenges faced by refugee communities, whose residents are frequently living in low-income and underresourced neighborhoods (Ellis et al., 2008). Furthermore, all TST-R services delivered across tiers are implemented with the support of a culture broker from the community in need—an essential element that is integral to the success of cross-cultural treatment (Anderson et al., 2003; Brach & Fraserirector, 2000). For Fathia and her family, a service model similar to TST-R that attends to the wide-ranging challenges associated with trauma and resettlement through a linguistically appropriate, culturally mindful frame is critical to stabilization and long-term success.

Conclusion

As long as global conflict persists, children—the most vulnerable members of our societies—will be affected. The multilayered effects of war on systems, communities, and individuals create a context of incredible adversity in which these children must navigate the tasks of psychological development and growth. The complex interplay of systems and development can create vulnerabilities; however, practitioners and policy makers can use this same interlocking of the environment and development to create positive change. Through concerted efforts to promote cultural understanding, reduce stress, and break down barriers to care, vulnerable youth such as Fathia can place the horrors of war in their past.

Notes

1. The role of a cultural broker differs from that of an interpreter in that a broker not only provides interpretation but also serves as a bridge, link, or mediator between groups or persons of different cultural backgrounds for the purpose of reducing conflict or producing change (Jezewski, 1990). This ultimately helps to increase engagement, facilitate cross-cultural communication, and strengthen the relationship between families and service providers, thereby improving quality of care.
2. Collectivist traditions are ones that emphasize community goals and needs over that of the individual.

References

Ahmead, M. K., Rahhal, A. A., & Baker, J. A. (2010). The attitudes of mental health professionals towards patients with mental illness in an inpatient setting in Palestine. *International Journal of Mental Health Nursing, 19*(5), 356–362. doi:10.1111/j.1447 0349.2010.00674.x

Ajdukovic, M., & Dean, A. (1998). Impact of displacement on the psychological well-being of refugee children. *International Review of Psychiatry, 10*(3), 186–195. doi:10.1080/09540269874763

Al-Krenawi, A., & Graham, J. R. (2003). Social work with Canadians of Arab background: Insight into direct practice. In A. Al-Krenawi & J. R. Graham (Eds.), *Multicultural social work in Canada: Working with diverse ethno-racial communities* (pp. 174–201). Toronto: Oxford University.

Al-Krenawi, A., Graham, J. R., Al-Bedah, E. A., Kadri, H. M., & Sehwail, M. A. (2009). Cross-national comparison of Middle Eastern university students: Help-seeking behaviors, attitudes toward helping professionals, and cultural beliefs about mental health problems. *Community Mental Health Journal, 45*(1), 26–36. doi:10.1007/s10597-008-9175-2

Anderson, L. M., Scrimshaw, S. C., Fullilove, M. T., Fielding, J. E., Normand, J., & Services, T. (2003). Culturally competent healthcare systems: A systematic review. *American Journal of Preventive Medicine, 24*(3 suppl), 68–79. doi:10.1016/S0749–3797(02)00657–8

Attanayake, V., McKay, R., Joffres, M., Singh, S., Burkle, F., Jr., & Mills, E. (2009). Prevalence of mental disorders among children exposed to war: A systematic review of 7,920 children. *Medicine Conflict and Survival, 25*(1), 4–19. doi:10.1080/13623690802568913

Barenbaum, J., Ruchkin, V., & Schwab-Stone, M. (2004). The psychosocial aspects of children exposed to war: Practice and policy initiatives. *Journal of Child Psychology and Psychiatry, 45*(1), 41–62. doi:10.1046/j.0021–9630.2003.00304.x

Betancourt, T. S., McBain, R., Newnham, E. A., & Brennan, R. T. (2014). Context matters: Community characteristics and mental health among war-affected youth in Sierra Leone. *Journal of Child Psychology and Psychiatry, 55*(3), 217–226. doi:10.1111/jcpp.12131

Birman, D., Ho, J., Pulley, E., Batia, K., Everson, M. L., Ellis, B. H., . . . Gonzalez, A. (2005). *Mental health interventions for refugee children in resettlement.* Retrieved from http://www.nctsnet.org/nctsn_assets/pdfs/materials_for_applicants/MH_Interventions_fo _Refugee_Children.pdf

Bolton, P., Bass, J., Betancourt, T., Speelman, L., Onyango, G., Clougherty, K. F., . . . Verdeli, H. (2007). Interventions for depression symptoms among adolescent survivors of war and displacement in Northern Uganda: A randomized controlled trial. *Journal of the American Medical Association, 298*(5), 519–527. doi:10.1001/jama.298.5.519

Bonanno, G. A., Brewin, C. R., Kaniasty, K., & La Greca, A. M. (2010). Weighing the costs of disaster consequences, risks, and resilience in individuals, families, and communities. *Psychological Science in the Public Interest, 11*(1), 1–49. doi:10.1177/1529100610387086

Brach, C., & Fraserirector, I. (2000). Can cultural competency reduce racial and ethnic health disparities? A review and conceptual model. *Medical Care Research and Review, 57*(4 suppl), 181–217. doi:10.1177/1077558700057001S09

Bracken, P.J., Giller, J.E., & Summerfield, D. (1995). Psychological responses to war and atrocity: The limitations of current concepts. *Social Science & Medicine, 40*(8), 1073–1082. doi:10.1016/0277–9536(94)00181-R

Cauce, A.M., Domenech-Rodríguez, M., Paradise, M., Cochran, B.N., Shea, J. M., Srebnik, D., & Baydar, N. (2002). Cultural and contextual influences in mental health help seeking: A focus on ethnic minority youth. *Journal of Consulting and Clinical Psychology, 70*(1), 44. doi:10.1037/0022–006X.70.1.44

Cronin, A., Shrestha, D., Cornier, N., Abdalla, F., Ezard, N., & Aramburu, C. (2008). A review of water and sanitation provision in refugee camps in association with selected health and nutrition indicators—the need for integrated service provision. *Journal of Water and Health,6*(1), 1–13. doi:10.2166/wh.2007.019

De Anstiss, H., Ziaian, T., Procter, N., Warland, J., & Baghurst, P. (2009). Help-seeking for mental health problems in young refugees: A review of the literature with implications for policy, practice, and research. *Transcultural Psychiatry, 46*(4), 584–607. doi:10.1177/ 1363461509351363

Delgado, M., Jones, K., & Rohani, M. (2005). *Social work practice with refugee and immigrant youth in the United States*. Boston, MA: Pearson.

Derluyn, I., Broekaert, E., Schuyten, G., & De Temmerman, E. (2004). Post-traumatic stress in former Ugandan child soldiers. *The Lancet, 363*(9412), 861–863.

Dossa, P. (2010). Exploring the disjuncture between the politics of trauma and everyday realities of women in Afghanistan. *Journal of Muslim Mental Health, 5*(1), 8–21. doi:10.1080/15564901003609414

Dyregrov, A., Gjestad, R., & Raundalen, M. (2002). Children exposed to warfare: A longitudinal study. *Journal of Traumatic Stress, 15*(1), 59–68. doi:10.1023/A:1014335312219

Ehntholt, K.A., Smith, P.A., & Yule, W. (2005). School-based cognitive-behavioural therapy group intervention for refugee children who have experienced war-related trauma. *Clinical Child Psychology and Psychiatry, 10*(2), 235–250. doi:10.1177/1359104505051214

Ehntholt, K.A., & Yule, W. (2006). Practitioner review: Assessment and treatment of refugee children and adolescents who have experienced war-related trauma. *Journal of Child Psychology and Psychiatry, 47*(12), 1197–1210. doi:10.1111/j.1469–7610.2006.01638.x

Ellis, B.H., Lincoln, A.K., Charney, M.E., Ford-Paz, R., Benson, M., & Strunin, L. (2010). Mental health service utilization of Somali adolescents: Feligion, community, and school as gateways to healing. *Transcultural Psychiatry, 47*(5), 789–811. doi:10.1177/1363461510379933

Ellis, B.H., Macdonald, H.Z., Klunk-Gillis, J., Lincoln, A.K., Strunin, L., & Cabral, H.J. (2010). Discrimination and mental health among Somali refugee adolescents: The role of acculturation and gender. *American Journal of Orthopsychiatry, 80*(4), 564–575. doi:10.1111/j.1939–0025.2010.01061.x

Ellis, B.H., Macdonald, H.Z., Lincoln, A.K., & Cabral, H.J. (2008). Mental health of Somali adolescent refugees: The role of trauma, stress, and perceived discrimination. *Journal of Consulting and Clinical Psychology, 76*(2), 184–193. doi:10.1037/0022–006X.76.2.184

Ellis, B.H., Miller, A.B., Abdi, S., Barrett, C., Blood, E.A., & Betancourt, T.S. (2013). Multi-tier mental health program for refugee youth. *Journal of Consulting and Clinical Psychology, 81*(1), 129. doi:10.1037/a0029844

Feldman, R., & Vengrober, A. (2011). Posttraumatic stress disorder in infants and young children exposed to war-related trauma. *Journal of the American Academy of Child & Adolescent Psychiatry, 50*(7), 645–658. doi:10.1016/j.jaac.2011.03.001

Haj-Yahia, M.M. (2005). On the characteristics of patriarchal societies, gender inequality, and wife abuse: The case of Palestinian society. *Adalah's Newsletter, 20*, 1–6. Retrieved from https://www.adalah.org/uploads/oldfiles/newsletter/eng/nov05/fet.pdf

Hobfoll, S.E., Watson, P., Bell, C.C., Bryant, R.A., Brymer, M.J., Friedman, M.J., . . . Layne, C.M. (2007). Five essential elements of immediate and mid-term mass trauma intervention: Empirical evidence. *Psychiatry, 70*(4), 283–315. doi:10.3402/ejpt.v4i0.21914

Howard, M., & Hodes, M. (2000). Psychopathology, adversity, and service utilization of young refugees. *Journal of the American Academy of Child & Adolescent Psychiatry, 39*(3), 368–377. doi:10.1097/00004583–200003000–00020

Hundley, G., & Lambie, G.W. (2007). Russian speaking immigrants from the commonwealth of independent states in the United States: Implications for mental health counselors. *Journal of Mental Health Counseling, 29*(3), 242. doi:10.17744/mehc.29.3.34016u53586q4016

Iaccino, L. (2014). *World refugee day 2014: Living conditions in the largest refugee camps*. Retrieved from http://www.ibtimes.co.uk/world-refugee-day-2014-living-conditions largest-refugee-camps-1453517

International Committee of the Red Cross. (1994). *Children and war*. Retrieved from https://www.icrc.org/eng/assets/files/other/icrc_002_0577k_children_in_war_kit.pdf

Jezewski, M.A. (1990). Culture brokering in migrant farmworker health care. *Western Journal of Nursing Research, 12*(4), 497–513. doi:10.1177/019394599001200406

Joshi, P., & O'Donnell, D. (2003). Consequences of child exposure to war and terrorism. *Clinical Child and Family Psychology Review, 6*(4), 275–292. doi:10.1023/B:CCFP.0000006294.88201.68

Karam, E.G., Fayyad, J., Karam, A.N., Tabet, C.C., Melhem, N., Mneimneh, Z., & Dimassi, H. (2008). Effectiveness and specificity of a classroom-based group intervention in children and adolescents exposed to war in Lebanon. *World Psychiatry, 7*(2), 103–109. doi:10.1002/j.2051–5545.2008.tb00170.x

Kinzie, J. D., Cheng, D. K., Tsai, D. J., & Riley, D. C. (2006). Traumatized refugee children: The case for individualized diagnosis and treatment. *The Journal of Nervous and Mental Disease, 194*(7), 534–537. doi:10.1097/01.nmd.0000224946.93376.51

Kirk, J., & Winthrop, R. (2007). Promoting quality education in refugee contexts: Supporting teacher development in Northern Ethiopia. *International Review of Education, 53*(5), 715–723. doi:10.1007/s11159-007-9061-0

Kirmayer, L. J., & Young, A. (1999). Culture and context in the evolutionary concept of mental disorder. *Journal of Abnormal Psychology, 108*(3), 446–452. doi:10.1037/0021–843X.108.3.446

Kulwicki, A., Aswad, B., Carmona, T., & Ballout, S. (2010). Barriers in the utilization of domestic violence services among Arab immigrant women: Perceptions of professionals, service providers & community leaders. *Journal of Family Violence, 25*(8), 727–735. doi:10.1177/1043659614524000

Kuterovac, G., Dyregrov, A., & Stuvland, R. (1994). Children in war: A silent majority under stress. *British Journal of Medical Psychology, 67*(4), 363–375. doi:10.1111/j.2044-8341.1994.tb01804.x

Kuterovac-Jagodić, G. (2003). Posttraumatic stress symptoms in Croatian children exposed to war: A prospective study. *Journal of Clinical Psychology, 59*(1), 9–25. doi:10.1002/jclp.10114

Laor, N., & Wolmer, L. (2002). Children exposed to disaster: The role of the mental health professional. In M. Lewis (Ed.), *Textbook of child and adolescent psychiatry* (3rd ed., pp. 925–937). Baltimore, MD: Williams and Wilkins.

Lavi, T., & Solomon, Z. (2005). Palestinian youth of the Intifada: PTSD and future orientation. *Journal of the American Academy of Child & Adolescent Psychiatry, 44*(11), 1176–1183. doi:10.1097/01.chi.0000177325.47629.4c

Layne, C., Olsen, J., Baker, A., Legerski, J. p., Isakson, B., Pašalić, A., . . . Arslanagić, B. (2010). Unpacking trauma exposure risk factors and differential pathways of influence: Predicting postwar mental distress in Bosnian adolescents. *Child Development, 81*(4), 1053–1076. doi:10.1111/j.1467–8624.2010.01454.x

Leshem, B., Haj-Yahia, M. M., & Guterman, N. B. (2015). The characteristics of help seeking among Palestinian adolescents following exposure to community violence. *Children and Youth Services Review, 49*, 1–10. doi:10.1016/j.childyouth.2014.12.022

Lustig, S. L., Kia-Keating, M., Knight, W. G., Geltman, P., Ellis, H., Kinzie, J. D., . . . Saxe, G. N. (2004). Review of child and adolescent refugee mental health. *Journal of the American Academy of Child & Adolescent Psychiatry, 43*(1), 24–36. doi:10.1097/00004583–200401000–00012

Machel, G. a. (1996). *Impact of armed conflict on children*. Retrieved from http://www.un.org/documents/ga/docs/51/plenary/a51-306.htm

Macksoud, M. S., & Aber, J. L. (1996). The war experiences and psychosocial development of children in Lebanon. *Child Development, 67*(1), 70–88. doi:10.2307/1131687

Masten, A. S. (2001). Ordinary magic: Resilience processes in development. *American Psychologist, 56*, 227–238.

Masten, A. S. (2011). Resilience in children threatened by extreme adversity: Frameworks for research, practice, and translational synergy. *Development and Psychopathology, 23*(2), 493–506. doi:10.1017/S0954579411000198

Masten, A. S., & Narayan, A. J. (2012). Child development in the context of disaster, war, and terrorism: Pathways of risk and resilience. *Psychology, 63*, 227–257. doi:10.1146/annurev-psych-120710–100356

Meffert, S. M., Abdo, A. O., Alla, O. A. A., Elmakki, Y. O. M., Omer, A. A., Yousif, S., . . . Marmar, C. R. (2014). A pilot randomized controlled trial of interpersonal psychotherapy for Sudanese refugees in Cairo, Egypt. *Psychological Trauma: Theory, Research, Practice, and Policy, 6*(3), 240–249. doi:10.1037/a0023540

Miller, K., Weine, S., Ramic, A., Brkic, N., Bjedic, Z., Smajkic, A., . . . Worthington, G. (2002). The relative contribution of war experiences and exile-related stressors to levels of psychological distress among Bosnian refugees. *Journal of Traumatic Stress, 15*(5), 377–387. doi:10.1023/A:1020181124118

Morgos, D., Worden, J. W., & Gupta, L. (2008). Psychosocial effects of war experiences among displaced children in southern Darfur. *OMEGA-Journal of Death and Dying, 56*(3), 229–253. doi:10.2190/OM.56.3.b

Nadeau, L., & Measham, T. (2006). Caring for migrant and refugee children: Challenges associated with mental health care in pediatrics. *Journal of Developmental & Behavioral Pediatrics, 27*(2), 145–154. doi:10.1097/00004703-200604000-00013

Neugebauer, R., Fisher, P. W., Turner, J. B., Yamabe, S., Sarsfield, J. A., & Stehling-Ariza, T. (2009). Post-traumatic stress reactions among Rwandan children and adolescents in the early aftermath of genocide. *International Journal of Epidemiology, 38*(4), 1033–1045. doi:10.1093/ije/dyn375

Papadopoulos, R. K. (2007). Refugees, trauma and adversity-activated development. *European Journal of Psychotherapy and Counselling, 9*(3), 301–312. doi:10.1080/13642530701496930

Raphael, B. (1983). *The anatomy of bereavement*. New York, NY: Basic Books.

Rousseau, C., Lacroix, L., Bagilishya, D., & Heusch, N. (2003). Working with myths: Creative expression workshops for immigrant and refugee children in a school setting. *Art Therapy, 20*(1), 3–10. Retrieved from https://doi.org/10.1080/07421656.2003.10129630

Sack, W. H., Him, C., & Dickason, D. (1999). Twelve-year follow-up study of Khmer youths who suffered massive war trauma as children. *Journal of the American Academy of Child and Adolescent Psychiatry, 38*(9), 1173. doi:10.1097/00004583–199909000–00023

Scheeringa, M. S., Zeanah, C. H., Myers, L., & Putnam, F. W. (2003). New findings on alternative criteria for PTSD in preschool children. *Journal of the American Academy of Child & Adolescent Psychiatry, 42*(5), 561–570. doi:10.1097/01.CHI.0000046822.95464.14

Schneider, W. (2000). Research on memory development: Historical trends and current themes. *International Journal of Behavioral Development, 24*(4), 407–420. doi:10.1080/016502500750037955

Schwab-Stone, M., Ruchkin, V., Vermeiren, R., & Leckman, P. (2001). Cultural considerations in the treatment of children and adolescents. Operationalizing the importance of culture in treatment. *Child and Adolescent Psychiatric Clinics of North America, 10*(4), 729–743.

Scuglik, D. L., Alarcón, R. D., Lapeyre, A. C., Williams, M. D., & Logan, K. M. (2007). When the poetry no longer rhymes: Mental health issues among Somali immigrants in the USA. *Transcultural Psychiatry, 44*(4), 581–595. doi:10.1177/1363461507083899

Shaw, J. A. (2003). Children exposed to war/terrorism. *Clinical Child and Family Psychology Review, 6*(4), 237–246. doi:10.1023/B:CCFP.0000006291.10180.bd

Smith, P., Perrin, S., Yule, W., Hacam, B., & Stuvland, R. (2002). War exposure among children from Bosnia-Hercegovina: Psychological adjustment in a community sample. *Journal of Traumatic Stress, 15*(2), 147–156. doi:10.1023/A:1014812209051

Summerfield, D. (1999). A critique of seven assumptions behind psychological trauma programmes in war-affected areas. *Social Science & Medicine, 48*(10), 1449–1462. doi:10.1016/S0277–9536(98)00450-X

Summerfield, D. (2000). War and mental health: A brief overview. *British Medical Journal, 321*(7255), 232–235.

Summerfield, D. (2001). Asylum-seekers, refugees and mental health services in the UK. *The Psychiatrist, 25*(5), 161–163. doi:10.1192/pb.25.5.161

Thabet, A. A. M., Abed, Y., & Vostanis, P. (2002). Emotional problems in Palestinian children living in a war zone: A cross-sectional study. *The Lancet, 359*(9320), 1801–1804. doi:10.1016/S0140–6736(02)08709–3

Thabet, A. A. M., Abed, Y., & Vostanis, P. (2004). Comorbidity of PTSD and depression among refugee children during war conflict. *Journal of Child Psychology and Psychiatry, 45*(3), 533–542. doi:10.1111/j.1469–7610.2004.00243.x

UNICEF. (1996). *The state of the world's children*. New York, NY: Oxford University Press.

UNICEF. (2005a). *Explosive remnants of war. Childhood under threat: The state of the world's children*. Retrieved from http://www.unicef.org/sowc05/english/conflictissue5.html

UNICEF. (2005b). *Childhood under threat: The state of the world's children*. Retrieved from http://www.unicef.org/sowc05/english/conflictissue.html

UNICEF. (2011). *Children in conflict and emergencies*. Retrieved from http://www.unicef.org/protection/armedconflict.html

UNICEF. (2015). *14 million children impacted by conflict in Syria and Iraq: UNICEF*. Retrieved from http://www.unicef.org/media/media_81172.html

Von Peter, S. (2008). The experience of "mental trauma" and its transcultural application. *Transcultural Psychiatry, 45*(4), 639–651. doi:10.1177/1363461508100786

Wexler, I., Branski, D., & Kerem, E. (2006). War and children. *Journal of the American Medical Association, 296*(5), 579–581. doi:10.1001/jama.296.5.579

Wooding, S., & Raphael, B. (2004). Psychological impact of disasters and terrorism on children and adolescents: Experiences from Australia. *Prehospital and Disaster Medicine, 19*(1), 10–20. doi:10.1017/S1049023X00001436

CHAPTER 11

Loss of a Parent or Primary Caregiver and Traumatic Bereavement

Vilma Reyes and Alicia F. Lieberman

Loss of a loved person, particularly a primary caregiver, may be a traumatic event for young children because their sense of self is inextricably connected to the attachment figures on whom they rely for a sense of safety and predictable continuity both in external circumstances and in inner states of being (Bowlby, 1980; Lieberman, Compton, Van Horn, & Ghosh Ippen, 2003). Responses to loss are greatly influenced by the circumstances surrounding the death, what the child witnessed, the child's developmental stage and constitutional characteristics, sources of support, and how the surviving parent and other adults cope with the loss. The death of a parent to a young child is very often premature and unexpected, leaving family members unprepared for the emotional upheaval and concrete demands that follow. When the child has witnessed the death as the result of violence or an accident and has been exposed to the overwhelming sensory experiences associated with the death, grief responses and traumatic responses may co-occur. In these situations, the child is grappling with both the loss of the parent and the fear and sensory overload from the circumstances of the death (Lieberman, Compton, Van Horn, & Ghosh Ippen, 2003).

A parent's death is often followed by other losses and stressors that place additional emotional burdens on the child. When the parent's death leads to extreme changes in life circumstances, this further adds to the financial pressure and emotional burden on the grieving surviving parent, and therefore his or her availability for the child (Lieberman et al., 2003). If the parent who died was a single parent, custody battles may ensue to determine a caregiving system and significant changes in everyday life and routine may follow. After the parent's death, the normative developmental anxieties surrounding loss, losing love and approval, body damage, and trust in one's intrinsic goodness are exacerbated because the child has learned prematurely that catastrophic events can occur unexpectedly.

Young children who are grieving may engage in self-blame in an effort to give meaning to the loss (Lieberman et al., 2003; Lieberman & Van Horn, 2008). They need trusted adults to provide a narrative that gives meaning to their loss and corrects possible misperceptions that they caused the death. Trauma in early childhood may disrupt every domain of development, but the highest cost is the impairment of trust in their primary care relationship and, as a result, their relational template for all future relationships. When the primary caregiver dies, the child loses the developmentally appropriate expectation of counting on the parent as a reliable protector and an organizer to his or her sense of self and well-being.

Considering the complexity of all the factors mentioned previously, a treatment approach needs to be firmly grounded on the lens of trauma, loss, and attachment while flexibly attending to the diverse circumstances of the death, the family's needs, and the social and cultural context they are embedded in. Child Parent Psychotherapy (CPP) facilitates the grief process within a primary relationship or supports the development of a new or emerging relationship with the surviving caregiver as a vehicle to restore their sense of trust and safety, regulate affect, and return to a healthy developmental trajectory (Lieberman et al., 2003).

CPP is an intervention for children from birth to age five who have experienced or witnessed a traumatic event such as witnessing violence or losing a parent to death and, as a result, are exhibiting attachment, behavioral, or emotional difficulties. CPP aims to give meaning and normalize grief- or trauma-related responses, support the parents in recognizing and contextualizing their children's behavior, and engage with the dyad in co-constructing a developmentally appropriate trauma narrative to help organize and integrate their experience (Lieberman, Ghosh Ippen, & Van Horn, 2016).

CPP objectives include (a) enhancing the child's healthy development by encouraging play, closeness, and communication; (b) providing reflective, culturally congruent, trauma-informed developmental guidance; (c) highlighting the surviving caregiver's protective behavior when it occurs and co-creating a narrative of his or her relationship to the deceased parent; and (d) offering case management, advocacy, and crisis intervention as needed (Lieberman & Van Horn, 2005). For young children who experience the death of a parent, the objectives expand to supporting the surviving parent or caregiver in addressing concrete circumstances and making concrete decisions, such as whether the child would participate in the funeral and what he or she may need, (b) what and how to tell the child about the parent's death, (c) explaining the idea of death to a young child, (d) alleviating the child's fears of death or other losses, and (e) integrating the positive and negative feelings about the deceased parent and maintaining a connection to their memory (Lieberman et al., 2016).

CPP preserved the foundational principles of infant–parent psychotherapy, a psychodynamic approach that aims to increase understanding of how the parent's current and past experiences shape their perceptions, feelings, and behaviors toward the infant and how the infant's temperamental characteristics interact with these perceptions (Fraiberg, 1980; Lieberman, Silverman, & Pawl, 2000). CPP added therapeutic goals based on a trauma perspective (Marmar, Foy, Kagan, & Pynoos, 1993) such as reestablishing trust in bodily sensations and internal cues, regulating affect, and restoring the ability to accurately perceive and respond to danger.

Ports of entry or clinical opportunities for interventions are chosen organically as the treatment unfolds. Clinicians should hold in mind any intervention's potential impact on the child, the caregiver, and ultimately their relationship; the overarching goal of enhancing the dyadic relationship should be prioritized. Ports of entry can be the child or caregiver's behavior, the interactions between them, the mental representations and attributions of each other, the child's play, the memories of the deceased parent, and the relationship to the clinician. Systemic ports of entry include offering concrete assistance with problems of daily living by providing ongoing consultation, advocacy, and a bridge to community resources, such as legal aid services, preschool centers, shelters, and medical providers (Lieberman et al., 2016).

Children's temperaments and constitutional demands contribute to their caregivers' attributions of who they are and what they need. In turn, the parent's caregiving history and psychological needs also alter perceptions of their children. These dynamic processes shape the "goodness of fit" in the parent–child relationship. When the parent's history includes traumatic events especially within the context of their caregiving relationships, the trauma-based expectations learned color their experience of parenting. If these dynamics remain unconscious, they can be reenacted in the relationship they are forming with their children. The clinician needs to attend to the child and the parent's traumatic grief reminders, attributions, and affect dysregulations. Clinicians encourage parents to reflect on the ways their own childhood experiences can serve as traumatic reminders that pose the risk of intergenerational transmission of trauma, referred to as "Ghosts in the nursery" (Fraiberg, Adelson, & Shapiro, 1975). Clinicians also encourage parents to recall moments in which they felt safe and protected in their own childhood, hoping to increase their capacity to draw upon these experiences when parenting their own children. These moments are referred to as "Angels in the nursery" (Lieberman, Padron, Van Horn, & Harris, 2005).

Holding in mind both the parent and the child's history and perspective not only creates one of the most significant challenges in CPP but also sets the stage for the greatest potential for deep, long-lasting transformation in two or more generations. When a loved one dies, this may be a traumatic event to both the surviving caregiver and the child, but each one may encode the multiple moments of the event and its aftermath in a different way or from a different perspective. As we are supporting the caregiver in his or her child's grief process, it is imperative to remember that the caregiver is also grieving the lost parent.

CPP brings awareness to the larger context in which the family is embedded, including the impact of historical trauma, racism, discrimination, and immigration experiences on parenting. Obstacles to the caregiver's ability to parent such as environmental stresses, socioeconomic factors, and parent mental health problems are recognized and addressed (Van Horn & Reyes, 2014). There is a robust body of literature showing associations between poverty and negative developmental outcomes in children (Garbarino, 1995). CPP considers the social context and its protective and risk factors and incorporates active assistance to caregivers including advocacy and appropriate referrals (Lieberman & Van Horn, 2005).

Treatment can take place in the client's home, a playroom at a clinic, or community setting. Clinic settings allow for consistency, safety, and more control around the therapeutic toys offered. Community settings such as childcare centers, resource centers, or churches have the advantage of extending the positive associations and trust the parent already has to the setting. It also creates more opportunities for collaboration with other providers and possibly increases consistency in attendance by increasing ease of access (Reyes, Stone, Hernandez-Dimmler, & Lieberman, 2016).

The course of treatment includes a foundational phase, a treatment phase, and a termination phase. The foundational phase involves weekly meetings with the caregiver alone for an average of five times. Depending on the caregiver's ability to meet consistently, this can take from one up to three months. This period is critical for building a strong alliance and thoroughly assessing the caregiver and child's trauma history and the caregiver's understanding of how these experiences impacted the child's functioning and their relationship. The assessment includes several trauma-informed instruments to assess symptoms and strengths. This process serves as the anchor for subsequent sessions by preparing the caregiver for the dyadic portion of treatment. The clinician supports the caregiver in creating an introduction of treatment to the child. This consists of an acknowledgment of the traumatic events the child has experienced, the ways in which these events have impacted the child, and the hope for what the parent aims to help with in treatment.

The treatment phase involves dyadic sessions with the child and surviving parent or closest caregiver. CPP does not determine a specific order of interventions, although clinicians are encouraged to start with simple and direct interventions, such as offering developmental guidance, highlighting the importance of physical and emotional safety, and normalizing the traumatic response. Moments of attunement in the caregiver–child relationship are highlighted, and the caregiver's attempts at restoring themselves as a protective shield are fostered. All interventions aim to promote hope, safety, and competence in both the caregiver and the child. Play and physical contact serve as vehicles to explore themes of death and loss and danger and safety, celebrate joy and mutual enjoyment, and co-construct a trauma narrative.

As the therapeutic relationship builds and trust deepens, clinicians can test more complex interventions such as addressing the generational transmission of trauma, challenging negative attributions about the child (Lieberman & Van Horn, 2005), and correcting possible misperceptions about the death of the parent. Clinicians must be mindful of the caregiver and the child's pace, as well as their ability to make use of the interventions. Young children have common fears after losing a parent such as worrying that other people they love may also die and they will be left with no one to take care of them. Many children also worry about their own mortality or worry that they caused the parent to die. If death is framed within a religious belief of an afterlife, children may also fantasize about their own death in an effort to reunite with their dead parent. Bereaved young children are forced to prematurely confront the painful questions that even adults struggle with. Treatment is a place where these questions can be tackled and their fears alleviated. For example, children can be explained that the illness or accident that caused the parent's death is rare and that most people live healthy lives until they are old (Lieberman et al., 2003).

The termination phase in CPP is an integral part of the treatment, and it should be carefully planned out with the caregiver over the course of around six weeks. The timing is mutually determined and often occurs once the caregiver feels capable to continue guiding the child through his or her healing process independently. Clinicians highlight a sense of hope, summarize the strengths they have shown in the process, and help the caregiver anticipate and prepare for traumatic reminders in the future. Once the caregiver and clinician have decided on the timing, they prepare the child by explaining the reasoning for ending, highlighting the caregiver's strengths in continuing the process independently, and normalizing their reactions to the goodbye. Clinicians may create a project such as a calendar for child to decorate and mark the weeks left to instill predictability to the goodbye or create a picture the family can take with them as a tangible reminder of their journey in therapy. Knowing that the loss of the clinician may be a significant traumatic reminder for the child and the surviving caregiver, thoughtful attention needs to take place to prepare the dyad for this transition.

The following case illustrates the use of CPP working with a mother and her son living at a temporary family shelter. We know from community attrition research that almost half of families referred to mental health services do not engage in treatment (Barrett et al., 2008). This case shows how the use of case management, advocacy, consultation, and mediation between the parent and community agency can be essential factors to engage families with multiple stressors.

Case Example

Reason for Referral

Joaquin, a 6-year-old boy, and his 38-year-old mother, Diana, were referred for treatment by their case manager at the emergency family shelter where they were living. VR was the CPP clinician offering services on-site as part of the community branch of the Child Trauma Research Program. Joaquin's father, Romelio, had died from prostate cancer one month prior to the referral. Romelio had lost his job four months earlier when his health had deteriorated, forcing the family into homelessness. Romelio and Diana were undocumented immigrants from Central America who lacked access to health care, and he had been working two jobs despite experiencing symptoms of prostate cancer for two to three years prior to his diagnosis. The last five months of his life required frequent hospitalizations, which Joaquin witnessed. Romelio had been using alcohol to cope with life stressors since Joaquin's birth, and his substance use escalated after his diagnosis. Joaquin had witnessed his father pass out on the floor from excessive alcohol use, and on at least two occasions, verbal arguments with Diana escalated to Romelio using physical violence such as pushing Diana against the wall and choking her.

As described by the case manager, Joaquin's symptoms involved simultaneous clinginess and aggressiveness toward his mother, disengagement from activities with other children at the shelter, and intense recurrent nightmares. The case manager attributed these difficulties to the mother's parenting style. At the time of referral, Diana and Joaquin had three weeks left at the shelter and an extension of stay was unlikely, in part due to the negative judgments the shelter staff had made about Diana's parenting. The case manager described the mother as someone who was unable to set boundaries for the child and who let him "run the show." Joaquin was obese and most of his teeth required significant dental work. However, Diana had consistently rejected referrals to community dentists, a response that was interpreted as neglectful by the shelter staff.

Without a grief and trauma frame to contextualize Diana and Joaquin's behavior, the service providers consistently misunderstood both mother and child. The shelter case manager could not understand why Diana continued to offer Joaquin as much candy as he requested every day. Similarly, Joaquin's kindergarten teacher could not understand why the mother insisted on traveling one hour each way to bring her son fast food for lunch and to supervise him during outside play. This kind of wide gap in perspective between service providers and the families referred often becomes a risk factor for families who may lose services for not following through with their providers' suggestions and is often the first piece of information that community clinicians need to grapple with.

Foundational Phase of Treatment

The family's room at the shelter offered an eloquent picture of Diana's emotional priorities. The first thing one saw on coming in was a large altar for Romelio with photographs of him, several of his belongings, dry flowers, and other mementos from his funeral. There was a bunk bed for Diana and Joaquin; however, the top bunk was used for storage and they shared the lower bed. The counter was overflowing with candy and a collection of video games. Diana greeted the clinician politely and rolled an oxygen tank she was using to sit on the bed. This was the first indication for the clinician that the mother had a medical condition and raised the dilemma of when and how to ask her about it. Joaquin asked if he could play in the shelter's common area, and Diana told him that he knew he had to ask his father first. Joaquin approached his father's altar, asked, "Can I go, Dad?" and then proceeded to leave the room. Diana started the meeting describing the judgment she felt from all the providers and her ambivalence about receiving mental health services. "They don't understand that it's my right to minimize any more pain for my son. He has suffered enough and I want to see him happy." The clinician told her that she understood her position and asked, "Please tell me more about what you mean." Diana started crying as she disclosed that she had been diagnosed with a terminal heart condition and was given an estimate of one to six months to live.

The clinician met with Diana alone for five weeks to assess traumatic history and symptoms, developmental history, parental stress, and the quality of their relationship. In addition to the assessment measures used for all CPP cases, Joaquin's experience of the death of his father including what he witnessed and what was explained to him was explored. The clinician asked about Joaquin's cognitive, social, and emotional functioning before and after his father's death; continuity versus disruption of family routines; cultural and family traditions regarding death; and Diana's response to the death of Romelio. As part of the assessment process, the clinician attempted to identify traumatic reminders by asking if any triggers provoke intense distress in the child. Diana was very clear that Romelio remained alive within them and reminders of him were welcomed, including the intense feelings that they could provoke. This commitment to remember and to feel the loss stood in contrast with Diana's stated intention to avoid any further pain or discomfort for her child. One possible interpretation could be that Diana was imparting to Joaquin how she wanted to be remembered after she died.

In conversations with the clinician, Diana showed insightfulness into the motivations for the decisions she was making about Joaquin. She reported that she traveled to the school at lunch time because Joaquin did not like the school cafeteria food and would otherwise choose not to eat for the day. She also wanted to supervise his recess time because Joaquin had reported that some children teased him. Diana was a fierce protector for her son as a way to compensate him for the pain that she could not protect him from. She wanted to let Joaquin enjoy the present moment, including eating candy and having any toy he desired, to alleviate the pain of losing his father and the impending loss of his mother. While her choices made sense when contextualized in a trauma frame, they were causing them further struggles. For example, Diana received some funds from Romelio's life insurance plan that she chose to spend on video games for Joaquin. This decision caused a further rift between her and the shelter providers, who saw it as irresponsible and denied her appeal for an extension of her stay at the shelter. It became clear that Diana needed a safe space to wrestle with the dilemma that while her protective choices delayed immediate discomfort and pain, they were also causing other struggles. The clinician was cautious not to be perceived like other providers who Diana had felt judged by. Any intervention would have to lie on a firm relational foundation in which Diana believed this clinician respected her, believed in her, and understood her choices.

Diana expressed a firm desire to only mention Romelio's death and its impact on the family and stated she did not feel ready to tell Joaquin about her terminal illness. A foundational value in CPP is to "speak the unspeakable" and bring voice to a painful reality many wish to avoid. We know that children often sense the reality that goes unsaid, and without a narrative with which to understand it, they are left on their own to make sense of what often does not make sense. However, it is also a CPP foundational value to respect the parents in their rightful place as the guide to their child's grief process. The clinician recognized the tremendous pain Diana and Joaquin were in, Diana's wish to alleviate any further pain for her son, and also the potential further confusion and uncertainty Joaquin may experience by not addressing his mother's illness. Diana agreed to mention her illness but refrain from speaking of her impending death unless Joaquin asked questions. The clinician and Diana agreed to maintain weekly one-on-one sessions, in addition to the dyadic sessions, to prepare her to share the news of her terminal illness and to make arrangements for Joaquin after her death.

Treatment Phase

The therapeutic setting continued to be the family's room at the shelter for the duration of treatment. Home visits provided unique opportunities to ascertain how the presence of Romelio's memory remained in the home and how family routines and structures were carried out. Home visiting also presented some unique challenges in how the physical space supported the treatment frame. There were more distractions such as other people unpredictably entering their room and access to nontherapeutic toys such as video games or TV. The clinician arrived to their room for the first dyadic session. Diana offered a warm greeting, and Joaquin was playing video games. Diana requested for the dyadic treatment to start the following week since Joaquin was busy playing video games that day. The clinician stated Diana's rightful place to decide when was the best timing for her son, "Joaquin, your mother loves you and is trying to decide what's best for you." Joaquin kept playing his game, and the clinician looked to Diana and asked if she would like to check in. Diana asked to speak in the hallway so that their talking didn't disturb Joaquin. She stated that it's hard to take away things he loves. The clinician acknowledged her protective stance considering how much he had already lost and also asked about how she set boundaries prior to Romelio's death. As Diana explored how she was able to set limits in the past, her voice became more empowered and confident. The clinician highlighted the shift in her confidence and wondered while losing his father, Joaquin also lost a confident mother who provided limits as well as love. Diana confessed she had not thought of it this way before; she walked back in the room and asked Joaquin to turn off his video game and he quickly complied. This moment symbolized a significant shift in Diana and Joaquin's relationship. It is common for surviving parents to overindulge or overprotect the child, to the point where expectations of appropriate behavior are suspended and daily routines are ruptured (Lieberman et al., 2003). In this dyad, this tendency was particularly present due to Diana's anticipation of further loss and pain. Reinstating predictability provided Joaquin with a sense of security.

Diana asked Joaquin to listen to the clinician as the previously agreed upon explanation was offered. "Joaquin, I have been meeting with your mother for a while, and she told me that you saw your father get very sick until his body stopped working. Doctors tried to help, but they couldn't help his body anymore, and he died. And now you may feel sad and miss him very much and sometimes you get nightmares." At this point, Joaquin intercepted and said, "They are not nightmares; they are dreams of my dad talking to me." Diana asked him why he wakes up screaming and crying, to what he responded, "Those are other dreams about you dying too." The therapist looked at Diana, and she became tearful and signaled for the clinician to speak. "You see your mother using a machine to help her breathe, and you worry about her being sick and dying too. She also worries about this, and this is a place you and she can talk about those things, right, Mom?" Diana nodded and hugged her son. "Don't you worry, *mijo*," she said, "your mama is strong and I am gonna get better." While clinicians should not collude with denial or dishonesty, it seemed that this dyad had taken an important step in facing a harsh reality, and this glimmer of hope for health was something they both needed at that time. The clinician knew that it would take the next months to continue preparing them both for the mother's terminal diagnosis.

Over the next month, treatment focused on the ways in which Diana and Joaquin held on to Romelio's memory. Diana had idealized Romelio and her relationship to him in the foundational phase, denying any struggles and identifying him as "the only person who ever loved her." During the weekly collateral sessions, Diana started to talk about Romelio's alcohol abuse, especially once he was diagnosed with cancer and he started losing hope in recovery. She stated that on one incident he got violent, pushed her against the wall, and choked her. The clinician normalized her desire to remember the good in him while also encouraging an integration of all that he was and space for Joaquin to process the moments in which he might have been frightened of his father. Idealization of the deceased parent is common and understandable, yet it can send a confusing message that the dark moments of the deceased parent are unspeakable or unbearable to talk about.

During one visit, Diana again prompted Joaquin to greet his father when entering the room, and he protested, yelling "Why? He wasn't even nice to us anyway!" While expressing anger toward the deceased parent is a typical emotional reaction, it was becoming evident that Joaquin needed space to create an integrated story of his father. The weekly collateral sessions with Diana were crucial in expanding her capacity to hold both sides of Romelio and eventually be able to tolerate Joaquin's anger and a desire for an integrated memory of his father. For children who have lost a parent to death, expressing their anger toward that parent is particularly challenging since they tend to fear that their anger may have caused their parent's death.

During the weekly collateral sessions, Diana realized that her insistence of only preserving positive memories of Romelio was a hope that Joaquin would only preserve benevolent memories of her when she dies. Once Diana realized this, she was better able to accept the negative memories Joaquin held of his father. The clinician recognized the difficulty in acknowledging the shadows of Romelio's memory and provided hope that often once the shadows are acknowledged, it creates a space for a more genuine light to enter. With support, Diana was able to normalize Joaquin's anger toward his father, which allowed more positive memories of him to also surface. During the 14th treatment session, Diana was talking about their stay at the shelter ending and Joaquin threw a toy toward his father's altar in their room and said, "This is all your fault for leaving us!" Where in the past, Diana would have discouraged his anger, she said instead, "I know you are mad. It's OK, but you know he didn't want to leave us." Joaquin approached the altar, fixed the picture frame that had fallen, and said, "Remember when Dad used to play soccer with me after school, Mom?" She smiled and said, "I remember."

As Diana's health deteriorated, Joaquin's anxiety worsened. This was manifested in somatization symptoms such as stomachaches and nausea. Diana responded by allowing Joaquin to stay home from school, which caused a further rift between Diana and the school administration. More time at home also meant that Joaquin accompanied Diana to her medical appointments and was exposed to more information about her health problems while still lacking a coherent narrative about her prognosis. Separation anxiety and fear of losing the surviving parent are very common reactions to losing a parent to death. This normative fear was significantly exacerbated by evidence of his mother's illness. He asked his mother in the session if she would always need the machine to help her breathe. Diana seemed anxious and asked Joaquin to continue with the drawing he was working on. The clinician acknowledged both mother's discomfort with talking about her health and Joaquin's anxiety from not knowing what to expect. "I know this is hard for you to talk about, Diana, but sometimes the uncertainty in children causes even more anxiety than the harsh reality," the clinician said. Diana looked at Joaquin and said, "I don't like to see you worry, mijo, but I will always need this machine." Joaquin hugged his mother, and they both cried. Diana wiped his tears and said, "No matter what, you are always gonna have me and Daddy in your heart." Joaquin said, "I know," and resumed his drawing. It was after this session that Diana started cooperating with the case manager's attempts to arrange custody plans after her death.

Once Diana was able to talk openly with Joaquin about her prognosis, his anxiety symptoms alleviated, and he started showing more sadness and anger. He would respond to directives from adults by saying, "It's not fair!" Over time, Diana became more confident in recognizing Joaquin's feelings and at the same time maintaining the expectation or limit she had already set. On one visit, Diana greeted this clinician excitedly and shared that she took Joaquin to the dentist. "He is gonna need a lot of work on his teeth; he didn't like it but he will live . . . and we are doing less candy, isn't that right, Jo Jo?" she asked her son. He hesitantly agreed with a smirk on his face. Aiming this balance of both compassion and predictable limit setting provided a healthy relational template for Joaquin and seemed to increase his sense of security.

Over time, Joaquin started using symbolic play to communicate his fears and anger, and Diana was better able to connect with him via this medium. Diana encouraged Joaquin to try painting and using the toys that were brought by the clinician. Joaquin used play to express the anger he felt toward his father for hurting his mother and for dying. Play made these feelings more tolerable to Diana, although she often joined play by rescuing father and stating that "he wasn't perfect but he loved us and he is dead now and deserves our respect." The clinician recognized Diana's cultural values about showing respect for the dead and helped find a mutual space in which Joaquin's anger could be expressed. As Diana deepened her understanding of the role and meaning of play, her tolerance for his feelings expressed via play grew.

The clinician brought toy family members that matched the family's skin color, a small dollhouse with furniture, a doctor's kit, an ambulance, paper and paint, a superhero, play cell phones, and a kitchen set with play food. When selecting toys, it is recommended to choose a variety of age-appropriate toys that may facilitate both posttraumatic play and nurturance and connection. The toys were selected in collaboration with Diana in a collateral session. Food was something that Joaquin and his father shared, and the play food was intentionally brought to provide opportunities for positive memories and hope to surface.

Once Joaquin started using symbolic play, his play themes centered on fears of separation, hopes for reunion, and rescue fantasies. For example, he would place the father doll on the roof of the house and say that "he is in heaven." Father would participate in conversations with the other family dolls from the roof. Conversations between them were about everyday routines such as their plan for the day or what they would eat. During one play sequence, he placed mother on the roof of the house with his father, and he asked the clinician, "Who will be down here with me?" The clinician repeated his question and invited Diana to speak for the mother doll. Mother took the doll, which was still on the roof, and tearfully said, "I wish I could have stayed down there with you. I love and miss you so much. I found very kind people that are down there with you and promised to take care of you." The clinician grabbed two new dolls from the box and invited her to introduce them to the story. Therapeutic play made it possible for Joaquin to ask the question they had both been dreading and for Diana to start preparing him for the next stage.

Termination Phase

After 10 months of CPP treatment, Diana had proudly surpassed the doctors' expectations on life expectancy and would jokingly say the doctors underestimated how stubborn she is. After persistent advocacy, Diana and Joaquin were granted permanent housing in a medical shelter for people who are terminally ill. They were both excited about the new apartment, which came stocked with a small kitchen. Diana expressed wishes to be able to cook healthier food for them. Diana had finalized and communicated the adoption arrangements for Joaquin after her death.

Diana expressed gratitude for the treatment and identified ways in which Joaquin was doing well, considering the circumstance. She stated that the new housing development required her to do therapy groups and her medical appointments were becoming more demanding, making it difficult to make time for mental health treatment. As much as goodbyes can be traumatic triggers for both parents and children, they can also represent valuable opportunities to provide a corrective emotional experience around separation and loss. The clinician aimed to work with Diana at planning the termination phase for Joaquin. This process typically involves an average of three sessions to process the goodbye. When presented options of how this phase could be, Diana confidently said, "I am sorry. I just can't drag on another goodbye for him." Diana decided that we would have one last session in which we would say goodbye. It occurred to the clinician that this goodbye was not only reminding her of losing her husband but of the last goodbye she would have to say to her son. Her wish was respected and treatment ended in one session in which the clinician invited a conversation that summarized their journey in therapy. Diana joked about how much she protected him at the beginning of treatment and commented on Joaquin's growing ability to be more self-assured and independent. She pointed to the top bunk, which was now occupied by him, as a concrete example of this. Joaquin prematurely waved goodbye and asked if he could play video games. Diana said he could, and she spent some time in the hallway with the clinician as she said goodbye.

"Separating from a person one loves ranks among the most difficult of human experiences. Losing a loved person is the most painful one. Both experiences, each in their distinct fashion, challenge the emotional foundations of the sense of self, and evoke powerful feelings of sadness, anxiety, grief, and anger" (Lieberman & Van Horn, 2004, p. 119). The clinician ended treatment by highlighting their incredible strength in light of the most painful experience of all. To this day, I am inspired by their courage and honored to have shared a bit of their journey.

References

Barrett, M. S., Chua, W.-j., Crits-Christoph, P., Gibbons, M. B., Casiano, D., & Thompson, D. (2009). Early withdrawal from mental health treatment: Implications for psychotherapy practice. *Psychotherapy: Theory, Research, Practice, Training*, 46(2), 248.

Bowlby, J. (1980). *Attachment and loss,* Vol. 3. New York, NY: Basic Books

Fraiberg, S. (1980). *Clinical studies in infant mental health.* New York, NY: Basic Books.

Fraiberg, S., Adelson, E., & Shapiro, V. (1975). Ghosts in the nursery: A psychoanalytic approach to the problems of impaired infant-mother relationships. *Journal of the American Academy of Child & Adolescent Psychiatry, 14*(3), 385–559.

Garbarino, J. (1995). *Raising children in a socially toxic environment.* San Francisco, CA: Jossey Bass Publishers

Lieberman, A. F., Compton, N., Van Horn, P., & Ghosh Ippen, C. (2003). *Losing a parent to death in the early years: Guidelines for the treatment of traumatic bereavement in infancy and early childhood.* Washington, DC: Zero to Three Press.

Lieberman, A. F., Ghosh Ippen, C., & Van Horn, P. (2016). *Don't hit my mommy: A manual for Child-Parent Psychotherapy with young children exposed to violence and other trauma* (2nd ed.). Washington, DC: Zero to Three Press.

Lieberman, A. F., Padron, E., Van Horn, P., & Harris, W. (2005). Angels in the nursery: The intergenerational transmission of benevolent parental influences. *Infant Mental Health Journal, 26*(6), 504–520.

Lieberman, A. F., Silverman, R., Pawl, J. H. (2000). Infant-parent psychotherapy: Core concepts and current approaches. In C. H. Zeanah (Ed.), *Handbook of infant mental health* (2nd ed., pp. 472–484). New York, NY: Guilford.

Lieberman, A. F., & Van Horn, P. (2004). Assessment and treatment of young children exposed to traumatic events. In J.D. Osofsky (Ed.), *Young children and trauma: Intervention and treatment* (pp. 111–138). New York, NY: Guilford Press. Retrieved from http://psycnet.apa.org/record/2004-21896-004

Lieberman, A. F., & Van Horn, P. (2005). *"Don't hit my mommy!": A manual for Child-Parent Psychotherapy with young witnesses of family violence.* Washington, DC: Zero to Three Press.

Marmar, C. R., Foy, D., Kagan, B., & Pynoos, R. (1993). An integrated approach for treating post-traumatic stress. In J. M. Oldham, M. B. Riba, & A. Tasman (Eds.), *American Psychiatric Press review of psychiatry* (Vol. 12, pp. 239–272). Washington, DC: American Psychiatric Press, Inc.

CHAPTER 12

Commercial Sexual Exploitation of Children in the United States

Emily F. Rothman and Megan H. Bair-Merritt

There has been increasing attention paid to the causes, consequences, and prevention of the commercial sexual exploitation of children in the United States since the passage of the U.S. Trafficking Victims Protection Act (TVPA) of 2000. As of 2016, more than three-quarters of U.S. states have passed laws to protect minors from being prosecuted for prostitution. Many providers are becoming more knowledgeable about CSEC, and there are reasons to hope that attitudes toward CSEC survivors[1] are becoming less judgmental and more supportive. However, there is still a dearth of tested, effective methods for intervening with CSEC survivors, CSEC perpetrators, and preventing high-risk youth from becoming involved in commercial sex.

Commercial Sexual Exploitation of Children: Definition and Epidemiology

Commercial sexual exploitation of children (CSEC) is a type of child sexual exploitation (CSE), which is a type of child sexual abuse (CSA) (see Figure 12.1). According to U.S. federal law, CSA is any employment, use,

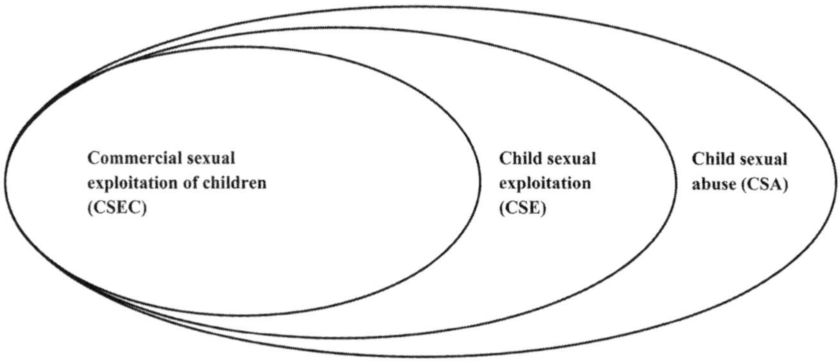

Figure 12.1 The relationship between CSEC, CSE, and CSA

persuasion, inducement, enticement, or coercion of a minor to engage in, or assist any other person to engage in, any sexually explicit conduct or visual depiction of simulated sexual conduct (42 U.S.C.A. § 5106g).

CSE is a type of CSA crime that entails a third party inducing a minor to have sexual contact with someone else. For example, if an adult arranges for a child to have sexual contact with, or simulate sex for, a patron at a strip club or an individual at a party, that person has engaged in CSE. Notably, it qualifies as CSE whether or not the adult in that scenario receives payment or not for having arranged the sexual encounter. "CSEC" is a term most commonly used to describe CSE that entails a third-party broker (i.e., a pimp or madam) arranging for a minor to have sexual contact with someone else in exchange for money or other things of value that accrue, at least in part, to the third party. For example, if a parent receives a payment for arranging for a stranger to have sexual contact with his or her child, that would qualify as CSEC. Another example of CSEC would be a boyfriend receiving cash, drugs, food, a place to stay, or other items of value, in exchange for arranging for someone to have sexual contact with his girlfriend who is younger than 18 years old. Importantly, there are cases of CSEC that do not involve direct physical contact between a buyer and a child but may involve a buyer paying a fee to watch or engage with a minor via an Internet webcam, live striptease act, child pornography, or erotic massage.

A synonym for CSEC is "domestic minor sex trafficking" (DMST). Many people hear the phrase "sex trafficking" and assume that it involves physically moving a trafficked individual from one place to another, but DMST can occur even if there is no transportation of a minor involved. According to the U.S. TVPA of 2000, recruitment, harboring, transportation, provision, obtaining, patronizing, or soliciting of a person younger than 18 years old for the purposes of a commercial sex act qualifies as a "severe form of human trafficking" and is a federal crime (22 USC § 7102). For an adult to be considered a victim of sex trafficking under U.S. federal law, the commercial sex act must be induced by a third party by force, fraud, or coercion. In contrast, according to federal law, *any* patronizing or soliciting of a minor child for commercial sex qualifies as sex trafficking, simply because of the victim's age. Importantly, CSEC/DMST victims may be from the United States or another country, may be of any gender, may be exploited by a relative or another person, and may assert that they have willingly participated in commercial sex.

One important difference between CSA and CSEC is the applicability of federal law and the severity of the criminal penalties that may be imposed. CSA is generally prosecuted under state law. The penalties for CSA vary by state, but typically maximum sentences for indecent assault and battery on a child younger than 14 years old range from 10 to 25 years in state prison for a first offense. In contrast, CSEC is prohibited by federal law 18 U.S.C. § 1591 and carries a mandatory minimum sentence of 15 years in prison if the victim was age 14 or younger, or 10 years in prison if the victim was 14–17 years old, and a maximum sentence of life imprisonment.

The prevalence of CSEC in the United States is unknown, and there has been debate about the validity of estimates. In 2001, a Department of Justice report by Estes and Weiner (2005) estimated that 326,000 children in the United States were *at risk* for a form of CSA because of their status as runaway, throwaway, homeless, unaccompanied minor immigrant, or gang-involved youth. Other data sources confirm that there may be thousands of U.S. CSEC victims each year. The U.S. Department of Justice reported that there were more than 1,000 reported allegations of CSEC to federally funded human trafficking task forces between 2008 and 2010, and of these, 25 percent ($n = 248$) were eventually confirmed to be CSEC cases (Banks & Kyckkelhahn, 2011). Similarly, in 2014 the National Human Trafficking Resource Center received information about 1,322 cases of CSEC (The Florida Legislature Office of Program Policy Analysis and Government Accountability, 2015). In 2014, the state of Florida investigated 826 cases of CSEC and confirmed that 170 were verified victims (The Florida Legislature Office of Program Policy Analysis and Government Accountability, 2015). Data from the Federal Bureau of Investigation (FBI) indicate that in 2014 there were a total of six CSEC cases prosecuted in the United States (U.S. Department of Justice, 2014). However, between 2011 and 2013, one hospital in Atlanta, Georgia, treated at least 27 CSEC victims in the emergency department (Varma, Gillespie, McCracken, & Greenbaum, 2015), so the number of prosecutions is very clearly a poor metric. In short, estimates vary widely and the prevailing assumption in the field is that only a small fraction of the true number of CSEC victims is ever identified. Innovative research methods that will permit more accurate estimates are urgently needed.

The risk factors for CSEC victimization appear to be similar to those for running away. One problem in understanding the etiology of CSEC is that the only way to study CSEC empirically is by asking questions of people who have already been identified as CSEC victims, or who are willing to report on a survey that they have exchanged sex for money or something else of value. These people may not represent all CSEC survivors, and it is not possible to tell how far off-the-mark research may be by using data only from these selected samples of individuals who have already been identified or choose to identify themselves. That problem notwithstanding, what research has revealed is that these factors elevate risk for CSEC victimization: experiencing childhood abuse or neglect (Brawn & Roe-Sepowitz, 2008; Choi, 2015) or other forms of interpersonal violence victimization prior to CSEC (Chohaney, 2016), being transgender or having a sexual orientation other than heterosexual (Martinez & Kelle, 2013), poverty (Klatt, Cavner, & Egan, 2014), history of running away (Choi, 2015; Cole, Sprang, Lee, & Cohen, 2016; Klatt et al., 2014), being expelled or suspended from school (Brawn & Roe-Sepowitz, 2008), feeling disconnected from school (Kaestle, 2012), having family members who are involved in commercial sex (Klatt et al., 2014), substance use (Brawn & Roe-Sepowitz, 2008; Cole et al., 2016; Klatt et al., 2014; Reid, 2014), feeling stigmatized (Reid, 2014), lower IQ (Twill, Green, & Traylor, 2010), and mental health problems (Cole et al., 2016; Twill et al., 2010). Importantly, youth who have multiple risk factors are not at all on an inevitable path toward exploitation, and the receipt of helping services can make a substantial positive difference in their life course.

Case Example: Lucy

Lucy was a 15-year-old, multiracial female who presented to the pediatric emergency department of a large, urban hospital with a fever, lower back pain, and symptoms of a urinary tract infection (UTI) one evening. She was average height and weight and dressed in jeans and a sweatshirt. Lucy was accompanied by an adult female whom she said was her aunt. Lucy reported that her parents lived in a nearby state and that she was visiting her aunt in the city on vacation. Neither Lucy nor her aunt was able to provide the name of Lucy's primary care physician, and her aunt reported that Lucy did not have health insurance. Lucy's aunt offered to pay cash for the hospital visit. Lucy did not have any identification, but her aunt had an out-of-state driver's license. Lucy reported that she had no chronic illnesses, had never had any surgery, and provided basic information about her parents' health when asked. She said that her parents live in a "good neighborhood," that she found school boring, and that she had three siblings with whom she did not get along.

When asked, her aunt left the examination room but was clearly reluctant to do so. Lucy reported that she was having frequent sexual intercourse with her boyfriend, which she thought was the cause of her symptoms. She could not recall the date of her last menstrual period. When asked if she felt safe in her relationship, she said, "I guess so." Upon further questioning, Lucy changed her story and stated that she did not have a boyfriend and actually had unprotected intercourse with multiple individuals in the past month, but she could not remember how many. She reported that she occasionally consumed alcohol and marijuana. She revealed that she had a criminal record for shoplifting and that she was afraid of police. She had a blunted affect.

The attending physician consulted with the department social worker. They agreed that "something didn't add up" about Lucy's story. Some of the things that struck them were that the aunt offered to pay for the medical visit in cash, that the aunt did not seem to be in touch with Lucy's parents or to be familiar with her health history, that they had come to an emergency department for a UTI, and that the aunt was hovering over Lucy in an odd way. The social worker spoke with Lucy again, without her aunt present, and Lucy eventually confessed that her parents did not know where she was and that the woman posing as her aunt was actually a friend whom Lucy had met in the past several weeks. The friend, whom Lucy called Sima, was demanding that Lucy pay rent for sleeping on her couch and had been using a website to find men for Lucy to have sex with to earn that rent money. Lucy reported that she was not permitted to keep or carry any of the cash she earned, so she was entirely dependent upon Sima for food, clothes, and other necessities. Lucy indicated that she began selling sex because she thought it would be an easy way to earn a lot of money fast, but that she had become unhappy with the situation. She was worried about getting a sexually transmitted infection (STI) or hurt by a client, but she also stated that she might rather sell sex than return home to live with her parents and attend high school.

The attending and social worker discussed safety options with Lucy, including the need to alert their Child Protective Services team. Lucy expressed concern for her immediate safety and also stated that she would rather go back and live with Sima than return to her parents. The team decided to admit Lucy to the hospital, both to treat her infection and establish a safe plan for discharge. Lucy reluctantly agreed. During the hospitalization, Lucy was treated for multiple STIs. The medical team involved Child Protective Services, law enforcement, and behavioral health professionals to work together to ensure safe discharge planning for Lucy.

Impact of CSEC on Physical and Emotional Health

In the case example, Lucy had a blunted affect, and an in-depth clinical interview during her hospitalization revealed that she was having trouble sleeping, was rarely eating, was experiencing frequent headaches and panic attacks, was using marijuana daily, and snapped in a hostile manner at the social worker several times during the clinical interview. She mentioned feeling suicidal, particularly at the prospect of having to return home to her parents. Lucy said that while she knew it wasn't safe to continue to sell sex, she felt like she had no choice because she was too young to get a decent job. She planned to drop out of school in four months when she turned 16 years old, so felt like it was pointless to attend school in the interim.

Lucy was experiencing several trauma symptoms common among CSEC survivors. The consequences of experiencing CSEC victimization are similar to those of CSA, but at least two studies have documented that the trauma symptomology can be even more severe (Cole et al., 2016; Varma et al., 2015). Consequences are also similar to those experienced by homeless and runaway youth. For those in Lucy's age group (i.e., 14–17 years old), some anticipated consequences of CSEC include depression (Hossain, Zimmerman, Abas, Light, & Watts, 2010; Oram et al., 2016), anxiety (Hossain et al., 2010; Oram et al., 2016), posttraumatic stress disorder symptomology (Hossain et al., 2010; Oram et al., 2016), panic attacks (Renner, Coohey, Ruch, & O'Leary, 2013), self-harm (Forsyth, Rogstad, & Interest, 2015), suicidality (Stanley et al., 2016), inattentiveness or attention-deficit hyperactivity disorder (ADHD; Weinstein, Staffelbach, & Biaggio, 2000), memory problems (Oram et al., 2012), insomnia (Wang, Raffeld, Slopen, Hale, & Dunn, 2016), unhealthy eating patterns (Dworkin, Javdani, Verona, & Campbell, 2014), aggressiveness (Deb, Mukherjee, & Mathews, 2011), unhealthy alcohol use (Cole et al., 2016), drug use or dependence (Brawn & Roe-Sepowitz, 2008; Cole et al., 2016), self-blame (Kaye-Tzadok & Davidson-Arad, 2016), dissociation (Cole et al., 2016), and conduct disorder (Cole et al., 2016; Maniglio, 2015).

Children as young as 10–13 years old, and younger, can also be victims of CSEC. In addition to the aforementioned trauma-related sequelae, young children who experience CSA and CSEC may exhibit precocious sexual behavior, age-inappropriate regressive behavior (e.g., thumb-sucking, urinary incontinence), and attachment disorder–related symptoms. Older adolescents and young adults who experience CSE may attempt to protect the person or people who have been exploiting them, profess love for or gratitude toward their exploiters, or insist that they are involved in commercial sex by choice. One of the most difficult aspects of assessing, referring, and treating adolescent and young adult CSE victims can be that many do not consider themselves abused (Smith, Vardaman, & Snow, 2009), may not want to discontinue aspects of their lifestyle (e.g., alcohol use, drug use, keeping no set schedule; Greenbaum, 2014), fear or dislike the child protection system and social service workers, and have reasons for not wanting to return to schools, particular friendships, or their families (Greenbaum, 2014). CSEC survivor youth may be emotionally labile and justifiably mistrustful of adults and social services systems, and they may be difficult to engage because their survival may have been dependent upon their capacity to evade authorities, deceive or manipulate people, and appear intimidating.

Responding to CSEC within Justice and Health Care and Engaging Survivors in Services

Historically, juveniles in the United States were treated no differently by the criminal justice system than adults who were arrested for prostitution. As of October 2016, there are now 38 states that have passed "Safe Harbor" laws that mandate that minor children who are identified as commercially sexually exploited be provided with immunity from prosecution and should instead receive rehabilitative social services (Barnert et al., 2016). In theory, it should not be necessary for individual states to pass Safe Harbor legislation, because the federal TVPA defines any commercial sex with a minor child as severe trafficking who is in need of services and not punishment. However, the reality is that states have been inconsistent about discontinuing to arrest juveniles for prostitution, so state Safe Harbor laws are necessary to reify the federal law for local law enforcement and juvenile courts.

Not all hospitals have protocols that guide physicians and other healthcare providers on what to do when a victim of CSEC is identified (Stoklosa, Dawson, Williams-Oni, & Rothman, 2016), but model protocols suggest that CSEC survivors be treated in a trauma-informed manner and that child abuse reporting procedures be followed as they would be in any other CSA case (Stoklosa, Showalter, Melnick, & Rothman, 2016).

If a CSEC case is reported to child protection, the first priority of the protection team should be to resolve immediate questions about where the minor should stay, whether contact with parents or guardians is in the best interest of the child, and whether law enforcement needs to be contacted. When immediate and urgent concerns are addressed, longer-term case management is usually needed. In many states and counties, multidisciplinary teams (MDTs) comprising a representative of the district attorney's office, Child Advocacy Centers (CACs) (Herbert & Bromfield, 2016), Child Protective Services, and local social service agencies that specifically aid CSEC survivor youth will conference about each CSEC case that is referred to the team and jointly decide how that youth should be supported. In some cases, CSEC survivors have committed crimes other than soliciting sex, such as illegal possession of firearms, possession of illegal drugs, theft, or assault and battery. In these cases, it is possible that youth will be referred to juvenile detention centers and may receive available CSEC recovery services while in detention. Some CSEC survivors are also involved with testifying against traffickers and need witness protection or other court advocacy help. Importantly, in some communities there are no CSEC recovery services at all, and few or no trained mental health professionals or social workers with expertise in CSEC and the capacity to treat underinsured youth. Ensuring that training on CSEC is available to those who come into contact with CSEC survivors or traffickers, or their family members, is a priority.

After Lucy was identified as a possible victim of CSEC by the hospital team and her case was referred to Child Protective Services, she was offered a choice between being transported back to her parents and being sheltered by a temporary foster family in the vicinity. Neither of those options appealed to Lucy. She explained that the reason that she left home in the first place was that her parents were physically and sexually abusive toward her and her siblings. Lucy indicated that the news that she had engaged in commercial sex would place her at further risk for harm by her parents. Lucy was also terrified of foster care—she had heard terrible stories from peers about how badly they were treated by foster families. Lucy felt unsafe remaining in the same vicinity as the exploiter and the exploiter's friends. She stated that she would not cooperate with any police investigation or testify about it in court because of fear of retaliation and because she felt that selling sex was her own choice. In her words, nobody held a gun to her head, so she didn't understand why people were acting like she was forced into anything. Lucy was unable to recognize that she was induced to sell sex because of structural disadvantages like parental abuse, homelessness, the limitations of foster care and her public school system, and lack of social service options for adolescents in need of assistance.

Lucy was offended at the social worker's suggestion that people had taken advantage of her. Even though Lucy didn't like selling sex and felt like she had no choice but to do it, she still saw Sima as a friend who was trying to help her. This is not atypical for CSEC survivors. Distinguishing trustworthy and supportive adults from exploitative ones is difficult for most people, and particularly for young people who have little practice determining whom to trust, for what reasons, and in what ways. For youth who have been abused or neglected at home, and live with chronic dual feelings of aversion and love for guardians, it can be particularly difficult to acquire the skill of discriminating between helpful and harmful adults. Many survivors of abuse also react negatively, like Lucy did, when they sense that they are being viewed as a victim. For some, accepting the label is tantamount to admitting personal failure and weakness and carries with it the possibility that they will be preyed upon because of it. For those who work in criminal justice or social services, the term "victim" is used factually to describe a person who has experienced a crime or abuse, and no judgment about the individual's inner character is implied. A CSEC survivor's refusal to "admit" that he or she has been victimized may frustrate people trying to help him or her, so it is important to understand that in some social networks acknowledging victimization of any sort may telegraph vulnerability and invite further abuse.

One other interesting comment that Lucy made to the social worker during the clinical interview was that she felt like she was already "damaged goods" because she had experienced sexual abuse as a child by a family friend and that other people could see that she was "broken" and so repeated sexual victimization was inescapable. This is not an uncommon sentiment for any sexual assault survivor. However, some CSEC survivors reason that if they are going to be forced to have unwanted sexual experiences anyway, they might as well be getting paid for it—because at least that way they get something out of it. This bleak logic can be difficult to challenge, particularly for helping professionals who simply cannot grasp why someone would ever view commercial sex as viable. Motivating a young person to make the effort to continue his or her education, make money in conventional ways, and adopt a more conformist lifestyle might be more easily accomplished by helping professionals who are deeply empathetic, able to explore genuinely both the "pros and cons" of disengaging from a commercial sex scene, and remain supportive even when the survivor has relapse episodes. It is for this reason that many of the community-based nonprofits that have been successful at helping CSEC survivors are staffed by "mentors" who are themselves former CSEC survivors who have fully recovered and are living stable lives.

In Lucy's case, the idea of reuniting with her parents was met with full opposition, and the child protection case manager assigned to her case on a temporary basis agreed that it could place her at risk of further harm. Because Lucy was using marijuana on a daily basis and had an outstanding warrant for petty theft in her home state, it was determined that she would go to a local residential school two hours away, which was a "partial lockdown" and treatment facility, meaning that the residents were not considered inmates and were not required to wear monitoring devices, and also were not permitted to leave any of the buildings without permission and were locked in their dormitories at night. There are over 1,000 such facilities in the United States as of 2016.

For some CSEC survivors, like Lucy, it is ultimately determined that it is in their best interest never to be reunited with parents and the process of terminating parental rights is initiated by Child Protective Services. For others, the process of reintegrating into their family can be accomplished but may be extraordinarily challenging. Some survivors feel so changed by their CSEC experience that they can no longer function in the family setting, and some parents and siblings cannot accept the CSEC survivor because of their exploitation experience. Many victims of CSEC face tremendous stigma and are rejected by relatives, peers, and former friends who treat them as though they are responsible for being exploited, lack morals, and deserve to be ostracized.

If Lucy's parents were determined to be fit to parent, and Lucy were going to return home, it is most likely that the reintegration would happen only after a period of separation with periodic, short-duration, trial visits leading up to reunification. CSEC survivors can find it difficult to resume a typical life after having been exploited—their sleep patterns may be irregular, they may be coping with substance dependence, they may be unaccustomed to following rules (or, conversely, accustomed to following rules imposed by an abusive trafficker, and therefore invested in living without rules), and they may no longer identify with the person that they used to be. Renewing an interest in hobbies or activities that they formerly enjoyed may be impossible.

While Lucy didn't return to living at home after being exploited, she did make several attempts to see her former friends and several teachers at her school with whom she had had a rapport. Even though she had only been gone for two months, when she saw her friends, it felt to her like she had been gone for a decade. Her friends weren't sure what to say to her and were intensely curious about what had happened to her. They had encouraged her to try to make money through sex, and they joked about being "hos" [whores], which made Lucy feel like they would think she was weak if she told them she didn't like it. Lucy also sensed that if she told them anything about that experience, they would have immediately leaked that information on social media. She realized that they had ideas about what prostitution was like from movies or videos, but that she would be unable to convince them about what it was really like. In short, she didn't feel like it was possible for any of the people she once considered friends to fathom what she had been through, and the inability to be honest with them made it impossible to sustain relationships.

A key clinical issue for many CSEC survivors who are exiting exploitation is that they may become socially isolated, feel that nobody but other CSEC survivors can understand them, and may feel compelled to return "to the life" because they miss the aspects of it that felt more fulfilling, thrilling, and emotionally intense than what they experience when living a conventional life and struggling with day-to-day challenges related to school or employment. The drawbacks of life "on the run" may seem diminished as compared to the loneliness and difficulties of rehabilitation, so many survivors return to exploitative situations repeatedly before something significant forces them to stop.

The fact that so many CSEC survivors disengage from helping services and choose to return to a dangerous life frustrates many well-intentioned social service workers. From the aid worker's point of view, it makes no sense that a victim who has been rescued from an abusive pimp and given a safe place to live, food, clothing, and even the friendship and social support of other survivors would give up those positive things in exchange for danger, homelessness, and violence. This can be particularly true for advocates who may expect CSEC survivors to behave precisely like other victims of CSA: in fact, CSEC survivors may come across as brash, proud, or seductive. They may continue to feel a mixture of pride and empowerment about their experiences "in the life," because they felt exhilarated or successful when they earned money. This is not at all common for other CSA survivors, so in comparison the CSEC survivor may appear "ungrateful," or even innately criminal, immoral, unwise, and selfish, because they contemplate returning to commercial sex. Advocates who have worked with survivors of domestic violence have useful insights upon which CSEC advocates can draw in these instances: there are myriad reasons, other than fear, why a person would return to a person who was abusive toward him or her or a situation in which he or she was in danger (Eckstein, 2011; Rhatigan & Axsom, 2006). Importantly, the inability to fit back in with peers and feelings of social isolation can be part of what drives some CSEC survivors back to the exploitative situations. Friendships that they establish with other survivors "in the life" may be emotionally fulfilling and even intensified by the shared experience of surviving abjectly dangerous situations.

Intersection of Race, Culture, and CSEC

It has been suggested that in the United States, CSEC victimization status is "racially coded" (Phillips, 2015). In other words, black individuals who have been exploited are less likely than their white counterparts to receive helping services when they come to the attention of social service providers or law enforcement as CSEC victims, and more likely to be perceived and treated as delinquent juveniles. According to Phillips (2015), the ongoing underprotection of black CSEC survivors is rooted in the fact that black people were legally enslaved in the United States until 1865 and had no legal recourse for rape or sexual assault. Because no protections from sexual assault or exploitation were extended, CSEC victims of color could not rely on government-run helping services and had to instead find alternative methods for remaining safe and coping with trauma. Over time, that reliance on community and oneself came to be interpreted by many in the social services and criminal justice fields as black survivors not needing, wanting, or deserving aid to the same extent that white survivors did. Stereotypes about black women and girls being immoral, sexually deviant, and hypersexual intensified perceptions that black girls who engaged in commercial sex were willful criminals rather than vulnerable victims. Racial biases that disadvantage black CSEC survivors persist, so it is imperative that professionals who serve or treat CSE youth receive training on the consequences of systemic, institutionalized, and individual racism.

There are few cultures in which men are not viewed as more powerful than women. However, it has been argued that the Latino cultural values of *machismo* (i.e., suggesting men are courageous, honorable, virile providers with authority over women), *marianismo* (i.e., division of labor according to traditional gender norms), *mujer decente* (i.e., remaining a virgin until marriage), and *familismo* (i.e., the duty to preserve the honor of the family) are so central that Latino survivors of CSEC may face particularly challenging struggles related to stigma and reintegration into the family (Flinn, 2012). In her 2012 report, Sarah Flinn writes, "It is important to remember that these cultural values do have an effect on Latina youth in situations of sexual exploitation, although that effect varies from case to case. Agencies and organizations working with Latina youth should have a thorough understanding of *marianismo* and *machismo*, both the expectations set forth by them as well as the results of adhering to those values."

While it is beyond the scope of this chapter to delve into the cultural dimensions of CSEC for every cultural subpopulation in the United States, family responsibility, pressure to preserve family honor, and spirituality have been cited as cultural factors that can impede East Asian and South

Asian CSEC survivors from receiving help (Hoffman, 2014). For American Indian/Native American youth, cultural factors such as distrust in social services systems, underfunded social services, generational trauma, cultural beliefs that most people are trustworthy, and cultural beliefs that the world is essentially good may affect susceptibility to CSEC traffickers (The Minnesota American Indian Women's Resource Center, 2009). Practitioners are well advised to understand the cultural backgrounds of the people whom they are most likely to serve and to seek information about the implications of their cultural beliefs on risk for CSEC and interventions for CSEC survivors.

Case Follow-Up

When Lucy was identified by health-care personnel as a CSEC survivor, she had already had numerous experiences with social services, other support entities, and multiple caring adults who tried to intervene on her behalf. Because none of these experiences had resolved the root cause of her problems, which was ongoing physical and emotional abuse by her parents, she developed a jaded, hopeless attitude about the capacity of even well-intentioned professionals to make a meaningful difference in her life. Ironically, the fact that she was raised in a middle-class suburb may have exacerbated some of her problems. Lucy didn't fit the stereotype of a "troubled youth"—she wasn't on a free or reduced lunch program at school, had mediocre but not failing grades in her classes, and was part of a peer group that didn't stand out to school administrators as particularly obstreperous. Her home life was assumed to be relatively stable because she didn't live in the most economically challenged neighborhood in her school district. As a result, intervention efforts were directed to the more obviously "at risk" youth at her school. The prior experiences she had with social services were the result of mandated reports that had been filed by a guidance counselor in elementary school, when her family lived in a different town, and had resulted in short-term stays with a relative. The art teacher at her junior high school had become someone in whom she felt comfortable confiding, but Lucy chose not to reveal that her parents were physically abusive because she wanted to avoid what she felt would be the subsequent, ineffective hassle.

Like many CSEC survivors and other runaway youth, by the time Lucy was identified as experiencing sexual exploitation, she was convinced that social services were unhelpful, intrusive, and caused embarrassment and that she had to rely on herself if she wanted the conditions of her life to change. It is developmentally normal for 15-year-olds to make choices that underestimate the potential for long-term adverse consequences. When service professionals puzzle over why or how an adolescent would choose to return to a sexually exploitative situation instead of a shelter or foster care home, they may be ascribing adult decision-making capabilities to adolescents.

Although it was ultimately determined that Lucy was not safe living at home, her parents had contacted her school to report that she was missing. They had not contacted law enforcement directly at first because they were afraid of getting Lucy in trouble and drawing attention to themselves. Lucy had told them she was going to stay with a friend and find work, and she texted them every few days, so they weren't too concerned. However, when Lucy continued to be absent from school, and her parents were unresponsive to school personnel's concern, they contacted law enforcement and Child Protective Services.

Supporting Survivors of CSEC with Trauma-Informed Practices

Conducting a clinical interview with a CSEC survivor requires preparation. All interactions should be guided by trauma-informed practice, as described by the Substance Abuse and Mental Health Services Administration (SAMHSA). Specifically, the six key principles of trauma-informed practice include: safety; trustworthiness, and transparency; peer support; collaboration and mutuality; empowerment, voice and choice; and consideration of cultural, historical, and gender issues (SAMHSA, 2016). Ideally, employing these principles when interacting with survivors creates a trusting environment and avoids retraumatization.

Regarding safety, conduct the assessment in a private place where the survivor feels comfortable. Consider who has accompanied the survivor, and do not make assumptions about this relationship (i.e., do not assume the adult is a parent or that the relationship is safe or supportive). It is important to ask, in a normative way that does not raise suspicion, to speak to the client alone. For example, clinicians may state at the start of the visit, "In our emergency department, the policy is to first speak to adolescents together with the adult, and then to ask the adult to leave and speak to him/her alone. So, we will start out talking together, and then we will ask you to leave so that I can spend some time talking to [client name] alone." During the discussion with the survivor, clinicians may notice that the person prefers to sit near the door or feel nervous if his or her direct access to an exit is blocked.

To most effectively establish trustworthiness and transparency, avoid writing notes while talking to the survivors and follow the survivors' lead when it comes to eye contact (i.e., social mannerisms may be unusual). In addition, be careful not to overpromise ("I will keep you safe no matter what"; "I will make sure you are placed with an amazing family who will love you."). Also, be very clear at the start of the conversation your duties to report—do not promise that you can keep information confidential if this is not true. However, clinicians can reassure survivors that they will always communicate openly with them about reporting requirements and will (if desired by the survivor) include them in this process.

Peer support is critical for trauma-informed care and may be particularly relevant for survivors of CSEC given the unique experience and common feeling that others do not understand "the life." Because of the central role of peer support, promising programs often employ peer mentors who are themselves former survivors of CSEC. If this type of mentorship program is locally available, using this peer support may be important in helping survivors stay safe and not return to a sexually exploitative situation.

The interview should be grounded in collaboration, empowerment, and cultural sensitivity. Clinicians should never ask a suspected CSEC survivor directly: "Are you a victim of sex trafficking?" Instead, they should ask questions such as "Did you ever have sex for things of value (for example money, housing, food, gifts, or favors)?" or "Did anyone ever pressure you to touch someone or have any unwanted sexual contact?" These and other recommended screening questions can be found in the Guidelines for Administering the Trafficking Victim Identification Tool (TVIT) disseminated by the Vera Institute for Justice (Vera Institute for Justice, 2014). When possible, involve survivors in decision making—for example, in Lucy's case, the Child Protective Service workers and social workers felt that several options would be acceptable including placement in foster care, return to Lucy's parents, or placement in a group home. Lucy's active participation in this decision likely resulted in increased safety. Having decision making ability may be particularly important for traumatized youth, who often have been isolated and stripped of control. Finally, be cognizant of implicit bias and the degree to which race, ethnicity, or gender may be impacting interactions or decision making.

Key Lessons within the Field of CSEC

Although research and program building within the field of CSEC are in a nascent stage of development, the following key lessons have emerged:

1. Sexually exploiting children leads to extensive and severe trauma symptoms and to adverse mental and physical health (Hossain et al., 2010; Oram et al., 2012).
2. CSEC occurs in children of all ages, including prepubertal children.

3. Oftentimes, children do not perceive themselves as being abused and may be reluctant to leave their situations (Smith et al., 2009). This phenomenon relates to a complex intersection of prior experiences, mental health issues, and lack of other safe supports; and, the child's perception of the situation relates intimately to his or her age and the related developmental lens.
4. Risk factors for being a CSEC survivor include personal histories of abuse, poverty, and social isolation. Therefore, survivors may not have established, nurturing families or social networks that can help them when removed from their current exploitative situation. They also may not view themselves as worthy of help.
5. The field needs to further develop and test strategies to prevent CSEC and to connect survivors with meaningful resources. Connecting survivors with peer mentors, who themselves are survivors, appears to be one promising practice.
6. Interactions with survivors should be based in principles of trauma-informed care and grounded in safety, relationship building, and trust.

Note

1. It is generally preferable to refer to those who have experienced CSEC as "survivors," though the term "victim" is used by criminal justice systems sources. In this chapter, we use the terms "survivor" and "victim" interchangeably.

References

Banks, D., & Kyckkelhahn, T. (2011). *Characteristics of suspected human trafficking incidents, 2008–2010*. Retrieved from http://www.bjs.gov/content/pub/pdf/cshti0810.pdf

Barnert, E. S., Abrams, S., Azzi, V. F., Ryan, G., Brook, R., & Chung, P. J. (2016). Identifying best practices for "Safe Harbor" legislation to protect child sex trafficking victims: Decriminalization alone is not sufficient. *Child Abuse & Neglect, 51*, 249–262. doi:10.1016/j.chiabu.2015.10.002

Brawn, K. M., & Roe-Sepowitz, D. (2008). Female juvenile prostitutes: Exploring the relationship to substance use. *Children and Youth Services Review, 30*(12), 1395–1402. doi:10.1016/j.childyouth.2008.04.011

Chohaney, M. L. (2016). Minor and adult domestic sex trafficking risk factors in Ohio. *Journal of the Society for Social Work and Research, 7*(1), 117–141. doi:10.1086/685108

Choi, K. R. (2015). Risk Factors for domestic minor sex trafficking in the United States: A literature review. *Journal of Forensic Nursing, 11*(2), 66–76. doi:10.1097/jfn.0000000000000072

Cole, J., Sprang, G., Lee, R., & Cohen, J. (2016). The trauma of commercial sexual exploitation of youth: A comparison of CSE victims to sexual abuse victims in a clinical sample. *Journal of Interpersonal Violence, 31*(1), 122–146. doi:10.1177/0886260514555133

Deb, S., Mukherjee, A., & Mathews, B. (2011). Aggression in sexually abused trafficked girls and efficacy of intervention. *Journal of Interpersonal Violence, 26*(4), 745–768. doi:10.1177/0886260510365875

Dworkin, E., Javdani, S., Verona, E., & Campbell, R. (2014). Child sexual abuse and disordered eating: The mediating role of impulsive and compulsive tendencies. *Psychology of Violence, 4*(1), 21–36. doi:10.1037/a0031779

Eckstein, J.J. (2011). Reasons for staying in intimately violent relationships: Comparisons of men and women and messages communicated to self and others. *Journal of Family Violence, 26*(1), 21–30. doi:10.1007/s10896-010-9338-0

Estes, R. J., & Weiner, N. A. (2005). The commercial sexual exploitation of children in the United States. In S. W. Cooper, R. J. Estes, A. P. Giardino, N. D. Kellogg, & V. I. Vieth (Eds.), *Medical, legal, and social science aspects of child sexual exploitation: A comprehensive review of pornography, prostitution, and internet crimes.* St. Louis, MO: G.W. Medical Publishing, Inc.

Flinn, S. (2012). *Latina youth in commercial sexual exploitation.* Retrieved from http://commons.pacificu.edu/cgi/viewcontent.cgi?article=1017&context=cassoc

The Florida Legislature Office of Program Policy Analysis and Government Accountability. (2015). *State and local agencies are in initial stages of addressing needs of child victims of commercial sexual exploitation.* Retrieved from http://www.oppaga.state.fl.us/MonitorDocs/Reports/pdf/1506rpt.pdf

Forsyth, S., Rogstad, K., & Interest, B.A.S. (2015). Sexual health issues in adolescents and young adults. *Clinical Medicine, 15*(5), 447–451.

Greenbaum, V.J. (2014). Commercial sexual exploitation and sex trafficking of children in the United States. *Current Problems in Pediatric and Adolescent Health Care, 44*(9), 245–269. doi:10.1016/j.cppeds.2014.07.001

Herbert, J.L., & Bromfield, L. (2016). Evidence for the efficacy of the Child Advocacy Center model: A systematic review. *Trauma Violence & Abuse, 17*(3), 341–357. doi:10.1177/1524838015585319

Hoffman, K. (2014). *Human trafficking at Asian massage parlors.* Paper presented at the Human Trafficking & Technology, Pittsburgh, PA.

Hossain, M., Zimmerman, C., Abas, M., Light, M., & Watts, C. (2010). The relationship of trauma to mental disorders among trafficked and sexually exploited girls and women. *American Journal of Public Health, 100*(12), 2442–2449. doi:10.2105/ajph.2009.173229

Kaestle, C.E. (2012). Selling and buying sex: A longitudinal study of risk and protective factors in adolescence. *Prevention Science, 13*(3), 314–322. doi:10.1007/s11121-011-0268-8

Kaye-Tzadok, A., & Davidson-Arad, B. (2016). Posttraumatic growth among women survivors of childhood sexual abuse: Its relation to cognitive strategies, posttraumatic symptoms, and resilience. *Psychological Trauma-Theory Research Practice and Policy, 8*(5), 550–558. doi:10.1037/tra0000103

Klatt, T., Cavner, D., & Egan, V. (2014). Rationalising predictors of child sexual exploitation and sex-trading. *Child Abuse & Neglect, 38*(2), 252–260. doi:10.1016/j.chiabu.2013.08.019

Maniglio, R. (2015). Significance, nature, and direction of the association between child sexual abuse and conduct disorder: A systematic review. *Trauma Violence & Abuse, 16*(3), 241–257. doi:10.1177/1524838014526068

Martinez, O., & Kelle, G. (2013). Sex trafficking of LGBT individuals: A call for service provision, research, and action. *The International Law News, 42*(4).

The Minnesota American Indian Women's Resource Center. (2009). *Shattered hearts: The commercial sexual exploitation of American Indian women and girls in Minnesota*. Retrieved from http://indianlaw.org/sites/default/files/shattered%20hearts%20report.pdf

Oram, S., Abas, M., Bick, D., Boyle, A., French, R., Jakobowitz, S., . . . Zimmerman, C. (2016). Human trafficking and health: A survey of male and female survivors in England. *American Journal of Public Health, 106*(6), 1073–1078. doi:10.2105/ajph.2016.303095

Oram, S., Ostrovschi, N. V., Gorceag, V. I., Hotineanu, M. A., Gorceag, L., Trigub, C., & Abas, M. (2012). Physical health symptoms reported by trafficked women receiving post-trafficking support in Moldova: Prevalence, severity and associated factors. *BMC Women's Health, 12*, 9. doi:10.1186/1472-6874-12-20

Phillips, J. (2015). Black girls and the (im)possibilities of a victim trope: The intersectional failures of legal and advocacy interventions in the commercial sexual exploitation of minors in the united states. *UCLA Law Review, 62*(6), 1642–1675.

Reid, J. A. (2014). Risk and resiliency factors influencing onset and adolescence-limited commercial sexual exploitation of disadvantaged girls. *Criminal Behaviour and Mental Health, 24*(5), 332–344. doi:10.1002/cbm.1903

Renner, L. M., Coohey, C., Ruch, G., & O'Leary, P. (2013). Self-reported panic attacks in adulthood: Relationship with injury, location and disclosure of childhood sexual abuse. *Journal of Social Work, 13*(3), 308–318. doi:10.1177/1468017311433429

Rhatigan, D. L., & Axsom, D. K. (2006). Using the investment model to understand battered women's commitment to abusive relationships. *Journal of Family Violence, 21*(2), 153–162. doi:10.1007/s10896–005–9013-z

SAMHSA. (2016). *Trauma-informed approach and trauma-specific interventions*. Retrieved from http://www.samhsa.gov/nctic/trauma-interventions

Smith, L., Vardaman, S., & Snow, M. (2009). *The national report on domestic minor sex trafficking: America's prostituted children*. Retrieved from http://sharedhope.org/wp-content/uploads/2012/09/SHI_National_Report_on_DMST_2009.pdf

Stanley, N., Oram, S., Jakobowitz, S., Westwood, J., Borschmann, R., Zimmerman, C., & Howard, L. M. (2016). The health needs and healthcare experiences of young people trafficked into the UK. *Child Abuse & Neglect, 59*, 100–110. doi:10.1016/j.chiabu.2016.08.001

Stoklosa, H., Dawson, M. B., Williams-Oni, F., & Rothman, E. F. (2017). A review of U.S. health care institution protocols for the identification and treatment of victims of human trafficking. *Journal of Human Trafficking*, 3(2), 116–124. doi:10.1080/23322705.2016.1187965

Stoklosa, H., Showalter, E., Melnick, A., & Rothman, E. F. (2017). Health care providers' experience with a protocol for the identification, treatment, and referral of human-trafficking victims. *Journal of Human Trafficking*, 3(3), 182–192. doi:10.1080/23322705.2016.1194668

Twill, S. E., Green, D. M., & Traylor, A. (2010). A descriptive study on sexually exploited children in residential treatment. *Child & Youth Care Forum, 39*(3), 187–199. doi:10.1007/s10566-010-9098-2

U.S. Department of Justice. (2014). *2014 crime in the United States, human trafficking 2014*. Retrieved from https://ucr.fbi.gov/crime-in-the-u.s/2014/crime-in-the-u.s.-2014/additional-reports/human-trafficking-report/human-trafficking.pdf

Varma, S., Gillespie, S., McCracken, C., & Greenbaum, V. J. (2015). Characteristics of child commercial sexual exploitation and sex trafficking victims presenting for medical care in the United States. *Child Abuse & Neglect, 44*, 98–105. doi:10.1016/j.chiabu.2015.04.004

Vera Institute for Justice. (2014). *Screening for human trafficking: Guidelines for administering the Trafficking Victim Identification Tool (TVIT)*. Retrieved from http://archive.vera.org/sites/default/files/resources/downloads/human-trafficking-identification-tool-and-user-guidelines.pdf

Wang, Y., Raffeld, M. R., Slopen, N., Hale, L., & Dunn, E. C. (2016). Childhood adversity and insomnia in adolescence. *Sleep Medicine, 21*, 12–18. doi:10.1016/j.sleep.2016.01.011

Weinstein, D., Staffelbach, D., & Biaggio, M. (2000). Attention-deficit hyperactivity disorder and posttraumatic stress disorder: Differential diagnosis in childhood sexual abuse. *Clinical Psychology Review, 20*(3), 359–378. doi:10.1016/s0272–7358(98)00107-x

CHAPTER 13

Medical Trauma

The Impact of Illness, Injury, and Medical Treatment Experiences on Children and Families

Nancy Kassam-Adams

Medical Trauma: Definitions and Background

When someone says "child trauma," what most likely comes to mind is a child who experiences abuse, lives with chronic violence, or is exposed to disaster. We are less likely to think of the child who is undergoing cancer treatment, admitted to the hospital after a car crash, or rushed to the emergency department with sudden unexplained abdominal pain. A growing body of research has established that illness or injury can lead to traumatic stress reactions in children (Kazak et al., 2006; Price, Kassam-Adams, Alderfer, Christofferson, & Kazak, 2016). What is it about medical events and experiences that may engender persistent traumatic stress for children and their families? How can doctors, nurses, and parents help children deal with traumatic stress due to illness, injury, challenging medical procedures, and treatment? This chapter will address the scope and impact of medical trauma and describe the ways in which health-care professionals, family members, and other support systems can help to address the potential psychological impact of illness and injury for children.

First, some definitions. When we talk about trauma and traumatic stress in the health-care arena, it is particularly important to clarify terminology. In the medical field, "trauma" refers to physical injury, and in common nonmedical usage, we often use "trauma" interchangeably to refer to *events* that are frightening and difficult or to the emotional *responses* elicited by those events. In this chapter, "medical trauma" refers to children's potentially traumatic medical events and experiences, and "medical traumatic stress" refers to the responses that a child and family may develop as a result of those events.

Medical events are among the most common potentially traumatic events experienced by children. In the United States, injury affects 20 million children each year (Agency for Healthcare Research and Quality, 2007; Centers for Disease Control, 2014b; Niska, Bhuiya, & Xu, 2010), leading to 8 million emergency department visits and 250,000 hospital admissions annually (Centers for Disease Control, 2014b). New diagnoses of life-threatening and chronic childhood diseases (e.g., cancer, diabetes, heart disease) affect more than 75,000 children each year (Center for Disease Control and Prevention, 2017; Hoffman & Kaplan, 2002; Ward, DeSantis, Robbins, Kohler, & Jemal, 2014). One in 285 U.S. children is diagnosed with cancer (American Cancer Society, 2014). Many children have chronic illnesses such as asthma or sickle cell disease that can involve disruptive, physically and emotionally challenging disease episodes and treatment regimens. In fact, each year 5 percent of U.S. children are admitted to the hospital (Agency for Healthcare Research and Quality, 2007) and about 20 percent have an emergency department visit (Centers for Disease Control, 2014a).

Why are these medical experiences potentially traumatic? Being in pain, feeling helpless and out of control, and feeling uncertain about what will happen next and not knowing how things will turn out, all contribute to the potentially traumatic nature of medical events. Certain aspects of medical care itself can, inadvertently, be traumatic. As one child told our research team about his experience in the emergency room after a serious injury, "Doctors crowded around and stuck stuff on me and cut my clothes off—I didn't know what was happening." Medically necessary procedures may involve physical pain or discomfort that is not easily controlled with pain medications, and in hospital emergency and inpatient settings, children can be exposed to other patients' pain or distress and to sights and sounds that they do not understand. Like other forms of child trauma, medical events can tear apart a child or family's sense of a safe or predictable world. One mother whose daughters faced serious, life-threatening illness wrote that parents who have gone through this, even when the outcome is positive for their child, know that they "have skirted the unthinkable and survived. That they have lost the illusion of safety and go on anyway, day by day" (Brown, 2008).

Acute or chronic pain, changes in one's body, or undergoing an invasive procedure can be challenging for children of any age. However, cognitive and socioemotional development plays a large role in children's understanding of their body, illness and injury processes, and how medical treatment works and how children interpret medical experiences (Myant & Williams, 2005). For example, a young child's unspoken misconceptions about the cause or implications of an illness or injury (i.e., thinking "I got sick today because I hit my little brother yesterday") may contribute to his or her fear or worry. Adolescents who have to restrict their usual activities (due to pain, fatigue, physical limitations) or who need help from their parents to manage illness- or injury-related demands may experience these changes as a threat to their growing sense of independence. Finally, individuals within the same family—the affected child, siblings, parents, others—often vary in which aspects of a child's illness or injury they perceive as most difficult or traumatic. A study that asked parents and children about potentially traumatic aspects of the child's cancer and treatment illustrates this point well (Kazak, Struber, Barakat, & Meeske, 1996). Parents in the study highlighted fear of their child dying or fear of the cancer recurring, while children more often focused on specific medical procedures or bodily changes such as losing their hair.

It is clear that medical events are often challenging, and have the potential to be traumatic, for a child and family. A case example may help to illuminate how this occurs.

Case Example: Anna Jones

Anna Jones is an active, athletic, and generally healthy 11-year-old girl who lives at home with her mother, father, and 5-year-old brother, Marco. On Monday morning, Anna wakes up complaining that she doesn't feel well, and her parents decide to keep her home from school. Over the next several hours, Anna develops a fever, becomes more lethargic, and continues to say that her belly hurts. By midafternoon, Ms. Jones becomes very concerned when Anna vomits repeatedly and her belly pain becomes much more severe. She calls the pediatrician, who advises her to take Anna to the emergency department at their local hospital. Ms. Jones tries unsuccessfully to reach Anna's father at work and leaves Marco with a neighbor.

At the hospital, the doctors and nurses quickly take Anna to an exam room while Ms. Jones stays outside to complete paperwork. As several different nurses come into the room to draw blood for lab tests and stick a needle in Anna's arm to prepare her for intravenous (IV) treatment, Anna is very quiet but asks repeatedly where her mom and dad are. She becomes visibly calmer when her mother joins her in the exam room. Several doctors examine Anna; she is diagnosed with appendicitis and admitted for surgery.

Surgery reveals that Anna had a perforated appendix. For the first 24 hours after surgery she continues to have pain and fever, and the medical team decides to continue IV antibiotics. At one point, when Anna overhears the nurses discuss the need to place a new IV, because of pain at the current IV site, she starts to cry. Mrs. Jones also gets teary and hugs her daughter. By Friday, Anna's medical condition has improved enough for her to go home from the hospital.

One week later, Anna's physical recovery is going well. But her parents notice that she seems withdrawn, and she has been reluctant to spend any time in her bedroom. When they ask Anna about this, she says she can't stop thinking about what happened, and being in her room just reminds her of the time she woke up sick and had to go to the hospital. Marco has been asking a lot of questions about what happened to Anna, and each night at bedtime he asks his dad to check his tummy to be sure it is OK. At a follow-up appointment with the pediatrician at the end of this week, both parents mention their concern that Anna is not ready for her planned return to school.

Impact of Medical Trauma

Anna and her family are a composite case illustrating the impact of pediatric medical trauma. Before we continue with Anna's story, it will be helpful to describe what is known about the impact of medical trauma. Pediatric medical traumatic stress is a set of emotional and physical reactions that children and family members may have in response to pain, injury, serious illness, medical procedures, and invasive or frightening treatment experiences (Kazak et al., 2006; National Child Traumatic Stress Network, 2004). These include traumatic stress reactions such as reexperiencing aspects of the trauma through memories or intrusive thoughts, avoidance of trauma reminders, changes in thinking or emotions (like feeling angry or feeling guilty), and hyperarousal (hypervigilance, sleep or concentration problems). Studies have documented persistent traumatic stress reactions in children facing a range of medical events or conditions including injuries, burns, cancer, organ transplantation, asthma, diabetes, sickle cell disease, and HIV/AIDS and in children admitted to the intensive care unit (Price et al., 2016). Traumatic stress reactions are also well documented in parents, often at equal or higher rates than for the children themselves (Price et al., 2016), and in the brothers and sisters of ill and injured children (Alderfer et al., 2010).

The impact of persistent medical traumatic stress can be substantial. There may be poorer adherence to follow-up medical care, slower physical recovery/return to functioning, poorer health-related quality of life, and overall poorer health outcomes (Holbrook et al., 2005; King et al., 2013; Landolt, Buehlmann, Maag, & Schiestl, 2009). Having a few traumatic stress reactions during or right after a medical event is not unusual—in fact, more than 80 percent of children and parents reported at least one acute traumatic stress symptom within the first month after the child was hospitalized for injury (Winston et al., 2002). For some, these early traumatic stress responses resolve over the course of a few weeks, with good support and the use of helpful coping strategies. But an estimated 20 percent of injured children, and 12 percent of children with serious illness, will go on to have traumatic stress reactions that last for months or years (Kahana, Feeny, Youngstrom, & Drotar, 2006).

There is no clear evidence that younger versus older children are more likely to develop medical traumatic stress. However, development does affect how children react to medical trauma. There are differences in the way that children process and adapt to medical trauma and exhibit medical traumatic stress reactions that mirror developmental differences observed for other types of trauma exposure (Pynoos, 1994; Salmon & Bryant, 2002). For example, the very youngest children will be more likely to show distress with their behavior; they often rely on parents and caretakers to help them regulate emotional distress arising from pain and other medical stressors. In our case example, when her parents ask her about changes they have observed, 11-year-old Anna has the ability (which would not be present in a much younger child) to explain how she is feeling and to reflect on her own mental processes, drawing a basic connection between thoughts and feelings (Salmon & Bryant, 2002).

In our case example, we saw that almost two weeks after she first became ill, Anna was experiencing acute traumatic stress reactions—she could not stop thinking about what happened, and she wanted to avoid things that reminded her of the day she got sick. Are Anna's early traumatic stress reactions a temporary response in the aftermath of a frightening medical experience? How can we assess the likelihood that she will have longer-lasting reactions that get in the way of her recovery, and for which we may want to implement preventive measures? Meta-analyses, combining results from multiple research studies, have begun to identify risk factors for persistent posttraumatic stress symptoms in ill or injured children. These factors include a sense of life threat, greater psychological distress (in children or their parents) in the early aftermath of a medical event, having less effective social support, and using problematic coping strategies such as social withdrawal (pulling away from friends and family) or trying to avoid thinking about the medical event (Alisic, Jongmans, van Wesel, & Kleber, 2011; Cox, Kenardy, & Hendrikz, 2008; Kahana et al., 2006; Trickey, Siddaway, Meiser-Stedman, Serpell, & Field, 2012). Having more severe pain, being separated from parents, and having a history of behavioral or emotional problems prior to the medical event also appear to be risk factors. Notably, research studies consistently find that objective medical severity does not predict which children will develop medical traumatic stress. It is important to remember this counterintuitive finding, as the practical implication is that we cannot rely on medical severity to tell us which children may need additional attention.

Case Example: Anna Jones (Three Months Later)

Three months after her hospital stay, Anna's physical recovery from surgery is going well, according to a recent follow-up visit with her pediatrician. Anna still tires a little more easily but has no ongoing pain. She feels anxious when anything reminds her of the day she got sick or of being in the hospital. Although she is back to sleeping in her own room, Anna wakes up many nights with nightmares about being in the hospital. She has not told her parents about this because she does not want to worry them. She tries to distract herself from thinking about it by keeping busy, although she is having a hard time concentrating on her schoolwork. Her grades are lower this quarter, even though she has more free time than usual after she had to drop out of soccer for the season while she recovers.

Anna's parents say that she seems "more like her old self," but they are concerned that she seems not to want to go out, even refusing to attend her friend's birthday party. Ms. Jones reports that, though she tries to keep herself from dwelling on it, she often has vivid memories of the day Anna got sick, reliving the feeling of rushing her to the hospital: "She was in so much pain and I didn't know what was wrong." Mr. Jones says that he is coping well now, but that he still feels bad that he was not able to be with Anna in the emergency department, and he sometimes worries about something else happening with his family when he is at work.

Key Clinical Issues in Medical Trauma

The clinical implications of medical trauma are best understood by considering the phases of medical events as these unfold over time (Kazak et al., 2006; Price et al., 2016). Figure 13.1 depicts these phases. For many illness or injury experiences, there is an acute or precipitating event. This may be the sudden onset of severe symptoms (as in our case example), an acute physical injury, or learning of a serious or life-threatening diagnosis. The first, "peri-trauma," phase, that is, the hours and days during and just after this acute event, brings stressors and demands related to emergency treatment, hospital admission, surgery, invasive procedures, pain, and physical symptoms that may challenge the coping capacities of any child and family. In the second phase, following the peri-trauma period, an ill or injured child may require active acute medical care in the hospital or as an outpatient for additional days or weeks. During this phase, many of the same stressors and challenges are present. Children and families begin to rally their existing support systems and coping capacities as

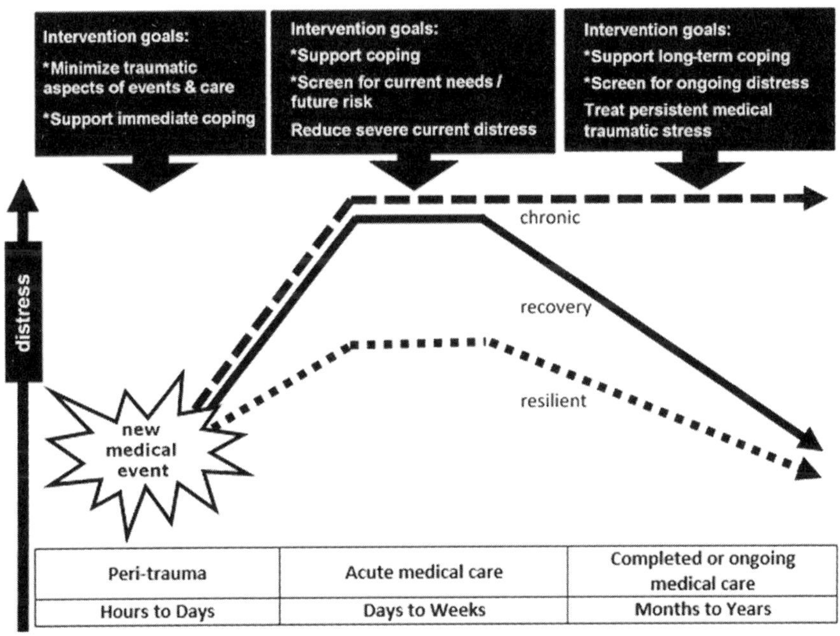

Figure 13.1 Phases of medical events, with potential trajectories of distress level over time, and goals for intervention during each phase

Note. Universal interventions are marked with an asterisk (*). Adapted from HealthCare-Toolbox.org and Price et al., 2016.

they adjust to the challenges. Depending on the type of illness or injury and the child's medical needs, the acute medical care phase ends with the child being discharged from active medical treatment, or with a transition to ongoing medical care that can last for months, years, or a lifetime. In this third phase, whether or not medical treatment continues, the impact of medical trauma can persist for children and family members. In the case of serious or life-threatening illnesses with aggressive treatment regimens (e.g., cancer), as well as chronic conditions with the potential for intermittent medical crises, these three broad phases of medical events do not always progress in a simple, linear fashion. New and potentially traumatic acute medical events may occur at any time due to the progression of the disease or condition or the challenges of ongoing treatment.

Studies with injured children find that the course of traumatic stress symptoms may follow several basic trajectories (De Young, Kenardy, Cobham, & Kimble, 2012; Le Brocque, Hendrikz, & Kenardy, 2010). More than half follow a "resilient" trajectory—the lower dotted line in Figure 13.1—in which initial distress, that is, medical traumatic stress reactions, in the peri-trauma period resolves relatively quickly as the child and family rally support systems and coping capacity. About one-third follow a "recovery" trajectory—the middle solid line in Figure 13.1—with significant early distress that decreases gradually over several months. A smaller group has a "chronic" trajectory—the top dashed line in Figure 13.1—in which medical traumatic stress reactions continue and may even escalate across many months.

Keeping these phases of medical events in mind helps us to understand how children's clinical needs and clinical presentation can evolve over time, and ultimately help ground our design of effective support and intervention for children and families at each phase. In our case example, three months after her sudden illness and hospitalization, Anna has been discharged from acute medical treatment, and yet she and her family are still experiencing the impact of her sudden illness. Both Anna and her parents have trauma reexperiencing and avoidance symptoms; Anna's symptoms are interfering with her sleep and her school performance. Anna's parents want to help her, but they are not fully aware of Anna's symptoms. In this phase, Anna's pediatrician or school nurse may be well situated to screen for and identify these concerns.

Age and developmental phase affect the range of cognitive and emotional strategies that children are able to employ to cope with distressing aspects of medical trauma (Zimmer-Gembeck & Skinner, 2010). A very young child who experiences painful or frightening medical events has not yet developed the cognitive and verbal skills to express and process emotional responses to these events and thus often uses more behavioral means (crying, becoming more clingy) of expressing distress or recruiting help from caregivers. Young children must rely on their parents or other adults to scaffold and support them in coping with distressing emotional responses. School-age children and adolescents are increasingly able to understand their own emotions and reactions and can use this understanding to help themselves cope with medical trauma. By the school-age years, children like Anna often have a much more developed repertoire of coping tools. At age 11, Anna has some understanding of her own emotional responses to painful or scary parts of what she experienced, and she has the verbal skills to tell her parents how she is feeling. Parent responses are essential for the youngest children, but they remain important for children and youth of any age. The role of parents and other adults in supporting effective child coping with medical trauma evolves as children grow (Power, 2004). For example, while they are in the hospital with an acute medical event, teenagers may temporarily need to depend more on their parents for emotional and practical support and then transition back to greater independence as they recover.

Cultural Considerations in Medical Trauma

Does illness or injury always happen for a reason? Who in the family should be involved in treatment decisions regarding a child's medical condition? Is it OK to ask a question when the doctor is explaining the expected course of treatment? Is it OK to mention fears or worries? Do the doctors and nurses look like my family? Do they speak our language? Culture shapes our beliefs, practices, attitudes, values, and interpersonal relationships and thus plays a role in how we understand illness, describe symptoms, perceive or express pain, and manage the challenges of a child's medical trauma (Gray, Szulczewski, Regan, Williams, & Pai, 2014; Kristjánsdóttir, Unruh, McAlpine, & McGrath, 2012). Cultural considerations, as well as ethnic and racial disparities in access to care and experiences of treatment (Johnson et al., 2013), also impact decisions of when and how to seek health care, relationships with health-care professionals, and trust in the health-care system. Each of these factors may impact the child's experience of medical events and treatment and thus the development of medical traumatic stress.

Relevant to medical trauma and medical traumatic stress, there appear to be cultural variations in communication styles and expectations, that is, what is appropriate to disclose to a child about his or her illness, diagnosis, or treatment course, in communication concerning death and dying (Gray et al., 2014). Culture also influences parent–child interactions as a family faces a child's illness or injury and the way in which families relate to their larger social support system in times of crisis related to a medical event.

Pain is a risk factor for persistent medical traumatic stress, and pain management is affected by children's expression of pain, as well as the ways in which health-care professionals interpret each patient's need for pain control measures. For example, there is some evidence that white American children display more verbal and behavioral responses (facial expressions, crying) to potentially painful medical procedures when compared to African American or Asian American children or to children from other countries in Europe or Asia (Kristjánsdóttir et al., 2012). Even when children across cultural groups rate procedure-related pain similarly, their expectations for how to behave within the doctor–patient interaction may influence the coping strategies they employ, that is, internal coping strategies such as thinking about positive things versus more overt strategies such as crying (Kristjánsdóttir et al., 2012). Research has not shown race or ethnicity to be associated with different rates of medical traumatic stress after illness or injury, but child and family experiences in the health-care system may be impacted by race, ethnicity, and language. Racial and ethnic disparities have been documented in provider treatment recommendations and in pain management for children in the emergency department or after surgery (Jimenez, Jackson, Zhou, Ayala, & Ebel, 2014; Johnson et al., 2013; Sabin & Greenwald, 2012). For example, some studies suggest that children of color, or children in families with limited English proficiency, may be less likely to receive pain medication, or may wait longer for pain medication, even when they rate their pain as severe.

The challenges of working across cultures, and the potentially traumatic consequences of cross-cultural misunderstanding in health care, have resulted in increased attention to culturally sensitive health care (Fadiman, 1997; The Joint Commission, 2010). For readers interested in exploring this topic further, Anne Fadiman's 1997 book *The Spirit Catches You and You Fall Down* provides a compelling exposition of the ways in which different understanding of a child's serious illness, between the child's family and a group of well-intentioned health-care and social service providers, can lead to unfortunate consequences including removal of a child from his or her family and suboptimal health-care and health outcomes. Providing pediatric health care that is both culturally sensitive and trauma-informed requires health-care professionals who are open to and curious about cultural variations in how children and families perceive and cope with medical events, and who are aware of their own susceptibility to unintentional biases and actively practice bias-reducing strategies (Chapman, Kaatz, & Carnes, 2013).

Who Can Help Children and Families Facing Medical Trauma?

Like Anna and her family, most families facing pediatric medical events do not seek mental health services, even if they begin to experience medical traumatic stress reactions. However, Anna and her family interacted with health-care professionals at each stage of her sudden illness and its aftermath—from the family's pediatrician to the emergency department doctors and nurses to the attending physicians, bedside nurses, and surgical team who took care of her during her stay in the hospital. After her discharge from the hospital, Anna had follow-up visits with the surgeon and with her pediatrician, and the school nurse checked in with her several times during her first weeks back at school.

Each of these professionals had the opportunity to provide trauma-informed pediatric health care. Their role is not limited to screening and making a referral to mental health professionals. Because many aspects of potentially traumatic medical events unfold within the health-care system, health-care professionals are the front line for providing care that could minimize the potentially traumatic impact of medical events and treatment (Marsac, Kassam-Adams, Hildenbrand, Winston, & Leff, 2016). In the emergency department when Anna appears quiet and anxious, in the hospital when both Anna and her mother struggle to cope with a new IV placement, a trauma-informed health-care team can respond in ways that impact the child and family's experience of unfolding medical events and support their competence in coping with these events. At the one-week follow-up visit, upon hearing Anna's parents' concerns about her return to school, the pediatrician can provide basic anticipatory guidance, interpreting Anna's avoidance as understandable but explaining the importance of helping her face her fears, thus helping this family understand and address early medical traumatic stress reactions before they become persistent.

Beyond provision of trauma-informed health care, an additional role for health-care professionals is to help connect children with social work or mental health professionals if more support or intervention is warranted. At three months, Anna's pediatrician might refer the family for further services based on learning that they are experiencing medical traumatic stress reactions that are impacting their daily functioning. Psychosocial services may be available within the medical setting itself, via psychology, psychiatry, social work, or child life services in the hospital or via mental health professionals integrated in pediatric or family medicine practices. Whatever their practice setting, mental health professionals working with children facing medical trauma need to learn about the child's medical condition and treatment regimen and understand the culture and expectations of the health-care system in order to interact effectively with the child's health-care team (Center for Pediatric Traumatic Stress, 2015).

General Intervention Principles for Medical Trauma

The single most important tool for addressing medical trauma is that of trauma-informed pediatric health care (Marsac et al., 2016). In a trauma-informed health-care setting, all staff recognize (a) the potentially traumatic impact of medical events and treatment for children and families and (b) the role that prior traumatic exposure may play in the child and family's response to new medical events. This basic recognition and understanding is integrated in health-care professionals' interactions with patients and reflected in institutional policies and practices. Trauma-informed pediatric health care complements and extends institutional practices and policies that are already emphasized in many health-care settings, notably patient- and family-centered care (Committee on Hospital Care, 2003; O'Malley, Brown, & SE, 2008; The Joint Commission, 2010).

A simple way for health-care professionals to remember the basic principles for trauma-informed care is the "D-E-F" protocol (Center for Pediatric Traumatic Stress, 2009; Stuber, Schneider, Kassam-Adams, Kazak, & Saxe, 2006). Health-care professionals are familiar with the A-B-C mnemonic—a reminder to attend first to *A*irway, *B*reathing, and *C*irculation to address immediate physical health needs. D-E-F adds *D*istress, *E*motional support, and *F*amily as the next crucial steps (after A-B-C) to address medical traumatic stress.

In addition to trauma-informed health care, which applies across all phases, the specific goals of medical trauma interventions evolve as the phases of medical events unfold over time, as indicated in Figure 13.1. In each phase, we can identify levels of intervention ranging from *universal* interventions (appropriate for all children facing medical trauma) to *targeted* interventions (for those at higher risk) or *mental health treatment* (for children or families with specific clinical needs).

In the peri-trauma phase, the primary *goal of intervention* is to minimize potentially traumatic aspects of medical events and treatment, keeping in mind that the child and the family's subjective experience of these unfolding experiences is key. Because prior trauma exposure is often unknown to the health-care team, trauma-informed care at this stage requires the awareness that any child may have a history of exposure to traumatic stress and that this prior exposure could impact the child's responses to the current medical events. Interventions in this phase may also have the goal of providing immediate support to help a child cope with acute physical symptoms or urgent medical procedures. *Universal* interventions in the peri-trauma period include attending to *distress* by optimizing pain management and providing age-appropriate information about what is happening during medical care and promoting *emotional support* for children, that is, giving specific suggestions to help a parent provide active distraction to reduce child anxiety during a medically necessary but challenging procedure (Blount et al., 2009; A. McCarthy et al., 2010). When Anna and her mother are both visibly upset at the prospect of Anna getting a new IV, the nurse who is taking care of Anna could coach Ms. Jones in how to help Anna focus away from the IV site and actively engage her in conversation or a game while the IV is placed. *Targeted* interventions in the peri-trauma phase may be appropriate in children with a known risk for severe medical traumatic stress reactions, that is, based on a history of medical or other trauma. Targeted strategies could include advance planning (coping skills training, specific plans for sedation, or pain management) to minimize or prevent distress during future medical events in children with chronic medical conditions. These interventions may require consultation from a mental health professional who works with the child and the health-care team.

In the second phase, during acute medical care, the primary *goal of intervention* is to reduce the chance that any emerging medical traumatic stress reactions will become persistent and impairing. In this phase, *universal* interventions continue to include attention to minimizing potentially traumatic aspects of care. A key focus in this period is screening to detect those children and families who need more assistance (Kazak et al., 2011; M. McCarthy et al., 2016), or to predict who is most at risk for a chronic trajectory with persistent traumatic stress symptoms that will impede emotional and physical recovery (Kassam-Adams, Marsac, García-España, & Winston, 2015). Based on formal or informal screening, *targeted* interventions in this phase can include anticipatory guidance to parents about ways to support the child coping over the expected course of illness, injury, or treatment. Innovative online or eHealth interventions show promise in this phase to reduce early traumatic stress symptoms and prevent the development of persistent medical traumatic stress (Kassam-Adams et al., 2016). There are widely accessible evidence-based resources that can help parents to understand their child's reactions to medical trauma and to support their child's coping with medical treatment (Marsac et al., 2012, 2014). For example, AfterTheInjury.org is a website available in English and Spanish that provides information and specific tips for parents of injured children (Marsac, Kassam-Adams, Hildenbrand, Kohser, & Winston, 2011). Health-care systems may also offer focused brief interventions to build family capacity for adaptation to predictable stressors and demands of illness and treatment; one such program has been developed for the parents of children newly diagnosed with cancer (Stehl et al., 2009). Formal *mental health* interventions would be implemented in this phase when severe acute distress interferes with the child's day-to-day functioning or the child's ability to participate in his or her care and to comply with medically necessary treatment regimens.

The primary *goal of intervention* in the third phase, when acute medical care has ended or has transitioned to ongoing longer-term care, is to reduce persistent medical traumatic stress reactions if these are present and to continue to build a child and family's capacity to cope with the ongoing demands of the child's medical condition or continued treatment. For Anna, it is not likely that her appendicitis and surgery will require extended medical care or have long-term physical consequences. But for a child with cancer, or with a severe traumatic injury, this period may be one in which active treatment or rehabilitation continues. For children with chronic conditions, this phase may represent the norm: periods in which the child is medically stable but remains at risk for a new medical event (the recurrence of symptoms that might signal a relapse, a frightening asthma attack, a severe pain episode in a child with sickle cell disease). *Universal* interventions in this third phase include ongoing monitoring of child and family medical traumatic stress during the child's contacts with the health-care system. For example, in the course of a routine checkup, Anna's pediatrician might ask how Anna and her family are managing and detect that she and her parents continue to struggle with medical traumatic stress reactions, months after her discharge from the hospital. Anna's continued anxiety, nightmares, and problems concentrating in school suggest that she and her family could benefit from talking further with a mental health professional who is knowledgeable about medical trauma. *Targeted* and formal *mental health* interventions are appropriate in this phase to treat persistent medical traumatic stress reactions.

Some interventions have been designed for and evaluated in specific medical populations, such as the Surviving Cancer Competently Intervention Program (SCCIP), which integrates cognitive behavioral and family therapy approaches for families facing pediatric cancer (Kazak et al., 1999). Evidence-based interventions that work well for children with other types of trauma exposure can be adapted for children with medical traumatic stress. Trauma-focused cognitive behavioral therapy has shown positive results in studies that included young children, school-age children, and adolescents experiencing medical trauma (Scheeringa, Weems, Cohen, Amaya-Jackson, & Guthrie, 2011; Smith et al., 2007).

Conclusion and Lessons Learned about Medical Trauma

Potentially traumatic medical events affect tens of millions of children each year in the United States alone. Because of these sheer numbers, the public health impact of unrecognized or untreated medical traumatic stress can be substantial. The research literature has provided initial evidence to help us understand and begin to address medical traumatic stress in ill and injured children and their families.

Two systematic reviews of the research on medical traumatic stress in children (Kazak et al., 2006; Price et al., 2016), a decade apart, have pointed to core themes arising from this body of work. Three of these themes are particularly relevant here. First, medical trauma happens to children and families who bring to this experience a range of prior life experiences, prior psychological functioning, and coping capacities. For many children, medical trauma is the primary exposure they have had to a potentially traumatic event. But medical trauma also intersects with other forms of trauma exposure in the lives of children. Trauma-informed pediatric care incorporates the awareness that any patient (and his or her parents) may bring a history of prior trauma to the present medical encounter.

Second, there is a range of normative reactions to children's potentially traumatic medical experiences, and these reactions often evolve over time. Traumatic stress responses in the peri-trauma phase are common and do not always lead to persistent distress. Families often benefit from basic information about medical traumatic stress in the context of discussing the child's medical condition, treatment course, and prognosis. Keeping in mind the phases of medical events provides a useful context for assessment of medical traumatic stress in an ill or injured child and his or her family members.

Third, medical traumatic stress appears to have an impact on health outcomes. Traumatic stress symptoms can delay physical recovery and get in the way of optimal engagement in needed medical treatment. Addressing traumatic stress is thus an essential part of promoting optimal medical as well as psychological outcomes in ill or injured children.

The research on medical traumatic stress suggests the importance of attention to coping, resilience, and competence in children and families. Many families have faced the devastating news of a life-threatening diagnosis for a child, dealt with the daily impact of a chronic illness that carries a continual threat of relapse or hospitalization, or had a day start out normally only to end in the emergency room or intensive care unit when a child is injured or becomes suddenly ill. These children and their families know that they are responding as best they can to what feels like an overwhelming stressor. Applying a traumatic stress framework to understand the impact of these medical events is not only useful to guide professional support or intervention, but it can also be empowering for children and families.

References

Agency for Healthcare Research and Quality. (2007). *Care of children and adolescents in U.S. hospitals*. Rockville, MD: U.S. Department of Health and Human Services.

Alderfer, M. A., Long, K. A., Lown, E. A., Marsland, A. L., Ostrowski, N. L., Hock, J. M., & Ewing, L. J. (2010). Psychosocial adjustment of siblings of children with cancer: A systematic review. *Psychooncology, 19*(8), 789–805. doi:10.1002/pon.1638

Alisic, E., Jongmans, M. J., van Wesel, F., & Kleber, R. J. (2011). Building child trauma theory from longitudinal studies: A meta-analysis. *Clinical Psychology Review, 31*(5), 736–747. doi:10.1016/j.cpr.2011.03.001

American Cancer Society. (2014). *Cancer facts and figures 2014—special section: Cancer in children & adolescents*. Retrieved from https://www.cancer.org/research/cancer-facts-statistics/all-cancer-facts-figures/cancer-facts-figures-2014.html

Blount, R., Zempsky, W., Jaaniste, T., Evans, S., Cohen, L., Devine, K., & Zeltzer, L. (2009). Management of pediatric pain and distress due to medical procedures In M. Roberts & R. Steele (Eds.), *Handbook of pediatric psychology* (4th ed., pp. 171–188). New York, NY: Guilford Press.

Brown, H. (2008, April 8). My daughters are fine, but I'll never be the same. *New York Times*, p. F5. Retrieved from http://www.nytimes.com/2008/04/08/health/views/08case.html?_r=2&pagewanted=print

Center for Pediatric Traumatic Stress. (2009). *HealthCareToolbox: D-E-F protocol for trauma-informed pediatric care*. Retrieved from https://www.healthcare

toolbox.org/what-providers-can-do/d-e-f-protocol-for-trauma-informed-pediatric-care.html

Center for Pediatric Traumatic Stress. (2015). *Working with children and families experiencing medical traumatic stress: A resource guide for mental health professionals*. Retrieved from https://www.healthcaretoolbox.org/images/TherapistResourceGuide.pdf

Centers for Disease Control. (2014a). CDC/NCHS: *National Health Interview Survey: Table 79. Emergency department visits within the past 12 months among children under age 18, by selected characteristics: United States, selected years 1997–2013*. Retrieved from http://www.cdc.gov/nchs/hus/contents2014.htm#079

Centers for Disease Control. (2014b). *Web-based Injury Statistics Query and Reporting System (WISQARS) [online]*. National Center for Injury Prevention and Control (producer). Retrieved from www.cdc.gov/ncipc/wisqars

Centers for Disease Control and Prevention. (2017). *National Diabetes Statistics Report, 2017.* Atlanta, GA: Centers for Disease Control and Prevention, U.S. Department of Health and Human Services; 2017. Retrieved from https://www.cdc.gov/diabetes/data/statistics/statistics-report.html

Chapman, E. N., Kaatz, A., & Carnes, M. (2013). Physicians and implicit bias: How doctors may unwittingly perpetuate health care disparities. *Journal General Internal Medicine, 28*(11), 1504–1510. doi:10.1007/s11606-013-2441-1

Committee on Hospital Care. (2003). Family-centered care and the pediatrician's role. *Pediatrics, 112*, 691–697.

Cox, C., Kenardy, J., & Hendrikz, J. (2008). A meta-analysis of risk factors that predict psychopathology following accidental trauma. *Journal for Specialists in Pediatric Nursing, 13*(2), 98–110. doi:10.1111/j.1744–6155.2008.00141.x

De Young, A., Kenardy, J., Cobham, V., & Kimble, R. (2012). Prevalence, comorbidity and course of trauma reactions in young burn-injured children. *Journal of Child Psychology and Psychiatry, 53*(1), 56–63.

Fadiman, A. (1997). *The spirit catches you and you fall down: A Hmong child, her American doctors, and the collision of two cultures*. New York, NY: Farrar, Straus, and Giroux.

Gray, W. N., Szulczewski, L. J., Regan, S. M. P., Williams, J. A., & Pai, A. L. H. (2014). Cultural influences in pediatric cancer: From diagnosis to cure/end of life. *Journal of Pediatric Oncology Nursing, 31*(5), 252–271. doi:10.1177/1043454214529022

Hoffman, J., & Kaplan, S. (2002). The incidence of congenital heart disease. *Journal of the American College of Cardiology, 39*(12), 1890–1900.

Holbrook, T., Hoyt, D., Coimbra, R., Potenza, B., Sise, M., & Anderson, J. (2005). Long-term posttraumatic stress disorder persists after major trauma in adolescents: New data on risk factors and functional outcome. *Journal of Trauma-Injury Infection and Critical Care, 58*(4), 764–769. doi:10.1097/00005373–200408000–00096

Jimenez, N., Jackson, D. L., Zhou, C., Ayala, N. C., & Ebel, B. E. (2014). Postoperative pain management in children, parental English proficiency, and access to interpretation. *Hospital Pediatrics, 4*(1), 23–30. doi:10.1542/hpeds.2013–0031

Johnson, T. J., Weaver, M. D., Borrero, S., Davis, E. M., Myaskovsky, L., Zuckerbraun, N. S., & Kraemer, K. L. (2013). Association of race and ethnicity with management of abdominal pain in the emergency department. *Pediatrics, 132*(4), e851–e858. doi:10.1542/peds.2012–3127

The Joint Commission. (2010). *Advancing effective communication, cultural competence, and patient- and family-centered care: A roadmap for hospitals.* Oakbrook Terrace, IL: The Joint Commission.

Kahana, S., Feeny, N., Youngstrom, E., & Drotar, D. (2006). Posttraumatic stress in youth experiencing illnesses and injuries: An exploratory meta-analysis. *Traumatology, 12*(2), 148–161. doi:10.1177/1534765606294562

Kassam-Adams, N., Marsac, M., García-España, J., & Winston, F. (2015). Evaluating predictive screening for children's post-injury mental health: New data and a replication. *European Journal of Psychotraumatology, 6*, 29313.

Kassam-Adams, N., Marsac, M., Kohser, K., Kenardy, J., March, S., & Winston, F. (2016). Pilot randomized controlled trial of a novel web-based intervention to prevent posttraumatic stress in children following medical events. *Journal of Pediatric Psychology, 41,* 138–148. doi:10.1093/jpepsy/jsv057

Kazak, A., Barakat, L., Ditaranto, S., Biros, D., Hwang, W., Beele, D., . . . Hocking, M. (2011). Screening for psychosocial risk at pediatric cancer diagnosis: The Psychosocial Assessment Tool. *Journal of Pediatric Hematology/Oncology, 33*(4), 289–294.

Kazak, A., Kassam-Adams, N., Schneider, S., Zelikovsky, N., Alderfer, M., & Rourke, M. (2006). An integrative model of pediatric medical traumatic stress. *Journal of Pediatric Psychology, 44,* 343–355.

Kazak, A., Simms, S., Meeske, K., Barakat, L., Hobbie, W., Foley, B., . . . Best, M. (1999). Surviving cancer completely intervention program (SCCIP): A cognitive-behavioral and family therapy intervention for adolescent survivors of childhood cancer and their families. *Family Process, 38*, 175–191.

Kazak, A., Struber, M., Barakat, L., & Meeske, K. (1996). Assessing posttraumatic stress related to medical illness and treatment: The Impact of Traumatic Stressors Interview Schedule (ITSIS). *Family Systems and Health, 14*, 365–380.

King, M., Mee, L., Gutiérrez-Colina, A., Eaton, C., Lee, J., & Blount, R. (2013). Emotional functioning, barriers, and medication adherence in pediatric transplant recipients. *Journal of Pediatric Psychology*, *39*(3): 283–293. doi:10.1093/jpepsy/jst074

Kristjánsdóttir, Ó., Unruh, A. M., McAlpine, L., & McGrath, P. J. (2012). A systematic review of cross-cultural comparison studies of child, parent, and health professional outcomes associated with pediatric medical procedures. *The Journal of Pain, 13*(3), 207–219. doi:10.1016/j.jpain.2011.12.008

Landolt, M.A., Buehlmann, C., Maag, T., & Schiestl, C. (2009). Brief report: Quality of life is impaired in pediatric burn survivors with posttraumatic stress disorder. *Journal of Pediatric Psychology, 34*(1), 14–21. doi:10.1093/jpepsy/jsm088

Le Brocque, R., Hendrikz, J., & Kenardy, J. (2010). The course of posttraumatic stress in children: Examination of recovery trajectories following traumatic injury. *Journal of Pediatric Psychology, 35*, 637–645. doi:10.1093/jpepsy/jsp050

Marsac, M., Hildenbrand, A., Clawson, K., Jackson, L., Kohser, K., Barakat, L., . . . Alderfer, M. (2012). Acceptability and feasibility of family use of the Cellie Cancer Coping Kit. *Supportive Care in Cancer, 20*(12), 3315–3324. doi:10.1007/s00520–012–1475-y

Marsac, M., Kassam-Adams, N., Hildenbrand, A.K., Kohser, K., & Winston, F.K. (2011). After the injury: Initial evaluation of a web-based intervention for parents of injured children. *Health Education Research, 26*(1), 1–12. doi:10.1093/her/cyq045

Marsac, M. L., Kassam-Adams, N., Hildenbrand, A. Nicholls., E, Winston, F. K., Leff, S., & Fein, J. (2016). Implementing a trauma-informed approach in pediatric health care networks. *JAMA Pediatrics, 170*(1), 70–77.

Marsac, M., Klingbeil, O.G., Hildenbrand, A.K., Alderfer, M.A., Kassam-Adams, N., Smith-Whitley, K., & Barakat, L.P. (2014). The Cellie Coping Kit for sickle cell disease: Initial acceptability and feasibility. *Clinical Practice in Pediatric Psychology, 4*(2), 10.

McCarthy, A., Kleiber, C., Hanrahan, K., Zimmerman, M., Westhus, N., & Allen, S. (2010). Impact of parent-provided distraction on child responses to an IV insertion. *Children's Health Care, 39*(2), 125–141. doi:10.1080/02739611003679915

McCarthy, M., Hearps, S., Muscara, F., Anderson, V., Burke, K., Hearps, S., & Kazak, A. (2016). Family psychosocial risk screening in infants and older children in the acute pediatric hospital setting using the Psychosocial Assessment Tool. *Journal of Pediatric Psychology, 41*(7), 820–829. doi:10.1093/jpepsy/jsw055

Myant, K., & Williams, J. (2005). Children's concepts of health and illness: Understanding of contagious illnesses, non-contagious illnesses and injuries. *Journal of Health Psychology, 10*(6), 805–819. doi:10.1177/1359105305057315

National Center for Chronic Disease Prevention and Health Promotion. (2014). *National Diabetes Statistics Report: Centers for Disease Control and Prevention.*

National Child Traumatic Stress Network. (2004). *Pediatric Medical Traumatic Stress Toolkit.* Retrieved from http://www.nctsn.org/trauma-types/pediatric-medical-traumatic-stress-toolkit-for-health-care-providers

Niska, R., Bhuiya, F., & Xu, J. (2010). *National Hospital Ambulatory Medical Care Survey*. Hyattsville, MD: Centers for Disease Control and Prevention National Center for Health Statistics.

O'Malley, P., Brown, K., & SE, K. (2008). Patient-and family-centered care of children in the emergency department. *Pediatrics, 122*(2), e511–e521.

Power, T. (2004). Stress and coping in childhood: The parents' role. *Parenting: Science and Practice, 4*(4), 271–317.

Price, J., Kassam-Adams, N., Alderfer, M., Christofferson, J., & Kazak, A. (2016). Systematic review: A reevaluation and update of the integrative (trajectory) model of pediatric medical traumatic stress. *Journal of Pediatric Psychology, 41*, 86–97. doi:10.1093/jpepsy/jsv074

Pynoos, R. (1994). Traumatic stress and developmental psychopathology in children and adolescents. In R. Pynoos (Ed.), *Posttraumatic stress disorder: A clinical review* (pp. 65–98). Lutherville, MD: Sidran Press.

Sabin, J. A., & Greenwald, A. G. (2012). The influence of implicit bias on treatment recommendations for 4 common pediatric conditions: Pain, urinary tract infection, attention deficit hyperactivity disorder, and asthma. *American Journal of Public Health, 102*(5), 988–995. doi:10.2105/AJPH.2011.300621

Salmon, K., & Bryant, R. (2002). Posttraumatic stress disorder in children: The influence of developmental factors. *Clinical Psychology Review, 22*(2), 163–188.

Scheeringa, M. S., Weems, C. F., Cohen, J. A., Amaya-Jackson, L., & Guthrie, D. (2011). Trauma-focused cognitive-behavioral therapy for posttraumatic stress disorder in three-through six year-old children: A randomized clinical trial. *Journal of Child Psychology and Psychiatry, 52*(8), 853–860.

Smith, P., Yule, W., Perrin, S., Tranah, T., Dalgleish, T., & Clark, D. (2007). Cognitive-behavioral therapy for PTSD in children and adolescents: A preliminary randomized controlled trial. *Journal of the American Academy of Child & Adolescent Psychiatry, 46*(8), 1051–1061. doi:10.1097/CHI.0b013e318067e288

Stehl, M. L., Kazak, A. E., Alderfer, M. A., Rodriguez, A., Hwang, W.-T., Pai, A. L. H., . . . Reilly, A. (2009). Conducting a randomized clinical trial of an psychological intervention for parents/caregivers of children with cancer shortly after diagnosis. *Journal of Pediatric Psychology, 34*(8), 803–816. doi:10.1093/jpepsy/jsn130

Stuber, M., Schneider, S., Kassam-Adams, N., Kazak, A., & Saxe, G. (2006). The medical traumatic stress toolkit. *CNS Spectrums, 11*, 137–142.

Trickey, D., Siddaway, A. P., Meiser-Stedman, R., Serpell, L., & Field, A. P. (2012). A meta-analysis of risk factors for post-traumatic stress disorder in children and adolescents. *Clinical Psychology Review, 32*, 122–138. doi:10.1016/j.cpr.2011.12.001

Ward, E., DeSantis, C., Robbins, A., Kohler, B., & Jemal, A. (2014). Childhood and adolescent cancer statistics 2014. *CA: A Cancer Journal for Clinicians, 64*, 83–103.

Winston, F., Kassam-Adams, N., Vivarelli-O'Neill, C., Ford, J., Newman, E., Baxt, C., . . . Cnaan, A. (2002). Acute stress disorder symptoms in children and their parents after pediatric traffic injury. *Pediatrics, 109*(6), e90.

Zimmer-Gembeck, M.J., & Skinner, E.A. (2010). Review: The development of coping across childhood and adolescence: An integrative review and critique of research. *International Journal of Behavioral Development, 35*(1), 1–17. doi:10.1177/0165025410384923

CHAPTER 14

The Developmental Consequences of Exposure to Complex Trauma in Childhood and Adolescence

Jana Pressley and Joseph Spinazzola

When 10-year-old Brian arrives at school on any given day, his primary objective is to remain invisible. As he shuffles from his locker to the classroom, his eyes are downcast and his expression remote in the midst of the loud, bustling hallway. When recognized as the "kid brother of the O'Connor twins," school personnel are typically perplexed that the younger sibling of the athletic, gregarious golden boys of the local high school on the outskirts of Boston could be this slight, melancholy boy. To Brian's fifth-grade teacher, however, his withdrawn demeanor barely catches her attention most days in comparison to his rowdy peers constantly demanding her redirection. It is only when he submits a writing assignment described by his teacher as "including dark themes and violent characters" that the adults in his life begin to take notice.

Alisha, on the other hand, is attracting plenty of attention in her rural north Georgia high school, as she begins the second semester of her sophomore year with a two-day suspension. In response to a peer conflict that escalated during basketball practice, Alisha struck a teammate after what she perceived as a demeaning comment about the coach's decision to promote her to the varsity starting lineup for an upcoming game. Although generally well liked by peers throughout her elementary school years, Alisha has increasingly struggled with a short fuse as the social, academic, and financial pressures in her life have compounded in her adolescent years. Both Brian and Alisha, as will be illustrated further in this chapter, are displaying warning signs indicative of much deeper internal distress resulting from the cumulative impact of chronic, interpersonal traumatic stressors.

Defining Complex Trauma

Youth like Brian and Alisha can be confusing to the adults in their everyday lives, who are often unaware of the prolonged and insidious nature of the early life experiences that have shaped the development of their behavioral responses and interpersonal style. Several decades of clinical experience and research have led experts in the field of traumatic stress to conceptualize the legacy of chronic violence, exploitation, and deprivation as a problem of *complex trauma* (Ford, 2017; Hopper, Grossman, Spinazzola, & Zucker, in press). Complex trauma is a two-pronged concept, emphasizing the interconnection between exposure to traumatic experiences and their disruptive effects on normative youth development, as children adapt in often increasingly problematic ways to survive dangerous or impoverished worlds and treacherous or unpredictable relationships.

Complex trauma is rooted both in acts of commission, overt forms of victimization including the infliction of physical or sexual violence, and in acts of omission, the repeated disruption or intentional denial of early nurturance and protection essential to meeting the basic emotional or physical needs of the child. Complex trauma prototypically involves pervasive exposure to multiple, often interrelated, developmentally adverse experiences, such as physical, sexual, and emotional abuse; domestic, school, or community violence; medical, educational, emotional, or gross neglect; and severe impairment of or repeated separation from primary caregivers (Cook, Blaustein, Spinazzola, & van der Kolk, 2003; Cook et al., 2005, 2007; Ford, 2017; Spinazzola et al., 2013). These experiences interfere with the child's ability to form secure attachment bonds, undermine safety and stability, and compromise healthy physical and mental development (Complex Trauma Workgroup of the National Child Traumatic Stress Network, 2017).

Research has identified several features of traumatic experiences that tend to lead to more complex problems with adjustment over time: *the age at which a child is exposed to traumatic events, the cumulative nature of the traumatic experience; and interpersonal forms of trauma.*

- **Age of Onset:** Initial research on the developmental timing or onset of trauma revealed higher frequency of symptoms of complex maladaptation in individuals exposed to maltreatment in adolescence versus adulthood and in childhood versus adolescence (Pelcovitz et al., 1997; van der Kolk, Roth, Pelcovitz, Sunday, & Spinazzola, 2005).
- **The Cumulative or Chronic Nature of the Traumatic Experience:** At least three large bodies of research spanning different subfields within public and mental health have amply demonstrated a "dose-response" association between the *amount* of trauma an individual is exposed to and severity of impairment. Research on *cumulative trauma* has linked complexity and severity of impairment to the number of different types of trauma one has experienced (Agorastos et al., 2014; Cloitre et al., 2009). Other studies have found similar outcomes associated with *frequency, duration*, or *chronicity* of exposure to singular forms of traumatic experiences (Manly, Cicchetti, & Barnett, 1994; van der Kolk et al., 2005). Taken separately or collectively, this research tells us that more trauma equals more trouble.
- **Interpersonal Forms of Trauma:** Interpersonal trauma may be defined as traumatic experiences perpetrated in the context of the child's immediate family or primary caregiving system. This type of trauma has been found to lead to more complex adaptation than *impersonal* forms of trauma such as serious accidents, injuries, or natural disasters (Pelcovitz et al., 1997; van der Kolk et al., 2005). This may be because impersonal traumas often occur randomly or by chance, tend to be publicly acknowledged or communally shared experiences, and lack malevolent intent. In contrast, interpersonal trauma often comes hand in hand with imposed secrecy or forced isolation and is typically accompanied by internalized shame, sense of being personally targeted, or perceived and often actual social injustice.

Within the category of interpersonal trauma, adverse experiences perpetrated in the context of the child's immediate family or primary caregiving system have consistently been found to have the broadest, most severe, and longest standing outcomes of virtually all forms of trauma (Cook et al., 2003, 2005, 2007). The lion's share of clinical and research attention over the past four decades has been devoted to the three most overt and tangible forms of caregiver-inflicted trauma: physical abuse, sexual abuse/incest, and domestic violence. However, increasing attention is being directed to the developmental impact of other more pervasive but insidious and often overlooked forms of caregiver-inflicted trauma, most notably psychological maltreatment, a form that has emerged as what may be the "sleeping giant" of childhood trauma (Spinazzola et al., 2013). The American Academy of Pediatrics recently released a special report identifying psychological maltreatment as the most challenging and prevalent form of child abuse and neglect (Hibbard, Barlow, MacMillan, & the Committee on Child Abuse and Neglect and American Academy of Child and Adolescent Psychiatry, 2012).

Accordingly, in this chapter we have intentionally selected vignettes based upon clinical case composites reflective of intervention with the many actual child, adolescent, and adult complex trauma clients from our trauma center who present for treatment with lives profoundly shaped by the most subtle forms of attachment trauma: emotional abuse and neglect. The case illustrations of Brian and Alisha are representative of the youth we serve at different developmental stages, genders, and racial and cultural backgrounds. Each vignette will examine the intersection between childhood experiences and the developing trajectory of behaviors, thereby illustrating and highlighting some of the manifold and complex dynamics of trauma exposure and adaptation.

In this book and elsewhere, readers can amply find other complex trauma case illustrations that are predicated around focal histories of childhood physical and sexual abuse.

Developmental Impact and Case Illustrations: The Complexity of Adaptation

The impact of complex trauma has been identified to span multiple overlapping domains of functioning: (1) attachment and relationships, (2) physical health and development: brain and body, (3) emotional responses, (4) behavioral responses, (5), cognition: thinking and learning, (6) dissociation, and (7) self-concept (Cook et al., 2003, 2005, 2007). It is important to understand trauma exposure within the context of a child's caregiving environment. A safe and nurturing relationship with a caregiver in early life imprints upon a child the belief that others can be trusted and relied upon and that the world is generally a safe place (Bowlby, 1969). However, when children experience relationships as rejecting, unsafe, or tumultuous, this experience often translates into long-term negative beliefs about self and others. Children exposed to relational trauma often have difficulties developing and sustaining healthy relationships, communicating needs, setting personal boundaries, and negotiating conflict or intimacy in relationships. Further, trauma-impacted youth often struggle with ongoing difficulty distinguishing safe from threatening interpersonal situations. They then adopt a default self-protective stance that assumes danger, and they act accordingly to avoid further suffering. For many, the inability to accurately discern safety from danger increases vulnerability for bullying or involvement with abusive partners later in life. Ironically, it is often the very same self-protective strategies that were functional at an earlier stage of development, which can later backfire and unwittingly prevent individuals from connecting to or maintaining the supportive relationships that would support healing.

A thorough understanding of complex trauma is also grounded in recognition of the biological impact of trauma on human development. Researchers have identified various interconnected systems of the brain and body that are highly vulnerable to the impact of chronic trauma exposure, particularly in the context of early childhood neglect (Fisher et al., 2016; Teicher & Samson, 2016). There is compelling data on the relationship between child maltreatment and potential risk of alterations in brain structure, brain function, and the stress response system, heightening risk for cognitive and emotional difficulties. When the body's stress response system has remained on high alert for extended periods of time, the intense physical and emotional arousal necessary for survival begins to erode the otherwise normative developmental tasks of childhood and adolescence. For some children, the body can feel constantly charged and on high alert, leading to hypervigilance and reactivity to even the most subtle cues of threat or rejection. One eight-year-old boy illustrated this experience vividly in a process he called "Hulking"—his daily experience of his body "always being stuck right in the middle of Bruce Banner turning into the Hulk." For other youth, survival strategies involving withdrawal from others, numbing of emotions, and disconnection from consciousness, or dissociation, have preserved life and safety most effectively.

When individuals are exposed to danger, whether real or perceived, we react with classic survival-based physiological responses, including fight, flight, freeze, and submit. These responses are necessary and adaptive in the moment, and often utilized in alternating patterns for any given individual, depending on the particular context of the threat. For those exposed to chronic trauma, however, these survival-based responses have often become so engrained in daily life that they become the predominant coping style later in life in response to any difficult situation. Children who are developing in the midst of a caregiving system that is overtly abusive, rejecting, or impaired and unable to protect are especially vulnerable to the early adoption and long-term reliance on survival-based stress responses. Such children experience fear, helplessness, anger, or despair, along with the accompanying bodily sensations, in the absence of a nurturing adult to help soothe and integrate these experiences and return to a calm state. *Emotional regulation* is the ability to identify, tolerate, manage, and appropriately express one's internal state of feelings, and this is an area of profound difficulty for the majority of trauma-impacted youth (Cook et al, 2005). For a child growing up in a relatively healthy and nontraumatic environment, there are opportunities throughout development to learn to manage emotions and behaviors in ways that fit the situational demands. For trauma-impacted children and adolescents, the highest developmental priorities have often centered around how to minimize danger, seek safety, and get emotional, physical, and relational needs met (Blaustein & Kinniburgh, 2007). As a result, children adapt to their environments by developing behaviors and interpersonal patterns that optimize survival and need fulfillment, but often to the long-term detriment of functional capacities.

When faced with current overwhelming stress or memories of past trauma, some children have significant difficulty staying focused on the present and might shift into a state of feeling disconnected from themselves and their immediate surroundings, a coping response known as *dissociation*. Occurring on a continuum of severity, youth with dissociative symptoms might seem to zone out and withdraw from their surroundings in order to manage or avoid overwhelming emotions or situations that seem threatening. For some trauma-impacted youth, past experience and current reminders can trigger reactive *behaviors*, such as oppositional or aggressive responses toward others, self-harm, substance use, or other compulsive behaviors. Early onset trauma can also put youth at risk, neurobiologically and functionally, for *cognitive* impairments, with potential negative impacts on memory processing, learning, and the executive functioning skills. Difficulties with executive functioning, involving skills such as concentration, sustained attention, delayed gratification, judgment, planning, problem solving, and engagement in goal-directed behavior, can lead to a cascade of behavioral, interpersonal, academic, and later vocational life struggles in the absence of intervention. Trauma exposure in the relational system, in combination with the aforementioned difficulties, often leaves youth with a profoundly altered *self-concept*. Trauma leaves behind a legacy of shame, self-doubt, negative body image, lack of a sense of agency, and identity disturbance. The trauma-impacted youth's view of self often overlaps naturally with the previously discussed relational difficulties, reinforcing perceptions of self as damaged, unlovable, or unmanageable.

Children subjected to ongoing maltreatment or impaired caregiving throughout their formative years are highly vulnerable to developing a variety of emotional, behavioral, and cognitive symptoms. Over time, this often results in a clinical profile characterized by numerous and at times contradictory psychological disorders (e.g. depression, anxiety, attention and behavioral disorders, eating disorders, or substance abuse) in an effort to capture the range of difficulties experienced by these youths. Use of systematic approaches and validated instruments to assess and measure the presence, severity, and developmental variation of symptom expression across these dimensions or domains of impairment is essential (for recommendations, see Briere & Spinazzola, 2005, 2009).

These difficulties may or may not coexist with the symptoms or diagnosis of posttraumatic stress disorder (PTSD; D'Andrea, Ford, Stolbach, Spinazzola, J., & van der Kolk, 2012). We have long known that PTSD is less common than other anxiety and behavior disorders in maltreated children (Ackerman, Newton, McPherson, Jones, & Dykman, 1998). In a national clinical database of nearly 15,000 children and adolescents with histories of exposure to trauma (National Child Traumatic Stress Network [NCTSN] Core Data Set), less than one-third meet criteria for a diagnosis of PTSD (Huang, Speicher, Habib, Silver, & Earle, 2017). In contrast, a national survey of clinicians from this network reported that for the traumatized children and adolescents in their caseloads ($N = 1{,}699$), the most prevalent difficulties (each observed in over 50% of clients) were affect dysregulation, problems with attention and concentration, lack of impulse control, aggression and risk-taking, and negative self-image (Spinazzola et al., 2005).

Considering these wide-ranging and complex symptom presentations, leaders in the field of trauma research have proposed a new diagnosis, developmental trauma disorder ([DTD] Ford, 2017; van der Kolk, 2005), to more accurately capture the experience and functional impairments resulting from chronic interpersonal traumatic stress.[1] Informed by the complex trauma categories described so far, youth fitting the DTD proposed diagnosis show dysregulation in the domains of emotions, bodily sensations, attention, cognition, behavior, identity, and relationships. Ongoing research conducted through a national multisite epidemiological and diagnostic field trial strongly supports the contention that DTD is a distinct and parsimonious clinical construct that captures an array of disturbances in affect and physiology, attention and behavior, and attachment and self-attribution beyond symptoms covered by PTSD. Moreover, these trials revealed DTD to be present most frequently in youth with chronic histories of severe attachment trauma (i.e., psychological maltreatment, neglect, impaired caregiving) in combination with one or more forms of "contact" maltreatment (e.g., physical or sexual abuse and assault, school or community violence; Ford, Spinazzola, van der Kolk, & Grasso, 2018, in press; Spinazzola, van der Kolk, & Ford, under review).

Case Example: Brian

Growing up in a family of four boys, flying under the radar is a skill Brian is learning to hone. At the age of 10, Brian is the next-to-youngest son to second-generation Irish American parents, living in an upper middle-class neighborhood on the outskirts of Boston. Their house is relatively modest given the surrounding community; however, Brian's father is proud of the business he has built as a contractor. Brian's twin older brothers are high school freshmen and star athletes, and although they sometimes evoke their father's critical postgame analysis, that pales in comparison to the harsh degradation that Brian has come to expect on a daily basis.

It began during his preschool years, when Brian displayed minimal talent and interest as the third son to participate in the local T-ball team. Brian was what the males in his family referred to as a "mama's boy." Throughout his early childhood, he preferred spending time flipping through books and coloring alongside his mother during the quiet hours of the afternoon before his older brothers and father would return home for the evening. This was in stark contrast to the rough and tumble early behavior of the twins, who from their earliest months of mobility embodied their father's temperament and interests in sports, cars, and the outdoors. Labeled early on as a "nerd" and a "geek" by his brothers, Brian became aware at an early age that his voracious appetite for reading and his interests in science fiction, comic books, and video games made him an outcast among the males in his family.

Brian's life was further complicated by his parents' growing conflict, which he remembers observing for the first time around the age of four. After his father started a new contracting business and the family moved to their new house, he recalls early memories of waking up at night to yelling, with his parents arguing about money and his father "being a bully with mean words" toward his mother. When his youngest brother was born that same year, Brian's mother became increasingly busy and preoccupied with the added care of an infant. Although he knew his mother cared about him, he felt very alone in the midst of the mocking rejection of his older brothers and the complicit reinforcement of this behavior by his father.

By the time he began elementary school, Brian's brothers became relentless at home in their harassment. When his mother was not around, they would pretend to bump into him or shove him into a wall "by accident" and then chide him for being a "sissy" who was not tough enough to protect himself. He spent most of his time retreating into books and games in his room or the basement, partly out of interest and partly with the intention to hide from the constant mockery. His father was often in the background during these daily interactions. He would either seem amused and passively support the behavior or join in with his own demeaning comments. When asked about his most painful memory, Brian describes the recurrent torment of riding the bus to elementary school along with his middle school brothers. One of his brothers would routinely trip him while getting onto the bus, loudly calling attention to an often-made-up problem with his appearance (e.g., food in his teeth, a stain on his shirt, a booger in his nose), or come up behind him, grab his book, and begin a game of keep-away. In each instance, they engaged their peers on the bus in a chant, taunting Brian to cry until eventually he would break into tears.

Brian approached school as a task to survive, despite his advanced intellect and the ease with which he completed his work. In second grade, he received rave reviews for his creative writing abilities. These skills blossomed over time as he developed in both academic skill and in the capacity to retreat into the fantasy world in his mind. Brian presented as quiet and reserved, with teachers often sharing the observation in parent–teacher conferences that he seemed "nervous" and "shy." Brian came to dread these meetings, which often provoked anger from his father, who was embarrassed by this feedback, stating to his mother with disgust "no boy of mine is going to be nervous! Maybe if he kept playing ball instead of wimping out, he would have gotten some confidence like his brothers!" Mr. O'Connor bitterly wondered aloud that it didn't make sense that an O'Connor would have such "nerdy interests like his futuristic comic books and games" and "not even try" when it comes to sports. To add insult to injury, Brian exhibited a slight hand tremor beginning in early childhood, which became increasingly pronounced in his elementary school years, impacting his handwriting. The tremor, which further embarrassed his father and heightened Brian's self-consciousness, added fuel to the shaming material of his older brothers. Overall, Mr. O'Connor seemed to experience Brian's differing interests and personality as a personal failure, lamenting that he and his extended family had "worked too hard to build a family and business in this country to have him moping around like some kind of weirdo."

Socially, Brian struggled with the ability to make friends, as he retreated further into himself each year. Brian dreamed about running away, but at the age of 10, his anxiety about getting caught and sent home to be berated by his father and brothers prevented him from following through with his escape fantasies. By fifth grade, he was described as a "loner," and if asked, he would have stated that he "just wanted to disappear." He would occasionally sit at the lunch table with peers from his science class lab group. However, he usually tried to get in and out of the cafeteria as quickly as possible, because of his experiences of being humiliated by his peers. Brian often appeared melancholy to anyone who paid attention; however, he worked to hold his emotional experience at bay. He recalls an experience in third grade when he was discovered in tears in the bathroom. This story was relayed to his brothers, inciting yet another bus chant about him being a "cry baby." After that day, Brian worked hard to not feel at all and learned, almost by accident, that picking the skin on his upper arms brought quick relief when he began to feel anxious and helped him "numb the bad feelings, almost like when they numb my teeth at the dentist." When triggered by interpersonal situations that suggested possible mockery or rejection, Brian experienced flashes of what some might describe as panic—heart racing, stomach in knots, and quickened breathing. He discovered that piercing his skin provided quick and powerful soothing from fear and bodily discomfort. Over the coming months, this behavior evolved into more severe forms of self-harm, including cutting and burning himself to increasingly achieve the desired level of affective anesthesia.

Brian felt the most relief, however, when he could withdraw into the safety and enjoyment of his favorite fantasy computer games. In his online world, Brian's unique talents were rewarded, while he simultaneously remained hidden from the scrutiny endured in his daily life. As he became more involved in the gaming world, Brian was befriended by someone who, along with the typical gaming banter, began to inquire into his life with what seemed like genuine interest and support. When this person, who gradually revealed himself as an adult male, began to ask Brian increasingly personal questions and express a sense of familiarity and fondness, Brian noted that he felt accepted and valued for the first time since he could remember.

Brian's narrative is a powerful narrative of chronic psychological maltreatment from caregivers, and the developmental adaptations and cumulative vulnerabilities often represented by youth who tend toward a more withdrawn, emotionally constricted coping style. In particular, Brian's online friendship could put him at risk of being exploited by an adult who was targeting his vulnerability, a pattern of revictimization all too common for children living in a context of emotional deprivation. For other trauma-impacted youth, externalizing behaviors and symptoms might emerge, creating a different set of challenges and subsequent reactions by adults or peers, as will be illustrated with Alisha's story.

Case Example: Alisha

Alisha Williams is a 15-year-old African American female, living in a rural community in Georgia with her mother, Sandra, and two younger sisters. When

Alisha arrives home from school on any given day, she has come to expect the sullen disengagement and unspoken antipathy of her mother. Their relationship has always been estranged. As a young child, Alisha would frequently cry herself to sleep at night wondering what she did to make her mother not love her and longing to be tucked in with a story and a kiss like she would see other parents do for their children on television. On one occasion after noticing her mother light up in response to a princess character in a movie musical, Alisha attempted to garner her mother's affections by dressing up and singing to her. She was devastated when her mother walked out of the room without once looking at her or acknowledging her efforts. Over time, desperate for any physical contact with her mother, Alisha would vigilantly track her mother's movements through the house and attempt to brush against her by passing through the narrow central hallway in the opposite direction. Reflecting on these experiences years later in therapy, Alisha would recount with great sadness the complex feelings of relief when her shoulder successfully contacted her mother's hip only to be followed by a deep sense of shame as she observed her mother visibly flinch and recoil at the contact.

Sandra Williams met Alisha's father when she was working in a coffee shop during her first year at a local community college. She recalls bitterly "how ridiculous it was to fall for his charm," as she laments the impact of their whirlwind romance on her long-term plans. Sandra planned to complete her first two years of college while saving money to finish her four-year business degree at a nearby state university. When she learned she was pregnant with Alisha, Sandra was devastated, although she initially hoped she could continue pursuing her academic goals. However, her boyfriend was not ready to settle down and eventually left shortly before Alisha's birth. With a limited social support network, Sandra dropped out of college at the end of her first year.

From the moment Alisha was born, Sandra struggled to connect to or feel warmth toward her daughter. Alisha was a constant reminder of the dreams she would never realize and confirmation of her own father's constant disparagement, including his derisive prediction that she would "end up pregnant and never leave this town." She was raised to take responsibility for her actions, so she committed to provide for her daughter's basic needs; however, her underlying resentment grew deeper and more pronounced throughout the first year of Alisha's life as she endured the tedious, sleep-deprived nights of single parenthood. At the end of most days, her daughter's seemingly endless need for emotional and physical input felt overwhelming to Sandra.

At the age of five, Alisha's mother met a new boyfriend, and her baby sister, Kim, was born in the coming year. Kim looked remarkably like her mother, while Alisha was described by her extended family as looking like her father, whom they described as a "deadbeat." Alisha grew up with the knowledge that her father ruined her mother's life but was also reminded that she shared both his good looks and his outgoing personality.

Alisha began kindergarten, as many children, with a mixture of risk and protective factors. Although subdued by an underlying sadness, she was a likeable little girl who longed for connection and was skilled at endearing herself to adults. It was midway through her kindergarten year when her little sister was born, and Alisha began to bear the additional weight of self-reliance and rejection. The mother whom she had always experienced as aloof and emotionally rebuffing was suddenly animated and loving toward her new baby sister. She observed her mother's beautiful smile and historically elusive laughter and wondered why she could never make her mother so happy.

Paradoxically, Alisha's greatest sense of satisfaction and competence began to grow in relation to caring for her baby sister, a pattern that continued throughout her adolescence when she ultimately became her mother's helper with the care of two younger sisters. The younger sisters were affectionate, playful, and seemingly looked up to Alisha, which felt good in the absence of such responses from her mother. Over the years, Alisha secretly harbored the hope that her mother would notice her helpfulness and skill in caring for her sisters, but such approval never emerged.

By the beginning of second grade, her growing sense of isolation and resentment at home began to manifest itself as irritability and disinterest at school. Alisha snapped at her peers, talked back to her teachers, and engaged minimally in learning activities. Over the coming years, her irritability escalated into periodic aggressive outbursts and subsequent behavioral interventions in school and after-school care settings, including detentions, parent–teacher conferences, her first suspension in eighth grade for a physical altercation in the cafeteria, and eventually truancy.

Alisha was in and out of trouble during her middle- and early high school years, although her natural athletic skill elicited some minimal support from coaches as she joined the freshman basketball team. Simultaneously, Alisha struggled in her academic performance, with a C grade average and weekly, unopened notes sent home about incomplete homework assignments. These struggles led to educational testing, which revealed Alisha's above-average intelligence along with a mild reading disorder. On the outside, the once-outgoing, curious little girl had evolved into an angry adolescent, whom teachers described as a "tough kid who is wasting her potential." Alisha often overheard adults lamenting her neglect to live up to her abilities, which only reinforced her belief that she was deficient and "didn't work hard enough, just like they say about my dad."

By high school, Alisha had fallen into a peer group perceived negatively by the adults in her life, and she began to experience the temporary relief found in alcohol and opioids. She maintained a low profile at home as she attempted to accept the reality of disconnection with her mother, which allowed for increasing freedom to sneak out of the house at night after her sisters were asleep to hang out with friends and get high. At the age of 14, Alisha began engaging in sexual relationships with older boys. She realized that romantic relationships provide a sense of connection and physical touch that is gratifying, even when short lived.

Key Clinical Issues in the Family and Cultural Context

The cumulative childhood experiences of Brian and Alisha, and the resulting trajectories of their adaptive behaviors, are powerful examples of psychological maltreatment and its impact throughout childhood and adolescence. For both, their behaviors created day-to-day struggles in educational and social environments, often leading to negative consequences such as school suspension or failure or alienation by peer groups. Such experiences can place trauma-impacted youth at risk for retraumatization and the reinforcement of survival-based behaviors. Brian's childhood was defined by chronic verbal abuse, parental rejection, isolation, and bullying, without access to a protector or advocate. He grew up in this context through the years when normative development would have fostered the cultivation of emotional and social skills. Brian's symptoms reveal struggles with self-regulation and reliance on coping strategies that support the avoidance of unsafe feelings and interpersonal engagement. He has learned to shrink into the background of his social world in order to minimize the chances of further humiliation. The mere day-to-day reminders of potential bullying often led to anxious feelings that were soothed through self-harming behaviors and escape into an inner world of fantasy.

Alisha's childhood experiences and the developing trajectory of behaviors also illustrate the dynamics of pervasive psychological maltreatment, adaptation, and ongoing vulnerabilities. Her experiences of emotional neglect have led to a developing interpersonal pattern at the age of 15 in which Alisha becomes quickly and intensely reactive to perceived rejection. Her irritability often leads to lashing out verbally toward authority figures, such as teachers and coaches, resulting in punitive responses that confirm her original belief that she is both a nuisance and too much to handle for those in her life. Although relatively socially skilled on the surface, Alisha maintains a guarded stance with her peers and does not let anyone close enough to truly get to know her, lest they discover her flaws at the level that she—and her mother—can see. At the same time, her growing sexual experimentation is putting her at increased risk for sexual exploitation, as she seeks to meet the emotional and physical needs that have never been met by her caregivers.

Opportunities and Goals for Intervention

Brian's pain and developing coping mechanisms went mostly unnoticed in his day-to-day world until he began turning in writing assignments reflecting dark and violent themes that his teachers found incongruent with his passive exterior. The writing assignments resulted in a referral to the school social worker, leading to an exploratory conversation with Brian, a phone call to his parents, and a follow-up family meeting.

The social worker's initial goal would be the development of trust and safety in the therapeutic relationship with Brian, who assumed that vulnerability was perceived as weakness, typically leading to shame and humiliation. Developing the capacity to tolerate and manage his painful experience in the presence of a safe and attuned adult would encompass a significant portion of treatment, as Brian's past adaptation was geared toward suppressing his emotions and numbing his physiological dysregulation. Given Brian's age and the ongoing relational context of his distress, change would be optimally addressed by incorporating Brian's parents into treatment. Perhaps the most important and simultaneously challenging part of the work would be identifying an inroad that could help Brian's father recognize the impact of his behavior. Through his own harsh criticism and contemptuous comments, Mr. O'Connor has perpetuated an emotionally abusive dynamic and implicitly condoned the bullying behavior by Brian's older brothers. Brian would benefit from his parents' ability to adopt a trauma-informed frame, recognizing the depth to which overt rejection and verbal abuse created an unsafe and damaging home environment, setting into motion a cascade of further vulnerabilities in his everyday world. This would ideally involve engaging with Mr. O'Connor in a manner that connects with the complexities of his own childhood in the midst of immigrating to the United States, his understanding of parenting, and what it means to raise a son.

Alisha's story reveals an adolescent who is coping the best that she can—but with significant gaps in her ability to identify, manage, and express her experience in a safe and regulated manner. Her suspension was both a crisis and an opportunity for intervention. With her two-day suspension threatening her ability to play basketball, which she loves, Alisha was desperate to do whatever she could to earn back the respect and credibility in her coach's eyes. When offered the opportunity to speak with the school counselor about the source of her recent outbursts, Alisha tentatively accepted the offer.

As was discussed with Brian, it would be critical for Alisha to experience a different kind of relationship with an emotionally attuned adult in order to feel safe enough to reveal the internal vulnerabilities she has worked so hard to protect from rejection. She will need support to build the capacity to tolerate and manage her painful experiences while also developing a more competent and empowered sense of self. Alisha's view of herself and others is deeply embedded in her persistent experience of unspoken contempt and profound shunning by her mother. Finding an avenue to engage Ms. Williams and help her explore the importance of her parental love and acceptance will be paramount to helping Alisha. The potential for an empathic connection with Ms. Williams would ultimately be rooted in acknowledging the reality of her own losses and lack of external support that likely left Ms. Williams vulnerable as a young parent to impaired and neglectful caregiving.

Principles of Intervention

For over two decades, various evidence-based treatment models have emerged, guided by a developmental understanding of complex trauma and summarized in the work of the NCTSN Complex Trauma Task Force (Cook et al., 2003, 2005, 2007). Specifically, intervention for complex trauma includes six core components: (1) safety, (2) self-regulation, (3) self-reflective information processing, (4) relational engagement, (5) traumatic experiences integration, and (6) positive affect enhancement. There is consensus among trauma-informed clinicians and researchers that effective treatment for survivors of complex trauma must be rooted in the cultivation of *safe* and reparative attachment relationships. Additionally, effective treatment involves building capacity for *self-regulation*. This involves supporting traumatized youth in the ability to identify and tolerate internal experience while building a repertoire of skills for managing and expressing emotions effectively. *Self-reflective information processing* involves the capacity for youth to learn to distinguish between past experiences and the ways in which those memories are triggering present-day reactions. Additionally, youth are supported in the enhancement of executive functioning skills such as present-focused planning, decision making, and problem-solving skills. *Traumatic experiences integration* is the treatment domain that incorporates the narrative processing of past experiences, along with the ability to incorporate past experiences into a sense of identity in the present. Treatment also acknowledges the ongoing need to build healthy *relational engagement*, by supporting both the interpersonal skills and self-perception of the client and the attunement and response of the caregiving system. Finally, comprehensive trauma-informed treatment seeks to go beyond symptom reduction by supporting and building on youth strengths, talents, and joy-enhancing activities (*positive affect enhancement*). (For additional reading on treatment of complex trauma in children and adolescents, see Blaustein & Kinniburgh, 2010; Ford & Courtois, 2013).

Complex Trauma: Key Lessons

Alisha and Brian's stories demonstrate several ways in which complex trauma survivors learn to cope with pain. However, these trauma-driven "survival" skills are often significantly misunderstood by those surrounding the survivor. Even more poignantly, these stories illustrate the important lessons that clinicians working with complexly traumatized youth and families have learned about trauma exposure, development, and adaptation. First, these stories illustrate the profound impact of psychological maltreatment, a term that encompasses both emotional abuse and neglect (Spinazzola et al., 2014). For many youth, the support and nurturance that did not occur during childhood may be as damaging as the more overt forms of abuse (Hopper et al., in press), and there is a growing body of evidence supporting the significant long-term impact of psychological maltreatment on development (Spinazzola et al., 2014; Trickett, Kim, & Prindle, 2011). Second, each story illuminates the subtle ways in which developmental adaptation to rejection, abuse, and isolation sets the child on a trajectory of behaviors and interpersonal interactions referred to by some as the "risk factor caravan" (Layne, Briggs, & Courtois, 2014). Ultimately, when we have access to the day-to-day interactions in the lives of youth affected by chronic interpersonal trauma, we recognize that the "small" interactions matter and are, in fact, not small at all. What might seem like typical insults between brothers, often answered by the societal reply, "boys will be boys," is actually a window into chronic bullying and parental rejection. What might appear to be teenage angst and oppositional behavior may reflect the erosion of a young woman's sense of self-worth and competence after a lifetime of feeling unloved at home. As these and countless other clients demonstrate through their stories and strategies for survival, complex trauma is deeply rooted in attachment disruption and the threats to our human need for connection represented in emotional abuse and neglect. These narratives illustrate the need for intervention grounded in a thorough understanding of how to effectively build capacity for youth to live and thrive in the present in the aftermath of chronic, interpersonal trauma exposure.

Note

1. A diagnostic construct capturing symptoms of complex maladaptation to childhood complex trauma in adults—*complex posttraumatic stress disorder* (*CPTSD*; Cloitre, Garvert, Brewin, Bryant, & Maercker, 2013)—is slated for inclusion in the next revision of the World Health Organization's *International Statistical Classification of Diseases and Related Health Problems* (*ICD-11*). While related in important ways to DTD, the CPTSD diagnostic construct covers a more narrow range of impact of complex trauma than DTD and is not developmentally anchored; that is, unlike DTD, CPTSD was not designed to capture the specific ways disturbances in affect and physiology, attention and behavior, and attachment and self-attribution are expressed in impacted children and adolescents.

References

Ackerman, P., Newton, J., McPherson, B., Jones, J., & Dykman, R. (1998). Prevalence of post traumatic stress disorder and other psychiatric diagnoses in three groups of abused children (sexual, physical, and both). *Child Abuse & Neglect, 22*(8), 759–774.

Agorastos, A., Pittman, J. O., Angkaw, A. C., Nievergelt, C. M., Hansen, C. J., Aversa, L. H., . . . Marine Resiliency Study Team. (2014). The cumulative effect of different childhood trauma types on self-reported symptoms of adult male depression and PTSD, substance abuse and health-related quality of life in a large active-duty military cohort. *Journal of Psychiatric Research, 58*, 46–54.

Blaustein, M. E., & Kinniburgh, K. M. (2007). Intervening beyond the child: The intertwining nature of attachment and trauma. *British Psychological Society* (Briefing Paper 26), 48–53.

Blaustein, M. E., & Kinniburgh, K. M. (2010). *Treating traumatic stress in children and adolescents: How to foster resilience through attachment, self-regulation, and competence*, New York, NY: Guilford Press.

Bowlby, J. (1969/1982). *Attachment and loss: Vol. 1. Attachment*. New York, NY: Basic Books.

Briere, J., & Spinazzola, J. (2005). Phenomenology and psychological assessment of complex posttraumatic states. *Journal of Traumatic Stress, 18*(5), 401–412.

Briere, J., & Spinazzola, J. (2009). Assessment of the sequela of complex trauma. In C. Courtois & J. Ford (Eds.), *Treating complex traumatic stress disorders: An evidence-based guide* (pp. 104–123). New York, NY: Guilford Press.

Cloitre, M., Garvert, D. W., Brewin, C. R., Bryant, R. A., Maercker, A. (2013). Evidence for proposed ICD-11 PTSD and complex PTSD: A latent profile analysis. *European Journal of Psychotraumatology, May 15*, 4, 20706.

Cloitre, M., Stolbach, B., Herman, J., van der Kolk, B., Pynoos, R. L., Wang, J., & Petkova, E. (2009). A developmental approach to complex PTSD: Childhood and adult cumulative trauma as predictors of symptom complexity. *Journal of Traumatic Stress, 22*(5), 399–408.

Complex Trauma Workgroup of the National Child Traumatic Stress Network. (2017). *Complex trauma definition*. Retrieved from http://www.nctsn.org/trauma-types/complex-trauma

Cook, A., Blaustein, M., Spinazzola, J., & van der Kolk, B. (Eds.). (2003). *Complex trauma in children and adolescents: White paper from the National Child Traumatic Stress Network Complex Trauma Task Force*. Retrieved from http://www.nctsnet.org/nctsn_assets/pdfs/edu_materials/ComplexTrauma_All.pdf

Cook, A., Spinazzola, J., Ford, J., Lanktree, C., Blaustein, M., Sprague, C., . . . van der Kolk, B. (2005). Complex trauma in children and adolescents. *Psychiatric Annals, 35*, 390–398.

Cook, A., Spinazzola, J., Ford, J., Lanktree, C., Blaustein, M., Sprague, C. . . . van der Kolk, B. (2007). Complex trauma in children and adolescents. *Focal Point, 21*(1), 4–8.

D'Andrea, W., Ford, J., Stolbach, B., Spinazzola, J., & van der Kolk, B. A. (2012). Understanding interpersonal trauma in children: Why we need a developmentally appropriate trauma diagnosis. *American Journal of Orthopsychiatry, 82*(2), 187–200.

Fisher, P. A., Beauchamp, K. G., Roos, L. E., Noll, L. K., Flannery, J., & Delker, B. C. (2016). The neurobiology of intervention and prevention in early adversity. *Annual Review of Clinical Psychology, 12*, 331–357. doi:10.1146/annurev-clinpsy-032814–112855

Ford, J. (2017). Complex trauma and complex traumatic stress disorder. In S. N. Gold (Ed.), *APA handbook of trauma psychology, volume 1: Foundations in knowledge*. Washington, DC: American Psychological Association.

Ford, J., & Courtois, C. (Eds.). (2013). *Treating complex traumatic stress disorders in children and adolescents: Scientific foundations and therapeutic models*. New York, NY: The Guilford Press.

Ford, J. D., Spinazzola, J., van der Kolk, B., & Grasso, D. J. (2018, in press). Toward an empirically-based developmental trauma disorder diagnosis for children: Factor structure, item characteristics, reliability, and validity of the developmental trauma disorder semi-structured interview (DTD-SI). *Journal of Clinical Psychiatry*.

Hibbard, R., Barlow, J., MacMillan, H., & the Committee on Child Abuse and Neglect and American Academy of Child and Adolescent Psychiatry. (2012). Psychological maltreatment. *Pediatrics, 130*, 372–378

Hopper, E., Grossman, F., Spinazzola, J., & Zucker, M. (in press). *Treating adult survivors of childhood emotional abuse and neglect: Reaching across the abyss*. New York, NY: Guilford Press.

Huang, L., Speicher, C., Habib, M., Silver, P., & Earle, L. (2017). *Complex trauma, children, and the health home option: Moving research and practice to policy* [Audio webinar and PowerPoint slides]. Retrieved from http://learn.nctsn.org

Layne, C.M., Briggs, E.C., & Courtois, C.A. (2014). Introduction to the special section: Using the trauma history profile to unpack risk factor caravans and their consequences. *Psychological Trauma: Theory, Research, Practice, & Policy, 6*(S1), S1–S8.

Manly, J.T., Cicchetti, D., & Barnett, D. (1994). The impact of subtype, frequency, chronicity, and severity of child maltreatment on social competence and behavior problems. *Development and Psychopathology*, 6, 121–143.

Pelcovitz, D., van der Kolk, B.A., Roth, S., Mandel, F., Kaplan, S., & Resick, P. (1997). Development of a criteria set and structured interview for disorders of extreme stress. *Journal of Traumatic Stress, 10,* 3–16.

Spinazzola, J., Ford, J., Zucker, M., van der Kolk, B., Silva, S., Smith, S., & Blaustein, M. (2005). National survey of complex trauma exposure, outcome and intervention for children and adolescents. *Psychiatric Annals, 35*(5), 433–439.

Spinazzola, J., Habib, M., Knoverek, A., Arvidson, J., Nisenbaum, J., Wentworth, R., Hodgdon, H., Pond, A., Kisiel, C. (2013). The heart of the matter: Complex trauma in child welfare. *CW360 Trauma-Informed Child Welfare Practice*, Winter 2013, 8–9.

Spinazzola, J., Hodgdon, H., Liang, L., Ford, J.D., Layne, C.M., Pynoos, R., & Kisiel, C. (2014). Unseen wounds: The contribution of psychological maltreatment to child and adolescent mental health and risk outcomes. *Psychological Trauma: Theory, Research, Practice, and Policy, 6*(Suppl 1), S18–S28.

Spinazzola, J., van der Kolk, B., & Ford, J.D. (2018). When nowhere is safe: Trauma history antecedents of posttraumatic stress disorder and developmental trauma disorder in the DTD field trial. Manuscript submitted for publication.

Teicher, M.H., & Samson, J. A. (2016). Enduring neurobiological effects of childhood abuse and neglect. *Annual Research Review, 57*(3), 241–266. doi:10.1111/jcpp.12507.

Trickett, P.K., Kim, K., & Prindle, J. (2011). Variations in emotional abuse experiences among multiply maltreated young adolescents and relations with developmental outcomes. *Child Abuse & Neglect, 35*(10), 767–782.

van der Kolk, B.A. (2005). Developmental trauma disorder: Toward a rational diagnosis for children with complex trauma histories. *Psychiatric Annals, 35*(5), 401–408.

van der Kolk, B.A., Roth, S., Pelcovitz, D., Sunday, S., & Spinazzola, J. (2005). Disorders of extreme stress: The empirical foundation of a complex adaptation to trauma. *Journal of Traumatic Stress, 18*(5), 389–399.

About the Editors and Contributors

Joy D. Osofsky, PhD, is a clinical and developmental psychologist and the Paul Ramsay Chair of Psychiatry and Barbara Lemann Professor of Child Welfare at Louisiana State University Health Sciences Center in New Orleans. She has published widely and authored or edited *Treating Infants and Young Children Impacted by Trauma: Interventions That Promote Healthy Development* (2017), *Clinical Work with Traumatized Young Children* (2011), *Young Children and Trauma: Intervention and Treatment* (2004), and *Children in a Violent Society* (1997). In 2017, she coauthored *Questions Every Judge and Lawyer Should Ask about Infants and Toddlers in the Child Welfare System* (National Council of Juvenile and Family Court Judges). Osofsky is past president of Zero to Three: National Center for Infants, Toddlers and Families and the World Association for Infant Mental Health. She played a leadership role in the Gulf Region following Hurricane Katrina and the Deepwater Horizon oil spill as codirector of the Louisiana Rural Trauma Services Center in the National Child Traumatic Stress Network (NCTSN) and clinical director for Child and Adolescent Services for Louisiana Spirit, Louisiana's Crisis Counseling Program. She serves as codirector of the Mental and Behavioral Health Capacity Project, part of the Gulf Region Health Outreach Program following the Gulf Oil Spill, and coprincipal investigator of the NCTSN Terrorism and Disaster Coalition for Child and Family Resilience, an NCTSN center. In 2007, Osofsky received the Sarah Haley Award for Clinical Excellence for trauma work from the International Society for Traumatic Stress Studies and in 2010 a Presidential Commendation from the American Psychiatric Association for her work in the aftermath of Hurricane Katrina. In 2014, she was recognized with the Reginald Lourie Award for leadership in infant mental health and outstanding contributions to the health and welfare of children and families.

Betsy McAlister Groves, MSW, LICSW, is a licensed clinical social worker and founding director of the Child Witness to Violence Project at Boston Medical Center, a program that has received national recognition for its work with young children affected by domestic and community violence. This program is one of four sites comprising the Early Trauma Treatment Network within the National Child Traumatic Stress Network. Within the Network, she serves on the Policy Task Force, and was cochair of the Domestic Violence Workgroup, leading efforts to create resources for parents and professionals on children affected by domestic violence. While at Boston Medical Center, Groves served as codirector of the Child Protection Team in the Department of Pediatrics. Her practice and research interests are on the impact of community and family trauma on young children, and on engaging the health and education systems in identifying and responding to children affected by trauma. She holds academic appointments as associate professor of pediatrics at Boston University School of Medicine and lecturer at the Harvard University Graduate School of Education, where she is coordinator of their Child Advocacy Program and teaches courses on childhood trauma. She served on the Massachusetts Governor's Council for Domestic Violence and Sexual Assault for 17 years and in 2010 was appointed by Attorney General Eric Holder to the National Advisory Commission for the US. Department of Justice—Office of Violence against Women. She has served as a consultant to the American Academy of Pediatrics, the National Council of Juvenile and Family Court Judges, Healthy Families America, and Futures without Violence. She is the author of *Children Who See Too Much: Lessons from the Child Witness to Violence Project* and has published extensively on topics related to child exposure to domestic violence, early childhood trauma and intervention.

Saida Abdi, LICSW, MSW, MA, is Associate Director for Community Relations at the Refugee Trauma and Resilience Center at Boston Children's Hospital (BCHRTRC) and a PhD candidate at Boston University.

Jaleel Abdul-Adil, PhD, is a clinical psychologist and associate professor of clinical psychology in psychiatry at the University of Illinois at Chicago. Abdul-Adil is the codirector of the Urban Youth Trauma Center, a SAMHSA-funded site in the National Child Traumatic Stress Network (NCTSN). Abdul-Adil's current research focuses on family-oriented rap music and hip-hop culture-based interventions for urban youth and families.

Megan H. Bair-Merritt, MD, MSCE, is associate professor of pediatrics at Boston University School of Medicine. She has conducted social epidemiology research for over 10 years at Boston Medical Center and has been Associate Division Chief of General Pediatrics. Bair-Merritt's long-term career goal is to lead multidisciplinary efforts to improve the health of children exposed to IPV.

Lawrence (Larry) Berkowitz, MPA, EdD, is the director and cofounder of Riverside Trauma Center in Needham, Massachusetts, and holds an appointment as a teaching associate in psychology at Harvard Medical School. He trains extensively on suicide prevention, assessment and management of suicide, and postintervention activities to contain suicide contagion in schools and communities.

Rebecca Brown, LCSW, is the clinical manager for the Department of Clinical Innovation at Maine Behavioral Healthcare in Portland. In her current work, she oversees implementation of evidence-based trauma treatments and interventions throughout the state of Maine. She has coauthored multiple national resources on the impact of domestic violence on children.

Emma Cardeli, PhD, is a research associate at the Refugee Trauma and Resilience Center (RTRC) at Boston Children's Hospital, an instructor in psychology at Harvard Medical School, and a licensed clinical psychologist with years of experience working with traumatized children and families from culturally diverse backgrounds.

B. Heidi Ellis, PhD, is an associate professor in psychology and psychiatry at Harvard Medical School and Boston Children's Hospital Boston, and a licensed clinical psychologist. She is also the director of the Refugee Trauma and Resilience Center at Boston Children's Hospital, a partner in the National Child Traumatic Stress Network. Ellis's primary focus is on understanding and promoting refugee youth mental health and adjustment, with a particular emphasis on understanding how trauma exposure, violence, and social context impact developmental trajectories. She is also codeveloper of the nationally recognized trauma treatment model, Trauma Systems Therapy.

Rebecca Hoffmann Frances is the Director of Clinical Innovation at Maine Behavioral Healthcare in Portland Maine and an assistant clinical professor of psychiatry at Tufts University School of Medicine. In her position, Ms. Hoffmann Frances manages multiple large federally funded projects that focus on providing care and treatment for children and families that have been exposed to violence and other types of trauma, including the Department of Justice Defending Childhood Initiative in Maine.

Abigail H. Gewirtz is the John and Nancy Lindahl Leadership Professor in the Department of Family Social Science and the Institute of Child Development and director of the Institute for Translational Research in Children's Mental Health at the University of Minnesota. Her research focuses on the development, effectiveness testing, and implementation of targeted prevention programs that promote child resilience among highly stressed families, including those affected by military deployment and war.

Krista Goldstine-Cole is an advanced doctoral student in human development at the Harvard Graduate School of Education where her research is focused on the nexus of social services policy, childhood adversity, and schools. She is a Presidential Scholar, Spencer Foundation Early Career Scholar in Civics Education, and Vision and Strategy Editor of the *Harvard Educational Review.*

Nancy Kassam-Adams, PhD, is associate director for behavioral research at the Center for Injury Research and Prevention at the Children's Hospital of Philadelphia and research associate professor in the Division of Emergency Medicine, Department of Pediatrics, University of Pennsylvania Perelman School of Medicine. Her research focuses on understanding how children and families respond to potentially traumatic events, such as medical emergencies, injury, and violence. She leads a team that is developing and testing secondary prevention protocols, which can be integrated into pediatric health-care settings.

Lucy S. King is a PhD candidate in Affective Science in the Department of Psychology at Stanford University. Broadly, her research focuses on the effects of variations in the early caregiving environment on the development of psychobiological stress response systems. She is the recipient of a Graduate Research Fellowship from the National Science Foundation.

Alicia F. Lieberman, PhD, is Irving Harris Endowed Chair in Infant Mental Health, professor and vice chair for Academic Affairs at UCSF Department of Psychiatry, and director of the UCSF-site Child Trauma

Research Program (CTRP). She is senior developer of Child-Parent Psychotherapy (CPP), an extensively tested evidence-based practice for young children exposed to trauma, and author of numerous publications related to young children and trauma.

Michele M. Many, MSW, LCSW, BACS, is Chief, Section of Social Work, and assistant professor, LSU Health Sciences Center, Department of Psychiatry. Ms. Many is a primary clinician for the Orleans Parish Infant Team and the Orleans Parish Safe Baby Court Team, working with infants and toddlers in the foster care system.

Jim McCauley, LICSW, is the cofounder and associate director of the Riverside Trauma Center, which provides critical incident response and suicide postvention services to schools, workplaces, and communities throughout Massachusetts and New England. McCauley has a special interest in suicide clusters and suicide prevention coalitions and has presented at national and international conferences on these topics.

Jana Pressley, PsyD, is the director of Education and Professional Development at the Trauma Center at Justice Resource Institute in Brookline, Massachusetts, where she oversees various components of the training program and holds a clinical role as a therapist and supervisor. She is a national trainer and consultant in both the Attachment, Regulation, and Competency (ARC) and Component-Based Psychotherapy (CBP) treatment models and serves as training faculty for the Complex Trauma Treatment Network (CTTN).

Vilma Reyes, PsyD, is an assistant clinical professor at University of California at San Francisco for the Child Trauma Research Program in the Department of Psychiatry at Zuckerberg San Francisco General Hospital. She is the assistant project coordinator of the community-based mental health initiative and provides training for the program.

Emily F. Rothman, ScD, MS, is an associate professor at the Boston University School of Public Health. She has a secondary appointment in the Department of Pediatrics at the Boston University School of Medicine.

Joseph Spinazzola, PhD, a national trainer and psychotherapist in private practice, is executive director of the Foundation Trust and Adjunct Faculty at Richmont Graduate University. Dr. Spinazzola co-founded the Complex Trauma Treatment Network and the Complex Trauma and

Developmental Trauma Disorder Workgroup of the National Child Traumatic Stress Network.

Liza M. Suarez, PD, is codirector of the Urban Youth Trauma Center, a Treatment Service Adaptation Center of the National Child Traumatic Stress Network, aiming to address the needs of youth impacted by community violence, and a clinical assistant professor of psychology in the Psychiatry Department at the University of Illinois, Chicago. At the Institute for Juvenile Research, she works on developing research and clinical programs for trauma-exposed and anxious youth and their families within the Pediatric Stress and Anxiety Disorders Clinic.

Na Zhang is a PhD candidate in the Department of Family Social Science at the University of Minnesota. Her research focuses on the prevention of emotional problems in children and adolescents.

Index

Note: *Italicized* page numbers indicate tables, figures, and boxed material.